LEGACY LETTERS

INSPIRATIONAL

NOTES TO MY

GRANDCHILDREN

A. T. SCOTT

BROOKSTONE
PUBLISHING GROUP

Birmingham, Alabama

Brookstone Publishing Group
An imprint of Iron Stream Media
100 Missionary Ridge
Birmingham, AL 35242
IronStreamMedia.com

Library of Congress Control Number: 2022911665

Cover design by Hannah Linder Designs

ISBN: 978-1-949856-77-4 (paperback)
ISBN: 978-1-949856-78-1 (eBook)

1 2 3 4 5—26 25 24 23 22

To Lois,
My Inspiration

FOREWORD

There seems to me to be a decided trend nowadays away from biblical truths, and toward man-made lifestyle standards. This is especially true I think among young adults. *Legacy Letters* is an attempt to help stem that tide. Accessing scripture daily is an obvious approach to doing that. So, to take selected Bible verses and provide for each one a short analysis of their relevance to our society seemed to be something that would help.

My goal in *Legacy Letters* was to make it simple to spend a few minutes each day in God's Word and come away with some Holy Spirit–inspired principles and thoughts on how to apply them in our daily lives.

Be assured of my prayers as you go forward.

A. T. Scott
August 2022

Scripture Index

1 JOHN 1:8–10

John the apostle wrote five books of the New Testament: the Gospel of John; 1, 2, and 3 John; and Revelation. There is a consistent general message throughout these five books emphasizing the love of God. That love resulted in His sending His only Son, Jesus Christ, to earth to save us from our sins. Thus, our response is to be acceptance of Him, by faith belief in Him, and obedience to Him. Such faith leads to our receiving God's free gift of eternal life. So confession of our need for forgiveness in humble acceptance of Jesus' sacrificial death for our sins is the only route to a proper relationship with Him. No one has ever been saved without first recognizing their sinful condition and need for a Savior. John points that out in this passage.

> If we say we have no sin, we deceive ourselves, and the truth is not in us. If we confess our sins he is faithful and just to forgive us our sins, and to cleanse us from all unrighteousness. If we say we have not sinned, we make him a liar, and his word is not in us. (1 John 1:8–10)

Notice John does not claim to have no sin in his life. He uses the word *we* to include himself in this passage. Even believers are guilty of sin, and need to confess their sin. Thus, all believers are to continually seek to live sin-free lives but confess their own sin when appropriate. God is faithful and just, infinitely so, and we can be assured He will keep His Word and forgive us if we are truly repentant when we confess our sin. And God goes even further. He cleanses us "from all unrighteousness." That concept has the sense of perfection implied. Picture yourself perfectly justified, that is, with all your sins completely removed "as far as the east is from the west" (Psalm 103:12). That's God's definition of removing the sin from our lives. Every element of unrighteousness is included. Only when we have this degree of purity within us will we be qualified for heaven. The phrase scripture uses to describe that condition is "we are glorified."

God will hold us accountable for our sins. It is, in fact, a lie if we maintain we are sin free, and our very act of claiming to be sinless is a blasphemous statement against God. We are saying God is a liar, for He has declared that "all have sinned and fall short of the glory of God" (Romans 3:23). All of us, therefore, dishonor God when we fail to meet His demands by sinning.

Notice the route to justification begins with our confession of our sin. Only a holy God could and would give us this privilege of confession. Only a God who loves us with an infinite love would want us to be cleansed to this degree. And only an all-powerful God has the authority to grant such a privilege as confession.

We are wise indeed if we take advantage of the availability of confession that leads to complete forgiveness. And complete forgiveness is what we need, and what we must have. In God's view there is no such thing as partial forgiveness. So, if we would grow spiritually, if we would become the witness God would have us be, and if our goal is to really know the joy of our salvation, then we need to become more steadfast in our confession of our sin. The fact of our sin is obvious to any true Christian, thus, the need for sincere, ongoing confession is mandatory. God knows this and loves us enough to make it available.

LUKE 3:21-22

At the very beginning of His ministry the Holy Spirit led Jesus to the Jordan river to be baptized by John the Baptist. This was for Jesus to identify with Israel's sin. See this event described by Luke:

> Now when all the people were baptized, and when Jesus also had been baptized and was praying, the heavens were opened, and the Holy Spirit descended on him in bodily form like a dove; and a voice came from heaven, "You are my beloved Son; with you I am well pleased." (3:21–22)

WOW!! Just imagine what that was like!! To be there and to see God's Son be baptized and praying, and to see something like a dove descend and land on Him. And then to hear a "voice come from heaven" and speak to Him, identifying Him as the Son of God, and expressing pleasure with Him. We can be sure this was something that those who witnessed it would remember for the rest of their lives. **But we know more. We know the "rest of the story."** We know things that we, too, are to remember for the rest of our lives. We know exactly who Jesus is, we know what He went on to do, and we know the significance of who He is and what He would do.

We were not there that day to see that dove, or to hear that voice from heaven. But by faith we can be sure it happened, and that Jesus went on to complete His earthly ministry, ending by dying on a cross to pay our sin debt, only to rise again on the third day. How and why do you think God orchestrated all these events? It seems too simple to say, "Because God loved us," but that is what scripture tells us. "For God so loved the world, that he gave his only Son, that whoever believes in him should not perish but have eternal life" (John 3:16).

The simplicity of this act of God in sending His Son to earth to save us from our sins, and the infinite significance of it, is hard for some people to grasp. And no one can grasp it without the aid of God's Holy Spirit as He opens their hearts to God's truth. Scripture tells us: "For the wages of sin is death, but the free gift of God is eternal life in Christ Jesus our Lord" (Romans 6:23).

So this one-time act of God was sufficient to satisfy God's wrath for the sins of all believers. Hallelujah! What a great God we have! And what a great story we believers have to tell. So go and tell it. It's the best news the world has ever heard. **Jesus Christ really is Lord!**

JUDE 24-25

Jude was Jesus' brother. Imagine being raised in the same family with almighty God. And yet he did not fully realize Jesus' deity until after His crucifixion and resurrection. But he finally did, and is probably writing here to an audience of other Jewish believers. Scholars conclude that since his writing seems to assume knowledge of Jewish customs and celebrations, Jude's message is one of encouragement in their faith in the midst of many false teachers who have infiltrated the church. Thus, Jude urges his readers to consistently defend the truth of the gospel against all who would deny Christ's identity as Messiah. This passage makes up the last two verses of the letter where Jude reemphasizes Jesus' identity and authority.

> Now to him who is able to keep you from stumbling and to present you blameless before the presence of his glory with great joy, to the only God, our Savior, through Jesus Christ our Lord, be glory, majesty, dominion, and authority, before all time and now and forever. Amen. (Jude 24–25)

Notice his message to his readers. Jesus Christ is the only one who can keep them from stumbling in their faith and present them blameless before almighty God at the judgment. By stumbling, Jude is referring to believers who fear falling into sin or error. Such a stumbling condition is always potentially present given Satan's continually evil influence. But, praise the Lord, Jude has already taught that God keeps those who are called to Him, thus assuring true believers they will never lose their salvation. Notice, too, that our blameless presentation will be accomplished with great joy. That's an understatement. Having been forgiven for all our sins, what other feeling could a believer have when he is presented to God the Father (by Jesus) than great joy? That is truly the culmination of God's grace and that believer's faith.

And who but Jesus Christ could present us blameless before God the Father? And how did that come about? It happened only through the love of God in gifting His only Son to die in our place to pay our sin debt. And it is to God the Father then, through Jesus Christ our Lord, that Jude urges praise and honor. See how complete Jude's mandate is to his audience. His instructions include the facts that the Father is worthy of all glory, all majesty, all dominion, and all authority, *and* that He already possesses those characteristics.

Notice the last sentence, "before all time and now and forever." Jude does not claim to give God those characteristics. He simply acknowledges God possesses them, and has always had them and always will have them. And he is urging his readers (including us) to acknowledge the same thing, and to live out those beliefs.

How could anyone (truly) believe in the kind of fatherly God Jude describes and not follow that with love, obedience, and proclamation of that truth? Most people believe in God and will admit to that. But unfortunately, they don't go as far as defining the kind of God they believe in, or give credence to the Bible as the revelation of who He is and what He has done for them.

PROVERBS 19:20

Proverbs 19 is one of many written by Solomon concerning living a good life. See the chart below listing some features we would be well advised to adopt in our lives.

Listen to instruction (vv. 16, 20)
Be kind to the poor (v. 17)
Be involved in your children's lives and discipline them (v. 18)
Avoid friendships with those who lack self-control (v. 19)
Acknowledge the rule of God (v. 21)
Understand that love and integrity are what bring real happiness (v. 22)
Fear the Lord (v. 23)

Verse 20 is a typical example:

Listen to advice and accept instruction,
that you may gain wisdom in the future.

So we are to be open to advice, and we are to accept instruction; good advice and good instruction that is. There is plenty of both around, but how do we discern which to listen to, for not everything we hear is good or worthy of following. God's Word is the obvious choice, and we know that already. So what is the new lesson for us here? The new lesson is for us to get and keep a proper prospective concerning the significance and the validity of these proverbs. We think we know them, but do we consistently live them out completely in our lives? Does obedience bring us joy? Are we burdened that others (especially those we love the most) are not aware of God's truth on these matters?

Notice verse 19:20, for example. We are to listen to good advice and instruction so that over time we will gain wisdom. Thus, we can correctly conclude these truths are not one-time events; they require consistency and patience to achieve the desired goals. Each one has a different goal in mind, and thus, taken together one achieves a good life. The Holy Spirit, who was behind Solomon's wisdom, is still involved in believers' lives helping us with proper priorities and obedience.

So living out the Christian life requires more thinking than many of us give it. We must beware the press of life that is apt to capture our focus and draw us away from God's perfect will, not so much to do bad things, but to not do the best things either. The whole process sort of "cries out" for us to be involved daily in times of prayer and devotion to the Lord. Studying (not just reading) God's Word would naturally be a part of that. Proactivity in making disciples would naturally also be a part of that.

God is aware of everything we do and all that we face, and that's a good thing. That knowledge gives us confidence that what Jesus said just before He ascended is true: "Behold, I am with you always, to the end of the age" (Matthew 28:20).

LUKE 24:36, 44–48

Jesus Christ, Son of God, had come to earth to save us from our sins. He had lived a sinless life, and yet was falsely accused of wrongdoing and crucified. But per prophecy He rose from the grave on the third day and appeared to His disciples several times. This scripture passage describes one of those appearances. The significance of His resurrection is lost on many because of their unbelief. Yet we read from the words of eyewitnesses that He did come and speak to them and assure them He was alive. Thus we, too, have the opportunity to believe; to trust Him, and to by faith live out our lives giving Him the praise, honor, and glory He deserves as Savior and Lord. See the description of this appearance:

> As they were talking about these things, Jesus himself stood among them, and said to them, "Peace to you!" . . . Then he said to them, "These are my words that I spoke to you while I was still with you, that everything written about me in the Law of Moses and the Prophets and the Psalms must be fulfilled." Then he opened their minds to understand the Scriptures, and said to them, "Thus it is written, that the Christ should suffer and on the third day rise from the dead, and that repentance for the forgiveness of sins should be proclaimed in his name to all nations, beginning from Jerusalem. You are witnesses of these things." (Luke 24:36, 44–48)

So Jesus appeared to His disciples, and reminded them of what He had taught them earlier, that He would be crucified and rise from the dead fulfilling previous prophecy. Notice what He told them would be said about Him, "that repentance for the forgiveness of sins should be proclaimed in His name to all nations." Thus, the concept of our truly repenting of our sins and God granting forgiveness is to be taught worldwide. That is still being done. In fact, believers are instructed to do so, wherever they go.

That's why I'm writing this.

God so loved the world that He sent Jesus to die on the cross to pay our sin debt. We are to believe that, repent of our sin, and trust Christ's sacrificial death for eternal life. It is that relationship we establish by our repentance and His forgiveness that God uses to provide us His free gift of eternal life. Good works are important, but real good works, done to glorify God, come after our salvation, not done before in an effort to earn our salvation.

Notice Jesus tells His disciples, "You are witnesses of these things." By faith, that applies to us too. Jesus did die and rise from the grave. His death did pay for our sins. Eternal life is available to everyone who believes. We are to go and tell others of that good news. And believers are to live out their faith.

Hallelujah! It really is true. Jesus is alive! And one day He will return to take all believers to heaven to live for eternity with Him.

MICAH 6:6-8

God selected the children of Abraham as His special people, protecting them, guiding them, forgiving them, and eventually bringing Jesus Christ, Messiah, into the world through their lineage. Thus, the Jews have always been God's chosen people, through whom He blessed the whole world with the opportunity for eternal life via Jesus Christ's sacrificial death on the cross for their sins. See what God had the prophet, Micah, tell the Jews concerning what God requires of them. This same truth applies to us Gentiles too:

"With what shall I come before the Lord,
  and bow myself before God on high?
Shall I come before him with burnt offerings,
  with calves a year old?
Will the Lord be pleased with thousands of rams,
  with ten thousands of rivers of oil?
Shall I give my firstborn for my transgression,
  the fruit of my body for the sin of my soul?"
He has told you, O man, what is good;
  and what does the Lord require of you
but to do justice, and to love kindness,
  and to walk humbly with your God? (Micah 6:6–8)

God has clearly told Micah to describe what God does *not* want, and what He does want. Notice the physical things that do not please God: burnt offerings, calves, rams, oil, or even their firstborn child. Even though there is personal sacrifice of some kind and to some degree involved with these offerings they are not what God requires from His children. What God does want, and what He merits is *us*, our hearts, our attitudes, our concentration, and our lifestyles, all reflected in our living justly, loving kindness, and our walking humbly before the world with our God. And these last things are often the things we find hardest to give over to God. We often hold ourselves most dear, who we are, what we do, how we look upon and respond to other people, and what we do with our time and talents. **We could accurately then say what God truly does want from us is for us to love Him, to glorify Him, to obey Him, and to consider Him worthy of all our praise, honor, and glory.**

These are what God considers good. These are what really matter. These are what are eternal. God has always known this, but sometimes we have a hard time understanding these truths. Thus, as much as we are tempted to try to earn our salvation, we can easily see from this passage, it is not good deeds that save us, but our relationship with Jesus Christ. Is He Lord of our life, is the question.

God has loved us since before we were born. Think of it as His loving us first, in spite of our unloveliness, thus defining His grace. And further, He has proved that love by blessing us in so many ways, particularly in His giving His Son to die in our place to atone for our sins.

What a story believers have to proclaim! What a message believers have to tell! What good news believers have to share! Nothing else the world has ever heard compares with the gospel of Jesus Christ, and nothing ever will.

1 JOHN 3:21-24

This passage comes under the heading of "Love One Another." God would have us love Him and each other (loving others as we love ourselves). There is a connection then between our loving others in obedience to God's command and Him hearing our prayers. Just as a parent would tend to answer the requests of an obedient child, God hears the prayers of His obedient children. Here John is reminding his readers (and us) we are to be obedient children of God. It's part of our relationship with God, if we love Him and others as He commands us, then He is pleased with us. Just consider the significance of that, as believers we can and should do things every day that please almighty God. And when we do, our relationship with Him is enhanced and we tend to more closely follow the leadership of the Holy Spirit within us. **Thus, the more obedient we are, the more obedient we will be, and that's the lesson God has John teaching his readers here.** See John's instructions:

> Beloved, if our heart does not condemn us, we have confidence before God; and whatever we ask we receive from him, because we keep his commandments and do what pleases him. And this is his commandment, that we believe in the name of his Son Jesus Christ and love one another, just as he has commanded us. Whoever keeps his commandments abides in God, and God in him. And by this we know that he abides in us, by the Spirit whom he has given us. (1 John 3:21–24)

As believers the Holy Spirit abides in us. We can know therefore, when we are in sync with the will of God in our actions. We don't have to wonder or guess, the Holy Spirit will (or will not) give us peace about given decisions we are making, and we need to (1) be honest with ourselves, and (2) be obedient to the leadership of the Holy Spirit. If there does seem to be doubt or questions about what we should do in a given situation then ask yourself the question, what course of action is most likely to glorify the Father? Such a question is usually easy to answer, although that may not lead us in the direction we wanted to go.

So, this concept of our heart condemning us is a very valid measuring stick for our decision making. Condemning us this way has to do with the Holy Spirit giving us peace or confidence in what we are about to do. Notice the two direct commands John passes on to us: (1) believe in the name of the Lord Jesus Christ, and (2) love one another. Obeying these two commands ripples out to almost everything we do. And most important when we do obey them, the result is God gets glorified, and that is to be our lifestyle goal.

John has an interesting way of teaching us Christians doctrinal principles. In the last verse, he tells us, "by this we know that God abides in us." But he hasn't told us yet how we know God abides in us. But then he does tell us how we know, it's "by the Spirit whom He has given us." Thus, we know that God abides in us because the Holy Spirit makes us aware of it. And then he also tells us God has given us His Holy Spirit to do just that, to continually make us aware of His presence. Isn't it awesome how God thinks of everything? He knows we always (badly) need to be aware of His presence with us. Right after Jesus gave us the Great Commission in Matthew 28:18–20 to go and make disciples, He told us, "Behold, I am with you always, to the end of the age." **And via the Holy Spirit, He is with us always.**

REVELATION 1:3

John the apostle wrote this letter toward the very end of the first century AD. Jesus had come to earth, lived a perfect life, and been crucified (and resurrected) about sixty years earlier. John is writing to the churches of Asia (now western Turkey) to encourage them in their faith, and to especially warn them of false teachers now out and about posing as authentic prophets of the gospel of Jesus Christ. The doctrine they promoted was self-generated, not literal, Satan-inspired, and of no worth to legitimate believers in Christ. John teaches a gospel focused on Jesus Christ without wavering in His identity as the Son of God, sent to earth to save us from our sins. See this verse for a summation of the importance of our giving these words full credence:

> Blessed is the one who reads aloud the words of this prophecy, and blessed are those who hear, and who keep what is written in it, for the time is near. (Revelation 1:3)

How we interpret the word *blessed* is key to the significance of this verse. Generally, we think the word means being provided favors, benefits, protection from evil, and prosperity over time. The inference is that these promised blessings come from a divine source, God almighty, and thus are guaranteed because of His power, and His nature as a promise keeper, who never fails to keep His promises. These blessings are not specifically defined, but again, considering their source, we have to believe they will be awesome indeed.

Notice we are also to read the words of this prophecy aloud, as if they gain credibility by being spoken so that others around us will hear. Think about the idea of reading God's Word aloud. In the first place making that small extra effort will cause what we are reading to mean more to us, we will be drawn more closely to what we are reading. Doing so ties us more directly to God, it adds a level of belief on our part, it communicates the message that we believe in our God, and that we are not ashamed to declare that to a world that for the most part does not believe in Him. Imagine being ashamed of your God, of not wanting others to know you are a believer, and being really worried about what others will think of you as a believer. See Jesus' thoughts on that: "For whoever is ashamed of me and my words, of him will the Son of Man be ashamed when He comes in His glory and the glory of the Father and of the holy angels" (Luke 9:26).

Notice, too, it is not enough to just know God's Word and to read them aloud but to hear and obey what we've read aloud and thereby announced that we believe. So, obviously, there is some responsibility inherent in declaring that we believe in Jesus Christ, that we've made Him Lord of our lives, and that we believe He is the Son of God. If we read these words of God aloud people who hear us will expect us to live up to what we've read. And when we start living that kind of lifestyle people will notice, because by definition some things in our way of thinking and acting will change.

See the ending of verse 3: "for the time is near." The events John was writing about are near (in God's way of thinking). To John and those whom he wrote to, their time left on earth was short (and ours is too). So, their time and our time to respond to John's message concerning Christ is short, our particular "time is near." That means our time to believe in Jesus (and obey) is *now*.

JOHN 2:11

Jesus provided many signs and wonders during His earthly ministry, and thus there had to be a first time. This passage describes the result of that first sign. Seemingly, Jesus had not planned on performing a sign on this occasion. He was drawn into it by His mother when, at a wedding they and His disciples were attending, the host ran out of wine. Jesus' mother asked Him to get involved and He did, easily turning some water into wine to solve the embarrassing problem. See what the result was:

> This, the first of his signs, Jesus did at Cana in Galilee, and manifested his glory. And his disciples believed in him. (John 2:11)

So from this verse, now we know Jesus did not perform signs during His childhood or early manhood. But suddenly, in what seemed to be an unplanned way a need arose, and He addressed the need. In the doing of that He manifested His glory. Now a sign is a miracle that gives evidence of Jesus' deity and identity as Messiah. Changing water to wine is clearly a miracle, but not nearly so dramatic as some Jesus would later perform. But it was enough to convince the disciples, they now believed Him to be Messiah. In one life-changing moment for them, they saw truth in Jesus. And all that they had heard all lifelong concerning a coming Messiah was played out before them. Now they could concentrate on following Him, learning from Him, obeying Him, and strengthening their faith. All things we are to do.

What about us? Many people today go into a first encounter of a sign from God with more background knowledge than those disciples had. But perhaps God shows Himself real to them in a simple, straightforward way that does not make waves in our society. Knowing from scripture what God can do and has done for others, are we willing to believe in Him from a "nonspectacular" event or experience? And does it take repeated reinforcement of our faith by ever more significant signs for us to grow spiritually? It should not.

Cana, a small town in Galilee will forever be known as that place where Jesus first gave evidence of His glory using such a sign. And the disciples believed in Him as a result. And we can, too, from that same event. It's not our call to select when or even if the Lord is going to show Himself to us regularly with signs. **But when and if we do what we already know to be His will, He will show Himself. That's the kind of God He is.** When we take even small steps in His direction (in obedience), He will bless that with progress in faith, and ever-increasing clarity of what He wants us to do next. So, it's no wonder scripture is full of commands, covering not all, but many of the decisions we make daily. And if we act in obedience when He clearly has dictated certain actions, then in those areas not covered specifically by scripture we will be able to discern what He would have us do. And as a matter of fact, we will be held responsible for that kind of obedience after discernment. Let us work hard at discerning His will.

2 TIMOTHY 2:15

God is a forgiving God. He forgives us of our sins when we sincerely turn to Him in faith, repentant of our sins. And He is also a just God, punishing those who deny Him. And praise the Lord, He is also a loving God, who loves us with a steadfast love even when we are unlovable. This love God has for us that we don't deserve is called grace. And it is that grace that led God to send His only Son, Jesus Christ, to earth to save us from our sins by dying a sinner's death in our place on the cross. In this letter to Timothy, his young disciple, the apostle Paul is reminding him to persevere in the faith even in the midst of suffering. That message is appropriate for us too. See the instructions Paul gives Timothy:

> Do your best to present yourself to God as one approved, a worker who has no need to be ashamed, rightly handling the word of truth. (2 Timothy 2:15)

Notice a commitment to Jesus carries with it the responsibility to put forth consistent effort to obey Jesus' commandments. The book of Matthew shows us how Jesus distilled his many commandments into two that are true for all of us in any era: **"You shall love the Lord your God with all your heart and with all your soul and with all your mind. This is the great and first commandment. And a second is like it: You shall love your neighbor as yourself. On these two commandments depend all the Law and the Prophets." (Matthew 22:37–40)**

When you look deeply into these two commandments it's easy to see how they apply to everything we do and say, and how appropriate they are to all of us in our daily lives. So, God is using Paul is tell Timothy to do His best to comply with these two commandments. And he is telling us to do that too. Thus, when we read here that we are to do our best to present ourselves to God as one approved, it's really God telling us to let our Christianity show in our lives. People will then see Jesus in us.

And we need to remember two important things about that instruction: (1) God never commands us to do anything that is impossible. (2) When He gives us a commandment, He always makes provision to help us comply. Therefore, we are to make clear to God we want to obey Him and sincerely pray for His help, guidance, and protection. We are to do this in a general way, and with regard to specific issues that we face every day. God will absolutely answer prayers that show we sincerely want to glorify Him.

In that way, when our main focus in life is to glorify God, our whole sense of values and priorities changes to reflect our love and obedience to Him. And people will notice the difference and God will be glorified, and we certainly will never be ashamed of our stand for Christ. Then Paul tells us all how to do that; it's by "rightly handling the word of truth." That is, by living in obedience to the Bible, God's Word. We rightly handle the word of truth when we live it out in our own lives, and when we share it with others. God's Holy Spirit worked in the hearts of over forty men spread over approximately two thousand years to have the Bible written exactly as He wanted it. So, it remains the one source of God's truth given to us by God Himself to guide us to Him and to lead us in the way of righteousness.

Notice Paul uses the word *worker* to describe the life of a Christian. And that's very appropriate, for there is work inherently involved with living the Christian life. But it's the most satisfying work an individual can undertake. God constructed a Christian's life to be that way because He loves us.

PROVERBS 2:1-6

The Lord is very adept at giving us "if-then" provisions; the kind where if we obey, then He will respond in positive ways. And since we are considering almighty God, we can be sure He will not fail to keep His commitments. Thus, it makes our decision-making process much simpler. We need only reconcile ourselves to God's identity as the almighty Creator who made everything that is, and humble ourselves before Him in complete obedience. Of course, that's easier said than done, but it for sure won't happen if we don't try. And that's the problem most people have. They don't give consideration to God's will or wishes. In fact, too much of the time, God's will does not enter the mind of unbelievers. See this classic example from Proverbs 2 of what God would have us do:

> My son, *if* you receive my words
>   and treasure up my commandments with you,
> making your ear attentive to wisdom
>   and inclining your heart to understanding;
> yes, *if* you call out for insight
>   and raise your voice for understanding,
> *if* you seek it like silver
>   and search for it as for hidden treasures,
> *then* you will understand the fear of the LORD
>   and find the knowledge of God.
> For the LORD gives wisdom;
>   from His mouth come knowledge and understanding.
>   (Proverbs 2:1–6, emphasis mine)

Notice the passage begins with the assumption that the reader is a child of God (son or daughter). Another point clearly made is that God has purposely made His word and commandments available to His children. So, we are to receive it with the knowledge God is providing it for our benefit; **and this because He loves us. Notice, too, that God reminds His children of the value of His truth. It is a treasure worth seeking and holding on to, and worth our attention and our understanding.**

So, there is some mental and spiritual work involved on our part. God never gives us commands without an inherent commitment to help us with obedience. So, we are to "call out," that is, pray for, insight. Insight (per Webster's dictionary) involves the "act or result of apprehending the inner nature of things, or seeing intuitively." Now doesn't that sound like an ability that we need a lot of times? God can and will provide that when we pray. We simply are not using all the resources God has made available to us when we fail to pray.

Thus, with diligence (like we were searching for silver) we are to reach out to God for direction in our lives. And then notice God's promise: we will come to know the fear of the Lord and find His knowledge. The "fear" used here is not as in being afraid but as in respect, assurance of God's involvement, and a certainty that God is not only able but willing to see to our needs.

So where are we to go to find the knowledge of God? Obviously to His Word, scripture. We won't ever find our name in the Bible, God does not personalize it that way, but it is very personal. And it's applicable to all our lives, in every era, and everywhere. Our prayers, study, and effort are then to be directed at applying God's principles to our situation. And God's Holy Spirit has been directed to indwell every believer to guide us in the personal application of what we find in scripture. God is the source of all truth, wisdom, and understanding, and He makes it all available to all His children. Thus, God not only provided us the route to eternal life via Jesus' death on the cross but also His commands to live by.

MATTHEW 5:8

If all we had of God's Word were the Beatitudes, we would have enough to guide us eternally. In His Sermon on the Mount Jesus gave His listeners, and us, the fundamental truths we need to plan our lives. Knowing this we are both without excuse and exceedingly blessed. As is always the case with the Lord, He blesses we believers with truth, and then holds us responsible for sharing that truth with the world. Notice the importance of this single Beatitude on being pure in heart:

> Blessed are the pure in heart, for they shall see God. (Matthew 5:8)

Having a pure heart is worth pursuing. And we are told why. We get to see God. What could be more gratifying than to see God? That's worth waiting a lifetime, and it's worth working a lifetime to achieve, not in the sense we can earn it, but in the sense we know God blesses those who glorify Him that way. So what exactly is a pure heart, and how do we get one? Or better, how do we purify the heart we have? Fortunately, God has told us how.

First, let us consider what makes up a pure heart. The dictionary maintains "pure" means to be "free from what does not belong." In a spiritual sense that's exactly right. Sin and spiritual impurities do not belong (per God's standards) in our heart. So if and when we come to be free from moral fault or guilt, we are pure in heart. Of course, when we speak of our hearts, we mean our spiritual makeup, our innermost conscience. The verse above tells us when we achieve that status we are blessed (happy, content, and at rest with our relationship with God). And those conditions result in our being rewarded by seeing God. **As hard as that is to imagine, it is true, because God's Word says it's true.**

Moses could not see God's face and live (Exodus 33:20–23), but Revelation 22:4 tells us we will see His face when we are completely sanctified in heaven. Evidently the sanctification process does the necessary purifying of our hearts to enable us to see God. And that, of course, applied to Moses too. God knows how important our being able to see Him is, even if we only think we do. And thus, because He loves us, He makes that available to us in heaven.

We then (here on earth) are to pursue purity and uprightness in every area of our lives. And although we are not likely to perfectly achieve that status by ourselves, that thought should not dilute our efforts at all. In fact, if we fail to pursue purity of heart because we realize in our own strength we can never achieve it, we have the wrong idea concerning God's purpose for our lives here on earth. We believers are to be His disciples and servants here on earth knowing we are God's children charged with making other disciples. We are to imitate Christ to the best of our ability using the guidance of the Holy Spirit as our driving force.

When we think about it, we realize what we say and do is initiated by what we think in our hearts. So the concept of cultivating ideal thoughts there is really what our goal should be. And we do that by filling our hearts with God's thoughts, His concepts, and His word. Therefore, the mental and spiritual sweat necessary to plant and grow Christlike thoughts is our challenge. God has provided His Word and prayer as the tools for us to use. His Holy Spirit will bless our efforts in those two areas, because **He wants us to have pure hearts.**

JAMES 3:1–2

James now provides some practical lessons for his readers beginning with a section on "Taming the Tongue." There is a sense in which what we say reflects our thinking and thus, our character. So, James correctly urges his Jewish Christian readers to discipline their thinking toward godly principles. As is so often the case in scripture, it is James' intention that such discipline become a virtual habit that believers are to live out every day. We've all experienced saying a thoughtless word that we regretted immediately, and we had to live with the consequences. Such instances do not bring glory to God and reflect that we are something less than the "perfect man" that James mentions in the passage. See James' guidance:

> Not many of you should become teachers, my brothers, for you know that we who teach will be judged with greater strictness. For we all stumble in many ways. And if anyone does not stumble in what he says, he is a perfect man, able also to bridle his whole body. (James 3:1–2)

First, James mentions the responsibilities inherent in becoming a teacher, for they take on greater responsibility by virtue of the greater influence they have on others. And they will be judged with greater strictness on "that" day. Thus, it is not a stretch to extend this teaching on responsible influence to the other roles we have as parents, employers, leaders in many places, and even as members of older generations. Therefore, James' teachings apply basically to all of us, for everyone has some degree of influence on those around them.

Then James gets even more practical, mentioning that "we all stumble in many ways." Stumble is a metaphor for sin as used here, and certainly that truth applies to us all. James lays out the sequence of our thinking, reflecting our words, which indicates what our bodies will actually do, which is stumble (that is, sin). And should there be someone who does not stumble, then that individual is a perfect man, having completely disciplined his thinking, and his words, thus leading to a sinless existence. But he says this facetiously, knowing his readers will understand no one lives sin free.

But this should be our goal and that's James' purpose: to encourage his readers (and us) to take care what we say. He later makes the point that a ship's rudder and a bit in a horse's mouth are both relatively small physical influences but they control large objects after their captain has applied them. Just so, a small word from us can have great influence (for good or bad) upon those around us.

We are wise to remember where small, relatively insignificant things (like rudders, bits, and words) have great influence, these conditions do not happen by accident. These are God-created scenarios which He uses (or allows) to control, guide, and sometimes dictate worldwide conditions for His glory. Thus, as believers committed to obedience to God's will, there are all the more reasons for us to (1) not underestimate the influence we can have on situations around us and (2) beware of speaking an idle word thoughtlessly, and (3) be forgiving of others when they obviously do such.

Knowing us completely, God has made provisions for help in this area via the influence of His Holy Spirit. Believers have been given God's indwelling spirit and are expected to obey Him. If we are wise, we will.

Isaiah 12:1–2

The Holy Spirit led Isaiah to write this letter in the midst of hard times. Isaiah lived around 700 BC and at that time Assyria was a serious military threat to Judah. The people of Judah had drifted away from God to sin, and between the threat from Assyria and their sinful condition, they needed encouraging to return to Him in obedience. So Isaiah speaks of a day when the Lord will return to gather the remnants of Israel to Himself for an eternal salvation. These words are also representative of the salvation that awaits believing Gentiles (us) in our day. See Isaiah's words:

> You will say in that day;
> "I will give thanks to you, O Lord,
>   for though you were angry with me,
> your anger turned away,
>   that you might comfort me.
>
> "Behold, God is my salvation;
>   I will trust, and will not be afraid;
> for the Lord God is my strength and my song,
>   and he has become my salvation." (Isaiah 12:1–2)

Isaiah describes for his readers what they will be thinking and saying in their day of salvation. In contrast with the fear and concerns they feel at the time of his writing, they will then feel only joy and peace. Only the Lord Himself can save them from their sin, and after a military defeat, and He will do that, supplying the only eternal comfort that is effective. They will trust in Him and no longer be afraid, with sin and any kind of defeat behind them. **When they, or we, are free from any type of fear or doubt that is an awesome state to be in. And only the Lord can provide**

that kind of condition. And the reason He can is because the people have (finally) recognized the truth: He is their strength and provider, and the reason they can sing a joy filled song of salvation. The Lord has always loved them and had the power to save them, but they had turned away from Him in disobedience.

Our society today is in a similar state. God loves us and still has the power to save us, and has provided the way to eternal life. But for whatever reasons, many people still live in denial and unbelief, choosing lives of distress and uncertainty filled with the same kind of fears and doubts Judah experienced in 700 BC. And the solution now is the same solution Isaiah spoke about then, trust in the Lord. Jesus Christ as the prophesied Messiah has come to live a perfect life and die a sacrificial death on the cross as payment of our sin debt.

Believers today can and should sing the same songs of praise and thanksgiving to the Lord that Isaiah encouraged in his day. We can have the same assurance and confidence those believers had then in their eternal life. Jesus offers us the same freedom from fear and doubt that Isaiah wrote about. **When we think about it, freedom from all fear and doubt and a heavenly assurance is the best kind of condition we could have, better than wealth, position, health, or anything else.** Our eternal life begins immediately upon our conversion, so we have such freedom available today.

Isaiah maintained that one day his readers would be boldly proclaiming, "Behold, God is my salvation, I will trust and not be afraid." That is exactly the same message God would have believers today give to the world.

ROMANS 6:12-14

This passage presents all-important good news concerning the significance of what God has done for believers (already) in Christ. **We see here the "why" we can triumph over sin in our lives** after our salvation. That fact should both encourage and empower us to become the disciples and the disciple makers God would have us be. See how God has Paul the apostle word this truth to us:

> Let not sin therefore reign in your mortal body, to make you obey its passions. Do not present your members to sin as instruments of unrighteousness, but present yourselves to God as those who have been brought from death to life, and your members to God as instruments for righteousness. For sin will have no dominion over you, since you are not under law but under grace. (Romans 6:12–14)

Note the emphasis on our own will in the process of escaping the power of Satan in our lives. We are told to "let not" sin reign in our lives here on earth as if we had control, and as believers WE DO. This, because we have died to sin and been raised to walk in the new life we have in Christ. God's Holy Spirit dwells within us and is now strengthening and guiding us. Every day we are to give ourselves to God as His instrument for use in this world (the one we live in every day). He knows exactly what we are facing and what our world consists of. See what God's position is in this matter of our daily living. Notice what we are specifically told: "Sin will have no dominion over you, since you are not under the law but under grace."

God's Word is telling us here that His power will dominate, "sin will have no dominion over us." And we are told why it will have no dominion over us. It's because we live now (as believers)

not under the law (a listing of what to do and what not to do), but under God's grace (the all-powerful love He has for us). What an awesome, awesome concept God conceived for our benefit. **This is not a command but a promise.** Certainly, we are to obey God's laws, but that comes as a natural outpouring of the love we have for Him in response to His first loving us as described in John 3:16–17: "For God so loved the world, that He gave His only Son, that whoever believes in Him should not perish but have eternal life. For God did not send His Son into the world to condemn the world, but in order that the world might be saved through Him."

If adherence to the law saved us, then faith would not be required. "Therefore, since we have been justified by faith, we have peace with God through our Lord Jesus Christ. Through him we have also obtained access by faith into this grace in which we stand, and we rejoice in hope of the glory of God." (Romans 5:1–2)

God's grace ensures our secure position with Him, and that one day we will be resurrected (as Jesus was) and glorified (made perfectly qualified for heaven). Such a position brings eternal joy to believers, starting now.

COLOSSIANS 1:15–20

Here the apostle Paul is writing to the church at Colossae, located in present-day Turkey. Paul did not found this church, but he did lead a disciple named Epaphras to the Lord while he was living in Ephesus for three years (mid-fifties AD) establishing the church there. Epaphras was from Colossae and after his conversion he returned to Colossae and began to share Christ with people there and the church was formed. Later Epaphras spoke to Paul of the zeal those Colossians had for the Lord, and thus, Paul is writing telling them of his prayers for them, and to ensure they continue to give preeminence to Christ. Notice how relevant Paul's words are to our day too. Speaking of Christ, Paul tells them:

> "He is the image of the invisible God, the firstborn of all creation. For by him all things were created, in heaven and on earth, visible and invisible, whether thrones or dominions or rulers or authorities—all things were created through him and for him. And he is before all things, and in him all things hold together. And he is the head of the body, the church. He is the beginning, the firstborn from the dead, that in everything he might be preeminent. For in him all the fullness of God was pleased to dwell, and through him to reconcile all things, whether on earth or in heaven, making peace by the blood of his cross." (Colossians 1:15–20)

This is the classic biblical description of Christ's role in creation and our redemption. This wording clears up the issue of the creation of Jesus. He is not a created being, for by Him all things in heaven and on earth were created. All nations, dominions, rulers and authorities, visible or invisible were not just created by Him, but for Him. Christ truly is King of Kings, and Lord of Lords. He was "there and here" before all things and holds everything together that was created. So He sustains what we know as the created order, this for our good, and His glory.

And to organize His doctrine and best describe His relationship to we believers, He established the church. Through His church we see illustrated how His relationship to us and we to each other is to play out in our society. We integrate His commands and our efforts through the church to best glorify Him, which is the essence of our purpose in being born.

Paul uses the phrase "fullness of God" to reflect, for our limited understanding, the complete extent of Jesus' identity, power, majesty, holiness, and involvement in the very existence of the universe (including us). And to that end, God chose to give His only Son to die in our place to provide atonement for our sins, and eternal residence in heaven for those who believe in Him. So, all things are reconciled through Him, "making peace by the blood of his cross." Only an almighty, loving God could and would make such provisions as these for us. "For God so loved the world, that He gave His only Son, that whoever believes in Him should not perish but have eternal life." (John 3:16)

Thus, though it may be difficult for some to grasp, we believers are the beneficiaries of God's steadfast love provided as the only way to eternal life. What a great, great God we have! Surely, we can justify telling others about His provisions for us.

1 PETER 4:16-19

Here Peter is writing to Christian churches in Asia Minor, modern-day Turkey, concerning standing up for their faith in Christ in an unbelieving world. There is a sense in which they (and we), are sometimes reluctant to proclaim our position with Christ for fear it will cause us to "stick out from the crowd." We don't know what that will lead to, or exactly what others will think of us, and we don't want to be conspicuous. Peter's position is that our glorifying God is much more important than the opinion of those around us. There is certainly no reason for us to be embarrassed or intimidated concerning our belief in Christ. Considering who Christ is and what He has done for us, a proper perspective would always cause us to be proactive in sharing our faith with others. See how Peter pictures our role as a suffering disciple of Christ:

> Yet if anyone suffers as a Christian, let him not be ashamed, but let him glorify God in that name. For it is time for judgment to begin in the household of God; and if it begins with us, what will the outcome be for those who do not obey the gospel of God? And

> "If the righteous is scarcely saved,
>   what will become of the ungodly and the sinner?"

> Therefore let those who suffer according to God's will entrust their souls to a faithful Creator while doing good. (1 Peter 4:16–19)

We are to not just be willing to suffer opposition for Christ's sake, but we are to look forward to those opportunities. Our suffering gladly in Christ's name is an expression of our belief in His sovereignty. "That name" as used here refers to Christ, in whose name Christians do everything. Peter explains such suffering among Christians is a normal thing. He says it is time for Christians (the household of God) to be responsible in their faith. And if in doing so, we face opposition, surely those unbelievers (who do not obey the gospel of God) will suffer one day, too, for their lack of belief. This concept applies in our day as well.

That the righteous are scarcely saved does not mean believers are saved, but only barely. The thought Peter has here is that even righteous people, who obey God, do suffer. Satan sees to that. After all, Christ suffered (though unjustly) to the greatest extent to pay our sin debt on the cross. Thus, if Christ suffered, and all believers do suffer, how much more suffering is due the ungodly and sinners? And one day they will. This principle of potential judgment is true for every person in every generation.

Thus, believers then and now are to remain strong in their faith. We are to entrust our souls, that is, our eternal destiny, to a faithful Creator. God is that faithful Creator. There is no inconsistency in Him. What He has said, He will do. The eternal life He promises is secure: "For God so loved the world, that He gave His only Son, that whoever believes in Him should not perish but have eternal life" (John 3:16).

And we are to go about life, suffering as we do, doing good in spite of our suffering. Bad things do happen to good people. God has organized things that way to bring both His love and His justice into play in our lives. But such a lifetime of suffering In Jesus' name is not to be compared with an eternity with the Lord in heaven that believers can anticipate.

2 CORINTHIANS 8:1-5

God blesses us and expects us to bless others. The criteria He uses is based on His love for us, and what He has gifted us to be able to do for others. He would have us be generous, as He has been generous to us. When we seriously sit down and total the gifts God has given us (especially including all the gifts we take for granted) we can only conclude God loves us very much. We are likely to take things like our health, our jobs, our family and friends who love us, when and where we were born, etc. for granted. Billions of people in this world don't have consistent food or shelter, and/or live under terrible conditions from governmental pressures. We know this from simply watching the news, but we don't give much consideration to what we might do to help. See this passage where Paul describes conditions where some people did do what they could to help others:

> We want you to know, brothers, about the grace of God that has been given among the churches of Macedonia, for in a severe test of affliction, their abundance of joy and their extreme poverty have overflowed in a wealth of generosity on their part. For they gave according to their means, as I can testify, and beyond their means, of their own accord, begging us earnestly for the favor of taking part in the relief of the saints—and this, not as we expected, but they gave themselves first to the Lord and then by the will of God to us. (2 Corinthians 8:1–5)

Paul was collecting money to be given to the poor church in Jerusalem. So, as he traveled through Macedonia (present-day northern Greece) he had made the churches there aware of the great need in Jerusalem. So now he is writing to the church in Corinth (southern Greece) telling them of the generous response from the Macedonian churches, who themselves were very poor. Paul especially points out how they gave out of their own need, sacrificing themselves for the benefit of the Jerusalem church. They apparently begged to be given the opportunity to be a part of the relief of the needs in Jerusalem. Those Macedonian churches had the right perspective. They gave themselves first to the Lord, and because of that their hearts were changed relative to how they pictured the needs in Jerusalem. Thus, they not only gave generously, but gladly.

The lesson for us is clear. We who have much are urged to give with the same kind of heart the churches in Macedonia demonstrated. And we are not to do this reluctantly or for personal reward, but simply for the sake of those in need and to glorify our heavenly Father who has been so good (for so long) to us. In a very real way, helping others is one way we thank God for what He has done for us.

There are unique benefits for people helping other people. If, for example, we give to help someone in dire need, we are much more likely to also pray for them and their relationship to the Lord. And having received a gift from you (even if they don't know where their gift came from) those people are much more likely to thank God and you for the gift they received and to begin to pray for you. So, now we see our gift has generated prayers to almighty God on behalf of others (from both groups). Picture that happening thousands of times; people getting help and lots of people praying for the situation. Surely, that's something God wants to see happening. And God rewards us accordingly.

PSALM 62:8

God has David title this Psalm "My Soul Waits for God Alone." That title sort of screams at us where our source of strength lies. He is writing to encourage people suppressed by their enemies and fellow countrymen alike. Those in positions of influence over them use their power and position to maintain their dominance, and thus, God's people tend to seek such authority themselves thinking that is the only way out from such oppression. Such is often the case in our day too. So an endless cycle of dominance and relief continues. See how David would stop this:

> Trust in him at all times, O people; pour out your heart before him; God is a refuge for us. (Psalm 62:8)

In David's time and in our day, the real source of relief from our troubles and depression is God alone. David has "been there," he has seen much in the way of trials and heartache. We think of him and his victory over Goliath as a teenager, and imagine God led him to victory in every battle. And with God's help he did experience many victories. But not all his days were victorious. He faced years of hatred by King Saul who tried to kill him on many occasions. He lost battles He could have won, but he failed at times to seek God's help. His own children turned against him, driving him from His throne in an attempt to overthrow him. He wound up with his army fighting against his son's army, resulting in his son's death, which broke his heart.

So what does such an experienced (with sorrow and defeat) man tell us to do? Answer: He tells us to "trust God at all times." We have the same God David had, and He loves us as He loved David. Notice what we are to do: "Pour out our heart before Him." To "pour out" implies deep-seated, heartfelt prayers of repentance

37

as we seek God's help and provision for whatever temptations and trials we face. The Psalm's instructions are open-ended, all problems are included, no time limit is mentioned, and it is God's limitless power and wisdom that are available to us.

Notice, too, David tells why we are to do this. It's because God is our only refuge. A refuge is defined as a shelter or protection from danger or distress. That is exactly what God makes available to us in our times of trouble. And how do we make the connection? Through sincere prayer, acknowledging God's position as sovereign Lord, and our position as a sinner saved by God's grace. Many times God does not address our situations as we have prayed or per our timetable, but He will respond and He always has our long-term good at heart. As it turns out God knows what we really need better than we do, and because He loves us, He works toward that end.

ACTS 5:38–39

Soon after His resurrection from the grave, Jesus returned to heaven. The disciples then continued to preach and teach as He had taught them to, hailing Jesus as Messiah and the Son of God. And as they did, they were also empowered to perform healing miracles. This gave the Jewish leadership credibility problems, because as they arrested the disciples in an attempt to get them to stop preaching, the healed person was often standing in the vicinity providing obvious proof of God's involvement in the event. Thus, the crowds who had witnessed the healings were a factor in the Jewish opposition to the disciples and their witness.

At one point as the disciples stood before the Pharisees charged with teaching in the name of Jesus, a well-respected Jewish Council member named Gamaliel spoke wisely to the council and senate concerning how to handle this problem. With the disciples out of hearing, he provided the Jewish leadership a logical solution to their dilemma. He recounted two different past occasions when rebel leaders had come against the council with some degree of military success. But eventually both rebellions ended when over time the leaders were killed and without strong leadership the rebellions came to nothing. See Gamaliel's words to the Council as God used him to accomplish His will:

> So in the present case I tell you, keep away from these men and let them alone, for if this plan or this undertaking is of man, it will fail; but if it is of God, you will not be able to overthrow them. You might even be found opposing God! (Acts 5:38–39)

His words were profoundly true, though not recognized as such at the time. The disciples were then beaten and released, having been told (again) not to speak in the name of Jesus. They left rejoicing that they had been deemed worthy to suffer dishonor in Jesus' name. And every day they continued to preach and teach Jesus as the Christ in the temple and from house to house. And the gospel spread. There is no way to measure (at this early stage of Christian growth) how much this unopposed freedom to share the gospel contributed to the rapid spread of the gospel worldwide.

Is this our attitude? Are we this zealous to share the gospel with the world? Fortunately for us, we do not live in such a restricted atmosphere, and are free to preach and teach the gospel (and live it out). God used Gamaliel that day purposefully. Neither is our present situation an accident. God has provided us this golden opportunity to share truth as His Word commands. And we have all the necessary tools to do so effectively, convenient air travel, the internet, email, television, etc. There are about seven billion people in the world, and it is estimated approximately one and a half billion of them have never heard the name of Jesus. Our task as believers is both challenging and obvious.

Surely, we are creative enough (with God's help) to clearly see ways we can contribute to the task of taking the gospel to the nations.

1 THESSALONIANS 5:14-15

As believers we have a responsibility to live daily as such. This, so that other people will have no doubt as to our allegiance to God and our eternal destiny in heaven with Him. Thus, Christianity is a full-time job, one that encompasses all we do and all we are. The main theme of this letter is the second coming of Christ. Thus, the apostle Paul, the author, is concerned his readers will not keep their focus on Christ and reminds them a proper relationship with Him will make itself known daily in all their personal relationships inside and outside their families. See some practical instructions Paul gives his readers.

> And we urge you, brothers, admonish the idle, encourage the fainthearted, help the weak, be patient with them all. See that no one repays anyone evil for evil, but always seek to do good to one another and to everyone. (1 Thessalonians 5:14–15)

We clearly see six mandates that we are to daily keep before us. Admonish the idle. Too many people, Christians included, do not stay busy doing the Lord's work. It's not as if there is nothing to do. We need only open our eyes and look around us to see more needs than we can meet, and there is not one need that God is unaware of. And there is not one needy person God does not love. And certainly we know what it feels like to be afraid, for we have all had our frightful moments, and know how traumatic they can be. Surely God would have us say a word of encouragement to the fainthearted.

All of us are blessed, some more than others and in different ways. Thus, when we know of or meet someone experiencing a weak moment, where stress and worldly issues have seemingly overwhelmed them (especially a Christian brother or sister), surely we can somehow lend our strength at that time. And then Paul mentions what is a common problem among believers, impatience. We often fail to exhibit to others the kind of patience we need so badly ourselves from God. Certainly, remembering how patient God has been with us will help us be patient with all others.

Believers in Paul's days were no more and no less likely to respond in kind to someone who has wronged them than we are today. The revenge motive, which is pride-oriented, is as rampant today as it was in Paul's time. This, and all the others of these instructions, are to be made a matter of prayer to God. Lastly, Paul urges a proactive attitude concerning good deeds. Let our minds gravitate to such thoughts on behalf of all others. How different our world today would be if all believers everywhere undertook to fulfill this command consistently within their own sphere of influence. And surely that is exactly what God would have us do, for how better can we glorify Him?

All these mind- and heart-sets mentioned above require proactive thought and intentions. We need to plan on this kind of lifestyle, thinking and living with our eyes open to the real world going on around us and thinking and living with our main goal being to glorify our heavenly Father. **Two things we can be sure of: (1) Our God is worthy of all our praise, honor, and glory. (2) We do praise, honor, and glorify Him, when we treat all others with the same kind of love He has for them.**

2 PETER 1:5-8

Here Peter is beginning to explain a very important principle that all believers need to understand, those in his day and those now. When we are saved by accepting Christ as our Lord and Savior, by faith we acknowledge Him as God incarnate, come to earth to save us from our sins. **God then grants us what scripture calls "all things" pertaining to life and godliness, including all of God's great promises.** And then here in verse five he urges us to actually live as Jesus taught us to live. Therefore, we are to understand that it is not our Christian lifestyle and good deeds that saved us, but they do prove that our faith that did save us is real. Beginning with faith and ending with love, Peter then lists eight qualities or virtues we are to live out in our daily lives. See how straightforward Peter is in his explanation. This is really God's word Peter is giving us:

> For this very reason, make every effort to supplement your faith with virtue, and virtue with knowledge, and knowledge with self-control, and self-control with steadfastness, and steadfastness with godliness, and godliness with brotherly affection, and brotherly affection with love. For if these qualities are yours and are increasing, they keep you from being ineffective or unfruitful in the knowledge of our Lord Jesus Christ. (2 Peter 1:5–8)

It's easy to understand how our lifestyles are the best and most accurate reflection of the purity of our hearts. Notice, too, improvement in these eight qualities comes by our own efforts (with the Holy Spirit's help). We are thus to make every effort to add to our faith by taking on these qualities. That can only mean we are to be "thinking" believers, always being sensitive to what Jesus would do in a given situation.

All these qualities are the result of our faith and reflect God's nature and Christlikeness. Our heavenly Father recognizes we need help in achieving growth in these areas, and He has sent His Holy Spirit to help us. This is a lifelong assignment for us, and Peter indicates that such growth is gradual. But such growth is the only way to be effective and fruitful in our spiritual influence.

If Peter tells us we are to make every effort to grow spiritually, **then it must be possible, and he tells us how, that is, by adding the various qualities listed. And if we do, the results are predictable, we are made effective and fruitful witnesses. Peter assumes that will be what we want. And if it is not what we want, then our commitment to the Lord is suspect.**

If we seriously consider what Peter is telling us, we realize that God must have a plan for our lives. He must have some things He will help us accomplish within His kingdom work. There is a real sense that believers are to let go, and let God have (complete) control of our lives. Consciously or subconsciously we often hold back from a total commitment to the Lord. Revelation 3:15–16 describes this condition: "Would that you were either cold or hot! So, because you are lukewarm, and neither hot nor cold, I will spit you out of my mouth."

We don't like coffee or ice cream lukewarm. Whatever should be hot, we want real hot, and whatever should be cold, we want real cold. It's not surprising then that God feels that way about our commitment to Him. There is no halfway commitment to God that satisfies Him, **and we know that.**

ISAIAH 9:6–7

Isaiah, the prophet, came with a message of hope and assurance, not to Israel only, but to the whole world. He spoke prophetic words that described Jesus Christ as Son of David, and Messiah, destined to rule the world, including Gentiles, forever. Isaiah lived during a time when Israel was far astray from God's will in sin, and threatened militarily by various powers of that time. He spoke as if Messiah was on the way and would arrive soon, but that was not to be. Isaiah lived about 700 BC, and Israel had much to suffer and learn in the interim before Messiah came. See these words describing the world's Savior:

> For to us a child is born,
>   to us a son is given;
> and the government shall be on His shoulder,
>   and His name shall be called
> Wonderful Counselor, Mighty God,
>   Everlasting Father, Prince of Peace.
> Of the increase of His government and of peace
>   there will be no end,
> on the throne of David and over His kingdom,
>   to establish it and to uphold it
> with justice and with righteousness
>   from this time forth and forevermore.
> The zeal of the LORD of Hosts will do this. (Isaiah 9:6–7)

Isaiah emphasized Messiah would come as an heir of David, a Jew, but with a mandate to rule over all Gentiles too. He would come as a child who would eventually head a government of peace based on justice and righteousness that would have no end. Notice the "zeal" of the Lord of Hosts is mentioned as the way He would do this. Zeal to us means eagerness, passion, and fervor. Thus, in our words we would say our Creator God was excited about His plans and what He would accomplish. And that's no wonder for His very nature is love, and we would describe all this by saying, "He loved us so much, He was anxious for us to get here."

If we are not careful, we will miss the point of these words recorded about 2,700 years ago. Here in God's Word, we are told of an almighty, loving, one true God of "all that is" who designed, created, and loved us all into being. He made infinite and indescribable provisions for our existence, and our life eternal with Him. To put that together He had to deal with our total depravity and unworthiness of the privilege of His presence. And He did that the only way possible by sacrificing His only Son on the cross to pay our debt of sin. We can't even come close to understanding the significance of these events, and that's because we can't come close to understanding the extent of His love. **But praise His name and hallelujah, He did it, and we believers have an eternity with Him to look forward to as a result.**

And to say that we should be grateful, and joy filled, is the understatement of all time. Obedience and sharing this truth should be our "all day, everyday" order of business.

PHILIPPIANS 2:9–11

God the Father sent His Son Jesus Christ to earth as man to save us from our sins. He came as the God-man who took on all our sins and died in our place on the cross to pay the sin debt of all who believe in Him. And hallelujah, He conquered death and rose from the grave for us. In this letter the apostle Paul wrote to the church at Philippi to encourage them in their faith. Christ only is worthy of all our praise, honor, and glory and Paul is describing the special position He has as Lord to remind the Philippians (and readers like us) of their need to follow Him. See Paul's description of Jesus' honored position:

> Therefore God has highly exalted him and bestowed on him the name that is above every name, so that at the name of Jesus every knee should bow, in heaven and on earth and under the earth, and every tongue confess that Jesus Christ is Lord, to the glory of God the Father. (Philippians 2:9–11)

From this description Jesus has clearly been given the highest of positions, and rightly so. He, only, merits the esteem and reverence due that one who came down from heaven to suffer and die a sinner's death that satisfied the wrath of God for our sin. And it is also clear that almighty God the Father is that only one who has the authority to exalt Jesus this way.

So, Paul's readers then, and we readers now, can be certain Jesus is worthy of all our worship and adoration. Thus, in a world of sin and ignorance God has seen fit to develop a plan of salvation that applies to all who will believe. Mankind now has a defined way to eternal life that is as certain as a sunrise, and as good as an infinitely good God can make it. So, a time of rejoicing is at hand. We can celebrate God's love shown in this gift of His Son.

We need not therefore become concerned and bothered by worldly issues that are only temporary in nature. This is one of the key reasons the Philippians needed this letter. They were under severe pressure from the Romans to submit to the lordship of Caesar. Paul needed to provide them this anchor for their faith, that would last throughout an extended Roman domination. We have a similar requirement today. Our society tries to dominate us in a very real way as well, tending to claim a Satan-oriented lifestyle as the preferred one. Our new life in Christ as a believer enables us to get and keep a perspective that focuses on heaven as our home, not this earth. Only true believers have an understanding of the significance of that heavenly perspective.

Notice the description of Jesus' glory. His name is above every other name, that we all should acknowledge and bow to, and that every tongue should confess as Lord. And the purpose of this adoration and praise is the glory of almighty God. And that, of course, is the "bottom line" purpose of all our lives: to bring praise, honor, and glory to God.

So, we can conclude the lives of the Philippians were not unlike ours, full of questions, trials, fears, doubts, and pressure from the powerful evil influences of the society around them. The solution then is the same solution now: salvation in Christ. No other way to eternal life has been devised or will ever be. No better approach to life has been created, or will ever be. No other Savior exists or will ever exist. Jesus really is Lord, God really did create us all in His image and love us enough to provide an eternity for believers with Him. Hallelujah! What a great God we have!

GALATIANS 3:7–9

A natural desire of every human is to find the (or "a") way to eternal life. So after creating man, and seeing the fall of that man into sin, God's love led Him to define a way to atone for man's sin, leading to his eternal salvation. John the apostle beautifully and simply defines that way: "For God so loved the world, that He gave His only Son, that whoever believes in Him should not perish but have eternal life." (John 3:16)

Then God was left with the task of how to communicate this path to the world. Notice God's plan is love-driven. It was because God loved the world that He would even care whether they found this way or not. And notice, too, belief in Jesus Christ is required. Thus, God chose Abram to be the father of a new nation, one given the task of sharing the fact of the way to salvation (there is only one way), and the way itself.

Key to God's salvation plan was the role faith was to play. Man's inclination was (and still is) to earn his own salvation with good deeds, and living a sinless life. But that was not to be. God's definition of holiness is such that mankind could never earn their way into heaven. See Paul's letter to the Galatian churches outlining how faith provides access to God's gift of eternal life.

> Know then that it is those of faith who are the sons of Abraham. And the Scripture, foreseeing that God would justify the Gentiles by faith, preached the gospel beforehand to Abraham saying, "In you shall all the nations be blessed." So then, those who are of faith are blessed along with Abraham, the man of faith. (Galatians 3:7–9)

See then how it is faith that defines the "sons of Abraham," not bloodlines. Thus, God makes provision to justify Gentiles, too, by faith. Hallelujah! John has told us that whoever believes can be saved, and now Paul reminds us God told Abraham that through him "shall all the nations be blessed." Of course, this phrase refers to Christ coming to make the supreme sacrifice on the cross to atone for the sins of all believers (Jew and Gentile).

So Paul's message here is that faith leads to salvation, not good deeds or pure lifestyles. Good deeds are important and are called for in scripture, but they are the result of our salvation, not the cause of it. Paul's theme in this letter to the Galatians was that justification (our acquittal by God from charges of sin) is by faith alone. Our belief, by faith, in Jesus' sacrificial death on the cross to pay our sin debt, defines the repentance we feel over the sin in our lives that required Jesus' atoning death to satisfy. It is that recognition on our part that we are sinners in need of a Savior that opens our hearts to God's Holy Spirit transformation.

The whole world urgently needs to know this. And the whole world includes those closest to us. In the first place, it's the best news anyone will ever hear. And second, ignoring this truth of God's provision would be the biggest mistake anyone could make, and that mistake would be eternal in scope.

HEBREWS 10:12–14

There has been much discussion for centuries concerning the sufficiency of Christ's sacrificial death on the cross as to whether it is the full payment for the sin debt of all believers. Praise the Lord, this unknown author of Hebrews addresses that issue and leaves us no doubt that Christ paid our full debt. See this passage declaring Jesus' qualifications to do that:

> But when Christ had offered for all time a single sacrifice for sins, he sat down at the right hand of God, waiting from that time until his enemies should be made a footstool for his feet. For by a single offering he has perfected for all time those who are being sanctified. (Hebrews 10:12–14)

Christ now being seated at the right hand of God reflects His work of redemption is complete. As Jesus said from the cross, "It is finished." Our sin ransom is paid. Nothing more is required. Human priests stood as they offered their sacrifices, indicating the incompleteness of that sacrifice. And they did it every year, again reflecting that the ongoing sin of the Israelites had to be repeatedly dealt with. So, on a once-for-all-time basis, God the Father offered His only Son as that means of perfecting believers.

This does not mean believers are immediately made sinless, but that Jesus earned their perfection, which will one day (at the judgment) be applied to them. So, human priests could not then and cannot now permanently atone for our sins with their sacrifices no matter how perfect the offered animal is. Jesus is now in "waiting" mode until that time when all unbelievers have had their chance to receive Christ's free gift of salvation by His grace and their faith. And as He waits, He intercedes on our behalf with the Father. All this per God's perfect plan of salvation. So Jesus, our high priest, is ever ready to receive our prayers of repentance, asking for forgiveness.

Thus, we believers do struggle with sin as we live out our lives here on earth, but God made provision for those struggles as well. Every believer is indwelt with the Holy Spirit to guide and protect us in our earthly journey toward compete sanctification. And then one day Jesus will return to complete that sanctification and take us to heaven for an eternity with Him.

There is the sense then that we both grow in sanctification here on earth after our conversion, and at the same time we are positionally assured at conversion that complete sanctification will be accomplished at Jesus' return. Thus, the perfection required for entrance into heaven will become ours. Hallelujah! God thinks of everything. Such is His love for us.

Significant in this process is the conviction (and comfort) all believers have that they can look to Christ for that perfection, and not to themselves. The passage clearly tells us Jesus perfected for all time those who are being sanctified. It is His righteousness that will be imputed to us at the judgment and that our heavenly Father will see in us allowing Him to welcome us into eternal fellowship with Him. And with that complete sanctification we become more like Christ, by far, than we are now. This, to enhance our natures to the point we truly are complete children (thus, heirs) of God and joint heirs with Jesus in His heavenly inheritance. Hallelujah again!

1 CORINTHIANS 15:20-23

This passage comes from that section of 1 Corinthians that discusses the resurrection of the dead who died as believers. All believers have doubtlessly reviewed this passage seeking information concerning their eternal destiny with Christ. Anticipating this search, God had Paul cover this subject in his letter to the church at Corinth, Greece. Like us, those believers wanted to know about their life after death. So, Paul answered their questions as he urged them to work together taking the gospel of Jesus Christ to a lost world. This, because Jesus' role in the eternal destiny of all believers is a major part of His gospel. Thus, we can rest assured this passage covers our eternal destiny too. See what Paul has to say:

> But in fact Christ has been raised from the dead, the firstfruits of those who have fallen asleep. For as by a man came death, by a man has come also the resurrection of the dead. For as in Adam all die, so also in Christ shall all be made alive. But each in his own order: Christ the firstfruits, then at his coming those who belong to Christ. (1 Corinthians 15:20–23)

Christ did rise from the dead after His crucifixion, as attested to by many witnesses. So, Christ was then said to be the firstfruits pointing to the resurrection from the dead of many others. "Firstfruits" is a common phrase of that day referring to the first samples that come from an agricultural crop indicating the nature and quality of the future harvest. Thus, as by a man (Adam) came sin (and thus, death), so by a man (Jesus Christ) came life (eternal), via belief in Jesus' death and resurrection. We can then identity what the resurrected bodies of all believers will look like by noting Jesus' body after His resurrection.

We find more information on that subject from 2 Corinthians 5:6–8: "So we are always of good courage. We know that while we are at home in the body we are away from the Lord, for we walk by faith, not by sight. Yes, we are of good courage, and we would rather be away from the body and at home with the Lord."

Here, Paul is teaching concerning the intermediate state of believers between their earthly death and the return of Christ. He felt that state for him and all believers would be as a spirit or soul at home with the Lord. Thus, he and all believers who die before Christ returns would remain in that spirit state without a body, until Christ returns, when Paul and all believers (those who had previously died, and those alive at Christ's return) would then be resurrected with resurrection bodies like Christ's. And thus, we then will exist in Christ's presence for an eternity with believers from every nation, in bodies not subject to weakness of any sort, without aging, or death.

So, what a future we believers have, what a message we have to share, and what a Savior we have to proclaim! In fact, that's our assignment, to (as the song says), "Go, tell it on the mountain. Over the hills and everywhere." No one and no place is to be exempted from the gospel of Christ.

JAMES 1:16–18

As believers we can expect to have our faith tested. Just as we lift weights, pushing against a resistance to develop stronger muscles. Just so are we spiritually tested, striving against trials and temptations, to develop stronger faith. God is behind this because He loves us and knows we need to grow in our faith. We are fortunate indeed to have a God who makes such provisions and explains clearly how and why we are to deal with our testing times. See how the Holy Spirit has James word our instructions:

> Do not be deceived, my beloved brothers. Every good gift and every perfect gift is from above, coming down from the Father of lights with whom there is no variation or shadow due to change. Of his own will he brought us forth by the word of truth, that we should be a kind of firstfruits of his creatures. (James 1:16–18)

If we think at all of where our blessings come from, we are tempted to think we have earned them, given our hard work and the time and money we wisely invest. But not so. The passage above clearly indicates that without exception every worthy gift comes to us from God the Father, worthy gifts being those with eternal implications and ramifications. So, all our gifts, particularly the good and perfect ones, come from above. Interestingly, God is referred to here as the "Father of light," that one who provides us the heavenly bodies who bring us light, which is a clear example of a godly type gift. We rarely consider the sun, moon, and stars as gifts, but they truly are as they provide light, warmth, weather, gravity, and the orbital motion that gives our world its stability and consistency.

God thinks eternally, with His gifts, even what we may consider small ones, having eternal implications for us. God is the very essence of consistency, always immutable, unchanging in every respect, especially in the love and mercy He shows us. The wording of the passage tells us to not be fooled by our selfish perspective and our shortsighted vision of the future, into thinking God is not involved in every facet of our lives. We tend to limit our consideration of God's gifts to tangible ones like food, shelter, health, wealth, and family. While these are all God's gifts, and worthy of our thankfulness, there is much more that we should also be thankful for, with our eternal salvation being our greatest and best gift. God's gift of His Son to die atoning for our sins is matchless.

And God did all this because of His total love for us. His incentive to provide us the gift of eternal salvation was always and only His love nature. We need to seriously consider God's love for us. It is not an abstract thing. It is alive and active, bringing blessings, benefits, guidance, and protection to us. First John 4:8 tells us God is love, meaning God continually gives Himself to others for their benefit. Notice it was God's idea to save us. His love for us motivated Him to give His only Son to die paying our sin debt, and His ongoing concern for us leads Him to give us daily direction and protection.

So, in a very real way, the tests God provides us are among His best gifts, and evidence of His great love for us. Such testing is to make us more Christlike, and what could be a better gift.

HEBREWS 4:14–16

All of us are born sinners and thus all of us need a high priest to act as our representative before a holy God. Jesus came to earth to fill that role. As our (great) high priest, He came and lived as a human, experiencing all the various temptations we face, yet without sin. Therefore, we can conclude Jesus understands our troubles, our temptations, and our trials having "been there" Himself. So, without hesitation we believers are to come to Him, sharing openly our needs, fears, and doubts. See this explanation of Jesus' position as our intercessor:

> Since then we have a great high priest who has passed through the heavens, Jesus, the Son of God, let us hold fast our confession. For we do not have a high priest who is unable to sympathize with our weaknesses, but one who in every respect has been tempted as we are, yet without sin. Let us then with confidence draw near to the throne of grace, that we may receive mercy and find grace in time of need. (Hebrews 4:14–16)

Not a single person ever lives without having to deal with troubles, trials, and temptations. So, the author (unknown) of Hebrews is on solid ground when he speaks of such common problems. Everyone has them. God, the Father, in His infinite love and wisdom made provision for our relief from these Satan-inspired ordeals. Jesus passed through the heavens, that is, He came from His high position in heaven to earth for our sake to specifically deal with our dilemma, and has now returned, sitting at the right hand of God the Father. So, we are to hold fast to our confession, that is, we are not to waver in our faith, but persevere to the end knowing Jesus identifies with our temptations.

We can persevere for we know our high priest, Jesus, is the high priest of heaven and earth, who has (already) experienced the same things we face. Jesus was appointed by the Father to suffer (and die) so that believers would receive the gift of eternal salvation. Jesus does not just acknowledge our weaknesses (in the face of temptation), He sympathizes with us. His heart goes out to us, and He prepares and delivers relief.

So, we can confidently "draw near to God's throne of grace." What a beautiful way to describe our access to God's love and provisions in time of stress. We can picture Him as King with all power and authority, and yet see Him also as the God who loves us infinitely, in spite of our unloveliness. So, mercy is available, grace (in abundance) is there for the asking, and the relief we need comes forth. What a great God we have!

So, what are we to do with this knowledge of so great a love? Is there no one we can share it with? Does our daily life reflect appropriate repentance of sin, and adequate remorse over our disobedience to God? For God's Word to urge us to draw near to God's throne would imply that it is possible, that we want to, and that we know how. And what are we to do "upon arrival?" Surely, repentance of our sinful condition and requests for forgiveness would be prerequisites for seeking communion with almighty God. Thus, prayer is key; it's that universal approach that God provided that is available to all of us, anywhere, at any time.

1 SAMUEL 12:24

Samuel had been sent to Israel as both a prophet and as a judge. The Israelites had a sort of "on again, off again" relationship with God. The people would obey God a while and then drift into idolatry, get into a crisis situation of some description with their pagan neighbors, and cry out to God for help. God would hear their cries and send a judge to lead them out of bondage; and once that was done, they would repent and obey God for a while, and then the cycle would repeat itself. We are very much like that today, tending to go our own way until a crisis comes. In this passage Samuel once again gives the Israelites (and us) instructions as to how they should be living, but this time he also gives them a clue as to how to accomplish this. Look at this verse:

> Only fear the LORD and serve him faithfully with all your heart. For consider what great things he has done for you. (1 Samuel 12:24)

The concept of acknowledging God's authority and sovereignty over all things is key to Samuel's instructions for them in that time and us in our day. **God is to be reverenced and served in all circumstances** for He is worthy of all our reverence and service. No mention is made of coloring these instructions with our present experiences and letting them help govern our reverence for God, or our serving Him. He simply tells us to fear and serve faithfully with a "no matter what" attitude. The word *faithfully* has two meanings here; to live full of faith, that is, with as much faith as possible, and secondly, to do so consistently. "With all your heart" speaks of our doing so with a "from the inside-out," intimate kind of effort.

And then Samuel gives us all the clue as to how to accomplish this: "Consider what great things He has done for you." Here we shape our perspective about all things after considering them alongside God's blessings and provisions for us. When we lay any worldly trial or temptation next to God's provision of eternal life through Jesus' sacrificial death in our place, we quickly conclude how much God loves us. And thus, we can sincerely praise and worship Him. Now we inherently know this truth, but it can only help for us to see it plainly put to us again by the Holy Spirit in light of today's world.

Proverbs 21:3

These proverbs, written by King Solomon as he was led by the Holy Spirit, furnish basic tenets of life, principles to live by to gain the most from life in any era. Some are subtle, some very straightforward, easy to understand and apply. This one fits that last description:

> To do righteousness and justice is more acceptable to the LORD than sacrifice. (Proverbs 21:3)

In the first place, this Proverb indicates our actions not only are known by God but also are (or will be) judged by God. We also see here that, evidently, we have a voice in what we do. Thus, if we decide what we do, and if God knows all that we do, and judges us, then the concept of responsibility is evident. So when we are in the process of choosing our actions, we are well advised to choose righteous actions, and just actions over sacrifices that tend to be things we do to attempt to make amends or atone for things we've done that we sense are wrong.

There is another (big) factor to add to this scenario: God's love. We are here because of God's love. So all the choosing, the actions, and the judging (and the results of that judging) are based on God's love. Because He loves us, God makes us aware of the criteria He uses to do His judging so that we have His basis of judging in front of us as we do our choosing. **So, in essence, we decide our destiny by how we choose.**

This particular Proverb speaks of the kind of principles God approves of (righteous principles, and just principles) over man-made activities like "after the fact" sacrifices. There are consequences resulting from our choices, good ones from right and just choices, and bad ones from sinful and unjust choices. Both kinds of consequences tend to still be in place after our actions, the good ones resulting in God still being glorified, and the bad ones still causing disruption and heartache to some degree for someone.

Thus, the obvious lesson from this Proverb is that God has constructed a cause-and-effect type of society on earth. But knowing our bent toward sin (the cause), and because of His great love for us, He saw fit to send Jesus Christ to earth to live a perfect life, and die a sinner's death on the cross in our place atoning for our sin by thus paying our sin debt (the effect). We gain complete forgiveness for our sin by our acknowledgment of our sinful status, our repentance for our sins, and our trust (by faith) in Christ's sacrificial death as payment for our sin. Notice we are saved then by God's grace and our faith, not any sort of "combo" of good deeds. Good deeds are the result of our salvation, not the cause, because only then will good deeds be truly done for the right reason, God's glory.

COLOSSIANS 3:17

The apostle Paul is writing here to the church at Colossae, giving them instructions as to how to live obedient lives. We might wonder why he wrote to them, and why they would listen to what he had to say. In the first place, he loved them. And that came across in his letter. Every one of us appreciates being loved, because consciously or subconsciously we recognize that as proof of our worth. And we all want to be thought of as having worth. And the people in the church at Colossae respected Paul. So, Paul wrote showing He cared enough about them to write to them as God gave him direction via His Holy Spirit. Paul knew that if his readers obeyed God's commands, they would benefit from doing so. Living godly lives will always work to our long-term good, especially in our day. **God blesses sincere obedience nowadays just as He did in the first century. He does this because our obedience is the best evidence we can provide that expresses our desire to give glory to God, and that is uppermost in importance to Him.** See our scriptural instructions on glorifying God.

> And whatever you do in word or deed, do everything in the name of the Lord Jesus, giving thanks to God the Father through him. (Colossians 3:17)

> So, whether you eat or drink, or whatever you do, do all to the glory of God. (1 Corinthians 10:31)

> Let your light shine before others, so that they may see your good works and give glory to your Father who is in heaven. (Matthew 5:16)

> Everyone who is called by my name, whom I created for my glory, whom I formed and made. (Isaiah 43:7)

Clearly then, God gives us all the proper sense of perspective we are to live by. And if we had to put it in one word, that word would be humility. We are therefore to take no credit for what we have or do. Nor are we to ever think of accepting the praise of men. We have been given everything we have and every talent we possess, thus, how could we justify accepting some kind of honor for something that came to us from above.

Notice how the Colossians passage tells us to give thanks to our Father God (through Jesus) for what He has provided. Thus, we are to be proactive in giving God any praise, honor, or glory that might come to us. **So, look at obedience to what you know (already) God would have you do as honoring God, as proof to any person who knows you that God is important to you, the most important person in your life**. Too many people run from being identified with Christ even though they might claim to be believers. Making that change in priorities will likely be the most important decision any of us ever make. After all, none of the worldly decisions we make will compare with making Jesus Christ our Lord and Master. And who in our life do we owe more allegiance to than that one who provided us eternal life?

2 SAMUEL 7:18–20, 22

Before time began David had been chosen by God to be king in Israel, but David did not know it until he was about thirty years old. And when God had Nathan the prophet tell him that he would be king and that his throne would be established forever, David was humbled by the thought. So he prayed, and we see his prayer beginning in verse 7:18. David used the phrase "your servant" ten times in this prayer, and he used the phrase "O Lord God" eight times in this prayer. Look at this part of that prayer:

> Then King David went and sat before the Lord and said, "Who am I, O Lord GOD, and what is my house, that you have brought me thus far? And yet this is a small thing in your eyes, O Lord GOD. You have spoken also of your servant's house for a great while to come, and this is instruction for mankind, O Lord GOD! . . . Therefore you are great, O Lord GOD. For there is none like you, and there is no God besides you." (2 Samuel 7:18–20, 22)

In reality, in this passage and others, God was telling David that Messiah, Jesus Christ, would come through his line, and thus, David's line would be honored in this special way. And David recognized that truth and was especially humbled, declaring, "You are great, O Lord GOD. For there is none like you, and there is no God besides you." Notice that what really humbled David is the significance of this truth, for here almighty God has told him news that is eternal in scope, and for all mankind. **The whole world was going to be blessed forever by one of David's descendants.**

And, of course, that is exactly what happened about a thousand years later. The lineage of Joseph, Jesus' earthly father, indicates Joseph is born as a direct descendant of King David. Now we may think a thousand years is a long time for God to wait before He fulfills His promise, but scripture tells us "a thousand years is as one day to God" (2 Peter 3:8).

And David was right, God is still great, and always will be, and there never will be a God like Him, and there never will be a God beside Him. So we can take joy in that fact, realizing the God who loved us so much He sent His Son to earth to save us from our sins is sovereign God, the only God of creation who created all that has been created. Let us give Him praise, honor, glory, and thanksgiving always and for everything.

PHILIPPIANS 4:5-7

There are certain attitudes God would have us take on and exhibit in our lives, and certain things He would have us do regularly to prepare ourselves for receipt of His Holy Spirit. This, because He desires we glorify Him with our lives, and He knows (far better than we do) what is involved in our obedience to His will and the results that will accrue to us if we do. See this special passage:

> The Lord is at hand; do not be anxious about anything, but in everything by prayer and supplication with thanksgiving let your requests be made known to God. And the peace of God, which surpasses all understanding, will guard your hearts and your minds in Christ Jesus. (Philippians 4:5–7)

Notice the first thing God has Paul assure us in this passage is that God is nearby, always ready and able to see to our every need. And thus, we are not to worry or be anxious about anything. If we assess this command properly, we realize it is an affront to God if we do fret and become afraid because of worldly cares and circumstances. Truly, such feelings are reflective of weak faith, or misunderstanding on our parts, of how powerful our God is, and how much He does love us.

Thus, we are to take everything (small and large problems) to God by prayer and supplication. Notice, too, we are to do this thankfully, fully acknowledging we know this is a privilege God has given us. As we do this, we also acknowledge we realize God already (intimately) knows and understands what our prayers and supplications are all about, yet He still tells us to voice our needs to Him in prayer. Obviously then there must be some benefit to our repeating to God, problems we know He knows about. **There is benefit to us in doing this; we then (over time) begin to see our**

requests as God sees them, and this leads us to a much greater understanding of His nature. And the more we understand Him the more we will love Him, and the more we then come to be Christlike. And, of course, this is our ultimate goal, to love and obey God as Christ does.

See the promised results of such obedient prayers and supplications. Supplications, by the way, describe how we pray, that is, humbly, earnestly, and consistently. When we pray this way, we are promised God's peace, which surpasses all understanding. We get the feeling this kind of peace can come to us no other way than via earnest supplications to God. And although we are told we will not fully understand such peace, it will guard our hearts and minds. And that, too, seems hard to completely understand, yet in guarding our hearts we sense protection and direction of our hearts and minds is included, and that we can grasp. We inherently understand our hearts and minds need to be protected and directed and who better than God can accomplish that?

So, we win when we pray (per God's direction) in several ways. First, we get help and relief with our problems. We lose the fear and anxiousness we had about those problems. And we gain God's peace that protects and directs our hearts and minds per Jesus' example. Perfection in these areas defines what heaven will be like. Isn't it just like God to begin now giving us ways we can start to understand and enjoy heaven? Then let us begin to pray God's way.

1 JOHN 2:3-6

Scholars think the apostle John left Jerusalem about AD 67 and settled in the vicinity of Ephesus in western Asia Minor, modern-day Turkey. His departure then came shortly before Jerusalem and the temple were destroyed by the Romans in about AD 70. This series of letters was then likely written to churches in cities in the general area around Ephesus, urging them to major in the three basics of the Christian life: true doctrine, obedient living, and fervent devotion. Obviously we, too, would do well to emphasize these same three principles in our lives. See how John words his instructions:

> And by this we know that we have come to know him, if we keep his commandments. Whoever says "I know him" but does not keep his commandments is a liar and the truth is not in him, but whoever keeps his word, in him truly the love of God is perfected. By this we may know that we are in him: whoever says he abides in him ought to walk in the same way in which he walked. (1 John 2:3–6)

The really good news of this passage is that it presents a description of how we may self-diagnose our relationship with Christ. Here the test is very straightforward: Have professing Christians experienced a changed life to the point they obey the Lord's commandments? See how John words that relationship. He says, "Whoever keeps God's Word, in him the love of God is perfected." Having God's love perfected within us would imply the very kind of relationship Jesus had with the world around Him is manifested in us also. That kind of care and concern for others is mature, ongoing, universally applied, and obviously visible. There would be no hypocrisy in our motives, no limit to our effort, and complete consistency of our love for the Lord our God, and our neighbors.

We can be assured then we know Him if the desire to obey His commandments is ever within us. Is that priority not "a" criteria we live by, but "the" criteria we live by? Per this passage, one's lifestyle, therefore, is the most accurate depiction of their relationship with the Lord.

When we think about this subject of assurance of salvation, words and phrases like *justification, propitiation*, and *glorifying God* come to mind. Justification is that act of God wherein He declares us not guilty, acquitted of all our sins (past, present, and future). This declaration comes only by God's grace through our faith in Christ's sacrificial death to pay our sin debt. Propitiation is the term referring to the sacrifice Christ made on the cross, including the provision that it was made specifically to satisfy the wrath of God, that wrath indicative of the abhorrence God has for sin of any kind. To glorify God is the basic reason any of us were ever born. All we do, say, or think (and our motives for all such) are to be aligned with that result of God's glory in mind.

So, Christ came to earth, specifically to save us from our sins. God made this supreme sacrifice because He loves us sinners with an infinite love, and it is by grace through faith we are saved. Thus, our good works do not save us, but done with the right motives, they are a reflection we are saved. And we can be assured of that. That's what John is saying in the last verse, "those who abide in Christ ought to walk in the same way in which He walked." Imitating Jesus is our goal because that best glorifies our heavenly Father.

LUKE 10:25-28

Every thinking person who has ever lived has considered the question, "What happens after death?" We all know inherently we cannot live forever, thus, the concept of eternal life is a viable concern for everyone. In this passage we see a lawyer putting Jesus to the test; that is, he is attempting to challenge Jesus' credibility before the people by asking Him a question concerning eternal life hoping Jesus will make some sort of doctrinal mistake. He is not really seeking to be taught by Jesus. But the lesson Jesus teaches him is one we need to learn too. See this conversation:

> And behold, a lawyer stood up to put him to the test, saying, "Teacher, what shall I do to inherit eternal life?" He said to him, "What is written in the law? How do you read it?" And he answered, "You shall love the Lord your God with all your heart and with all your soul and with all your strength and with all your mind, and your neighbor as yourself." And he said to him, "You have answered correctly; do this and you will live." (Luke 10:25–28)

Note the lawyer asks Jesus a question he already knows the answer to. So he answers his own question correctly, and Jesus confirms that before the people. **But Jesus also points out to him that intellectual knowledge of how to inherit eternal life is not enough.** Jesus also tells him (and us) to "do this and you will live." The lawyer must know what to do and then do it. That same criteria is true for us.

Notice what the criteria for eternal life is: to love the Lord your God with all your heart, soul, strength, and mind, and love your neighbor as yourself. These commands are both taken from the Old Testament (Deuteronomy 6:5 and Leviticus 19:18).

Jesus considered the Old Testament to be the definitive source of correct doctrine. Nothing that Jesus taught or lived was in conflict with Old Testament doctrine. Notice how beautifully the concept of loving the Lord and our neighbors encompasses the complete giving of ourselves to others. We cannot love God with everything we have and are, and also disobey His commands. And we cannot love our neighbors as we love ourselves and not see to their needs when necessary. **And it's these total "love" commitments God wants to see in us.** Thus, these commands translate into our living lifestyles sincerely given over to God and others **and not ourselves.**

If the lawyer that day was required to live out these two commandments to inherit eternal life, so are we. So, we know what is required. The problem is, we are unable to do it. No one lives a completely sinless life. We are born sinners and therefore something must be done about our sin condition. But, hallelujah, God knew that and because He loves us, He made provision for it. He sent Jesus to earth to live a sinless life and save us from our sins by His substitutionary death in our place on the cross. **Jesus' sacrifice paid our sin debt completely. We take on His righteousness by faith when we repent of our sins and trust His death as payment for our sins.** Such a transformation is life changing, and if authentic it shows. Other people will see Jesus Christ in our lives when we prayerfully live them "sold out" to Him.

EPHESIANS 4:29–32

In this passage Paul urges those members of the church in Ephesus to mind their ways. Recognizing that God the Father, through Christ, has reconciled all of creation to Himself, and united all believers of every nation together in His church, then they are to live lives evidencing proper gratitude for all His many blessings. There is no room for idolatry, selfishness, or pride in their lifestyles, given their great God's love and provisions. See Paul's very practical instructions for his readers in that day and ours:

> Let no corrupting talk come out of your mouths, but only such as is good for building up, as fits the occasion, that it may give grace to those who hear. And do not grieve the Holy Spirit of God, by whom you were sealed for the day of redemption. Let all bitterness and wrath and anger and clamor and slander be put away from you, along with all malice. Be kind to one another, tenderhearted, forgiving one another as God in Christ forgave you. (Ephesians 4:29–32)

Obviously, when we are saved, we are given new life in Christ, and thus, certain different attitudes and actions are to prevail in our lives. Paul lists characteristics we are to lose, and others we are to take on. Our new status in Christ is to show by our concern for others. Building others up, then, is to be our mindset, and giving them grace our goal. To give grace to someone is a worthy purpose and is not to be taken lightly. We do, in fact, have responsibility for how our influence affects others.

There is a sense in this command that if we can give grace or benefit someone with what we say, God will hold us accountable for doing it. And why not? Who are we to withhold beneficial information or encouragement from someone without thinking?

Therein lies the crux of the matter: do we think before we speak? And what is our purpose when we do speak? Discipline in what we say is thus to become a habit with us.

And we are not to grieve the Holy Spirit. Of course we are not. We know that without even trying to define what Paul means when he uses the word *grieve*. No doubt Paul, at the very least, means we are not to speak or act counter to the will of the Holy Spirit. But all of us do so thoughtlessly and need to give more consideration as to the consequences of what we say and do. Paul seems to be saying we surely will not want to grieve the Holy Spirit given the key role He plays in our salvation. He indwells all believers and is there to guide us and remind us of what we have in Christ, which is the same inheritance of eternal life He has. **Thus, the real essence of our not grieving the Holy Spirit is that we don't do it "for Christ's sake" and that's the most important reason we could ever have for doing (or refraining from doing) anything.**

Note the list of "do not's" and "do's" Paul then adds. Notice, too, that the word *all* is specifically telling us to not let any bitterness, wrath, anger, clamor, or malice become a part of our lifestyle. Paul's message is surely that if we are guilty of even a small amount of any of those, we are apt to become guilty of a lot of all of them. Sin is like that, some sin leading to much more sin. But conversely, we are to "put on" kindness, tender hearts, and forgiveness, especially since God in Christ has forgiven us of so much. And, of course, this is how we glorify the Father.

MARK 4:26-29

There are a number of ways God communicates His message to us, His children. Perhaps the most distinct way is though His Word. He has gone to great lengths to provide the Bible for our knowledge and benefit. Written over a period of about fifteen hundred years by at least forty different authors, the Bible presents the timeless truths God intends for us to learn and obey. It is not, however, simply a listing of do's and don'ts for us to memorize and try hard to comply with. There is a certain God-provided power and wisdom within God's Word that captures our subconscious mind and can transform our very nature. Thus, when over time we read and study the Bible with our minds and hearts open to the truth God alone put there, we are able ever increasingly to understand His nature and His plan for our lives. That mysterious power God has is exampled in a story Jesus told His disciples that has come to be known as the parable of the seed growing. See that story and how it plays out in our day:

> And he said, "The kingdom of God is as if a man should scatter seed on the ground. He sleeps and rises night and day, and the seed sprouts and grows; he knows not how. The earth produces by itself, first the blade, then the ear, then the full grain in the ear. But when the grain is ripe, at once he puts in the sickle, because the harvest has come." (Mark 4:26–29)

The passage encourages us to picture someone sowing seed in a field. After the sowing, the man can only wait while the seed grows and matures. The man cannot see this happening, nor does he really understand what God is doing beneath the ground. But it is definitely God at work, not man. The man has done what he can do, and now God is at work doing what He only can do. The man goes about his life, sleeping and rising, day after day, while mysteriously God is involved, growing the seed.

And so it is with God's Word. Man reads the Word, as the man sowed the seed. God then does the work of mysteriously growing the man spiritually, and the man does not know how this happens, BUT he sees and feels the results and knows his spiritual growth has happened. **Something within our spiritual awareness and our nature has come to be exercised by the truth and power of God's Word. The best way for you to understand this phenomenon is to dive as deeply as you can into God's Word yourself. This experience is very, very real and some of the greatest minds on earth stand as witnesses to the truth of this process.**

Think now of the farmer who planted the seed. Even though the invisible process of seed maturing happened outside his view, he can see the result and is ready to benefit from God's work. So, he harvests the crop, for harvest time has come. And that same analogy works for the jealous Bible reader. They have matured spiritually, and are now ready and able to harvest the result as mature disciples of Jesus Christ. Their natures have been transformed and are continuing to be transformed. They are enjoying a relationship with Christ that can only come from obedience to the Holy Spirit within them. And mature believers are ever increasingly open to the Holy Spirit's leadership.

Thus, we now can better understand the "why" of God's Word: to guide us, to encourage us, and to prepare us for what lies ahead in our lives. God knows what lies ahead for us and as mature believers we can confidently face the future knowing our goal is what God wants it to be, to glorify Him. Our lives then are more complete, more satisfying, and more enriching to others. And that's what God wants.

TITUS 3:4-7

Here, the apostle Paul is writing to his disciple, Titus, concerning what happens to affect the salvation process in a lost person's heart. So, God is really communicating through Paul to the believers on the island of Crete (and us now) how His love for them led Him to send His Son Jesus to earth as a man to live a perfect life and die a sinner's death on the cross to pay the sin debt of all who believe in Jesus. We believers today experience salvation and eternal life the same way Paul's readers did, that is, through faith in Jesus Christ. Thus, our assignment is the same as Titus', to "go (wherever we go) and make disciples," teaching them to observe all that Jesus commanded us. See Paul's words:

> But when the goodness and loving kindness of God our Savior appeared, He saved us, not because of works, done by us in righteousness, but according to his own mercy, by the washing of regeneration and renewal of the Holy Spirit, whom he poured out on us richly through Jesus Christ our Savior, so that being justified by his grace we might become heirs according to the hope of eternal life. (Titus 3:4–7)

So, it is simply out of God's goodness and loving-kindness that anyone is ever saved. These characteristics of God are identified in other verses of scripture as God's grace; love we get (from God) for no reason other than He chooses to love us, as unworthy as we are. So, it is a truism to say: "For by grace you have been saved through faith. And this is not your own doing; it is the gift of God, not a result of works, so that no one may boast" (Ephesians 2:8–9).

So, there is great reason to celebrate when Titus received this letter, and when we read it today. Literally, if we don't celebrate, we don't really understand the significance of what Paul has described.

Or we do understand, but just don't believe it. When you think about it, there is no better news than the gospel of Jesus Christ and no better gift than eternal life. Notice we cannot earn God's salvation. If we have it, it's because we received it as a free gift through God's grace and our belief (faith) in Jesus.

In his Titus letter, Paul speaks of our regeneration and renewal when God pours out His Holy Spirit on us. What else could that mean other than that we are filled and anointed with God's spirit as we respond in belief to the Holy Spirit's movement in our hearts. In other scripture verses, that transformation is referred to as our being born again, as we experience a new birth when we believe in Jesus. We have died to self and been baptized with God's Spirit. That is symbolized in water baptism, where a person is recognized as being buried with Christ (as He was crucified and buried) and we are raised (from the baptismal waters) to walk in newness of life, as Jesus was raised from the dead. And then as a baptized believer, we live forever with Jesus Christ, on this earth, and later (after our physical death) with Him in heaven.

Especially should we notice the status we gain at conversion. **We become heirs, not of Christ, but heirs with Christ. That means we will share the same inheritance He has.** In spite of our sinful condition, at conversion our ransom is paid, all our sins are forgiven (those committed before conversion, and those afterward). Such is the completeness of Jesus' atoning death in our place. To be justified is to be "found not guilty" (completely). As the gospel hymn title says, "Jesus Paid It All"; "it" being all our sin debt.

How could we respond properly to these truths other than with belief and salvation? Hallelujah!

REVELATION 22:18-19

We find this passage at the very end of the book of Revelation, and because of that, if it be possible, we sense these words deserve even more credibility. Here John the apostle begins closing this final chapter of the last book of God's Word describing His revelation of Himself, His love for mankind, and His provisions for their eternal life. So as you read this, take special note of the warning given to readers:

> I warn everyone who hears the words of the prophecy of this book: if anyone adds to them, God will add to him the plagues described in this book, and if anyone takes away from the words of the book of this prophecy, God will take away his share in the tree of life and in the holy city, which are described in this book. (Revelation 22:18–19)

Obviously, God has had this "whole Bible" written and organized exactly as He wants it to remain. He has said exactly what He wanted to say, and given us all the revelation we need to accomplish His will for His glory forever. When you think of the significance of these words, and who they come from (not John, but almighty God), that very thought renews our faith, excites our visions of heaven, calls us to more and consistent study, and burdens our hearts to spread the good news of Jesus to a lost world. So no wonder a God who loves us would provide us this strict warning not to change His message.

Two things really excite me about this passage, other than the obvious holy content of scripture in general, and these words specifically. And that is that these decidedly strict warnings sort of "scream at us" that (1) God's Word is valid and worthy of our greatest attention and earnest compliance and sharing, and

(2) God's Word can be understood as written. By definition, God would not have seen fit to put anything in scripture that we cannot understand. God loves each of us enough to not only provide His Son to die a sinner's death in our place to pay our sin debt, but to communicate that truth to us (many times in many ways) in His Word. Thus, we can conclude these words are worthy of our best efforts to study and understand, they are significant enough for us to strive to live them out, and most assuredly they are important enough for us to share with others (in our families, and throughout the world). And praise the Lord, He thinks of everything, He even provides His Holy Spirit to live within we believers to guide us as required in our efforts to understand, comply, and share.

What a great, great God we have.

HEBREWS 11:4–40

Certain men and women were called by God and responded in faith. They are presented here as examples of people who lived out their faith, and yet at the end did not see (in this life) fulfillment of all God's promises. But even so they persevered and did not flinch during tough times and before strong opposition. The author of Hebrews makes the point these individuals were specifically called by God to special assignments and were commended for their faith-filled responses, **but we received something better. See these passages that describe how our eternal destiny was provided also:**

By faith Abel offered to God a more acceptable sacrifice than Cain. (v. 4)

By faith Enoch was taken up so that he should not see death. (v. 5)

By faith Noah, being warned by God concerning events as yet unseen, in reverent fear constructed an ark for the saving of his household. (v. 7)

By faith Abraham obeyed when he was called out to go to a place that he was to receive as an inheritance. (v. 8)

By faith Sarah herself received power to conceive when she was past the age. (v. 11)

By faith Moses, when he was grown up, refused to be called the son of Pharaoh's daughter. (v. 24)

By faith the people crossed the Red Sea as on dry land. (v. 29)

By faith Rahab the prostitute did not perish with those who were disobedient. (v. 31)

And all these, though commended through their faith, did not receive what was promised, since God had provided something better for us, that apart from us, they should not be made perfect. (vv. 39–40)

Suffering as they did, and as faithful though they were, these stalwart champions did not receive what we did. Our reward came later, when we believers were made perfect (that is, saved) through faith in Christ, and His redemptive death on the cross to pay our sin debt. Just think of all that is implied when we refer to Jesus' redemptive work at Calvary. It's His eternal provision for our salvation including all His actions—past, present, and future—in heaven as creator, on earth as our sacrificial lamb, and as our judge and redeemer one day.

Hallelujah! We were not left out. Our heavenly Father did not provide for those others without provisions for us. When we read of the exploits of those heroes of the faith listed, we wonder how we could measure up. But praise the Lord for the New Covenant. It was provided for us. **By faith in Jesus we are as saved as those listed in the Hebrews passage.** We, too, are heaven-bound. Our faith is in Jesus' sacrificial death in our place. And by faith we believe in the resurrection and Jesus' ascension back to heaven to the right hand of God. And by faith we believe in Jesus' second coming. And by faith we know this earth is not our home, but heaven is where we will spend eternity with our Lord and Savior, Jesus Christ.

What a great, great God we have. How blessed are we as believers and what a story we have to tell!

GENESIS 22

God is the creator of everything and is powerful enough to do anything He wants. Because of this, once upon a time long ago God chose a man named Abraham to be the father of a huge nation. Here is the true story of how that came about.

When God told Abraham what He had decided to do, Abraham was already seventy-five years old, too old to have children. His wife's name was Sarah, and she was old too. Both of them did not believe God, because they knew they were too old to have children. God waited twenty-five more years until Abraham was one hundred years old and Sarah was ninety and again He told them they would have a child and they were to name Him Isaac. And sure enough, within a year they had a son and named him Isaac. You can imagine how much they loved Isaac, having him so late in life.

Then one day when Isaac was about twelve years old, God told Abraham to take Isaac and go to a certain mountain and there sacrifice Isaac on an altar. Now Abraham was obedient to God and took Isaac and went to that mountain. On the way Isaac said to his father Abraham, "Father, we have wood for the sacrifice but where is the lamb for a burnt offering?" Abraham answered him saying, "God will provide a sacrifice."

When they got to the mountain, Abraham tied Isaac up and laid him on the altar because he was to be the sacrifice. We can't imagine how hard that was for Abraham to do. Isaac had been born when he was one hundred years old and now here at age 112 Abraham had been told by God to sacrifice him, his only son, on this altar. Abraham must have wondered how he could become the father of a huge nation if he sacrificed his only son that he loved very much. But he was obedient to God and took out his knife and raised it above Isaac there on the altar and was about to stab him when an angel called to him from heaven and told him not to touch Isaac. The angel told Abraham, "Because you obeyed God and were going to sacrifice your only son, I now know that you have an obedient heart." Then Abraham looked and saw a sheep caught by his horns in a thicket nearby. No doubt that sheep had been placed there by God. So, Abraham sacrificed the sheep.

Afterward, the angel spoke to Abraham again, and told him that God was going to bless him with many descendants like the stars in heaven, and that through his line the whole world would be blessed. And God kept His word. Today we know that Abraham did have millions of descendants through Isaac, and they are the Jewish nation living in Israel. And the whole world has been blessed through them because Jesus Christ was born within the Jewish nation, and we know He is God and came to earth to save us from our sins. The world could not have been given a greater gift than for Jesus to sacrifice Himself to pay for all our sins. God does keep His promises even if sometimes it takes a long time.

We should thank God today for His gift of His Son Jesus on the cross to give us a path to eternal life. God did it because He loves us and always will. So, we can know for sure God hears our prayers and will look after us if we just trust him like Abraham did.

JOSHUA 24:16–18

At this point in the book of Joshua, the children of Israel are in the promised land, having spent forty years in the wilderness since they left Egypt. There have been many ups and downs in their commitment to obedience to Jehovah God. And Joshua, their leader, now an old man, is giving them a last encouragement to continue obedient lives, with a warning as to what will happen if they don't. Look at their response:

> Then the people answered, "Far be it from us that we should forsake the LORD to serve other gods, for it is the LORD our God who brought us and our fathers up from the land of Egypt, out of the house of slavery, and who did those great signs in our sight and preserved us in all the way that we went, and among all the people through whom we passed. And the LORD drove out before us all the peoples, the Amorites who lived in the land. Therefore we also will serve the LORD, for He is our God." (Joshua 24:16–18)

Without doubt the people knew what God had already done for them. Thus, ignorance of this would not be an excuse for disobedience in the future. Yet we know that once Joshua and those who led alongside him died, the people again fell into disobedience. How could this be? That ought to be easy for us to answer for we do the same thing. **We, like the Israelites, know how to live more obedient lives than we live. Nor do we pass God's ordinances and their significance along to the next generation as we should.** Over time there seems to be some kind of memory lapse and commitment failing that comes upon us and too many people lose that understanding of the significance of how important obedience to God is.

We would make a perfect score on any "Jesus Quiz," and we could fill up a page with listings of the blessings God has provided us. So what is the answer? It may well be that we try to do too much in our own strength. God has provided us help from the Holy Spirit, tools and information to use in His Word, and ways to access them both through prayer. And He has told us clearly that the two greatest commandments are to love the Lord our God with all our hearts, souls, and minds, and our neighbors as ourselves (Matthew 22:36–40). So it's highly likely daily devotional times of Bible study and prayer, along with consistent involvement with like-hearted believers, would reorient our perspectives regarding our lifestyles of disciple making. And building up our love for the Lord and others will surely motivate us toward obedience. The more we understand God's nature and His love and provisions for us the more we will love Him. Remember He loved you first. For that we ought to praise Him daily.

HEBREWS 12:5-6

In this passage we find instructions as to how to deal with God's discipline. All believers have felt God's discipline from time to time and sometimes it seems quite harsh and hard to understand. The author of Hebrews quotes from Proverbs to give us God's concept of discipline and how He uses it for our good. We will relieve ourselves of much pain and discomfort if we learn God's perspective on discipline.

> And have you forgotten the exhortation that addresses you as sons? "My son, do not regard lightly the discipline of the Lord, nor be weary when reproved by him. For the Lord disciplines the one he loves, and chastises every son whom he receives." (Hebrews 12:5–6)

Notice the potential we believers have of forgetting even the very good things we hear from God. So here we are reminded not to do that. As believers we are to be thinking individuals, mindful of God's laws and the importance of our being obedient to them in front of a sinful world. The concept taught here is that godly discipline comes to us for a purpose, that of teaching us lessons that make us more Christlike. More often than not, godly discipline comes to us because God has simply chosen to let us suffer the consequences of our own sin. Thus, we are told "not to regard lightly the discipline of the Lord." We are to give extra weight to our suffering, by considering whom we have sinned against, for all sin is against the Lord. We are not to grow weary when reproved by Him. Now reproved means to "show or express disapproval of." So being reproved by God indicates to us how He feels about our sin. He disapproves, He is disappointed in us, and we are not to grow weary of recognizing that. That is, we are not to be so shallow in our repentance of our sin as to not truly always feel the need of making things right between us and God, even as we suffer trials.

Scripture tells us the "wages of sin is death." There are two ways we can deal with our sin: either we die in our sins and spend eternity paying that sin debt, or we by faith receive Christ's free gift of eternal life. Jesus died a sinner's death on the cross to atone for the sins of all believers. See Romans 6:23: "For the wages of sin is death, but the free gift of God is eternal life in Christ Jesus our Lord."

Thus, we are to look for the lessons present in the disciplines we experience. God disciplines us because He loves us, as a godly parent disciplines their children, to teach them needed lessons. God chastises all His children. To chastise means to "inflict punishment." God does this out of a love motive. Thus, that One in authority (God) punishes those of us within His care (believers) for our own good. Often God's punishment comes to us in the form of trials we suffer that we have created ourselves by our sins.

So we come again to the basic principle found in John 14:15: "If you love me, you will keep my commandments."

By obedience to God's Word we remove the need for discipline and the suffering that comes with it. Thus, when we are disobedient, our loving God steps in with the discipline we need, and though it may be painful, we emerge having learned God's lessons.

JAMES 3:5-10

James, the earthly brother of Jesus is writing here to Jewish believers concerning the importance of our controlling what we say. This whole section is titled "Taming the Tongue." When you think about it, this is as great a problem today as it ever has been. It may be even worse nowadays, since now with all our modern means of communication we "talk" more with different people than society ever has. So, there is all the more reason for us to be careful what we say, for we may well not know the extent of the influence we have, and we surely want our influence to be positive. Notice James' practical advice:

> So also the tongue is a small member, yet it boasts of great things. How great a forest is set ablaze by such a small fire! And the tongue is a fire, a world of unrighteousness. The tongue is set among our members, staining the whole body, setting on fire the entire course of life, and set on fire by hell. For every kind of beast and bird, of reptile and sea creature, can be tamed and has been tamed by mankind, but no human can tame the tongue. It is a restless evil, full of deadly poison. With it we bless our Lord and Father, and with it we curse people who are made in the likeness of God. From the same mouth come blessing and cursing. My brothers, these things ought not to be so. (James 3:5–10)

We would have a hard time debating the wisdom of James' words. Consciously or subconsciously we recognize he is right. Influence is important and we all influence others. Thus, we all carry this responsibility with us every day. James likens the tongue and its use to a small fire, that, once started, can grow and cause great harm. Clearly then, the analogy is, it only takes a single word to start a harmful thinking and action process that also does great harm.

Notice James points out how the tongue "stains the whole body." That is, it dictates action, and starts in motion events that affect our whole bodies (lives). He words that description as "setting on fire the entire course of life." And he follows that statement making the point that fire is set by hell. Evil speech is so terrible and destroys so completely because its origin is hell, that is, Satan himself.

Over time, mankind has learned to tame all kinds of living creatures, but we can't contain and tame our own tongues. We do sin. We are born sinners, filled with the deadly poison of sin, facing evil temptations every day. Thus, with the same tongue we praise and honor God, we curse our fellow men, which, of course, is the height of hypocrisy. How could such polar-opposite actions come forth from the same source? They can because we fail to take God at His Word. We fail to live out the good we already know to do, and we let worldly priorities dictate our motives and actions.

In a real sense, our unbridled tongues are an expression of all the wickedness in the world. Our words (triggered by our precious thoughts and motives) lead to the wickedness we see acted out everywhere. We are wise then to let God's Holy spirit guide what we say, seeking to glorify Him in all our ways.

See this same wisdom clearly spelled out again in Proverbs: "From the fruit of his mouth, a man eats what is good . . . Whoever guards his mouth preserves his life" (Proverbs 13:2–3).

2 TIMOTHY 1:8-10

Paul the apostle is writing here to Timothy, his young disciple, to encourage him in his Christian walk. Paul is writing from prison, and probably was martyred shortly after he wrote this letter. Knowing what lay ahead, Paul's words are strikingly brave, and therefore should be all the more significant to us. Paul tells Timothy and us to continue in the faith no matter our circumstances. Jesus Christ suffered for His faith, so did Paul, and so will believers today. Paul's message, though, is that the suffering is worth the cost. Eternity with the Lord is valuable beyond measure, and we need to keep that in mind. See Paul's words:

> Therefore, do not be ashamed of the testimony about our Lord, nor of me his prisoner, but share in suffering for the gospel by the power of God, who saved us and called us to a holy calling, not because of our works but because of his own purpose and grace, which he gave us in Christ Jesus before the ages began, and which now has been manifested through the appearing of our Savior Christ Jesus, who abolished death and brought life and immortality to light through the gospel. (2 Timothy 1:8–10)

So, given all that God has provided us, we are not to be ashamed of the gospel of Jesus. As a matter of fact, just the opposite should be true. We should be singing His praises. And our lifestyle should give first priority to God's will and His glory. We who have been saved, of all people, should be dedicated to the heavenly calling we have been given, not because of our works and worthiness, but because of God's purpose and grace in what He has done for us already.

God's love for us came early, very, very early for we believers, even before the ages began. Could that be true, we, as sinful as we are, before we were born being predestined for salvation and for an eternity with the Lord? Yes, not only could such a destiny be defined (already) for believers, but God proved it was so. He made His love for us abundantly clear when He sent Jesus to earth to live a perfect life, but yet die a sinner's death on the cross in our place. Now, as believers who by faith have trusted Jesus' atoning death for payment of our sin debt, we are assured we, too, will rise from the grave (as Jesus did) to live forever with Him in heaven.

The last verse of this passage sums up the awesome extent of God's love: Jesus abolished death (for believers) and brought (eternal) life and immortality to light through the gospel. This gospel of Jesus Christ was true in the first century when Jesus lived it, and when Paul preached it, and it is true when we hear it and believe it today. **No wonder we are told not to be ashamed of the gospel.** No truth ever meant so much to all mankind. No news ever is as good as this news of God's love expressed in Jesus Christ. Given what we have received, how could any believer ever feel reluctant to stand up for the Savior we have in Jesus Christ?

And how could we ever feel love for anyone and not share the magnificent truth of Jesus we've heard about and believed? If our love for them is real and our faith in Christ is true, then nothing would keep us from telling them about the love of God we've experienced. And that is exactly the attitude Paul has that he is sharing with Timothy, and exactly the attitude we are to have as we share with those we care about.

ACTS 2:22-24, 36

Fifty days after Jesus' resurrection and ascension back to heaven, it was time for the Day of Pentecost, the second of the Jewish Feast Days celebrating the coming harvest. Many Jews then returned to Jerusalem to commemorate this feast. During these days, 120 Christian believers were gathered together in one room when God's Holy Spirit suddenly descended upon each of them in a mighty outpouring of thunder and fire. A flame of fire appeared and reached out to touch each one, indwelling them with God's Holy Spirit and enabling them to do things they could not do before, like understand and speak in foreign languages, and to prophesy future events. Many people gathered near the temple out of curiosity at what caused the loud noise and witnessed what these believers could now do. The apostle Peter took this opportunity to preach to the people gathered there concerning who Jesus was and what had happened to Him. See the significance of this sermon to us in our day.

> Men of Israel, hear these words: Jesus of Nazareth, a man attested to you by God with mighty works and wonders and signs that God did through him in your midst, as you yourself know—this Jesus, delivered up according to the definite plan and foreknowledge of God, you crucified and killed by the hands of lawless men. God raised him up, loosing the pangs of death, because it was not possible for him to be held by it. . . . Let all the house of Israel therefore know for certain that God has made him both Lord and Christ, this Jesus whom you crucified. (Acts 2:22–24, 36)

Clearly, through the leadership of the Holy Spirit, Peter called the people to task for their treatment of Jesus as they turned Him over to lawless men (the Romans) to be crucified. He identified Him as both Lord and Christ who conquered death by His resurrection from the grave, all per God's plan and knowledge. The Holy Spirit did a "work" among the crowd that day and over 3,000 people were saved.

That same information, about that same Jesus, does the same thing in our day when people believe it. God's love and interest in our eternal destiny has not lessened one bit. The good news of Jesus (the gospel) still has that same power and influence on those who take it to heart. Belief in Jesus' death on the cross to pay our debt of sin is still required for salvation. Thus, God's provision for the atonement of our sin is still relevant. His free gift of eternal life is still available to repentant believers, and the message of Ephesians 2:8–9 is still true: "For by grace you have been saved through faith. And this is not your own doing; it is the gift of God, not a result of works."

We need to do what Peter did, use the available power of God's Holy Spirit and take the gospel to the nations wherever we find them, in our country, or in theirs. We are to pass on the truth of Jesus, the Holy Spirit will do the work of transforming the hearts of those who hear. This is both the privilege and the responsibility of all believers.

PSALM 105:1–6

Psalm 105 is a song celebrating God's involvement in the lives of His people, meaning Israel in the days of this psalmist, and believers of all nations in our day. Notice the psalmist is talking about lifestyles, not random acts of worship by believers. He urges that ongoing, enthusiastic praise, honor, and glory be lifted up to the Lord. See this psalmist excitedly pouring out his heart to his readers then and now.

> Oh give thanks to the LORD; call upon his name;
>   make known his deeds among the peoples!
> Sing to him, sing praises to him;
>   tell of his wondrous works!
> Glory in his holy name;
>   let the hearts of those who seek the LORD rejoice!
> Seek the LORD and his strength;
>   seek his presence continually!
> Remember the wondrous works that he has done,
>   his miracles, and the judgments he uttered,
> O offspring of Abraham, his servant,
>   children of Jacob, his chosen ones! (Psalm 105:1–6)

Key to this passage is verse 5, recall of all God has done for His children. Such recall is to be exhibited many ways: gratitude to the Lord, calling on His name, singing praises to Him, glorying in His name, and seeking Him, His strength, and His presence (continually). No way could this kind of attention and adoration of the Lord be done "in a corner." Such devotion will show, such enthusiasm will be contagious, such consistency will be evident in the lives of all believers who follow the psalmist's lead, reflecting the "sold out" to the Lord attitude the psalmist had.

Could we do this? What if 100 percent of any church, anywhere, large or small, lived out this model? In thirty days their growth and ministry would be making headlines in the local newspaper. In six months, national news agencies would be in town taking note of what is happening. And likely also, by then, opposition of all sorts would be working against them.

Our required response is obvious. God doesn't add instructions in His Word needlessly. The understood subject of every sentence in this Psalm is "you," the reader, and "we," His church.

NUMBERS 6:22-27

God loved His chosen people Israel, and He still does. As they wandered in the wilderness between leaving Egypt and getting to the promised land of Canaan, God protected them, guided them, and made all necessary provisions for them, enabling them to accomplish the mission He had given them. This passage describes a prayer Aaron (the first high priest) is to pray over all Israel (for all time). Simply put, God's love for these people caused Him to want them to be blessed in the best ways possible. And perhaps just as important, **God wanted them to know they were blessed, and that it was He who had blessed them. See these verses, understanding they apply to we believers today as well:**

> The Lord spoke to Moses, saying, "Speak to Aaron and his sons, saying, Thus you shall bless the people of Israel: you shall say to them,
>
>> The Lord bless you and keep you;
>> the Lord make his face to shine upon you and be gracious to you;
>> the Lord lift up his countenance upon you and give you peace.
>
> "So shall they put my name upon the people of Israel, and I will bless them." (Numbers 6:22–27)

Notice the ways they were to be blessed. First, they are to be generally blessed, that is, God desires (and will provide) their highest good, short- and long-term. Remember, He gets to define what our highest good is. He will also keep them, that is, He will guard and protect them. The Lord will make His face shine upon them, meaning He will purposefully and deliberately provide them specifically His personal favor, indicated by his "smiling face." Just imagine having almighty God smile at you. What an awesome thought. And there is more. The Lord will be gracious to them, providing His mercy (though they and we don't deserve it) completely and forever. And He will give attention to them, and notice them always, ever aware of their need for assurance of His love and approving countenance. And for them and us all the result is perfect and everlasting peace.

We need to stop a moment and consider again what this prayer tells us. I think God has just described for us what heaven is going to be like. Keep in mind, we believers are spiritual Israel, thus, this prayer applies to us. We can and should take it to heart, believe it, rejoice in it, and share it with others (so they can do the same thing).

GALATIANS 2:15-16

Paul traveled through the region of Galatia in southern Turkey on his first missionary journey in about AD 47. There he preached the gospel, establishing churches along the way. However, soon after he left these churches evidently false teachers came behind him teaching a different gospel. Paul preached salvation by faith in Christ alone, while these false teachers required new believers to convert to Judaism, following the various Jewish ritual and diet laws, before they were accepted into the churches. So when Paul heard this, he wrote to correct this mistaken theology. These false teachers struck at the very heart of the gospel of Jesus Christ. They promoted a salvation by adherence to the law and works, not through faith and the grace of God. See how Paul promotes justification by faith, not works:

> We ourselves are Jews by birth and not Gentile sinners; yet we know that a person is not justified by works of the law but through faith in Jesus Christ, so we also have believed in Christ Jesus, in order to be justified by faith in Christ and not by works of the law, because by works of the law no one will be justified. (Galatians 2:15–16)

To be justified is to be found not guilty of sin, acquitted of our guilt and sin. We call that being saved, forgiven of our sins, and thereafter bound for heaven. So this passage is telling us we are saved by the grace of God and faith in Jesus' sacrificial death on the cross as payment for all our sin debt. Thus, we do not have to go to church to be saved, or be baptized, or to do good deeds, or any other such actions. **However, before we stop doing such things (or never start) we ought to read further in scripture.** See these for typical commands for believers:

See that no one repays anyone evil for evil, but always seek to do good to one another and to everyone. Rejoice always, pray without ceasing, give thanks in all circumstances; for this is the will of God in Christ Jesus for you. Do not quench the spirit. Do not despise prophecies, but test everything; hold fast what is good. Abstain from every form of evil. (1 Thessalonians 5:15–22)

You shall love the Lord your God with all your heart and with all your soul and with all your mind. This is the great and first commandment. And a second is like it: You shall love your neighbor as yourself. On these two commandments rest all the law and the prophets. (Matthew 22:37–40)

Go therefore and make disciples of all nations, baptizing them in the name of the Father and of the Son and of the Holy Spirit, teaching them to observe all that I have commanded you. (Matthew 28:19)

Not neglecting to meet together, as is the habit of some, but encouraging one another. (Hebrews 10:25)

Saving faith involves a heart transformation, a sense of acknowledgement of our sins against God and a sincere repentance for them. Thus, if our faith is real, sincere, and authentic, then we will want to do everything God suggests or commands, for we know He understands what is best for us, and that obedience is not a chore or unnecessary, but vital to our growth as Christians, and what truly brings us the joy of our salvation.

ISAIAH 30:1–2

Around 700 BC God sent Isaiah out to preach and write to the Israelites to warn them of what continued sin and rebellion against God would lead to. Their ancestors had been delivered out of Egypt once, they had been given salvation and set free from captivity. Yet they had not learned their lesson, and now about 800 years later (after Moses died) they were again more or less imprisoned by surrounding countries and were leaning again toward seeking to purchase military help from Egypt. They had been freed once from Egypt's control and now they were returning seeking again to give control to Egypt. **In essence then they were reversing their salvation.** Against God's will they were turning their backs on His protection and seeking their own solution using their plan, not God's. See God warning them and us through Isaiah:

> "Ah, stubborn children," declares the LORD, "who carry out a plan, but not mine, and who make an alliance, but not of my Spirit, that they may add sin to sin; who set out to go down to Egypt, without asking for my direction, to take refuge in the protection of Pharaoh and to seek shelter in the shadow of Egypt!" (Isaiah 30:1–2)

They were called stubborn children and they surely were. They would not listen to God's messenger or His Spirit. They had (what they called) a plan, but it was theirs only, not God's. They claimed it was God directing them, but it was not of His Spirit. Their plans did not glorify Him. In fact their plan led the people to sin and more sin. It was not an accident that their plans failed and led the people into hardship, trouble, and pain. It's always like that in the long run when we go our way, away from God's way.

They had thought long and hard about their predicament. They considered other approaches to their problems, that is, other countries who might help. They did all the things worldly people do, then and now, to gain relief from their troubles. That is, they sought relief everywhere but from God. That's true today, too, for countries and individuals. And even when God made His way clear through men like Isaiah, they still did not respond with obedience.

The "pharaohs" of today's world that we individuals use to try to gain relief from our "captivity" position don't help us now any more than the Egyptian pharaoh of that day helped Israel. Today's pharaohs take the form of trusting the wrong people, making up our own theology, associating with the wrong groups, denying the truth of God's Word, and claiming wisdom and knowledge we don't really have.

God has provided a real salvation plan to protect us from those types of mistakes, He sent Jesus Christ to die in our place to pay the sin debt of all those who will believe, and He provided His word to instruct us all in the revelation of the Father. True believers will seek to obey the Lord, they will see God's Word as their road map for life, applying all of it, to every aspect of their lives. And they will feel a burden for the lost of this world who do not yet know the truth of the gospel of Jesus.

1 JOHN 2:1-2

One of Jesus' disciples, the apostle John, wrote this passage to some small churches outside the city of Ephesus in present-day Turkey. He wanted to encourage them in their Christian faith. God saw to having it recorded here in the Bible to encourage us in our day too. See this important passage:

> My little children, I am writing these things to you so that you may not sin. But if anyone does sin, we have an advocate with the Father, Jesus Christ the righteous. He is the propitiation for our sins, and not for ours only but also for the sins of the whole world. (1 John 2:1–2)

John's purpose in writing this letter is made clear. He desires that his readers not sin against God. His goal is not to ease their consciences when they do sin, or to somehow make it easier for them to recognize sin, or to claim that it is OK for them to sin, but that they don't sin. Our gratitude to God for making forgiveness available should not lead us into carelessness toward sin, but toward sinlessness.

But if we do sin, we can know we have an advocate with the Father: Jesus Christ, who earned that position when He was crucified on the cross. Notice the concept of family in the wording of these verses, Jesus Christ is the Son, our advocate with our heavenly Father, for we believers who are children of God.

We might ask, "What does Jesus do as our advocate?" An advocate is one who pleads the cause of another before a tribunal or judicial judge. That is exactly what we need, Jesus pleading the case of our sin charged against us before our heavenly Father, the judge of all judges. And who could be a better advocate than Jesus

Christ, that one who lived a perfectly righteous life yet died a sinner's death on the cross paying our sin debt to God.

Notice the verses say Jesus is the propitiation for our sins. That means He is the sacrifice made to God for our sins. But the word has an added feature; a propitiation is a sacrifice made for one reason, and that reason is to appease the wrath of God caused by our sins. Jesus died for the sins of the whole world. But only those who believe in Him, that is, those who believe that He is God the Son come to earth to save us from our sins on the cross will receive that forgiveness made available by His death. No one has ever been saved from their sins until they acknowledge they are sinners and thus in need of a Savior, and that Jesus is that Savior for anyone who trusts in Him.

Thus, there is no route to salvation (eternal life in heaven with God) except via faith in Jesus Christ. Jesus confirmed it in His own words: "I am the way, and the truth, and the life. No one comes to the Father except through me." (John 14:6)

Jesus Christ really is Lord, who came to earth to save us from our sins, and He accomplished that through His death on the cross in our place where He paid the sin debt we owe. What a Savior He is!

2 PETER 1:16–18

Numerous times in scripture God interjects Himself into our world in a dramatic fashion. The children of Israel crossing the Red Sea on dry land (Exodus 14:21), that same group forty years later crossing the Jordan River into the promised land, when God stopped the river flow (Joshua 3:14), and when God brought water from a rock for the Israelites (Exodus 17:6), are examples. In this passage we see another example, God speaking from heaven directly to several of the disciples. Here Peter is writing to various churches about an incident that happened when Jesus took him, James, and John up on a high mountain by themselves, and Jesus was transfigured before them. His face "shone like the sun and His clothes became as white as light," and Moses and Elijah came to talk with Him. And then the voice of God came from heaven with a significant message. See this message God had for them and for us:

> For we do not follow cleverly devised myths when we made known to you the power and coming of our Lord Jesus Christ, but we were eyewitnesses of his majesty. For when he received honor and glory from God the Father, and the voice was borne to him by the Majestic Glory, "This is my beloved Son, with whom I am well pleased," we ourselves heard this very voice borne from heaven, for we were with him on the holy mountain. (2 Peter 1:16–18)

So, we have here the testimony of a creditable witness of God authenticating Jesus as His Son. We can only imagine the feelings of Peter, James, and John during that episode. We, about two thousand years later, are to read this believing it is true, and that Jesus is truly Messiah, God come to earth to save us from our sins.

Matthew's version of that same incident adds these words to the message from God: "Listen to Him" (17:5). How could we not listen to Him after hearing that command from heaven?

Peter's message to his readers is that his description of Jesus is literal, real, authentic, and eternal. We can take his message that way too. If we are looking for reality in our faith, and for true direction for our lives, we can do no better than to take on holy scripture as our guide. In Peter's day there were many false teachers preaching myths concerning Jesus, denying His deity, and refuting the promise of His second coming. Sounds just like our day. Peter wants to eliminate doubt in the minds of His readers.

We are saved by God's grace through faith, and it's that faith we are to live out. We weren't there at the Transfiguration, and only three of the disciples were. But the others believed when they heard about it, and so should we. God promises to and does bless our faith when we take steps to reflect it in our lives.

Peter and the disciples did not have to add anything to the gospel message. And we don't either. It's love-filled and miraculous enough as it stands. We need only live out what we teach and preach for others to get the true message. And that's our assignment from the Lord.

Notice the title Peter gives almighty God as He evidenced Himself to those three disciples: "Majestic Glory." That has to be representative of the Father's transcendent presence as He lowers Himself to earth to verify the honor and glory due His beloved Son. There is nothing the Father could have done or said to authenticate Jesus more clearly as Son of God. So, yes, Jesus is worthy of all our praise, honor, and glory, and we are so blessed to have Him as our Savior and Lord.

PSALM 119:55, 62, 147–148

God provides His Holy Spirit to help and teach us twenty-four hours a day. When we are awake or asleep, He does His work in our hearts. So we should not ever be surprised at suddenly being made aware of some precept of God as it might apply to a particular event that comes to mind, or that we see playing out before us. See these verses as they reflect these concepts:

> I remember your name in the night, O LORD,
>   and keep your law. . . .
> At midnight I rise to praise you,
>   because of your righteous rules. . . .
> I rise before dawn and cry for help;
>   I hope in your words.
> My eyes are awake before the watches of the night,
>   that I may meditate on your promise. (Psalm 119:55, 62, 147–48)

Notice God provides the psalmist physical and mental promptings, so that he might be led to spiritual activities, growth, and direction. He remembers God's name in the night, he rises at midnight and cries for help, and his eyes are awake before the night watches. Notice what spiritual activity God has in mind for the psalmist to do: keep His law and righteous rules, praise Him, hope in His words, and meditate on His promise. We get the feeling God provides our physical and mental world for the purpose of feeding our spiritual growth. We can only conclude from this how important our spiritual growth is. And that would only be logical given that this world is not our home and is only temporary, while heaven with the Lord is eternal.

And why would God establish this type of order and priority in the world? It's because He knows best. He knows His will and His way lead to eternal peace, rest, and life, while our will and our way lead to turmoil, disappointment, and death. And fundamentally it's because of His steadfast love for us. "By grace you have been saved through faith. And that is not your own doing; it is the gift of God, and not a result of works, so that no one may boast" (Ephesians 2:8).

God loves us even though we are unworthy of His love (grace), a point we need to remember and rejoice in, and a point we need to share with others.

ROMANS 1:16–17

Here is a passage that touches on a most important subject, the righteousness of God, and why an understanding of it is so necessary in every believer's understanding of God's plan of salvation. Here we have Paul writing to the church in Rome to clarify this doctrine. See this passage:

> For I am not ashamed of the gospel, for it is the power of God for salvation to everyone who believes, to the Jew first and also to the Greek. For in it the righteousness of God is revealed from faith for faith, as it is written, "The righteous shall live by faith." (Romans 1:16–17)

Paul recognizes that the gospel (the truth of Christ's coming to earth to save us from our sins) has been authored, authorized, and initiated by almighty God as the only way to salvation (eternal life) for all, both Jews and Greeks. In explaining God's righteousness Paul refers to God's right and moral character as made known by His love and His justice. So this concept shows us more fully why God saw fit to have His only Son die in our place as the only method and provision for our sins that would completely and justly atone for them, while at the same time reflecting His great love for us. Only Christ's death could satisfy the debt our sin incurs, and yet how better and more effectively could God have shown His great and steadfast love for us than to offer His only Son to die in our place, erasing our sin debt. Thus, we see God's righteousness both as coming to us *from* God and being characteristic *of* God.

So this act of the gospel lived out by Christ on our behalf really does come from God and is His power in action on display in the world. We can conclude the phrase "from faith for faith" to mean that the right standing with God our faith leads to, extends from start to finish, that is, from the point of our salvation to the time of our glorification when Christ returns. Therefore, we need to see our faith as ongoing, growing daily as we live it out before the world. And why not, Paul begins by saying he is not ashamed of the gospel, and neither should we be ashamed of it. God's love for us as shown by the cross is so great, so pure, and so steadfast we could never begin to understand it, much less earn it.

And praise the Lord, too, for the phrase "and also to the Greek." That's where we come in. God's salvation plan therefore includes we Greeks (all non-Jews). Notice, too, the point made on how we are to live. At the point of salvation, we took on Jesus' righteousness, and thus are to live from then on by faith. Our faith triggers words, motivations, and actions beyond our capacity to generate. That's God's Holy Spirit leading us to be the witnesses, the servants, the shepherds, the ambassadors, the disciples, and the disciple makers God would have us be. Praise the Lord!

MATTHEW 25:26-30

All of us are given a certain number of talents and opportunities during our lifetime. That's the way God has ordered things. We will then one day be judged and held responsible for what we have been given, not what we have not been given. Jesus gave us what has come to be a very familiar parable to illustrate this.

A wealthy man was going on a long journey and before he left, he gave three of his servants a number of "talents" to be responsible for while he was gone: one got five talents; one, two talents; and one, one talent. During his absence the servant given five talents and the one given two talents each invested their talents, and each doubled what they had been given. When the master returned and saw this he was pleased and rewarded these two faithful servants with much more than they had been given and an important place in his household.

But the servant who had been given one talent had not invested that talent and had thus, earned nothing for his master. The master chided him, and his judgment on that servant serves to provide a very important lesson for us. See how the master judged the unfaithful servant:

> You wicked and slothful servant! . . . You ought to have invested my money . . . and at my coming I should have received what was my own with interest. So take the talent from him and give it to him who has the ten talents. For to everyone who has will more be given, and he will have an abundance. But from the one who has not, even what he has will be taken away. And cast the worthless servant into the outer darkness. In that place there will be weeping and gnashing of teeth. (Matthew 25:26–30)

WOW!! God is obviously very seriously interested in what we do with what He gives us in the way of talents, time, and opportunity. Notice while the master was gone the talents still remained his, and the servants were simply stewards of what they produced. And notice, too, the servants were rewarded for doing what they could with what they were given, not for what they had not been given. And isn't it interesting that the master gave that one talent to the servant who already had ten. He did not give it to the servant who only had four, or split it between the two faithful servants giving them another one-half talent each. God's accounting principles are His alone. But praise the Lord, He does explain them to us, and so we are without excuse for misuse of what He provides us just as the unfaithful servant was without excuse.

The rewards the two faithful servants received are not defined, but without question the story communicates that they were well worth their diligence (forever). And notice, too, that "the outer darkness" destiny of the unfaithful servant is not completely defined either, but we quickly conclude we don't want any part of that.

So as always, we see Jesus communicating His message very effectively. Let us not be foolish but be consistently diligent in living fruit-filled lives for God's glory.

MARK 9:38-41

Here is a passage discussing how the gospel makes progress, how people share it with a right attitude or with something less than a perfect attitude. We tend to be judgmental of others who do not use exactly the same words or methods we do as they share the love of God with the world. When we are judgmental, we forget the involvement of the Holy Spirit in all we do. God can take any word, any action, or any person, and use them for His glory and His purposes. See this passage as an example:

> John said to him, "Teacher, we saw someone casting out demons in your name, and we tried to stop him, for he was not following us." But Jesus said, "Do not stop him, for no one who does a mighty work in my name will be able soon afterward to speak evil of me. For the one who is not against us is for us. For truly, I say to you, whoever gives you a cup of water to drink because you belong to Christ will by no means lose his reward." (Mark 9:38–41)

Evidently, there were others empowered by God out in the communities preaching and healing in Jesus' name. Perhaps they were disciples of John the Baptist. We are not sure, but God was obviously in their ministries at least to some extent. Who were the disciples (or us in our day) to judge those ministers? Jesus did not seem to be worried about how the gospel was shared, just that it was shared.

This passage is really good news for believers. Notice who Jesus points out is "in line" for rewards, those who do something as simple as giving a cup of water to those who share the gospel. Each of us can surely "pass out water." Surely, we know of someone who is actively out and about in this world sharing God's love and truth concerning the giving of His Son to pay our sin debt. Clearly Jesus is telling us to go and support them a little bit. They may be across the ocean or operating out of our local church. Perhaps they could use a few extra dollars for their ministry, or a simple note of encouragement. The point is all of us can and should do something (consistently) in the way of kingdom work. Even believers can sometimes get caught up in the daily grind of life and fail to see the simple ministry opportunities right before their eyes. And before we know it, years have passed, and we've missed out on the joy of service and on many rewards.

As we prayerfully consider our involvement in such ministry, the word *proactive* is likely to come to mind. That should be our approach. We are to be looking for ways to serve, asking questions about ministries we hear about, reading books on serving, and noticing those around us who seem (already) to be involved in God's work, etc. **God will absolutely bless our openness to obedience to participation in sharing His gospel.**

JOB 38:2; 41:11; 42:3, 6

The man Job had suddenly experienced terrible losses in his life. He had gone from having family, friends, health, and wealth, to having none of those in a very short period of time. And he challenged God, saying he had done no wrong worthy of such punishment, and he cried out for the opportunity to speak with God and to make his case, for he was sure he had been treated unjustly. For the first thirty-seven chapters of this book Job discusses his fate before his friends, hearing their thoughts on why this had happened, maintaining his innocence all the while. Finally, in chapter 38 we begin to see God's response. Look at these several excerpts from God's response, and of Job's reaction for clues as to how we should see God's actions in our lives that are not what we expected, or what we want:

> Who is this that darkens counsel by words without knowledge? (Job 38:2)

> Who has first given to me that I should repay him? Whatever is under the whole heaven is mine. (Job 41:11)

> I had heard of you by the hearing of the ear, but now my eyes see you; therefore, I despise myself, and repent in dust and ashes. (Job 42:5–6)

God had listened to all of Job's "logic" and cut him off in one sentence, saying in reality, "Who are you to speak given your lack of understanding anything at all of my works, my ways, and my purposes?" In the second verse God clearly indicates He owes no man anything, for He is God almighty who created and owns everything that is. Having heard these statements and several more such from God, Job's perspective about his situation is changed completely, and he repents before God.

As harsh and insensitive as God seems to be sometimes, He is neither. He operates in a different realm with higher, better, and more perfect purposes. His worldview is individually oriented, and yet takes all of mankind into account. And best of all His steadfast love is the source and power of all He creates and accomplishes. Thus, we, God's children are, and forever will be, the beneficiaries of all His thoughts and actions. In the end Job understood this, and his story gives us an example to follow.

LUKE 10:20

At one point in His ministry Jesus empowered some seventy-two of His followers with the ability to heal the sick and call demons out of those possessed. And He sent them forth in pairs to visit cities all over Galilee to heal those in need, and to announce the coming of the kingdom of God. And so they did, successfully. And they returned with joy saying, "Lord, even the demons are subject to us in your name." Jesus' response was to give them (and us) a valuable bit of wisdom concerning the priorities in our lives. See Jesus' words:

> Do not rejoice in this, that the spirits are subject to you, but rejoice that your names are written in heaven. (Luke 10:20)

Simply put, Jesus is telling us to beware of rejoicing too much in what we see as God's use of us in this world. Obviously, there are all kinds of mental and physical needs in this world that need our attention. Some close at hand, and some across the oceans. And we are to be the "Lord's hands" as we seek to do what we can to relieve pain and suffering. And even in the humblest person, such service is fulfilling and satisfying. But Jesus warns us not to lose perspective. We can do good deeds for worthy reasons, but they are not the best reasons. A far, far greater blessing for us to seek is our eternal salvation (having our names "written in heaven").

Our focus is to be on our relationship with the Lord, and that of those we serve. Spiritual well-being is what is really needed in this world, for there eternal issues are involved. As the only person who has ever lived who knows the (complete) future, Jesus is giving us eternal advice. **And He is doing this because He loves us**. He (only) knows how critically important it is for us to settle our relationship with Him while we can here on earth. He knew, too, that one day soon He would pay our sin debt on the cross.

And notice Jesus is telling believers to rejoice in their status as heaven-bound saints. This is not to be a "silent" condition, one we keep to ourselves and that no one else sees in us. By definition, a saving relationship with Jesus Christ will show, as we exhibit the peace and love for others the Holy Spirit has installed in us. And that's a "joy-filled" condition, and it turns out to be the best way to live. And that's no accident. Our loving heavenly Father created such conditions. A believer's eternal life begins the moment they receive Jesus' free gift of eternal life, and thus, they begin then growing toward becoming the completely glorified saint they will one day be in heaven. That's good news worth sharing.

PSALM 142:1–2

This Psalm to God, by David, is titled "You Are My Refuge." We are not told of the actual conditions David is facing when he voices this prayer, but obviously he is under much stress. When we read it, we cannot help but notice the sincerity of David's heart. An important principle taught here is that God *is* our refuge, our source of strength in times of stress. But we note that just as important is that David recognizes that fact. What if God were David's refuge, but David did not know it, or had heard of it, but did not believe it? Thus, he would go blindly on in life fearful and suffering without relief because he did not know where to go for help, or did not trust God. See the result of the fact of God's love and power, and the fact David is aware of that love and power.

> With my voice I cry out to the LORD; with my voice I plead for mercy to the LORD. I pour out my complaint before him; I tell my trouble before him. (Psalm 142:1–2)

Four times we see David voicing his request to God: he cries out to the Lord, He pleads for mercy, he pours out his complaint, and he tells God of his troubles. Now David was "a man after God's heart." Other scripture tells us that. "[God] said, 'I have found in David the son of Jesse, a man after my heart'" (Acts 13:22).

So we can be sure if, before he prayed, you had asked David if God knew of his situation, he would have answered, "Yes, God does already know." So we see here David telling God of circumstances he knows God is already aware of. Why then is his prayer (or ours) necessary? We have problems and bring them to God, but if He is all-powerful (and He is) and if He loves us (which He does) why doesn't He just go ahead and solve our problem, or better yet not let the problem come up in the first place? The classic question then comes to mind, "Why do bad things happen to good people?"

The answer is, "Because there is more to prayer than just getting God to take care of a given need." When we pray, by definition, we have condensed our problem into a given set of words. Our problem then is not just a certain sense of pain, or fear, or a certain troubling situation that we feel sharply, but a set of undefined, vague hurts that we have not truly analyzed so as to really know what our need is. By praying like David we begin to see our prayers (needs) as God sees them, and thus, we can better understand Him and His nature, and His responses. Most of the time there are lessons we need to learn, that will enable us to "go from here" better equipped to be the disciple God would have us be.

So don't waste a trial, determine what God is teaching. Nothing happens by accident, and He always knows best. Learn to continually pray, trusting Him and His love and provision for you.

EPHESIANS 5:1-2

The subject of this chapter in Ephesians is "Walk in Love." So we are to walk, yes, and not just move around, but be specifically motivated and directed by God's love. Thus, our lives become purposeful and dedicated, creative and meaningful. It is God's love then that makes the difference between just activity and God's will being accomplished. And thus do we bless God, and thus are we blessed in return. Paul tells us how:

> Therefore be imitators of God, as beloved children. And walk in love, as Christ loved us and gave Himself up for us, a fragrant offering and sacrifice to God. (Ephesians 5:1–2)

There is a difference between copying and imitating. To copy is to make something so that it resembles an original thing. To imitate is to follow as an example or pattern. Thus, to copy is more static in nature, and to imitate is to imply more action and movement. And we are to imitate God, to be "out and about" applying His love in His world through our lives. This, so that His love is seen, felt, and experienced by others. And we are to do this as beloved children, His family members beholden and gifted with His love, representing Him in all we do and are. And Jesus was the classic example of this. He told us: "Whoever has seen me has seen the Father" (John 14:9).

That does not apply to us, but we are to live such that there is no doubt whose we are, what family we belong to, and who is Lord of our lives. To tell us to "walk in love" implies a daily consistency to what we do and why. And what we are to do is to love Him with all our hearts, souls, and minds, and the why of it all is to bring praise, honor, and glory to God.

Notice Paul reminds us Christ did not just love us. He proved His love when He gave Himself up for us. We are to seriously consider what this verse is saying: **almighty Creator God loved each of us so much He sent His beloved Son to earth to save us from our sins by paying our sin debt with His death on the cross.** And the verse tells us to "walk in love" **as Christ loved us.** So it is that kind of love we are to imitate. And the fact that the word *love* is used in the past tense in no way implies God has stopped His love for us.

Notice the description of Jesus' gift to us Paul provides. It was (and still is) a "fragrant offering and sacrifice to God." We are the ones who sin, and our sins are against God. So, it is to Him offerings and sacrifices are due. And only the gift of Jesus' life is sufficient to atone for our sin debt, and Christ provided that. The word *fragrant* implies sufficiency and *offering* implies the love-driven motive for which Jesus gave His life. So the sin debt for believers is fully and gladly paid. What a great God we have.

So Paul's message from God is clear. In loving response back to God for His first loving us, we are to imitate His kind of love to others. God does not need our love as we think of need. But He wants it, He merits it, and He has earned it. Who are we to withhold any part of our self from full allegiance to Him? God freely gives His love and so should we.

REVELATION 22:12-13

In this passage, John the Apostle has been led by the Holy Spirit to put in writing the description of the visions God has given him. Now he is almost through and here he begins to sum up his message concerning the end times, when Jesus returns to gather all believers to take them to heaven. We believers can take this as good news, while unbelievers need to understand the specific warning given. See how God has John explain these truths:

> Behold, I am coming soon, bringing my recompense with me, to repay everyone for what he has done. I am the Alpha and the Omega, the first and the last, the beginning and the end. (Revelation 22:12–13)

This is Jesus speaking, telling us He is coming quickly, suddenly, and when no one expects Him. Thus, the message is, "Be ready." And when He comes, He will bring our rewards with Him; the concept being that all people will be accurately judged; believers rewarded as appropriate, and all taken to heaven to spend eternity with the Father and the Lamb (Jesus). Unbelievers will also be judged, and all of them will be separated from God to spend eternity in hell. So it is by God's grace and our faith that we are saved, and by the same criteria we are all to be judged, those having a saving relationship with Christ being rewarded and taken to heaven, and all others separated from God forever.

Notice the three references to Jesus' authority given that authenticate His power and right to do this judging. "Alpha and Omega, the first and the last, and the beginning and the end," all reference the same thing, that is, Jesus' position as God, creator and sustainer of the universe, here before the universe was, and forever Lord over all of it. God is completely thorough in all He does. He has told us what is coming, what will be the disposition of all our eternal destinies (and why), and He advises us by what authority He will do these things. He has made His authority and position clear.

We have the option of belief or unbelief, that of establishing a relationship of our servanthood and His Lordship or not. Surely there are those you know and care about who need to hear of God's love and provision in Christ. Their eternal destiny is at risk.

MATTHEW 6:19–21

In our society there is much too much emphasis placed on material things, things that we think are permanent, but that are actually temporary. Things that if they don't fail us short-term, and well they might, they surely will fail us long-term. God would have us keep a proper perspective concerning everything in this world, keeping our focus on Him and eternity. See this passage and its message for us:

> Do not lay up for yourself treasures on earth, where moth and rust destroy and where thieves break in and steal, but lay up for yourselves treasures in heaven, where neither moth nor rust destroys, and where thieves do not break in and steal. For where your treasure is, there your heart will be also. (Matthew 6:19–21)

God knows the temptations we face and warns us here of the danger of emphasis on possessions. Notice the main point here is that we have a choice as to how we use the time, talent, possessions, and opportunities God provides us. So we are to remember this earth is not our home, and thus, emphasis on our heavenly status should be our focus. The worldly things people work so hard to acquire will not last and they will eventually disappoint. There is a real sense that our worldly activities will tend to store up either earthly rewards in the present, or heavenly rewards in the future. And God has provided us information in scripture that will enable us to differentiate between the two.

The last phrase concerning where our heart is, thus, becomes particularly potent. In short, in this passage God advises us that our heart will be eternally where those things that are most important to us are now. So the key questions are: What do we treasure? And, where is our eternal destiny going to be? Will we spend eternity with God in heaven, or separated from God in hell? Those are the only two options, and our choices made now are key in the process of determining our eternal future.

Ephesians 5:15–16 speaks to this same subject: "Look carefully then how you walk, not as unwise but as wise, making best use of the time, because the days are evil."

Surely this is good advice. The older we get the more we realize how time really does "fly by." So our limited time here on earth is to be used properly. We do well to be involved in activities that have eternal implications, that benefit others, and that glorify God. That is why we were born. The verse in Ephesians says it well: "Walk not as the unwise, but as the wise." So be wise.

PROVERBS 27:17

God has brought mankind together in this world to live among each other in harmony and support of one another. In fact, we cannot live without influencing others to some degree and in some manner (for good or for evil). As we interact with others, God would have we believers glorify Him with our lifestyles. And He provides instructions in His word as to how we are to do so. See this classic example of such direction for us:

> Iron sharpens iron, and one man sharpens another. (Proverbs 27:17)

The image is of one man being of positive influence on another man. For one piece of iron to do any proper sharpening, it must be brought into contact with another section of iron with vigorous, intentional, and purposeful action. Just so are we to give similar planned, ongoing, and intense effort to our positive influence on someone else. The concept of Christian disciple making comes readily to mind here. Let me list some observations and several results of such efforts for individual believers as they go about making disciples:

1. Both participants must be willing subjects for meaningful discipling to take place.
2. Both participants receive benefit from the process.
3. At least one of the participants must have the required credentials for such discipling, else the process may become a "pooling" of ignorance.
4. Consistent interaction over time will be required for proper results.

5. Growth in the process is to lead to both participants continuing the process with others.

6. Prayer-filled preparation will bring God's Holy Spirit into the equation, for without question God will support such sincere efforts.

7. God commands us to make disciples, thus, we are without excuse for not doing it.

8. Since God commands such disciple making, He will, therefore, bless our efforts.

Scripture presents many examples of this principle of disciple making. Jesus is the classic disciple maker. He lived the process with His twelve. Paul went into seclusion right after his conversion to prepare himself, but he did not stay there. He returned to present the gospel wherever he went. Until his old age, John taught, lived, and wrote of the gospel for the benefit of many. And there are many other examples.

So let us take seriously this privilege and the responsibilities inherent with it. God loves us and presents the disciple making command for our benefit, and for the benefit of the whole world.

1 THESSALONIANS 5:9-11

Paul's purpose in writing to the church at Thessalonica is to encourage them in their faith. Given their lives living under Roman oppression, the extent of poverty among them, and the general temptations to sin all humans face, they needed encouragement. And so do we. And we can take heart for the same reasons the Thessalonians could. Jesus is Lord, and He will never be anything less than Lord. And as He loved the Thessalonians, He loves us too. And praise the Lord, we believers will spend eternity with Him in heaven alongside the Thessalonica believers. Note the promises God has made.

> For God has not destined us for wrath, but to obtain salvation through our Lord Jesus Christ, who died for us whether we are awake or asleep we might live with him. Therefore encourage one another and build one another up, just as you are doing. (1 Thessalonians 5:9–11)

God has a plan for each of us as individuals and as a group. He developed those plans before time began and has not varied one bit from His original plan. These plans incorporate our relationships with each other, and take into account every single variation of time, place, talent, condition or circumstances any of us could ever face. And that plan is based on the fact of eternal salvation accruing to all those who believe in Jesus Christ as Savior and Lord. And at God the Father's appointed time, Jesus will return to earth from heaven to collect all believers for their journey with Him to heaven to spend eternity with Him there.

Thus, because Jesus' sacrificial death on the cross paid the complete sin debt of all who believe, no believer will ever face God's wrath, but obtain salvation through Jesus Christ. In those days of this letter, which was only about twenty years after Jesus' crucifixion, not everyone who had witnessed Jesus' miracles, heard His sermons, and accepted Him as their Savior, had died. But some had. Thus, naturally the question arose as to the present circumstance of those believers who died before Jesus' promised return. And Paul clears that up for his readers then, and especially us now (who die two thousand years after Christ's death and resurrection). Whether "awake" (that is, alive) at Jesus' return, or "asleep" (that is, dead) at Jesus' return, **believers will live with Him.** Hallelujah! We can rest easy that God has taken all these time issues into account.

So, Paul tells his readers to encourage one another, and to build one another up. It follows then that we are to be good examples of godly believers. We may not feel qualified to build up other believers. But we don't have to fulfill this assignment in our own strength. God never assigns us anything without making provisions for helping us obey His commands. When God is our helper, then we need not worry about our own lack of ability or capacity. Specifically, God has assigned the Holy Spirit to indwell us and see to our recollection of everything Jesus said or did during His earthly ministry.

And God has done two more things to assist us in compliance with encouraging and building one another up. (1) He has seen to the provision of His Word for our edification and instruction. (2) He has established the institution of the church. This, to facilitate our association with other believers who have the same assignment we have, that is, "to go and make disciples." So, as we build up each other, we go out into the world both singly, and as a group, to take the gospel to the nations. Scripture tells us in Matthew 24:24 after that is accomplished, the end will come, that is, Christ will return.

COLOSSIANS 3:16–17

The good news of Jesus Christ is not news we are to keep to ourselves. Paul the apostle was preaching and teaching in Ephesus, modern-day Turkey, about AD 52 where a man named Epaphras was converted to Christ. He was from the town of Colossae and went back home telling others about his conversion. Eventually he founded a church in Colossae and now ten years later while under house arrest in Rome, Paul writes to that church to encourage them in their spiritual growth. It is this practice of one believer telling other people about Jesus Christ that both Paul and Epaphras exampled, that leads to the spread of the gospel around the world. That same process still works today. Look at some key things Paul writes to the church in Colossae, that we, too, are to apply:

> Let the word of Christ dwell in you richly, teaching and admonishing one another in all wisdom, singing psalms and hymns and spiritual songs with thankfulness in your hearts to God. And whatever you do, in word and deed, do everything in the name of the Lord Jesus, giving thanks to God the Father through Him. (Colossians 3:16–17)

Jesus Christ is key, and scripture concerning Him is to "dwell in us richly." That has to involve our letting His truth grow within us, as we live it out in our lives and tell others about Him, especially those we love the most. Singing Psalms and spiritual songs would seem to mean joining with other believers in regular worship meetings to praise the Lord and engage in teaching and preaching sessions. Notice we are to have thankful hearts for what God specifically has done for us, and for what we are learning and experiencing over time. Certainly, the free gift of eternal life God provides to all believers is worthy of all our gratitude and thankfulness of heart. **It's the best gift anyone can ever receive.**

See the emphasis Paul gives to focus on the Lord Jesus. If we don't do anything else right, we are to do whatever we do "in word and deed" in the name of Jesus Christ, who paid our sin debt with His sacrificial death on the cross. He obviously is central to the Christian faith and our lives are to reflect total commitment, loyalty, and allegiance to Him. And why not? He is God, come to earth to save us from our sins, and resides now in heaven at the Father's right hand, interceding for us. One day He will return to gather to Himself all those who believe for an eternity in heaven.

Again, in the last sentence of the passage we notice thanksgiving is again mandated. This time God the Father and Jesus Christ are connected. We are to thank the Father through Jesus. Our emphasis on getting thanksgiving to God through Jesus does not diminish the Father, but provides Him glory. And in the final analysis glorifying the Father is why we were born. In His infinite love and wisdom God has commanded consistent thanksgiving from us for a reason. That reason is, He loves us with an infinite love. And He knows when we have proper perspective, gratitude, and love to and for Him, we establish an eternal relationship with Him that begins in this life when we are saved, and extends on into heaven for an eternity. And the more we love and thank Him for our earthly experience of salvation, the closer will be our relationship to Him, and the richer will be our inheritance there.

PHILIPPIANS 2:13

In this verse Paul provides one of the most basic truths in all of scripture. The very concept that God not only knows what is best for us and leads us to make decisions that work toward that end, absolutely proves His infinite love for us and the thoroughness of His salvation process. The very thought of that degree of involvement by God in our lives should bring us to our knees in gratitude. Paul is explaining that doctrine to the Philippians, and praise the Lord, at the same time is explaining it to us. See this awesome verse:

> For it is God who works in you, both to will and to work for His good pleasure. (Philippians 2:13)

Talk about a verse we should highlight in our Bible, this is one. If there was ever a thought we should never forget and promote among those who mean the most to us, this is that thought. In the first place we are far, far from worthy of such love and provision from God. That fact speaks volumes about God's grace, that is, His undeserved love that we have. Born in sin, from birth we work toward self-preservation, to the exclusion of others. Jesus, Son of God, King of Kings, and Lord of Lords, had to come to earth as man to die in our place to properly illustrate obedience to the Father, and love for our neighbors. And still we resist His two greatest commandments, love for Him, and for our neighbors.

And now about two thousand years after Jesus came, we are still adjusting to the "New Covenant" God made with mankind whereby with His sacrificial death on the cross Jesus pays all the sin debt of those who believe in Him. While God has provided many commands for us, those laws identify sin, but are not listed to furnish the route to eternal life. In fact, we cannot comply with those laws and, thus, earn our way to heaven. The only way is by God's grace through faith. (Ephesians 2:8). And God provides both of those.

Notice in this verse who provides us the "want" for obedience: our heavenly Father God. This ongoing urging on God's part gives us the motives and the incentive to live out our faith. That is, to make obedience to God's laws paramount in our lives, and to make glorifying the Father the reason for our living. Interestingly, Paul defines our goal in life to be God's good pleasure. We don't use that phrase often, but we do get the message. Implied in this goal is not one particular command, or one unique occasion, but a consistent Christian walk, a lifestyle of Christlikeness, and a lifetime of decisions for God's glory.

Notice, too, God does not provide just the will to obey, but the incentive to work. That type of work takes on many forms and has an ongoing quality about it. So, as obedient believers we can expect challenges. "Smooth sailing" does not describe a Christian's life. Jesus suffered, and we can expect suffering as well. We can be sure, however, of help along the way. God in His infinite love and wisdom provided His Holy Spirit to see to our every circumstance. He is there, indwelling us, leading us, and as the verse says working in us. We are to take that assurance of the Holy Spirit's presence to heart; never forget it, count on it, and live out His presence. In fact, His presence should be a source of our confidence and joy as we live for God's good pleasure.

2 CORINTHIANS 3:2-3

Here Paul the apostle is writing to the church at Corinth, speaking about their roles as witnesses for the Lord. Those believers have come to a knowledge of Christ as the Holy Spirit used Paul to share the truth of the gospel with them. Hearing, and by faith believing the gospel led to their heart transformations and their receiving God's free gift of eternal life. That gift carries with it the responsibility to "go and do likewise." And we have that responsibility too. Thus, Paul is reminding the Corinthians and us that we are to do what He did, make disciples, wherever they went. See how Paul describes his ministry:

> You yourselves are our letter of recommendation, written on our hearts, to be known and read by all. And you show that you are a letter from Christ delivered by us, written not with ink but with the Spirit of the living God, not on tablets of stone but on tablets of human hearts. (2 Corinthians 3:2–3)

In those days there were many spokesmen who traveled the world preaching "a" gospel. It was easy enough for them to claim Paul had sent them and thus gain the confidence and (financial) support of the local churches. To combat such actions Paul often wrote letters of recommendation for those he knew to be authentic disciples of Christ. As he wrote this letter concerning himself and his ministry, it was his position that changed hearts were the true authentication of someone's ministry, not some signed document. So, it was Paul's contention that his readers could know his ministry was legitimate by the way each believer felt about their own relationship with the Lord.

Paul makes a critical point concerning his ministry, that what he preached could be understood, evaluated, and believed, by all.

That is, his ministry was consistent, his doctrine was the same wherever he preached, not modified somehow to accommodate given different physical circumstances in the various cities he visited. And the route to eternal life he preached was the same for everyone, by God's grace through faith. Thus, the true believers in Corinth were living and breathing testimonies of God's saving grace, just as we should be.

Notice, too, how Paul attributes the presence of the Holy Spirit in each believer to be the driving force behind their lives. Paul calls the Corinthians a "letter from Christ." What a neat all-encompassing phrase to describe the lives of these believing Corinthians as they went about influencing others for Christ. Would that the same thing could be said about us, that we are true witnesses for the Lord to the nations, living and consistently sharing what we know to be true concerning Jesus.

Paul clearly reminds us that we are all "letters" written not with ink, but with the influence of the Holy Spirit in our lives. Such life letters will be "read" by those around us. We, thus, do and will influence other people. It is impossible to live and not do so. When we think of letters being carved on tablets of stone the idea of permanence comes to mind. But even stone letters are not as permanent or as effective as those written on our hearts. Knowing this, it is no surprise God provides His Spirit to indwell every believer to be with and in us 24/7 in all circumstances, always available to guide us.

2 TIMOTHY 4:7-8

Paul is writing from prison what is likely the last letter he ever wrote. In it, he urges Timothy to persevere in his faith in spite of suffering and opposition. Using himself as an example, Paul also covers the concept of rewards believers will be given on that Day; that Day being the time and point when we stand before God and are judged on our lives. All believers since, in every society, have wondered about how that will play out. So, it's not surprising that the Holy Spirit led Paul to share information on this subject. The news is good for those who persevere:

> I have fought the good fight, I have finished the race, I have kept the faith. Henceforth, there is laid up for me the crown of righteousness, which the Lord, the righteous judge, will award me on that day, and not only me but also to all who have loved his appearing. (2 Timothy 4:7–8)

Paul is awaiting death and he knows it. Thus, it is amazing that he can write such encouraging words to Timothy and those he is ministering to in the church at Ephesus. Paul is confident that there is a "crown" of righteousness "laid up for him" in heaven. That may be an actual crown, or a reference to the glorious state all believers will have in heaven. What we can be sure of is that our status in heaven will be joy-filled beyond our present understanding. Notice the three points Paul makes concerning this crown. (1) Paul's crown is prepared already and will be given to him at the proper time. God already knows how all believers will finish their earthly "race," and thus our appropriate reward(s) will be provided. (2) It is the Lord Jesus, the righteous judge, who will make the decisions relative to our award. No one else is better qualified. And (3) all believers will also receive their awards on that (same) day, although to think of *day* as a twenty-four-hour period is probably inaccurate. The point is that rewards are in store for all believers. The time, place, type, and conditions are God's to decide. We can simply be assured the almighty God of heaven will not fall short in showing us His level of love.

Notice how Paul describes believers (of any era): "those who loved His appearing." What a completely descriptive phrase for indicating our relationship to Jesus. We know He came to earth (appeared). We know it and we rejoice in His coming. We are grateful for it, and we trusted Him as our Savior and Lord, who died on the cross to pay our sin debt.

Paul fought the "good fight," likely one that was a lot more difficult than ours. Consistently then, for decades, Paul stayed the course in His Christian walk. We can do that too. God helps those who persevere, and He expects us to persevere.

So, what is the lesson we can learn from this passage? Certainly, we can learn from Paul's diligence in his faith. He set a good example, and that's the lesson we must learn. Paul walked the Christian walk, encouraged others to do so, and supported them in their efforts. We can do this in many ways. We do so verbally, with sympathy for the stress of life others might be facing. We can do this financially, by supporting mission efforts locally and globally. We can do this via prayer, which is the most important approach we can take. **Nothing speaks more vividly of our love and support for someone and their Christian walk than consistent prayer. God will bless such prayer efforts more than we can imagine.** We can be sure Paul backed up his letters to Timothy with many hours of prayer for him. There is no way Paul could have written such meaningful letters otherwise.

EXODUS 15:2

When Moses led the children of Israel out of Egypt it was a very stressful time, filled with fears and doubts, needful of God's help every step of the way. We sometimes have episodes in our lives also filled with fears and doubts, and needful of God's involvement. This passage reflects a prayer and song that Moses lifted up to God on this occasion that we, too, can "sing." Notice his dependence on God and his acknowledgement of that need leading to him praising God in the midst of his trial.

> The Lord is my strength and my song, and he has become my salvation; this is my God, and I will praise him, my father's God, and I will exalt him. (Exodus 15:2)

Notice how worthy God is of our praise and exaltation even while our trials are playing out. In the middle of his fears and frustrations God brings a perspective to Moses that we would be well advised to emulate. He recognizes God's position as his salvation, that is, the source of his relief, safety, and restoration. At this point he is not even praying for relief, he is simply acknowledging God's sovereignty.

When Jesus gave His disciples, and us, His model prayer, He began it with the phrase, "Our Father who are in heaven, hallowed be thy name" (Matthew 6:9). When we pray those words, we are not praying for our heavenly Father's name to be hallowed; **it already is hallowed** because of who He is. Jesus tells us to begin our prayers this way so as to establish our trust in God's love and power, and His willingness to attend to our needs.

So we are to pray, praying for strength, stamina, and perseverance; for faith, hope and assurance. God already knows we want and need those things, but He wants us to pray them anyway. This, so that over time we begin to see our prayers as God sees them, and that is, us as His children (whom He loves) coming to Him (first and only) confident He can and will provide us everything we need. It's that kind of relationship He wants us to have with Him.

The last line of Moses' song is very comforting, telling us how available the Lord always is: "The Lord will reign forever and ever" (Exodus 15:18).

ROMANS 10:9

Here in this passage is the essence of God's plan of salvation, what mankind needs to understand and believe for salvation. God not only provides the way of salvation, but saw to the recording of His plan so that all may know and believe the truth. Paul is writing here to the church at Rome about thirty years after Jesus' death and resurrection. Notice how God has Paul word this so simply for us all:

> If you confess with your mouth that Jesus is Lord and believe
> in your heart that God raised Him from the dead, you will be
> saved. (Romans 10:9)

This verse does not mean this one work on our part of confessing Jesus as Lord is adequate to merit our justification (that word describing God's finding of us as not guilty of our sins). But it does give evidence of our inward faith in Christ's substitutionary death on the cross in our place to pay our sin debt, and **that is key to God's salvation plan**.

We are to believe also that God raised Jesus from the dead; not just that one act, but all it indicates. And it clearly indicates that God approved of the "why" of Jesus' sacrifice (to save us from our sins), and proves His death was sufficient to atone for all our sins. Thus, our heavenly Father has made all the necessary provisions for our salvation and made us aware of them.

Jesus had already provided us from His own lips the certainty of His deity and purpose of His coming to earth: "I am the way, and the truth, and the life. No one comes to the Father except through me" (John 14:6).

We might well wonder why God made all these provisions. And scripture explains that too. Again in one sentence we see this most significant truth described. "For by grace are you saved through faith" (Ephesians 2:8).

Grace defines that (undeserved) love God has for us. Now that can be hard to understand. How could God love us at all (given our unworthiness), and especially how could He love us first, while we were deep in sin as unbelievers? But He did, and He does. That, we do have to believe by faith. But we see His love evident every day in our lives by all He does, all He provides, and all the protections He gives us.

Thus, God describes in scripture how we come to be saved. That word "saved" sounds all inclusive, and praise the Lord, it is all inclusive. By these verses we see how all our sins (before and after our conversion) are forgiven and not counted against us. We will never hear of any better news.

REVELATION 22:6–7

John the apostle is writing here and almost finished with his letter we call the book of Revelation. He is now an old man writing near the end of the first century. John's vision of the end times has been led by an angel from heaven, and this passage begins with the angel speaking to John, and ends with Jesus speaking to John. See this passage and take note of the significance of what is said to us.

> And he said to me, "These words are trustworthy and true. And the Lord, the God of the spirits of the prophets, has sent his angel to show his servants what must soon take place. And behold, I am coming soon. Blessed is the one who keeps the words of the prophecy of this book." (Revelation 22:6–7)

We should not have to be reminded that the words of God contained in the Bible are trustworthy and true, but here that very thing happens. Such reminders only emphasize how important it is for us to observe all that God has put in His scripture for our benefit. In His Word, God has described how He has made provision for our eternal life via Christ's sacrificial death on the cross in our place, and has repeatedly urged (and even warned) us to believe and take to heart what He has said. And now in this last letter of the Bible we are told again what will happen soon. The word *soon* as used here does not mean in a short length of time, but it means quickly or suddenly. So we can see the message for us from God here is to "get prepared now" for we don't know when Christ will return.

And then Jesus speaks saying, "Behold, I am coming soon. Blessed is the one who keeps the words of the prophecy of this book." *Behold* means to be aware of, or "open your eyes," "get ready." We are wise if we heed these words of scripture, for as Jesus says,

He is coming quickly. We are not told here exactly what the word *blessed* (for keeping the words of these prophecies) means, but for the twenty-one chapters in front of this one God has described the heaven He is preparing for those who are obedient. Surely the meaning of "blessed" is that obedience to Jesus' words will lead to the blessing of residence in heaven with God and Christ forever. Just a few verses before this passage we are told that in heaven God's servants will worship Him, and **See His Face**. Seeing God's face is the definition of heaven.

EPHESIANS 2:4–6, 19

Multiple times throughout scripture, God has seen fit to record the route to eternal life for anyone who will believe in Jesus Christ. This is one of those passages. Paul is reminding the believers in the church at Ephesus that at one point they were unbelievers; lost, and bound for an eternity separated from God. But that then God stepped in and provided them a way to escape condemnation. That way is still available in our day, with the same stipulations, that is, belief in Christ as the Son of God, and that He did, in fact, come to earth to save us from our sins through His sacrificial death on the cross in our place. Look again as Paul describes this awesome provision:

> But God, being rich in mercy, because of the great love with which he loved us, even when we were dead in our trespasses, made us alive together with Christ—by grace you have been saved—and raised us up with him and seated us with him in the heavenly places in Christ Jesus . . . So, then you are no longer strangers and aliens, but you are fellow citizens with the saints and members of the household of God. (Ephesians 2:4–6, 19)

God is obviously rich in mercy, and obviously loves us with a great love. And amazingly, this was true even when we were "dead in our trespasses," that is, before we had any belief in God's provisions for our eternal life. Paul describes that transition on our part from unbelief to belief as God making us "alive together with Christ." Thus, in this way God's grace came into play, grace being that love God has for us that we've done nothing to deserve. So, reality is, if we are saved, it is by God's grace and nothing else. So the famous song title "Amazing Grace" hits the nail on the head, God's grace is amazing.

Paul goes further to describe what the new relationship believers have (after salvation) looks like. We are figuratively (spiritually) raised to heaven and seated alongside Jesus Christ even while we remain physically alive here on earth. Once saved, the salvation that God provides us is so secure, so permanently in place, so certain, that our eternal life begins here on earth the moment we by faith receive God's free gift of eternal life. Our physical death here on earth is only a temporary interlude between our earthly death and Christ's return to earth to gather all believers who have been born again. We will be raised from our graves exactly as Jesus was raised from His grave.

And notice our new status after salvation: we are adopted permanently into the household of God, along with our fellow saints who came to know Jesus Christ as Lord in any era. No longer are we outsiders, strangers, or aliens to God's family. Now we can truly claim God as Father and Jesus Christ as brother.

Nothing trumps membership in God's family in heaven for an eternity. Nothing presupposes an existence anywhere close to the peace, love, serenity, and joy God offers with He and Christ in heaven. Surely that message is worth our repeating over and over to a lost world.

JAMES 3:17-18

All of us would like to be wise, to have the kind of wisdom that only God provides. This section of James describes that kind of wisdom, calling it "Wisdom from Above." So, what we find here is God's definition of wisdom as it applies in our lives. Thus, we can come to this passage to determine the characteristics the world will see in us as we exhibit godly wisdom from above. The passage even concludes with a summary of what will be the result of our living out such wisdom.

> But the wisdom from above is first pure, then peaceable, gentle, open to reason, full of mercy and good fruits, impartial and sincere. And a harvest of righteousness is sown in peace by those who make peace. (James 3:17–18)

See the eight characteristics listed that make up godly wisdom. First, we find purity, that trait meaning unmixed or untainted with any other matter or condition. Pure wisdom in the ultimate sense then is godly, perfect in quality, longevity, and application. It's peaceable, finding its place as a solvent to strife and discord among men. Godly wisdom is also gentle, and we would expect that from our loving heavenly Father. Notice, it's open to reason, so as to broaden its application in all instances. Godly wisdom is full of mercy, too, and we praise God for that. Who, more than we, needs mercy, given our sinful condition? We might wonder what godly wisdom leads us to, and we are advised that good fruits are that end point. And we are grateful to God His wisdom is impartial, as we might apply it, and thankfully as it is applied to us. And who would doubt God's wisdom is sincere, marked by genuineness, everlasting and equally offered and applied to those who seek it?

Given these worthy characteristics, what is the end result of our habitually living this way, exhibiting them throughout our lives? James gives us that result, and it is a worthy goal, indeed. Our lives become a "harvest of righteousness." Picture your life being described as a "harvest of righteousness" leading to your being classified as a peacemaker. The image is one of total dedication to the Lord and His will in our lives. Surely, such a life that sows peace would be reflected in peacemaking. Notice what happens to peacemakers, and what they are called. "Blessed are the peacemakers, for they shall be called sons of God" (Matthew 5:9).

And sons (and daughters) of God are blessed. Knowing the God who loves us so much He sent His only Son to earth to save us from our sins, we need not be concerned about the validity of that promise, or the nature and timing of those blessings.

If godly wisdom originates in Him (and it does), then it is available only from Him. Thus, by definition, He is the source and where we are to go seeking such wisdom. God has given us the means to request such wisdom via prayer, and we can be assured God will hear our sincere prayers for His wisdom. God does not need us as His peacemakers. However, He loves us and knows we need to be peacemakers, and that we benefit from living out these eight characteristics. God has constructed the world including His love-driven provision for the eternal life of those who believe, even given our birth condition in sin. What a great God we have!

PROVERBS 28:9;
PSALM 66:18

We are told by God to "pray without ceasing" (1 Thessalonians 5:17), giving us clear indications as to the importance of the role God feels that prayer should play in our lives. The concept of the need for consistent fellowship between God and man is obvious. Yet there are right and wrong ways to pray. Look and see some specifics here for how to pray:

> If one turns away his ear from hearing the law, even his prayer is an abomination. (Proverbs 28:9)

> If I had cherished iniquity in my heart, the Lord would not have listened. (Psalm 66:18)

God does not promise to hear the prayers of those who refuse to pray with sincerity, willing ahead of time to take heed to the answers God provides no matter their direction. God has gone into great detail in His word to provide us all we need in our search for righteousness. Certainly, all of us have many questions, requests, and needs to lay before our heavenly Father. Still, we all have a given level of knowledge given us in our consciences of God's will and directions for our lives. Are we in compliance now with what we know already of God's purposes for our lives? What is our daily attitude concerning glorifying God by obedience to His commands?

It is likely most people already believe in (some sort of) God. But is that God the one revealed in scripture, creator of the universe, that one who loved us so much He gave His only Son to die a sinner's death on the cross in our place? We might well sincerely desire to know God's will for our lives, and pray that prayer. But the truth is we could probably readily take out pen and paper and fill the page with a listing of commands we are already familiar with that God has given us in His Word. Where do we stand with regard to possessing hearts that want and try to comply with our own list?

Jesus' model prayer (Luke 11:2–4) tells us to request forgiveness of our trespasses **"as we forgive those who trespass against us."** Clearly, we need to consider seriously the question, "Is forgiveness of others consistently a part of our lifestyles?" Perhaps our first prayer should be for a forgiving heart?

Praise the Lord, God loves us with a steadfast love. He knows of and understands our many failings and trespasses. And He would have us be humble and repentant of those trespasses, ever mindful of our need for His forgiveness and mercy, always seeking to glorify Him by all we say, and do, and are. That's why Jesus' model prayer also includes the request, "Thy kingdom come, thy will be done on earth as it is in heaven."

HEBREWS 12:28-29

The title of this section of scripture is "A Kingdom That Cannot Be Shaken." That refers to the kingdom God has established for those who believe. It exists in the heart of believers and will last forever no matter what our physical circumstances here on earth may temporarily be. It is available to us all, and involves our receipt of God's free gift of eternal life though His grace and our faith in Jesus Christ's sacrificial death on the cross to pay our sin debt. See how the Holy Spirit has directed this author to word this vital message for us all:

> Therefore let us be grateful for receiving a kingdom that cannot be shaken, and thus let us offer to God acceptable worship, with reverence and awe, for our God is a consuming fire. (Hebrews 12:28–29)

God has promised eternal salvation to believers and refers to that condition as them living in a kingdom that cannot be shaken, that is, with a permanency about it that will never end. That heavenly home coming to believers is where God will share companionship with them forever in eternal bliss. And given that is true, then the passage tells us we should offer God acceptable worship now, here on earth. After all, He created us all, and now promises an eternity with Him.

Such a God is surely worthy of all our gratitude, our reverence, and awe. God is worthy, He knows He is worthy, and He wants us to know it too. He loves us and has made a way for us to come to Him through faith in His Son Jesus Christ that leads to our receipt of His free gift of eternal life. Perhaps the most well-known scripture verse in the Bible is John 3:16 that describes this provision God has made. "For God so loved the world, that

He gave His only Son, that whoever believes in Him should not perish but have eternal life. For God did not send His Son into the world to condemn the world, but in order that the world might be saved through Him" (vv. 16–17).

In essence, because of His great love for us, God has made every provision for our eternal life. Notice though, the passage closes by telling us God is a consuming fire. That refers to the fact He is a loving God, a just God, and He is a jealous God. **He merits our praise, honor, glory, and obedience and He requires it of us.** Thus, as we live out acceptable worship of God, we show our relationship to Him by our lifestyles, and other people will see that in us. The things we do (and don't do) will reflect our priorities and our life perspectives.

God is God and we are not. He is both the standard for us to live by, and the judge of our obedience. We have been given His revelation of Himself in Holy Scripture, and are without excuse as to what His will for us is. We need only respond in obedience to the love He has so graciously shown to us in John 3:16.

JOB 2:9–10

Scholars are not sure when Job lived or who wrote the book, but we do know it is one of the most profound books in the Bible, filled with eternal truths and principles for us to learn and live by. We know he was a godly man, and these two verses reflect his response to his wife's rebuke when she challenges his stoic and resolute attitude about his painful conditions. He has lost his family, his possessions, and his station in life, yet he resolves to maintain his integrity and relationship to God. Notice his heart reflected here, and how appropriate such humility would be for us:

> Then his wife said to him, "Do you still hold fast your integrity? Curse God and die." But he said to her, "You speak as one of the foolish women would speak. Shall we receive good from God, and shall we not receive evil?" In all this Job did not sin with his lips. (Job 2:9–10)

Integrity has to do with one's sense of moral values, and Job's was oriented around God's truths. In his times of wealth and prosperity he had maintained a clean heart and a right spirit, and adversity did not change that perspective. His wife had lost her children, wealth, and reputation, too, and Satan used her to tempt Job further. But Job was not moved. Job 27:5 tells us Job said, "till I die I will not put away my integrity from me." Satan took away his family, worldly goods, health, and status, but could only tempt his heart. The same is true for us. Beware his temptations of your heart, likely disguised as worldly pressures, disturbing circumstances, troubling conditions, and especially prideful attitudes. That last temptation is likely to be the most difficult to deal with for most people, especially ardent believers. Do not let them control what you know to be God's truth and righteousness in your life. God either provides or allows all of what we might classify as good and bad experiences. In every case He has some lesson for us to learn, some principle He knows we need to absorb and apply. Look for them knowing His steadfast love for us is involved in every single thing He does. Praise His name for that.

1 PETER 5:6–7, 10–11

Peter the apostle is writing to Jewish Christians and Gentile believers too. His purpose is to encourage them to persevere in their faith. His message has to do with them being steadfast during suffering knowing that God's will for their lives is best even though at times it is difficult to remain faithful. That's true in our day too. Peter reminds believers in all eras that God has not forgotten them and that the joy of an eternity with the Lord will more than make up for any earthly pain and trials. See Peter's wording of God's promises:

> Humble yourselves, therefore, under the mighty hand of God so that at the proper time he may exalt you, casting all your anxieties on him, because he cares for you. . . . And after you have suffered a little while, the God of all grace, who has called you to his eternal glory in Christ, will Himself restore, confirm, strengthen, and establish you. To him be the dominion forever and ever. Amen. (1 Peter: 5:6–7, 10–11)

Peter suggests we all humble ourselves within God's awesome power knowing He has total control of the universe. Since we can be assured He cares for us then His power will eternally play out for our benefit as at the proper time He exalts us. Thus, every anxiety we ever have is properly dealt with when we turn them over to God. **Who better could we trust with our problems and even eternal life than an all-powerful God who loves us? That's a truth we need to grasp, live out, and share with others.**

So, yes, there is apt to be suffering in every life. But when you think about it, the temporary earthly trials we experience simply better prepare us to appreciate the eternal joy God has promised us in heaven with Him. And notice the personal attention God does and always will provide us. The passage tells us specifically that "**the God of all grace** . . . **WILL HIMSELF** restore, confirm, strengthen, and establish" us. He is described as "the God of all grace." That phrase is so all-encompassing that we are likely to pass over it without realizing the significance of it. Grace is a unique word that refers to the love only God has for us that comes to us undeservedly, and unexpectedly, and it is unbending, unchanging, and everlasting. And if that were not enough, it is infinite in scope. **We have it all.**

See the depth of God's makeover for each believer. He will restore us. Nothing about us will be the same. We will be made new, and without blemish. We will be confirmed, that is authenticated, and especially designated a child of God and, thus, an heir to the throne. And we will be strengthened. No matter the level of weakness or strength we now have *we will have added strength*. And God will establish us, that is, He will "set us in place"; that's the place we ought to be, per God's will. We will become confident of that new established place, and find peace there.

And because of these changes we will come to realize more than before about God's worthiness of all our love, praise, honor, glory, and admiration. But we must never think we can ever add to any of these characteristics God has. HE ALREADY HAS ALL HONOR, GLORY, POWER, WISDOM, MAJESTY, ETC. We CAN ONLY add to OUR appreciation of God's nature, but never come close to total understanding.

Peter is right in closing this passage, saying, "To Him be the dominion forever and ever. Amen." **That's the almighty God we have and whom we are to worship.**

ACTS 8:4–8

Now after Jesus' ascension back to heaven there arose great oppression of those of His believers left behind, and because of this, they scattered throughout Judea and Samaria, taking the gospel with them. So in essence this persecution served to help spread the gospel. Here we see one more example of how God uses our circumstances (some of them bad) to work His will in the world. Philip, one of the first deacons, illustrated this. See how God used him for His glory:

> Now those who were scattered went about preaching the word. Philip went down to the city of Samaria and proclaimed to them the Christ. And the crowds with one accord paid attention to what was being said by Philip, when they heard him and saw the signs that he did. For unclean spirits, crying out with a loud voice, came out of many who had them, and many who were paralyzed or lame were healed. So there was much joy in that city. (Acts 8:4–8)

Notice how the Holy Spirit chose to bless the preaching of Philip. He used the signs Philip did to prove the authenticity of his words. And people believed in Christ. And why not? Such miracles surely caught people's attention, giving credibility to the message Philip preached. The same thing would be true today. God's obvious involvement in the world always gets our attention.

The Samaritans were a mixed-race people, part Jewish and part Gentile, generally looked down on by both groups. Yet God saw fit to provide them the gospel and to have someone record the results for us to read about. So Philip's witness to them had to be surprising to those who heard about it. But because God blessed Philip's witness, people understood the gospel was not just meant for the Jews. In those days that was a hugely significant truth. It's a significant truth in our day too. We are not to restrict our gospel witness to people "just like us."

The Holy Spirit empowered Philip's witness. We know this because people "with one accord" paid attention and were saved. Philip must have been led by the Holy Spirit to go to Samaria in the first place, for he would not normally see the gospel as appropriate for anyone other than Jews. Yet when he did go and preach to them the Holy Spirit moved among them as He had done among the Jews.

So the lesson for us in this passage is clear: trust the Holy Spirit's leadership. We've been commanded to go and make disciples. Thus, any leading we get in that direction must be God speaking to us via His Holy Spirit. So obedience to God's commands is **always** appropriate for us. And see the results, there was much joy in that city. We need to remember the Jews did not like the Samaritans, but the Samaritans did not like the Jews either. So when a Jew came to a city in Samaria with a message that results in great joy, that was a newsworthy event. God had to have been involved to break down these cultural barriers.

God uses His truth to break down society's barriers and melt hard hearts in our day, too, if His disciples will follow His leadership. Let us be diligent in doing so. God will bless the results.

2 Timothy 4:5

Paul has written this letter from prison in Rome to his young disciple, Timothy. He has left Timothy in Ephesus ministering to the church there. The time is the mid-sixties AD, about thirty years after Jesus' death, resurrection, and ascension, a time when many false teachers have come to plague the church of Jesus Christ everywhere with their lies, myths, and distortions of scripture. So Paul encourages Timothy to stay true to the gospel, and consistent in his lifestyle as a disciple of Jesus Christ. See how this verse summarizes his instructions to Timothy and really to us in our day too:

> As for you, always be sober-minded, endure suffering, do the work of an evangelist, fulfill your ministry. (2 Timothy 4:5)

Paul has been describing the various activities of these false teachers, and of the danger in letting them go unchallenged. And now he particularly addresses Timothy with instructions in four areas of ministry. First, he mentions being sober-minded. To be sober-minded is to exhibit an earnestly thoughtful character at all times, seriously considering our actions and their ramifications. This is a more difficult assignment than we might imagine. It presumes "heavy" thinking, and an ongoing evaluation of the effects of what we do and say on others. Consciously or subconsciously we tend to avoid this kind of mental activity. Our habit of watching television is an excellent example of how not to be sober-minded. One of the main reasons watching televisions is so popular is in doing so, we don't have to do anything, we don't even have to think. We just sit there absorbing whatever we are watching, showing how mentally lazy we often are. Paul is telling us all to discipline ourselves to give ongoing consideration to patterning our lives after God's will for us, and to be about that work consistently.

Paul would have Timothy endure suffering. It's one thing for us to endure suffering not of our own making, but Paul is describing a lifestyle that deliberately comes into contact with people and situations that are apt to be painful, frustrating, and unrewarding. That's what sin brings into the lives of the world and what separates us from God. Any time we separate ourselves from God's will, we can be sure that pain and discomfort will eventually come to us. As witnesses and disciple makers we put ourselves at risk of suffering, and that's what we must expect. That's what happened to Jesus and what will happen to us as well. But hallelujah! It also leads to our relationship with Him on earth and eternally.

We are to do the work of an evangelist. By definition, that would mean taking on the responsibility of sharing the gospel of Christ with the world. It implies doing so with accuracy, enthusiasm, and zeal. It carries with it the thought of promoting Jesus Christ as Son of God, Savior, and Lord, who died on the cross to save us from our sins. It speaks to the concept of mankind gaining the free gift of eternal life by God's grace and our faith.

And thus we are to fulfill our ministry. This is the way Paul lived, and the way he urged Timothy and all believers to live. To live such lives will involve much in the way of giving of ourselves, and much in the way of putting God and others first. This was the example Jesus set for us, and our relationship with Him assures us of an eternity in heaven with Him forever.

MATTHEW 15:10-11

There was much that Jesus wanted to teach His disciples (and us). He and His disciples had been challenged by the Pharisees on their eating habits, and the very type of food they ate. Thus, Jesus took that opportunity to expound on the principles involved with food intake through the mouth, and what actually comes out of our mouths. See how relevant this passage is to us today:

> And he called the people to him and said to them, "Hear and understand, it is not what goes into the mouth that defiles a person, but what comes out of the mouth; this defiles a person." (Matthew 15:10–11)

So the real principle Jesus teaches here does not involve what we eat, or how we eat, but concerns defilement, that is, what is it that actually does defile us? What then makes up sin? What causes it? How are we to deal with sin? And how does this teaching apply (if it does) to the Old Testament food laws?

To take the last question first, Jesus taught here that the Old Testament food laws were to be abandoned. All food is clean in a nutritional sense, and His hearers then, and we now, are free to eat all foods. But the subject of what goes into our mouths is not nearly so important as what comes out of our mouths. Jesus refers here to our speech, our thoughts, where those thoughts originate, and the influence our words have on others.

The concept, of course, speaks of our hearts as the origin of our thoughts, and our words, and our actions. Jesus even later lists evil thoughts, murder, adultery, sexual immorality, theft, false witness, and slander as examples of sins originating in our hearts. **And those are what defile us. So if we can somehow deal with our heart problems, then defilement and sin will also be alleviated.**

As he was expressing his remorse over the Bathsheba episode, King David prayed this way: "Create in me a clean heart, O God, and renew a right spirit within me" (Psalm 51:10).

David realized that his heart condition led to his sin with Bathsheba. He knew (and so should we) that clean hearts and right spirits lead to obedience to God. And he also knew (and so should we) that clean hearts and right spirits originate with God, and that (1) only God can provide them and (2) God will absolutely hear prayers requesting these kinds of hearts and spirits that only He can provide. This because He very much wants us to have clean hearts and right spirits. We then glorify Him. Hallelujah!

Bottom line: let us pray sincerely, and often, for clean hearts and right spirits. Then let us keep our hearts and spirits filled with God's Word, His truth, His directions, and His will, all as outlined in scripture. God will use that kind of "nourishment" to develop clean hearts and right spirits within us.

ISAIAH 40:9

This verse is one we might read and quickly pass over if we are not careful. It begins a section on "The Greatness of God," a subject we can never study too much. Isaiah is writing to the people of Israel to remind them of their responsibilities in the area of worship. Israel was in trouble during the time Isaiah traveled the country preaching and teaching. Nearby countries, particularly Assyria, were threatening it with military action, and the people and their leaders were looking for help. God had Isaiah preach a simple message, "Behold your God." See how he did that with emphasis.

> Go on up to a high mountain, O Zion, herald of good news; lift up your voice with strength, O Jerusalem, herald of good news; lift it up, fear not; say to the cities of Judah, "Behold your God!" (Isaiah:40:9)

The concept is clear: the Israelites have a great God, and a great story to tell. It's worthy of everyone hearing (then and now). "Zion" refers to the Israelite people, every single one of them. Isaiah is urging all of them to go tell the world about their great God. The news is good, and the message is important. It needs to be lifted up, that is, proclaimed loud and clear to the masses.

And they are not to fear. Such a message is apt to be controversial, especially in a land now given over to idolatry. So, Isaiah urges the people not to be afraid. Their God is worthy of the highest praise and worship, and they are to be bold in that proclamation. And they are to go everywhere, that is, to all the cities of Judah. No one and no place is to be excluded, for whether the people realize it or not, they all need to hear this message.

And what is the message? It's "Behold your God." What does that really mean? First, it means their God exists. It means they and we are to notice our God, to recognize Him, to consider Him, to obey Him, to worship Him, and to do all this consistently and with a whole heart. It means to do so (right now) and not stop. The implication is their God is the only God, and has always been. And it implies they have been especially chosen as His people, and that they should recognize their unique position.

There is certainly the sense communicated that we, too, are to do all this with a glad heart, a joy-filled heart, and with the expectation that God will hear our worship and praise, and respond with the love, guidance, and protection that only He can provide.

So, talk about good news, this is the greatest news the world will ever hear. It was in Isaiah's day, and it is now too. And yes, the command to get out and about spreading this good news applies to us. There is no person, no situation, no assignment, and no condition that supersedes these instructions. We are to beware losing the perspective Isaiah is calling us to.

Isaiah is challenging us all to reorient our lives around the concept of beholding our God. Knowing God should be the most important concept we give time and effort to. And it's not as if that is impossible. God would never assign us an impossible task. And He never assigns us a task that He does not help us achieve. That's the kind of God Israel had, and that's our God too.

1 TIMOTHY 6:10–12

Paul has left Timothy in Ephesus as a leader of the church there. He writes him with instructions as to how to deal with the common problems that arise in any church, in the first century and today. Thus, this passage is relevant to church groups and individuals in any era. Notice how practical Paul is:

> For the love of money is a root of all kinds of evils. It is through that craving that some have wandered away from the faith and pierced themselves with many pangs. But as for you, O man of God, flee these things. Pursue righteousness, godliness, faith, love, steadfastness, gentleness. Fight the good fight of the faith. Take hold of the eternal life to which you were called and about which you made the good confession in the presence of many witnesses. (1 Timothy 6:10–12)

Notice Paul's instructions are for any of us in any particular situation. Our Christian witness will be felt by those we work for, those we work with, and those who work for us. And that's as it should be, for everyone needs a Savior, some perhaps a lot more than they realize. Timothy was a young man and likely was not given the credibility Paul had, but still Paul urged him to preach and teach and live the gospel. Once I shared the gospel with a young man who was changing the oil in my car. It turns out he was a pastor working there part time, already saved, and who knew a lot more about scripture than I did. He thanked me for sharing with him, and noted he should have been sharing with me.

Keeping a proper perspective concerning money is just one of the values a believer should be careful about. Our financial focus will be noticed by others and is likely to be a good source of Christian witness. When Paul tells us to flee such things, he means to keep such potential sins regularly on our minds so we can make proper decisions when the needs arise. As we flee negative influences, we are, on the other hand, to pursue right thinking to achieve righteousness, godliness, faith, love, steadfastness, and gentleness. To pursue something implies we have made the decision that thing or concept is worthwhile, and we give it continuous rigorous effort, sacrificing some other things to continue that pursuit. And if we pursue wisely, God will surely bless us.

Obviously those six characteristics are worthy of our greatest efforts. Paul likens such a pursuit as a fight wherein the adversary (Satan) opposes every effort we make. Doubt it not, Satan is alive and well and works continually to dilute, change, turn, and diminish every godly thought and action we originate. And praise the Lord, we have a divine resource in such a fight. It is the eternal life we received when we by faith came to know Jesus Christ as Lord. As we engage Satan daily using our God-supplied eternal life condition, then we, by definition, will be a daily example in the presence of many witnesses.

It's amazing how the decision for Christ we made at one point in time leads to such lasting and beneficial blessings. God's grace, that is, His unconditional love for us is what makes eternal life possible. That's the message Paul is urging Timothy to preach, teach, and live out. That's our task too.

Notice Paul refers to Timothy as a "man of God." What a title!!! Would that we all could merit that title by the way we live. And we can. The Holy Spirit has taken up residence in the heart of every believer, and is there always to provide the leadership and protection we need. Jesus promised us, "Behold, I am with you always, to the end of the age" (Matthew 28:20). And the Holy Spirit is the helper He uses.

PHILIPPIANS 3:7–11

Here Paul the apostle is teaching the principle of justification by faith alone. To be justified is to be acquitted, thus, to be found not guilty of sin. No one achieves that status by good deeds, or by compliance with all the law. Romans 3:23 tells us, "For all have sinned and fall short of the glory of God." We cannot achieve the perfection necessary to be considered guiltless. But Jesus did, He lived a perfectly sinless life, thus qualifying as the only adequate sacrifice for our sins. So, Paul is correct in placing all his dependence on Christ as his Savior and Lord. So should we. See Paul's teaching on this:

> But whatever gain I had, I counted as loss for the sake of Christ. Indeed, I count everything as loss because of the surpassing worth of knowing Christ Jesus my Lord. For His sake I have suffered the loss of all things and count them as rubbish, in order that I may gain Christ and be found in Him, not having a righteousness of my own that comes from the law, but that which comes through faith in Christ, the righteousness from God that depends on faith—that I may know Him and the power of His resurrection, and may share His sufferings, becoming like Him in His death, that by any means possible I may attain the resurrection from the dead. (Philippians 3:7–11)

A long passage but powerful in its message. No list of good deeds will provide us eternal life. Only a relationship with Christ, the perfect One, will do that. How does this work? **Because of His steadfast love for us, God, in His infinite power and wisdom, imputes Jesus' perfection to every person who by faith trusts in Him for salvation. Thus, all our sins are covered and forgiven, those committed before our conversion and those afterward.**

Still, some people see this as too simplistic. Consciously or subconsciously (if they consider their eternal life at all), they feel they must somehow earn their salvation. Paul tries to "short-stop" that concept, telling us we cannot generate a "righteousness of our own that comes from the law." That kind of thinking automatically indicates they are attempting to put themselves on God's level, making the eternal decisions only God can make. He is creator, not us, He controls all that happens, not us, and He knows the real "why" of all we think and do, and we cannot fool Him. But stubbornly, to their eventual sorrow, many people try.

Notice how Paul concludes any human goals and achievements we might make pale alongside a relationship with Christ. He calls them rubbish. Citizenship in heaven requires the righteousness of Christ, not some imitation we might offer. Notice, too, how much credence Paul gives to the resurrection of Christ. Because Jesus rose from the dead, so will all true believers.

Thus, Paul has given up all earthly ends as shortsighted and worthless compared to an eternity with His Lord. He has gained Christ and intends to be found in Him. His relationship with Christ then is permanent, eternal in its scope and that eternity begins with conversion. To be "found" in Christ implies someone, at some point, will be looking, searching, evaluating, and assessing, Paul's relationship with Christ. That same Savior will be judging us one day too. Will we be found in Christ?

MARK 3:32–35

We should be fully aware of our relationship to Jesus. That thought is a serious one and should be uppermost in our minds. We believers know the whole story of Jesus' coming to earth to save us from our sins. We know about His birth, His life, His miracles, and His death and His resurrection. And praise the Lord, we know about his return one day to gather believers for transport to heaven. God has had this whole plan in place since before time began. And in God's eyes we each are an important part of it. See Jesus' comments about His family that pertains to us.

> And a crowd was sitting around him, and they said to him, "Your mother and your brothers are outside, seeking you." And he answered them, "Who are my mother and my brothers?" And looking about at those who sat around him, he said, "Here are my mother and my brothers! For whoever does the will of God, he is my brother, and sister, and mother." (Mark 3:32–35)

Jesus had left His family when He began His earthly ministry, not to the point of denying their relationship, but indicating His higher calling to go and teach the gospel. The main point of this passage is the availability of a close kinship to Jesus that accrues to all believers at the point of their salvation. **Notice the criteria for membership in Jesus' family: "doing the will of God." That is still true.**

We might ask then, what is the will of God with respect to joining Jesus' family? God's will is that we love the Lord our God with all our hearts, souls, and minds, and that we love our neighbors as we love ourselves (Matthew 22:36–40). That plays out in our lives as we trust and obey Jesus. Being saved, that is, being adopted into Jesus' family, comes with our faith in Christ's sacrificial death on the cross as payment for our sin debt. All of us are born sinners in need of a Savior. Thus, once we acknowledge our sinful condition, repent of those sins, and believe in Christ as God's Son sent to earth to save us from our sins, we are given God's free gift of eternal life. Our eternal life begins at that moment, right here on earth wherever we are, and is all encompassing in scope and eternal in length.

Thus, membership in Jesus' family is available to all those who believe, made available through God's grace and our faith. Jesus' earthly family would be given eternal life that same way. So, in this passage when Jesus maintains "Here are my mother and my brothers," He is referring to all those around Him who believe, and all those who will ever believe (including us).

Romans 8:16–17 provides us an even deeper picture of our saved family relationship with Jesus: "The Spirit Himself bears witness with our spirit that we are children of God, and if children, then heirs—heirs of God and fellow heirs with Christ."

Could this be true, we become actual children of God and thus, "brothers" with Christ, with an inheritance like He has in heaven forever with our heavenly Father? Yes, hallelujah, it is true!

So, let us live lives worthy of our family membership, telling others of this amazing provision of eternal life God has made for all who believe.

1 PETER 2:9-10

Here Peter the apostle is writing to believers who make up the churches in what is now Turkey. He sees the church as a new Israel, made up of those who by faith have trusted Christ as Savior and Lord. These chosen ones then are especially designated by God to take the gospel of Jesus Christ to the nations even amidst the persecution they were experiencing. So, this letter is one of encouragement for believers in any era, for there are always challenges for Christians. Peter emphasizes the fact that believers are chosen, selected by God as His children destined to spend eternity with Him.

> But you are a chosen race, a royal priesthood, a holy nation, a people for his own possession, that you may proclaim the excellencies of him who called you out of darkness into his marvelous light. Once you were not a people, but now you are God's people; once you had not received mercy, but now you have received mercy. (1 Peter 2:9–10)

Thus, we see the group believers join when they accept Christ. And what a select, responsible, group it is. Notice what Peter calls them: a chosen race, a royal priesthood, a holy nation, and a people for Hs own possession. This only partially describes the relationship Christians have with God. Imagine those kinds of relationship **with almighty God. And inherent in those relationships is eternal life.** This is what God promises and provides His children. **And the most amazing thing about it is that these relationships and positions Peter describes COME AS A FREE GIFT FROM GOD. They cannot be earned. They accrue to believers when via God's grace and their faith (which God provides them)**

they trust Jesus' sacrificial death on the cross as payment for their sin debt.

We might wonder what comes next. What does it mean to now exist in God's marvelous light? It has to include at least understanding more about His love and eternal provision for us in heaven. It has to include now having a better feel for what Jesus actually did do for us on the cross. It has to include more knowledge concerning sin and how abhorrent it is to God. And it has to include more of a burden to share the truth of the gospel with those who have never heard it.

And what are we to do given our new relationship with God? Peter gives us that answer. We are to "proclaim the excellencies of Him who called us out of darkness"; that is, we are to live out actually and verbally God's excellencies. And what might those be? They are, of course, God's traits, His characteristics, His nature, and His will. God being perfect in love, power, mercy, and hope gives us a lot to talk about. We can share our whole lives and not ever come close to covering the subject of God's excellencies.

Peter reminds his readers that as believers at one point they were unbelievers, without mercy, bound for an eternity in hell. Then they met Christ, repented of their sins, and accepted Jesus' payment of the ransom for their sins, which was His sacrificial death on the cross. In short, they were given mercy, unbelievable, eternal, mercy. They had been separated from God, and now they were a people of God, His children, adopted into His family with all the inheritance privileges that being God's children provides.

HEBREWS 12:5-6

This chapter of Hebrews begins to speak specifically on the subject of believers dealing with their own sins. Believers in the first century and believers in our day are alike in their salvation, and alike in their imperfections. They then, and we now, were advised to guard against sin in our lives. This author (unknown) reminds all readers that God does discipline believers on an "as appropriate" basis. And He does this because He loves them. **It is most significant that the Hebrews author notes that scripture refers to them as sons. And that applies to us. As believers we are children of God, therefore, joint heirs with Jesus, eligible for an inheritance like His.** See this passage on the discipline of sons:

> My son, do not regard lightly the discipline of the Lord, nor be weary when reproved by him. For the Lord disciplines the one he loves, and chastises every son whom he receives. (Hebrews 12:5–6)

This passage is a quote from Proverbs 3 on the subject of trusting in God. To believe in God does not automatically provide us the trust that helps so much during our times of trials. The Hebrews author is encouraging his readers then, and us today, to take the step of trusting in God. God does discipline us as a loving earthly father disciplines his sons. Our earthly fathers do this out of love, knowing that long-term we will be better off for having been disciplined. And God does so, too, for the same reason. In this passage we are told to keep a proper perspective about God's discipline. We are to remember God knows our situation and has our best interests at heart, and that involves our trust.

Trust in the midst of trial is easier said than done. And God knows that. That's part of the reason we are advised in passages like this to persevere during trials. Thus, when trials come (and they do come to all believers) we are to look for the meaning involved. Many times our trials are the direct result of sin on our part, but sometimes they seem to come for no reason. But there is purpose behind God either directing or allowing us to face difficulties. We live lives in which nothing happens by accident. Our almighty heavenly Father is directing everything for everyone.

We cannot help but regard the disciplines life brings, and this passage reinforces the concept of taking them seriously, learning whatever lesson from them that God provides. The passage tells us to stand fast when reproved by God. Reproved is not a word we use often. It adds the flavor of gentleness to the correction someone gives us. Thus, it implies their goal is to correct us, but to help and benefit us as well. That fits God's discipline too. If we just listen, God will teach us something from out trials.

Sometimes though, God chastises us for sin, which involves a harsher type of punishment, no doubt because that's what we need. The way this is worded in the Hebrews passage implies all of us will evidently need chastising at some point.

In total then, this passage serves as both a warning (that discipline is coming) and as counsel (on how to deal with it). We are foolish indeed if we ignore such instructions. It is both noteworthy and encouraging though to hear that God loves all believers. Thus, in a very real way we can take joy in the fact that we suffer discipline. From this passage we learn that proves God loves us.

All believers then have the same hope and assurance. Knowing that God loves them and He has made provision both for their daily lives and for their eternal home in heaven with Him. That's worth sharing.

PSALM 142:5–7

There is not one single person who has ever lived that has not at some point had strife, trouble, fear, or doubt come into their lives. Sin inhabits our world, and it affects us all. So it should not be surprising that about three thousand years ago David wrote, praying to God, concerning such conditions in His life and titled it "You Are My Refuge." And it should not be surprising either for the God of love David prayed to, to see fit to have his prayer recorded for us to benefit from now. See what David prayed:

> I cry to you, O LORD; I say, "You are my refuge, my portion in the land of the living." Attend to my cry for I am brought very low! . . . that I may give thanks to your name! (Psalm 142:5–7)

When we reach the point of crying out, we truly are "very low." But David recognizes the Lord as his source of relief and calls Him "my refuge, my portion in the land of the living" (that is, in this life). Refuge means a person or place that provides shelter and protection from danger or distress, and that is exactly what David is seeking. Notice that David commits to giving thanks to God when he sees the result of his prayer.

So we see two clear takeaways from this Psalm: first, that when we are in need, the Lord is our source of help and relief. And secondly, our response to His help should be a thankful heart. Yet there is more implied in this Psalm. God is not a heavenly "Santa Claus" readily supplying presents of help and support at our beck and call. David had a long-standing, ongoing relationship with the Lord. He had long before recognized and surrendered to the Lord as his God in all circumstances. He was certainly (like we believers) not a perfect man, but his heart was inclined to God, and he sought to be the individual God would have him be.

As believers, we have the same privilege David had of going to God with all our needs. And we are blessed with even more knowledge than David; we know the specifics of Christ's life and sacrifice for our sins. Our privilege has been to receive Christ's free gift of eternal life by simply recognizing our sinful status, repenting of our sins, and trusting Christ's sacrificial death as payment for our sin debt. The apostle Paul said it this way: "For by grace you have been saved through faith. And this is not your own doing; it is the gift of God, not a result of works" (Ephesians 2:8).

So clearly, like David, God would have us seek His face, and pray to Him without ceasing. He has a plan for our lives involving how He would have us spread His truth to the nations. Let us be part of that.

PROVERBS 28:13-14

All of us are born as sinners in need of a Savior. Worse off though, are those people who deny their sinful condition and work to hide their sins and keep them from others as they continue their life of sin. God knows of all these people (and loves them) and has made provision for their forgiveness and restoration. There is hope for them amid God's plan of salvation that provides for their complete atonement. Thus, there is a way to achieve a relationship with God that leads to eternal life, and a certainty of an eternity with Him in heaven. See these verses addressing such willful attitudes:

> Whoever conceals his transgressions will not prosper, but he who confesses and forsakes them will obtain mercy. Blessed is the one who fears the Lord always, but whoever hardens his heart will fall into calamity. (Proverbs 28:13–14)

No person has ever been forgiven of their sins unless they first acknowledge their need of forgiveness. Only then do they indicate the repentant heart necessary for God to forgive them. Trying to conceal our sins from others is foolish and will only end in a worse condition. Especially is it foolish to deny our sin before God who knows us better than we know ourselves. On the other hand, sincere repentance before God will lead to complete forgiveness, for His mercy is both infinite and everlasting.

We are to fear the Lord. This is not fear as in "afraid," but fear as in "respect" and "reverence." Notice the verse says we are to fear God always. Thus, our ongoing attitude toward God is to be consistently respectful and reverent. He is surely worthy of such feelings given His position as creator, Lord, and master of the universe. But some people see fit to ignore the truth of God's love and position, consciously or subconsciously, hardening their heart against God's offer of eternal life. Believers sometimes have difficulty understanding how people could take such a position and sort of "shake their tiny fist in God's face," as they stubbornly go their own way. Obviously, their perspective concerning eternity is wrong, or more likely they have never seriously considered what their eternal destiny is and why. They have likely not considered either that no decision in this matter is a decision, and that decision is a "no" to God's offer of eternal life.

The answer is clearly spelled out in the verse above: confess and forsake the denial that has led to a heart hardened against the truth of God's love. Given the eternal significance of such decisions the timing of them must be now. How could anyone see fit to delay? To delay is indicative of unbelief and a lack of faith in the God of the Bible and His provision for eternal life for all who believe. The significance of such decisions cannot be overstated. God's provision for eternal life not only involves the most important decision anyone will ever make, but it also contains the best news they will ever hear.

God proved His love for mankind when He provided the only payment for our sin debt that would suffice, the sacrificial death of His Son, Jesus Christ, on the cross. John 3:16 says it all: "For God so loved the world, that He gave His only Son, that whoever believes in Him should not perish but have eternal life."

MATTHEW 11:11

In this verse Jesus is speaking to the crowds concerning John the Baptist, telling them of his credibility and importance to kingdom work. But He then adds a strange comment that is really good news to all His listeners that day and to us now. See how this comment benefits us:

> Truly, I say to you, among those born of women there has arisen no one greater than John the Baptist. Yet the one who is least in the kingdom of heaven is greater than he. (Matthew 11:11)

Notice how glowingly Jesus speaks of John the Baptist, and yet tells us those least in God's kingdom is greater than he. This is true because those in the kingdom of heaven have already experienced the relationship to God heaven provides due to their belief in Jesus' sacrifice for their sins (which has not happened yet). Thus, this far ahead faith they had in God's grace, as exampled by Abraham, has gained them entrance into God's presence. Like Abraham, their "far ahead" faith changed their "right now" lives. All this, of course, speaks volumes concerning the majesty and glory of God that all believers will one day enjoy for an eternity with the Lord.

Paul speaks to this same subject as it applied to Abraham:

> For the promise to Abraham and his offspring that he would be heir of the world did not come through the law but through the righteousness of faith.... That is why it depends on faith, in order that the promise may rest on grace and be guaranteed to all his offspring—not only to the adherent of the law but also to the one who shares the faith of Abraham. (Romans 4:13, 16)

When God spoke to Abraham, he "went as the Lord told him." God had various assignments for him to accomplish and none of them were in Ur where God originally spoke to him. He had to be obedient and move out in faith. He had experiences in Egypt, in the future promised land, in battles to rescue Lot, and with Sarah and Hagar. He was not always completely obedient to God, and he (and his family) suffered for it. Notice though, this promise (of an eternal destiny with the Lord) *is guaranteed* for Abraham, yes, but all of the rest of us believers too.

So clearly God has plans for all his children, John the Baptist, Abraham, and you and me. And it is the faith of all of us in God's everlasting grace that saves us in the first place and motivates us to live lives of obedience after our salvation experience.

God had plans for John the Baptist and Abraham, and He does for you and me. It behooves all believers to "live looking." That is, to begin every day seeking God's will for us that day. He may send us across the world or down the street, but He will send us. God always has as us getting involved with other people. Always God would have us love Him. Always He would have us love our neighbors. We are to live as Jesus did, witnessing to those whose paths crossed His. There is this kind of consistency to Jesus' life, and that same consistency of love should be representative of our lives too.

Since we believers have been told our status in the kingdom of heaven will be great, that tells us much about how we are to live now. **Thank God now for that guaranteed position then, and live out that thanksgiving every day.**

JAMES 2:18-19

In this passage James, the author, is telling both his readers in his day and us in our day about the connection between our faith in God and our actual lifestyles. The concept is, we cannot say one thing and live another way, and have any kind of consistent witness to those around us, for they will see the hypocrisy inherent in us. If we are to be the witness God would have us be, then our lives must reflect obedience to His laws. We can easily visualize the necessity of that requirement. God would have us love and respect Him enough to not only seek to be obedient to Him, but to share His truths with other people. However, God recognizes we have difficulty in obeying all of His commandments. Thus, when we believe in Christ and make Him Lord and Savior of our lives, then sincere obedience is honestly our will and our goal, and we feel remorse, embarrassment, and a need for forgiveness when we disobey Him. See how James words this requirement:

> But someone will say, "You have faith and I have works." Show me your faith apart from your works, and I will show you my faith by my works. You believe that God is one; you do well. Even the demons believe—and shudder! (James 2:18–19)

James was addressing Jewish Christians who believed in God, but felt no connection in that belief (faith) and their daily decision making. When you think about it, such thinking really does not "compute." If almighty God is anything, He is just, and He looks on our heart. Thus, He not only monitors what we say and do, He knows why we act that way.

The classic argument against such inconsistency (that's claimed belief without corresponding obedience) is that demons (Satan's agents in this world) absolutely are convinced Jesus Christ is Lord.

They know He is God come to earth to offer mankind atonement for their sins, but their allegiance is to Satan and obeying God's laws is far from any requirement they honor. These demons do readily acknowledge Jesus as God, but don't even claim obedience to him and do no good works, and thus are definitely not saved, though the necessity for them to deal with their sins (before Jesus Christ as judge) one day does frighten them. We are told they do believe, but shudder at the thought. So, James is correct, when anyone consistently lives in opposition to God's laws, then any claim they might make to salvation and eternal life is suspect. Their actions prove their claims are false.

We are to understand, though, the obedience to God's law requirement for salvation is not to be considered a burden, a chore we detest, and wish we did not have to comply with. If Jesus Christ truly is Lord of our lives, if we really do believe Jesus died in our place for our sins, and to atone for every sin we ever commit, then we won't see obedience as a chore, but a heartfelt effort we make every day. Obedience then does not save us. It simply reflects we are saved, having by faith trusted Christ's death on the cross as payment for our sin debt. And sincere repentance on our part for sins we do commit brings quick forgiveness by God.

There is a line in a popular hymn we sing concerning Jesus' substitution for us on the cross that goes, **"God looks on Him and pardons me." Hallelujah!**

1 JOHN 1:1-4

When we read scripture, we are apt to believe it because we have been taught to believe it. But there are more concrete reasons for our belief. These words are God's truth that He has made available for our benefit. God used over forty authors writing through two thousand years of history to bring His revelation of Himself to the world. The experiences of the biblical authors of scripture are real, they lived what they have recorded. They were there to see and hear Jesus' teachings and the miracles He performed. In our day, eyewitness testimony is what gives credibility to decisions made in our court system. Nothing has more weight than what a witness saw and heard personally. It is just that kind of validation that scripture carries and provides for us. See John clearly spelling out what he and the other apostles experienced.

> That which was from the beginning, which we have heard, which we have seen with our eyes, which we looked upon and have touched with our hands, concerning the word of life—the life was made manifest, and we have seen it, and testify to it and proclaim to you the eternal life, which was with the Father and was made manifest to us—that which we have seen and heard we proclaim also to you, so that you too may have fellowship with us; and indeed our fellowship is with the Father and with his Son Jesus Christ. And we are writing these things so that our joy may be complete. (1 John 1:1–4)

Notice the different references John makes to Jesus. He refers to Him as "that which was from the beginning," the life made manifest, the eternal life, which was with the Father, and lastly, as "his Son Jesus Christ." Notice, too, in just these four verses, thirteen uses of the personal pronouns *we, our,* and *us.* John could not have been more emphatic in his declaration of the apostles' witness to Jesus' identity, presence, and actions.

Initially, He establishes Jesus as eternally real, and thus, involved in the creation. He then outlines the various real-life experiences he and the other apostles had with Jesus. They took those experiences with Jesus as expressions of the "word of life," that is, the very essence of why Jesus came to earth as man. They saw Him, they touched Him, they heard Him, and they now proclaim it. And they had good reason for doing so. They definitely wanted others to experience the fellowship with the Father and Jesus that they had. And so now John writes to them to share with them the truth of Christ providing him complete joy. It's obvious that John did not consider a relationship with someone complete until he has shared the truth of Christ with them. Would that we felt that same way.

It is the divine perspective being with Jesus gave John and the others that brought home to them the significance of His influence. He only could be the Son of God, Messiah, and King of Kings. He only could save them from their sins. And he only can save us from our sins. What a message we have to share.

LUKE 13:22–24

This passage is not familiar to most believers and yet it should be, for it contains the powerful truth concerning what individuals must do to be saved. In this passage, we find Jesus and His disciples making their way to Jerusalem for the last time, and along the way He teaches them concerning His coming kingdom. See Jesus' words:

> He went on his way through towns and villages, teaching and journeying toward Jerusalem. And someone said to him, "Lord, will those who are saved be few?" And he said to them, "Strive to enter through the narrow door. For many, I tell you, will seek to enter and not be able." (Luke 13:22–24)

Jesus does not directly answer this question concerning the quantity of believers, but focuses on the more important question, "What shall we do to be saved?" Jesus says we should strive to enter though the narrow door. See verses 13:3 and 5. Twice Jesus uses the exact same words to tell us how to be saved. "Unless you repent, you will all likewise perish." We might ask, "What is involved with repentance?" First, it means we are to acknowledge we are sinners in need of a Savior. No one has ever been saved unless they first realize they are lost. Second, repentance involves how we feel about our sinful status. We are to be remorseful, recognizing our sins are against Holy God. This last becomes increasingly clear to us over time as we become more and more familiar with God's holy characteristics and nature.

Using the phrase "narrow door" depicts a difficult assignment ahead when we seek to enter the door of God's kingdom. And notice the last phrase of the passage, "for many . . . will seek to enter and not be able." This sort of screams at us that there will come a point beyond which we will lose the opportunity to trust Christ for salvation. Yet, see John 6:37: "All that the Father gives me will come to me, and whoever comes to me I will never cast out."

So, if we come to Jesus, He will not turn us away. The concept is so simple, many people miss it, because they read more into the requirements of salvation than simple repentance, belief (through faith) in Jesus' substitutionary death to pay our sin debt, and acceptance of Jesus' free gift of eternal life. Thus, the time of decision is now, the situation is urgent. Surely we all know someone who needs to hear this message before it's too late.

MARK 8:34-35

Following Christ involves establishing a whole new set of priorities in our lives. It involves a whole new perspective, it involves having the worldview that Jesus had, and a focus on others rather than a focus on self. Jesus puts this very plainly:

> And calling the crowd to him with his disciples, he said to them, "If anyone would come after me, let him deny himself and take up his cross and follow me. For whoever would save his life will lose it, but whoever loses his life for My sake and the gospel's will save it." (Mark 8:34–35)

Jesus wanted the disciples and the general public to hear this important principle. It's critical that we understand this truth is one we need to live out daily, right where we are. We must, therefore, know what "to come after Jesus" is all about. "To come after" means to follow and "be like," to do the same things, with the same motives, with the same results. So we are then to deny self, putting others and their well-being ahead of our own. Jesus calls that emphasis "taking up His cross," that is, suffering as He did. Here Jesus is not referring to doing miracles as He did, and not necessarily dying as He did, but living a life completely focused on glorifying God as He did, no matter the opposition.

So given our talents, time, and opportunities we are to make the fruit of our lives sharing the gospel with the world. If we seek to save our lives, that is, gain worldly treasure, esteem, and position, then we lose our lives in this pursuit. On the other hand, if we lose our lives for Jesus' sake and the gospel's, that is, if we give focus, emphasis and priority to sharing the good news of Christ with the world, acknowledging Him as Lord and Savior, then we save our lives in that pursuit.

So there is the choice for us to make: a self-centered lifestyle, or a Christ centered lifestyle. We may live a self-centered lifestyle and do good things, but consciously or subconsciously that type of lifestyle will be lived for our glory, not God's. Notice we do have the wherewithal to make such decisions, else Jesus would not be commanding us to do so. But, praise the Lord, believers have God's Holy Spirit within to guide us along the way.

Following Jesus is a full-time occupation. It's an all-day, everyday activity. It is, therefore, applicable in every area of our lives. And that is not bad news, it's very good news. God does not slice our lives into various segments, some requiring His involvement and others not so much. So let us confidently, gladly, and consistently, love the Lord with all our hearts, souls, and minds, and our neighbors as ourselves. That's how authentic followers of Christ live.

PHILIPPIANS 4:8–9

These two verses sum up Paul's instructions to the church at Philippi. Paul's purpose in this letter was to encourage them in their faith and to urge them to give evidence of that faith through their lifestyles. See how appropriate these instructions are for us in our day too:

> Finally, brothers, whatever is true, whatever is honorable, whatever is just, whatever is pure, whatever is lovely, whatever is commendable, if there is any excellence, if there is anything worthy of praise, think about these things. What you have learned and received and heard and seen in me—practice these things, and the God of peace will be with you. (Philippians 4:8–9)

Paul lists six characteristics of a society or of any individual that we should strive for. Then he urges his readers to evaluate these characteristics to see if any are excellent and/or worthy of praise. If so, then we are to consider them, that is, make them a part of our own personalities. Notice Paul makes the assumption we would recognize these traits when we see them, and that we know how to acquire them. We do recognize them, and thus, it remains for us to put forth the effort to attain them.

Then, as Paul often does, he recommends they recall what he has been teaching them and what he has been living before them, urging them to do likewise. "Practice these things" is easy to understand. Paul wants them to imitate Him. He even tells them the result of obedience to these instructions: "the God of peace will be with them." He leaves it to them and we readers to conclude what God's peace will mean to us. We can be sure God's peace is worthy of all our efforts.

Paul wants them and us to begin to think, to consider (now) how to implement these verses. They describe characteristics of people, particularly believers. But just how do we believers live true, honorable, just, pure, lovely, and commendable lives, all oriented to glorify the Father? We want to live excellent and praiseworthy lives, but it's easier said than done. It involves our small, medium, and large decisions, all of them, all the time. **There is only one way to do it; one decision, and one day at a time.** It requires constant vigilance, ongoing prayer, courage, patience, and the help of the Holy Spirit. That last is key. The Holy Spirit's job description is just that, to guide us to be the disciples and disciple makers Jesus told us to be. Jesus is not about to give us unattainable goals, nor is He going to give us any command that He does not help us obey. So seek His help.

It's important that we accept the fact these instructions are for us, and that God expects obedience from us. And if God expects obedience from us, then our obedience is doable. Some people are farther along this path than we are, and the reason for that is they are more willing than we are to give of themselves to the Lord, following the leadership of the Holy Spirit. And we recognize those people for what they are, God's children who are living as if heaven is their home and not this earth. Let us do that.

So, it comes down to our daily perspective concerning whatever we are dealing with that day. Plenty of both good and bad news will come our way. Look for and expect the good news. Be thankful for it and give praise to God. Trust Him when what seems like bad news arrives. Rest assured God understands our trials and will love us through them. Jesus has always been Lord and always will be. Trust Him.

MATTHEW 27:3–5

It's one thing to do something you later realize was wrong and feel remorseful about it. But it is quite another to repent of that wrong to the point you seek forgiveness from those involved and feel led to make restitution for the wrong. The difference in these two approaches to dealing with our sins is what describes how Judas felt about his betrayal of Jesus Christ. See the passage that describes this:

> Then when Judas, his betrayer, saw that Jesus was condemned, he changed his mind and brought back the thirty pieces of silver to the chief priests and the elders, saying, "I have sinned by betraying innocent blood." They said, "What is that to us? See to it yourself." And throwing down the pieces of silver into the temple, he departed, and he went and hanged himself. (Matthew 27:3–5)

Judas evidently was sorry for what he did, but no mention is made of any repentance on his part. He certainly realized he had made a mistake, and that Jesus was not guilty of anything. But to repent is more than acknowledging a mistake. It involves our heartfelt turning from our sin and our sinful orientation, to dedicating our lives to amending our ways and thought processes. To repent is to work at never again committing a given sin or any others, in order to comply with God's will for our lives. And repentance is step two in the process leading to forgiveness (step one being in the first place to acknowledge we have sinned). And step three is asking God for forgiveness.

Notice Judas' approach to relief from how he felt. He attempted to return his payment (thirty pieces of silver) back to the chief priests. He seemed to feel that if he were not rewarded for his sin that would relieve him of guilt. But sin does not work that way. What he had done had already negatively affected some other people (whether he was rewarded or not), making restitution difficult or even impossible. In Judas's case, millions of people were and are involved. We wonder how after hearing three years of teaching from Jesus his perspective could have been so far askew. But then we know the end of the story, how Jesus died and rose again and is coming back one day. And yet many, many people today (like Judas) deny this truth and give it no credence. And many others have yet to even hear of Jesus' gospel.

Notice the priests gave him "zero" relief, thus attempting to blame the whole incident on him. It's interesting that Judas threw the coins back at them. Picture the chief priests picking up the thirty pieces of silver, stooping down to gather the "thirty reasons" that Judas had betrayed the Son of God. At that time, thirty pieces of silver were equivalent to about four months' wages, not much for a man's life, especially Jesus' life. Remember, these chief priests and elders should have been the ones who were urging people to believe in Jesus, not seeking to kill Him.

So what can we learn from Judas' misunderstanding of Jesus' identity and purposes? First, that Jesus really is Lord. He really is God, that person of the Trinity who loved us to the point of coming to earth to take our place on the cross. His purpose in coming was to save us from our sins if we would only believe in Him, trusting His death as payment for all our sins. The beauty and simplicity of God's salvation provisions become a stumbling block for some people. They are convinced inwardly they must somehow earn their salvation. But if we *do* believe in Jesus, then by definition we are to go and make disciples, giving others the benefit of what we know to be true about Him.

ROMANS 1:18–20

These verses begin a passage describing God's wrath on unrighteousness. Since we are all sinners (see Romans 3:23) it certainly is applicable to us all. See what the Holy Spirit has had Paul put here for us to read:

> For the wrath of God is revealed from heaven against all ungodliness and unrighteousness of men, who by their unrighteousness suppress the truth. For what can be known about God is plain to them, because God has shown it to them. For his invisible attributes, namely, his eternal power and divine nature, have been clearly perceived, ever since the creation of the world, in the things that have been made. So they are without excuse. (Romans 1:18–20)

God's wrath refers to His personal anger against sin (any sin). It is His loving response to our sin. He abhors sin of any description and any nature. When we sin (before or after a salvation experience) we, by definition, suppress His truth. The truth we suppress has to do with His position as Lord and sovereign creator of all that has been created. By sinning we express our desire (in front of the world) that we (and not He) control our destiny, that we have the ability and wisdom to do so and can provide for ourselves what is best for us. That only reflects our poor perception of the significance of what we see around us, and how and why it came to be. Practically speaking, it is a very shortsighted view of life, and of God's position and authority.

Almighty God loves the world. And because He does, He has seen fit to create a world that reflects His existence and character in front of us day by day. And He has provided within us a capacity to see and understand this by showing us His power and divine nature in what He created. But when we are blind to His creation, and reject this example of His power and love, we incur His wrath and punishment.

Thus, we need not be surprised when our own plans fail to materialize, and we suffer for our misdirection. But praise the Lord, one of the characteristics of His divine nature is His steadfast love and mercy. He has made a way for us to turn from our sin and receive His free gift of eternal life through the gift of His Son. Through belief in Him we may "not perish but have eternal life" (John 3:16).

What more could God do than create us and all we see around us (reflecting His power and love), give us the knowledge and capacity to understand this (through His Holy Spirit), and provide a way for us to recover from sin and error on our part (via Christ's sacrificial death in payment of our sin debt)? What a great, great God we have. Tell someone you care about of God's love and provision for them.

Matthew 13:47–50

Jesus often taught using parables, stories, and illustrations of common events in people's lives that had important spiritual significance. This passage describes one parable whose hidden meaning involves the judgment that will come to all people one day when Jesus returns. Note how the application of the truth in this parable should be understood by all people in all societies in all eras. **That includes us.**

> Again, the kingdom of heaven is like a net that was thrown into the sea and gathered fish of every kind. When it was full, men drew it ashore and sat down and sorted the good into containers but threw away the bad. So it will be at the end of the age. The angels will come out and separate the evil from the righteous and throw them into the fiery furnace. In that place there will be weeping and gnashing of teeth. (Matthew 13:47–50)

It's easy to see that Jesus is teaching that all people will one day be sorted (that is, judged). And that everyone is destined for one of only two eternal destinations: evil people for the fiery furnace (which we designate as hell, separated from God) and the righteous for the kingdom of heaven (where God reigns). The joy in heaven is not described here, but the misery in hell is. There will be weeping and gnashing of teeth in hell for an eternity.

Now we don't like to consider such stark realities, but Jesus Christ, Savior, and creator of the universe, saw fit to bring this truth to our attention. And He did so because He loves us. And that's how we should look at this revelation, thanking Him for making it clear.

Evil, as used here, does not necessarily refer to really bad people as much as it designates that group that have no relationship with Christ. That may recognize Jesus' existence (even Satan does that), but they have not by faith trusted Him as Lord of their lives, believing their sins have been forgiven via Jesus' sacrificial death on the cross in their place. Such a commitment has been made by those indicated here as righteous. So it is our relationship with Christ that determines our eternal destiny, not how many good deeds we do, or how few bad deeds we do. It is therefore not bad people who will go to hell, it is lost people who will go to hell. Conversely, it is not good people who will go to heaven, it is saved people who will go to heaven. Of course, these saved people will do good deeds, but they do them now for God's glory, not their own glory. Those good deeds come as the result of their salvation, but are not the reason for it.

So, if we really believe the truth of this passage, then it will transform our lives, and it will transform them now. If these truths are worth believing, then they are worth believing now, and worth sharing with those we care about now. People we know and love will absolutely see the difference. Our feelings for them will change and be reflected in our attitudes, our perspectives, and our priorities. Jesus Christ will be first in our lives, others second, and we somewhere after that.

HEBREWS 2:14-18

The author of the book of Hebrews is unknown. But what we can be sure of is that God's Holy Spirit rested on that author as he penned these words to first century believers. His message is Christ-oriented, and His basic theme is that Jesus is both fully God and fully man. Thus, as fully man, Jesus was subjected to the same trials and temptations we are, and can therefore relate to our pain, confusion, and doubts. He is truly qualified then as Messiah, Son of God, sent to earth as a man to save us from our sins. This portion of the letter describes how Jesus meets those qualities as Founder of our Salvation:

> Since therefore the children share in flesh and blood, he himself likewise partook of the same things, that through death he might destroy the one who has the power of death, that is, the devil, and deliver all those who through fear of death were subject to lifelong slavery. For surely it is not angels that he helps, but he helps the offspring of Abraham. Therefore, he had to be made like his brothers in every respect, so that he might become a merciful and faithful high priest in the service of God, to make propitiation for the sins of the people. For because he himself has suffered when tempted, he is able to help those who are being tempted. (Hebrews 2:14–18)

To qualify as our high priest Jesus therefore had to come to earth as man and be subjected to the same issues and temptations that we are. Satan is Prince of this World, and for a time Jesus allowed Himself to be subject to his earthly reign without yielding to the sin of obedience to him. Given that the wages of our sin is death, though sinless Himself, Jesus gave Himself on the cross to die in our place in order to pay our sin debt, thus earning the position as Founder of Salvation. Jesus, our Savior, merciful and faithful, and without sin, became our high priest in the service of God; this to make propitiation for the sins of the people. The act of propitiation Jesus performed reflects His sacrifice on the cross for the express purpose of satisfying the wrath of God for our sins. As believers, our sin debt is paid, and our sins are atoned for completely by Jesus' sacrificial death. At judgment we will be pardoned simply (and only) because by God's grace through faith, we have received God's free gift of eternal life. Our good works are appropriate, but not necessary for salvation. We do good works because we are saved, not to earn our salvation.

Thus, Jesus understands our pain, our temptations, our difficulties, and our shortcomings. He experienced them all without sin. So, we believers are figuratively offspring of Abraham, that is, not Jews, but more importantly children of God, adopted into His family at the moment of our salvation. Thus, our salvation is accomplished, a completed act, eternal in scope, and heavenly in orientation. **Believers are already living their eternal life and our words and deeds are to reflect that.**

So we've a message to communicate. Jesus is Lord, sent to earth to save us from our sins. In fact, it's the most important message the world will ever hear, appropriate to all who will receive it, and by faith trust Jesus Christ as Savior and Lord.

PSALM 96:1–4

Almighty God is creator of the universe and all that is in it. This Psalm celebrates that fact and proclaims that everyone on earth should love and worship Him. And they should do so with all their hearts, without pretense or falsehood, but with sincerity and enthusiasm. And it tells them why they should do so. See the first four verses as they "jump start" this message:

> Oh sing to the LORD a new song;
>   sing to the LORD, all the earth!
> Sing to the LORD, bless his name;
>   tell of his salvation from day to day.
> Declare his glory among the nations,
>   his marvelous works among all the peoples!
> For great is the LORD, and greatly to be praised;
>   he is to be feared above all gods. (Psalm 96:1–4)

Notice the psalmist's readers then (and we now) are to sing to the Lord. Of all the commands we are given in scripture, to "sing to the Lord" is the one given us most often. That says something significant concerning how we are to worship the Lord. What an awesome gift our heavenly Father gave us when He gave us the ability to sing. When you think about it, there really is something additionally majestic about singing our prayers, and not simply just saying them. Notice, too, we are to bless His name, that is, we are to ascribe to Him (alone) all honor, glory, and majesty. We are also to tell the world of His salvation "all day, every day." And why not? His provision for us to spend eternity with Him is proof positive of His power and His steadfast love for us. So that gospel is to be the gist of our message to the world. And lastly, we are told to "declare His glory among the nations." Here we see God's

Great Commission (Matthew 28:19–20) given to us in different words. As for His marvelous work, what could be more marvelous than His provision for Christ's sacrifice to pay our sin debt? We are told to take this message to all the earth, among the nations, and to all the peoples. Everyone is worthy of hearing of God's love, and we believers have been selected to take the message to them.

And why are we to do this? God has the psalmist make that very clear: "For great is the Lord and greatly to be praised; He is to be feared above all gods." Simply put, there is none beside Him, He is God, and we are not. He and He alone is worthy of all our praise, honor, glory, and worship. He and He alone deserves all our love, respect, reverence, and obedience. That means all our time, talents, energy, and hearts are to be directed to Him and His kingdom work, all for His glory.

So our assignment is obvious. Our task is well defined. And the time to begin is now. In this passage and many others God has seen fit to outline His plan for us, and why it is to be a priority in our lives. Would that we take it to heart and urge others to do so as well.

JAMES 1:22-25

Our heavenly Father saw fit to create us, and as he did, to make us in His image. Thus, we are the only created beings with the potential of becoming like God. Still, we are prone to sin, and thus, to qualify us for Christlikeness and an eternal destiny with Him, there must be some provision made for our sins. God provided that completely via the gift of His Son Jesus Christ. Jesus' death on the cross paid the sin debt of all those who believe in Him. To further guide us through life, He saw to the writing of scripture wherein we find God's revelation of Himself. This Word of God then constitutes "the way, the truth, and the life" (John 14:6), describing that person (Jesus Christ), and the route to eternal life. See the relationship between God's Word and our lifestyles reflected in this passage in James:

> But be doers of the Word, not hearers only, deceiving yourselves. For if anyone is a hearer of the Word and not a doer, he is like a man who looks intently at his natural face in a mirror. For he looks at himself and goes away and at once forgets what he was like. But the one who looks into the perfect law, the law of liberty, and perseveres, being no hearer who forgets but a doer who acts, he will be blessed in his doing. (James 1:22–25)

There is an obvious sense in this passage that we are to live out the truths God provided us in scripture. The mirror illustration presents a classic analogy for us. When we look in a mirror, we see the truth of what we look like. When we look into God's perfect law, His Word, we see the truth of who we are, a sinner in need of a Savior. How foolish we are then, if, after looking at God's Law and seeing what we are like, to walk away with no understanding or will to make changes. Thus, we are hearers of the word (we have looked into the mirror), but not doers of the word (we forgot what we saw in the mirror) and make no attempt to obey God's Word.

The Old Testament Law defined sin with its list of "thou shall nots," but provided no power we could use to comply with the Law. Therefore, that law did not liberate believers but made slaves of them. However, praise the Lord, when the Law is coupled with the gospel, the good news of Jesus and his sacrifice at Calvary, we are freed and liberated from slavery to sin. Jesus died in our place paying our sin debt for us. We are not to just hear and know and understand God's Word, we are to persevere in obedience to it by faith. This is not to say our deeds save us, but our deeds simply reflect that we are saved, and that Jesus is in fact our Lord and Savior. We are not then hearers who forget, but doers who act on what we have heard. And those actions constitute a lifelong journey walking with the Lord.

Notice God monitors our actions. He knows what we do and why. And those who persevere in their faith, God blesses. He defines and provides those blessings consistent with His mercy and His love for us. As believers, there are certain things we do (or don't do) because we have a relationship with Christ. Our saved lifestyles are not sin free, but we are forgiven. We will not habitually or premeditatedly sin, but when we do sin, we feel the remorse that sin brings to believers, and we will seek the Father's forgiveness, which He has promised to provide. Basically, it is as if Jesus has paid our sin ransom, once and for all on the cross. Thus, His sacrifice dealt with all our sins forever. Hallelujah!!

PSALM 107:1–2

The idea of this Psalm is we are to recognize God's presence in our lives and we are to let those feelings of freedom and peace His presence brings be known to those around us by our words and the way we live. Look how the psalmist words this concept:

> Oh give thanks to the LORD, for he is good,
>   for his steadfast love endures forever!
> Let the redeemed of the LORD say so,
>   whom he has redeemed from trouble. (Psalm 107:1–2)

God is good, very good. James 1:17 tells us, "Every good gift and every perfect gift is from above, coming down from the Father of lights with whom there is no variation or shadow of change." God is good, He has been good, and will always be good, without changing ever. So we owe Him gratitude that His ongoing love for us will last forever.

See that next phrase, "Let the redeemed of the LORD say so." Those whom God has saved are to say so, that is, our lives are to reflect the salvation He has provided, and our trust in Him should show. We are to voice our praise and our thanksgiving regularly, such that we are known as a people whom God has redeemed from troubles. So when troubling times do come, we have a basis for hope, and a foundation of faith to fall back on knowing this world is really not our home, heaven is.

We need to remember, too, this Psalm is written to the children of Israel, God's chosen people. And they were well-known for their unfaithfulness. They often transgressed against the Lord and when things got really bad, they would repent and cry out to God for relief, and He would always forgive them and bless them again. So the lesson for us here is God knows what is going on in our lives and if and when we sin, we are to repent and seek His face for forgiveness; He will also always forgive us as He did Israel. So believers are never without hope.

Thus, we have every reason to be excited about our relationship with the Lord and our eternal destiny. The psalmist was excited, and he wanted to communicate this excitement to his readers. Imagine a whole nation of people in love with God, expressing that love every day, and seeing those around them doing the same thing. That's what heaven will be like.

ROMANS 11:33–36

As Paul closes this chapter on the salvation of God, the ultimate significance of it causes him to break into praise:

> Oh, the depth of the riches and wisdom and knowledge of God! How unsearchable are his judgments and how inscrutable his ways!
>
> "For who has known the mind of the Lord,
>   or who has been his counselor?"
> "Or who has given a gift to him
>   that he might be repaid?"
>
> For from him and through him and to him are all things. To him be glory forever. Amen. (Romans 11:33–36)

Paul reminds us that God's judgments and ways are far beyond the understanding of man. We would readily agree, but do we often really think about the significance of these words? He is perfect in power (He proved that by creating all that is), perfect in love (He proved that by giving His Son to die in our place for our sins), and perfect in purity (Jesus proved that in His life and in His Word).

Quotes in this passage from Job (35, 36, 41) tell us again that unless God reveals Himself, no man knows His mind. And who can claim to be a counselor to God, or who has anything God does not have, and can thus give Him a gift? "Every good gift and every perfect gift is from above" (James 1:17). Everything we humans have is a gift from Him, and is to be used in ways that glorify Him.

We cannot question Paul's comments for we feel the same way. So what is our response to our great God to be? How are we to adequately and properly relate to God who is so far above us in every respect? If we think very much on this subject the word *obedience* will come to mind. God knows who He is, and what He has done for us and why. He also knows everything there is to know about us, our strengths, our weaknesses, our motivations, and our tendencies. And given all that He still loves us, and thus, He tells us what He requires of us in His Word.

1. We are to love Him with all our hearts, souls, and minds, and others as ourselves. (Matthew 22:37–39)
2. We are to pray, and He gave us a model prayer. (Luke 11:2–4)
3. We are to be obedient, and He gave us a Great Commission. (Matthew 28:19–20)
4. And most of all we are to believe, to trust Him in all He has promised. (John 3:16)

All these involve moment-by-moment, day-by-day commitments. Through the ups and downs of life we are to persevere. And praise the Lord, He promises to help us as we do.

REVELATION 4

John the apostle had been exiled to the island of Patmos for preaching the gospel of Jesus Christ. While there, God gave him a vision of heaven. In that vision he was called up to heaven and saw things there no man had ever seen before. And John described what he saw for us to get a feel for what heaven will be like. See this description:

The Throne in Heaven:

After this I looked, and behold, a door standing open in heaven! And the first voice, which I had heard speaking to me like a trumpet said, "Come up here and I will show you what must take place after this." At once I was in the Spirit, and behold, a throne stood in heaven, with one seated on the throne. And he who sat there had the appearance of jasper and carnelian, and around the throne was a rainbow that had the appearance of an emerald. Around the throne were twenty-four thrones, and seated on the thrones were twenty-four elders in white garments, with golden crowns on their heads. From the throne came flashes of lightning, and rumblings and peals of thunder, and before the throne were burning seven torches of fire, which are the seven spirits of God, and before the throne there was as it were a sea of glass like crystal.

And around the throne, on each side of the throne, are four living creatures, full of eyes in front and behind: the first living creature like a lion, the second living creature like an ox, the third living creature with the face of a man, and the fourth living creature like an eagle in flight. And the four living creatures, each of them with six wings, are full of eyes all around and within, and day and night they never cease to say,

"Holy, holy, holy is the Lord God Almighty,
   who was and is and is to come!"

And whenever the living creatures give glory and honor and thanks to him who is seated on the throne, who lives forever and ever, the twenty-four elders fall down before him who is seated on the throne and worship him who lives forever and ever. They cast their crowns before the throne saying,

"Worthy are you, our Lord and God,
   to receive glory and honor and power,
for you created all things,
   and by your will they existed and were created." (Revelation 4)

A long passage, but what a picture! We can visualize some of it and other parts of it are beyond what we can imagine. But we certainly do get the idea of splendor and majesty and power and authority and God reigning on a throne, and angelic-like beings in secondary positions of authority all worshipping God.

So, God does rule and will reign forever and ever. And He (only) is worthy of all glory and honor and praise. And all beings around Him will and do worship Him and pay homage to Him. Later in Revelation John describes Jesus and an infinite number of angels and the time of judgment there and much more.

So, via this long vision John is given insight into what God has in store for believers in heaven. To be in heaven at all is beyond our ability to grasp, trying to take in all God has provided there for believers. But to also see Jesus and experience His presence forever will be awesome beyond words. But then God is an awesome God and praise His name; He loves us with an infinite love. We believers have much to enjoy here on earth, much to look forward to in heaven, and much to share with those who don't know Jesus Christ. What a great, great God we have.

1 JOHN 2:15-17

This section of scripture is titled "Do Not Love the World." The concept is we are not to love the world system that is opposed to God. So, we are to go about life with God's purposes in mind. It's one thing to say we believe in God. But that is not nearly enough to please God. Satan believes in God and likely knows more about Him than most believers. We must also believe what God says, and we most also make efforts to be obedient to what He says. Without question then we are to seriously consider our relationship to God as being the most important relationship we have. And we cannot and will not accomplish that without putting some "mental sweat" into the equation. And why not? He created us, and thinking about Him should be the most important subject we have on our mind. His love, His mercy, His will, and His purposes are to be uppermost in our minds and hearts. See this passage where the apostle John contrasts love for the world with love for God.

> Do not love the world or the things in the world. If anyone loves the world, the love of the Father is not in him. For all that is in the world—the desires of the flesh and the desires of the eyes and pride of life—is not from the Father but is from the world. And the world is passing away along with its desires, but whoever does the will of God abides forever. (1 John 2:15–17)

We inherently understand what "love of the world" means. It has to do with our priorities and focus, it's about what is important to us and what is not. If our thoughts and purposes are on worldly things, then, by definition, they are not on God, and love for Him "is not in us." Worldly things are in and of the world. Things of the flesh are physical things, material things, and things measurable by human standards and not from God in the sense that He would have us focus on them to the exclusion of obedience to Him. Notice the mention of pride of possessions. We all are touched by this temptation. Somehow, we have come to the point where we often measure ourselves and others by the size of our bank account. God would have us drop that standard of measurement. Wealth is often the poorest measure of a person's character there is.

Notice, too, John's assessment of the world. He says it's temporary, that it is passing away, that its appearance of permanence is wrong. At some point scripture tells us the world and its desires will be gone, changed so as to be unrecognizable. Even our desires and what brings us joy and peace will be different. We have trouble grasping that idea. What else could the phrase "the world is passing away" mean but that one day it will be gone? God has a better idea. A new earth is coming.

See Revelation 21:1: "Then I saw a new heaven and a new earth, for the first heaven and the first earth had passed away."

Using the same phrase "passed away," we see Revelation saying the same thing as 1 John says about the future of the world. The old world is to be replaced by a new heaven and a new earth. We cannot imagine what that will involve. But praise the Lord we don't have to know. We can simply trust God to keep His promises in the most wonderful way possible.

And see the conclusion to John's thoughts concerning the future for believers: "Whoever does the will of God abides forever." Talk about an awesome future, believers have the greatest inheritance possible, an eternity with the Lord in heaven.

1 TIMOTHY 2:1–4

Paul has left Timothy in the church at Ephesus to deal with the various issues present there (like false teachers and disobedient lifestyles) and is writing with guidance in how to do that. Further, his goal is to encourage Timothy in his own faith. The main theme of this letter is that God's holiness lived out in the lives of believers will shape their lives into the image of Christlikeness. It could be said (then and now) true belief in the gospel produces holiness in the lives of believers. Our beliefs actually dictate our behavior. Thus, to proclaim belief in Christ, but not exhibit a Christlike lifestyle, reflects a questionable spiritual state. See, then, how Paul's instructions with regard to prayer should become part of a believer's example before the world.

> First of all, then, I urge that supplications, prayers, intercessions, and thanksgivings be made for all people, for kings and all who are in high positions, that we may lead a peaceful and quiet life, godly and dignified in every way. This is good, and it is pleasing in the sight of God our Savior, who desires all people to be saved and to come to the knowledge of the truth. (1 Timothy 2:1–4)

Notice, first of all, Paul addresses the general subject of communicating with almighty God. And under that general heading of communications with the Lord God, Paul lists various types of prayers: (1) supplications (defined as requests of God both specific and general), (2) prayers (a broad term reflecting any and all our efforts to speak to and with God), (3) intercessions (requests on behalf of someone else), and (4) thanksgivings (wherein we express gratitude to God for past, present, and future blessings).

Led by the Holy Spirit, in this passage Paul is urging that all these types of prayer be made for and by people of both high and low estate. There seems to be no doubt in Paul's mind that such praying by the whole of society would lead to all living peaceful and quiet lives, godly, and dignified in every way. Paul advocates that this is good and pleases God our Savior. For given His love for the world, God desires all people to be saved and to come to the knowledge of the truth. This is not to say that eventually everyone will somehow be saved, for throughout scripture that is clearly taught not to be true (see 1 Timothy 4:1; 5:24; and 6:10 as examples). Scripture teaches that mankind (as individuals) must respond (by faith) to the gospel concerning Jesus Christ. See John 3:16. "For God so loved the world, that he gave his only Son, that whoever believes in him should not perish but have eternal life."

But this letter to Timothy does provide assurance of salvation for all those who do trust and obey, that is, believe (by God's grace through faith) in Christ's sacrificial death on the cross as payment of their sin debt, and who sincerely seek to live out that faith.

The key thought, therefore, in this passage is that God will honor the participation of all faithful believers in the kind of prayer-filled lifestyles mentioned: peaceful, quiet, godly, and dignified. Such consistent use then of the tools God has provided (supplications, prayers, intercessions, and thanksgivings) pleases God, and facilitates His blessing believers toward the end that all who believe will receive the free gift of eternal life. Hallelujah! What a great God we have!

1 JOHN 5:1–5

God knows the difficulties we face in overcoming the world. He understands exactly what we are facing and has made provision for anything that we might encounter. He does this because He loves us, and He does this because He is all-powerful. His love is behind all that He does for us, and thus, He merits our responding love. If we are wise, we will acknowledge His love and respond in kind by loving God and our neighbors. Notice the precise wording in this passage how our love of God verifies our position as children of God. So, it's not what we claim, but what we live out that proves our love of God.

> Everyone who believes that Jesus is the Christ has been born of God, and everyone who loves the Father loves whoever has been born of him. By this we know that we love the children of God, when we love God and obey his commandments. For this is the love of God, that we keep his commandments. And his commandments are not burdensome. For everyone who has been born of God overcomes the world. And this is the victory that has overcome the world—our faith. Who is it that overcomes the world except the one who believes that Jesus is the Son of God? (1 John 5:1–5)

To be born of God is to be God's child, and a member of His family. And that position is provided us as a free gift through our belief that Jesus is the Christ, Son of God, come to earth to save us from our sins. And those who believe this come to love the Father for His provision of His Son to save us. Those who believe have much in common with other believers, particularly the love they have for each other instilled in them by God's indwelling Holy Spirit. In this passage, John is reminding his readers then and we now, of their special position as adopted children of God.

Such a relationship should serve to build up our faith and help us overcome the world. What could the phrase "overcome the world" mean? It references the problems, pain, fears, doubts, and frustrations we have all experienced from just living in this world.

This kind of overcoming relief comes from a love for the Father and other believers leading to our compliance with God's commandments; not reluctant obedience, but an eager obedience, eager to please the Father. Notice John points out that these commandments are not burdensome. The very fact that the Holy Spirit saw fit to have John include that statement indicates the tendency of believers to sometimes fall short of full obedience to God's commands. And John goes further to remind us that not just a few select believers are given this position in God's family, but every one of those born of God (saved believers) are thus able to overcome the world's influences. What could be better news for all believers than to know that almighty God is aware of their problems and has made a way of relief.

And that overcoming power comes to us as a result of our faith, a faith provided us by God Himself. Our Father, then, has chosen faith as the route to victory over our worldly troubles. **Our loving Father has not only provided us His Son's sacrificial death to pay our sin debt and give us eternal life, but He has also provided us the faith to be sure of it.**

What a great God we have that loves us so much He has made every provision for our eternal life. That kind of God wants us to share that good news with the world around us, for as 2 Peter 3:9 tells us, His will is that none be lost. "The Lord is . . . not wishing that any should perish, but that all should reach repentance." So, our instructions are clear.

PSALM 31:1–2

Most of us need to learn to thank God for making known His demands. How else are we to know what He would have us be and do? And further, we need to learn to thank Him for making known what is available to us in His love. This latter fact is the subject of this Psalm. We are not told which episode in David's life is the cause of this lament, but it would apply to many incidents in his and our lives. See the wisdom of it as applied to us:

> In you, O LORD, do I take refuge;
>   let me never be put to shame;
>   in your righteousness deliver me!
> Incline your ear to me;
>   rescue me speedily!
> Be a rock of refuge for me,
>   a strong fortress to save me! (Psalm 31:1–2)

Notice there is no defined need described here. That the psalmist's need is omitted is no accident by God. We can pray this prayer on many occasions to meet any need, and God will hear it. Neither does this psalmist claim to deserve God's attention and help, yet that is exactly what David is praying for. As a child of God such privilege is always available to us, and we can and should praise the Lord for that. We are thus allowed the presumption of going before our heavenly Father with all our needs and of expecting His notice.

It would be hard to describe this Psalm without using the word *faith*; it's on display throughout this passage. David is quite sure his prayer will be heard. We, too, can be assured God will hear us. He prays for God to "incline His ear to him," that is, as if he wants God to bend down, to get close to him, to listen attentively, and respond quickly, and that is what he wants, for his need is great and urgently required (like ours). The two phrases "rock of refuge" and "strong fortress" are synonyms for God's power and involvement in our lives, and we can think of God's help that way too. There is permanent (not temporary) safety with the Lord and David is counting on that. His beginning words, "In you, O LORD, do I take refuge," prove he will go nowhere else for help with his prayers, and we need not either.

So what we've known for a long time is still true, Jesus Christ is Lord, fully worthy of all our praise, honor, and glory, always ready to be of help. Matthew 28:20 says it well where Jesus tells us, "Behold, I am with you always, to the end of the age." We can take joy in that!

ISAIAH 25:8–9

The Holy Spirit came upon Isaiah the prophet about 700 BC with a vision describing what lay ahead for Israel, God's chosen people. They had fallen into idolatry and were threatened by strong neighboring countries that did not fear God. So, Isaiah's prophecies represented a warning from God of the defeats and death that were coming. But he also brought promises from God of the coming Messiah and spoke of a time when death would be defeated, and their tears would end. So, there was hope, and in this passage, Isaiah urged his readers to rejoice. See his encouraging words:

> He will swallow up death forever;
> and the Lord GOD will wipe away tears from all faces,
> and the reproach of his people he will take away from all the
> earth,
> for the LORD has spoken.
> It will be said on that day,
> "Behold, this is our God; we have waited for him, that he
> might save us.
> This is the LORD; we have waited for him;
> let us be glad and rejoice in his salvation." (Isaiah 25:8–9)

Life expectancy in those days was much shorter than today, and death was an ever-present concern. People were old at fifty and along with much more vulnerability to sicknesses and disease, the ongoing threat of defeat and captivity by foreign nations increased the tendency for ignorant people to take refuge in idol worship for protection (from every kind of threat) they could not provide for themselves. Thus, the worship of idols naturally came about for help with everything from harvests to wars.

So, Isaiah's words claiming involvement by an almighty God who could end death and pain were what the people wanted to hear. But like many people today they grew to take God's love and provisions for granted (especially when they thought of themselves as God's children, particularly chosen for recognition and help). So now Isaiah is renewing God's promises in an effort to resurrect sincerity of worship from Israel.

When Israel discredited God by idol worship, God turned His back on them and they received the just rewards for their trespasses, which was military defeats, and physical hardships. Thus, for a country to claim their God was the all-powerful God, and for the world around them to see them in defeat and despair, did not compute. Other people obviously thought their God was either not all-powerful, or that they had somehow earned the wrath of their God and He was punishing them. But Isaiah promised days when such reproach would end along with death and pain.

Certainly, when they come, such days would be recognizable by all, and with that recognition would come proper gratitude to God for His provisions. People would naturally be thankful that God had kept His promises. And here Isaiah is calling the people to prepare to be glad and rejoice. Gladness is what we feel in good times, and rejoicing is what we do when those glad times come.

And finally comes the punch line of this passage. Notice the phrase Isaiah uses to describe what Israel will receive: "His salvation," new life, eternal life even. That's what is at issue here in Isaiah's day. And it's the main issue in our day too. God has made provision for eternal life for all those who believe, and it is His salvation, coming no other way than through faith and trust in Christ's sacrificial death to pay our sin debt. As Isaiah predicted way back then, we, too, will claim, **"Behold, this is our God, we have waited for him that he might save us."**

MATTHEW 21:42-43

The nation of Israel is God's chosen people with much history of association with God. They always have been chosen. In His infinite wisdom and His divine decision-making process, God selected them to be the means by which the good news of the gospel would be taken to the nations. That gospel is the truth of God's love for the world illustrated by Jesus' substitutionary death on the cross to pay the sin debt of all believers. But Israel saw fit to reject Jesus (even to the point of crucifying Him) when He came to earth as the promised Messiah and walked among them, doing many miracles and teaching them concerning His identity as the Son of Man. The analogy in this scripture passage presents Jesus speaking to some Jewish leaders as He describes Himself as the cornerstone of a great building (His coming kingdom) and describes how the kingdom of God would be taken away from them and given to "a people producing its fruits" (the church). See how God describes this process and the inherent responsibility given to we believers as members of God's church:

> Jesus said to them, "Have you never read in the Scriptures:
> "The stone that the builders rejected
>   has become the cornerstone;
> this was the Lord's doing,
>   and it is marvelous in our eyes'?
>
> Therefore, I tell you, the kingdom of God will be taken away from you and given to a people producing its fruits. (Matthew 21:42–43)

Thus is described how believers have come to be given the task of making disciples of Jesus among all the world's nations through the only institution Jesus established and left on earth when He returned (temporarily) to heaven. And that institution is His church, made up of believing Gentiles and Jews. So it is no wonder the church still plays such an important role in kingdom work in the world. And thus, it is also no wonder we, as believers in Jesus Christ as our Savior and Lord, are tasked with the job of sharing what we know of Christ with the whole world. That involves us going "next door" and across the ocean with the message of Christ, to people we know, and people we don't know. So, yes, we believers are to "go to church." There we are trained, equipped, and encouraged to fulfill our God-given task of disciple making, and at the same time we worship, giving praise, honor, and glory to our heavenly Father for His outpouring of blessings on us.

Church membership is then not a chore to be dreaded and a waste of time. Contrary to what many people use as an excuse for not going to church, you and they cannot worship the Lord as well seating alongside a lake with a fishing rod in your hand as you can gathered with like-hearted believers singing God's praises, and hearing His Word taught by a godly pastor. We need the influence and help of other godly believers, and they need our influence and help. God knew what He was doing when He established the church, and we are (very) unwise when we ignore His commands to participate.

EXODUS 16:9-12

As the children of Israel, led by Moses, wandered in the wilderness, they naturally needed food and water. Since there were so many of them (about two million) they moved slowly, and the quantity of food and water needed was huge. And when their needs were not quickly met, they grumbled. Not too many days before, they had seen the power of God reflected in their path (on dry ground) through the Red Sea when God rolled back the waters, and when He returned the waters to their original place on top of the pursuing Egyptian army, saving them all. Yet even in the face of such miracles, they now grumble as if God did not know of their circumstances, as if He had no power, and as if He did not care for them. This story sounds a lot like us; we receive God's blessings for years, and yet when troubles come, we complain, acting as if God has never heard of us, and has no idea of our needs. Read what then happened to the Israelites:

> Then Moses said to Aaron, "Say to the whole congregation of the people of Israel, 'Come near before the LORD, for he has heard your grumbling.'" And as soon as Aaron spoke to the whole congregation of the people of Israel, they looked toward the wilderness and behold, the glory of the LORD appeared in the cloud. And the LORD said to Moses, "I have heard the grumbling of the people of Israel. Say to them, 'At twilight you shall eat meat, and in the morning you shall be filled with bread. Then you shall know that I am the LORD your God.'" (Exodus 16:9–12)

And it happened just as the Lord described. We cannot help but wonder what the glory of the Lord looked like in a cloud. It must have been awesome. And we don't know whether the Israelites heard God's words to Moses, but we do know they got the message,

He is their God. God had heard their grumbling, and was sending food that very evening and the next morning. And He provided daily food for them for the next thirty-eight years.

So God did know about their problems, He did have the power to deal with them, and He did care enough about them to provide them daily food for the next thirty-eight years. And He still does. So when we grumble this same God hears us, and better, when we pray in faith, this same God hears us, and provides for our needs today. All this happened with the Israelites about thirty-five hundred years ago in 1500 BC. And, praise the Lord, about two thousand years ago, God sent His son into the world to save us from our sins. So now God has completed His provision for our eternal life. We need only believe, acknowledge that is, that we are sinners in need of a Savior, and believe that Jesus Christ is that Savior, who died on the cross in our place to pay our sin debt. There are not many ways to eternal life, but hallelujah, there is one way, and that's by God's grace and our faith in Jesus Christ (see Ephesians 2:8).

1 THESSALONIANS 5:8-11

This letter to the church in Thessalonica is equally relevant to us believers today. Its purpose is to encourage believers to continue (even in the face of trials) to walk in faith, confident of their relationship to the Lord, and of their eternal destiny with Him in heaven forever. In it Paul refers to believers as "children of the light," that is, children of the day, not asleep, but awake and actively participating in life within God's will and wearing God's armor; that is, faith, hope, and love. See this explained:

> But since we belong to the day, let us be sober, having put on the breastplate of faith and love, and for a helmet the hope of salvation. For God has not destined us for wrath, but to obtain salvation through our Lord Jesus Christ, who died for us so that whether we are awake or asleep we might live with him. Therefore, encourage one another and build one another up, just as you are doing. (1 Thessalonians 5:8–11)

Paul is confident of the salvation of his readers, and wants to encourage them in their faith. And he begins to tell them how to keep up their courage. His instructions are timeless and just as relevant for us as for those first-century Christians living in Thessalonica. We are to put on faith, love, and hope. To "put on" means to actively and consistently take on those characteristics, living them out daily. This is how we are to relate to others. This is how we are to think of others. And this is how we are to exhibit Christlikeness before others.

Paul reminds the Thessalonians they are already saved, and thus assured of escaping the wrath of God that is reserved for unbelievers. And Jesus sealed that covenant through His sacrificial death on the cross. What better confirmation of our eternal safety

223

could we have than the atoning death of the Son of God in our place? Thus, whether we are alive (awake) or dead (asleep) when Jesus returns, our eternal position with the Lord is secure. So Paul simply tells the Thessalonians to take that truth and share it with each other, building up each other's faith. It's something we can (and should) get excited about.

So, literally, we are to "turn off" our sad dispositions in the face of trials and exhibit the secure hope we have in Christ. We are not to let even severe trials rob us of the joy of our salvation. See the Psalm King David prayed:

> Create in me a clean heart, O God,
>   and renew a right spirit within me.
> Cast me not away from your presence,
>   and take not your Holy Spirit from me.
> Restore to me the joy of your salvation,
>   and uphold me with a willing spirit. (Psalm 51:10–12)

Imagine having the clean heart and right spirit David prayed for. What if we really knew Jesus' presence was with us to the end of the age (Matthew 28: 20), and what if we could actually hear the Holy Spirit within us as David prayed? And what if we could sense the "joy of our salvation" ever increasingly upholding us? Here is a prayer we should make our own. God would have us always be this transparent before Him with regard to our relationship to Him.

PSALM 63:1-4

This Psalm by David is titled "My Soul Thirsts for You." The application would seem to be during a time of stress in his life when he is fleeing from a powerful enemy. The message to us then would be that comfort, relief, and rest is available to us during times of trouble. See these first four verses:

> O God, you are my God; earnestly I seek you;
>> my soul thirsts for you;
> my flesh faints for you,
>> as in a dry and weary land where there is no water.
> So I have looked upon you in the sanctuary,
>> beholding your power and glory.
> Because your steadfast love is better than life,
>> my lips will praise you.
> So I will bless you as long as I live;
>> in your name I will lift up my hands. (Psalm 63:1–4)

Wow! What an outpouring of love and commitment on David's part! What a recognition of God's love and provision for His children by David. His soul thirsts, and his flesh faints, so he is spiritually and physically exhausted, but he knows where relief is found. And he earnestly goes there (before God) confidently and expectantly, knowing God's love for him abounds and is never failing. And he concludes the obvious: God's love is better than life, and He is thus worthy of David's praise and blessings as long as he lives.

When questions, situations, and trials seem overwhelming in our lives this same God of David is available to us. And why not? His love for us is just as steadfast, just as powerful, and just as effective. We can and should draw the same conclusions David did: our God is both adequate and accessible in any circumstance. He is worthy of all our praise, honor, and glory too. Notice David's response, he commits to "lifting up his hands in God's name." There is clearly presented here the idea of love, humility, commitment, and faith. That's the kind of heart God wants to see in us.

2 Timothy 2:11-13

Paul the apostle is writing from prison in Rome to Timothy in Ephesus. So, as he awaits his own death Paul encourages Timothy to be strong in his faith. What an expression of Paul's faith, and his love for Timothy! Thus we, too, are to persevere in our faith even amid whatever troubles may be happening in our lives. God had not forgotten Timothy or Paul, and He has not forgotten us. This passage comes in a section of Paul's letter titled "A Good Soldier of Christ Jesus." The analogy is clear, we are to fight the good fight of faith here on earth. Notice the conclusions Paul draws that also apply to us:

> The saying is trustworthy for:
>   If we have died with him, we will also live with him;
>   If we endure, we will also reign with him;
>   If we deny him, he also will deny us;
>   If we are faithless, he remains faithful—
> For he cannot deny himself. (2 Timothy 2:11–13)

Paul wants Timothy and any others who see this letter to believe him. And that is certainly applicable to our day too. We see here four "if-then" statements that remain true for all believers. If we are saved (that is, if we have died to self, and now live for Christ), then we will "also live with Him" (in heaven). Believers, therefore, spend an earthly lifetime trusting Christ and in obedience to Him, and are rewarded with an eternity in heaven with Him.

And if we endure (that is, if we persevere), then "we will also reign with Him." To endure is to be consistent in our Christian walk. That does not imply we will live perfect sinless lives, but it does imply we want to do that, and that we will make every effort to do that. And it does imply we are repentant when we do sin.

Endurance also leads to reigning with Christ. When we become Christians, we are adopted into the family of God. We literally join God's family as His chosen children and become joint heirs with Jesus Christ. We then have an inheritance like that of Jesus and will somehow reign with Him in heaven. We cannot imagine what that will be like, but we can be sure it will be awesome. Notice Paul's emphasis at the beginning of this passage on the truth of these statements. Thus, these statements concerning living (forever) with Jesus and reigning with Him are absolutely true.

On the other hand, if we deny Christ (that is, if we turn away from the truth of Christ's sacrificial death on the cross for our sins), He will also deny us. We then would be responsible for paying our own sin death, which amounts to an eternity in hell. And these conclusions are also true.

Lastly, we see Paul make the point of Christ's faithfulness. If (as believers) we fail in our Christian walk, then Christ is faithful to forgive us. Again, Paul is writing about truths that are hard for believers to understand. But, hallelujah! We can be sure they are true. God does keep His promises. Jesus' sacrificial death on the cross was sufficient to pay the sin debt of all those who believe in Him. Therefore, it is true that "by grace we are saved through faith" (Ephesians 2:8). God's love then is the basis for the salvation of all believers.

Finally, see Paul's concluding statement: "Jesus cannot deny Himself." Jesus is Lord, God come to earth to save us from our sins. He cannot and will not fall short in that effort. What a great God we have!

JUDGES 3:31; 5:6

When the children of Israel occupied the promised land, they soon began to take on the habits and worship styles of the pagans who lived there, not completely driving them out as the Lord had commanded them to do. And so they sinned, and God punished them for those sins by allowing these pagans to torment the Israelites daily, and defeat them in battles fought here and there in the promised land. As this scenario played out over time it got worse and worse and God provided various men and women as judges to lead Israel against those pagans. One such judge was a man named Shamgar. See the two short passages describing what Shamgar did:

> After him was Shamgar the son of Anath, who killed 600 of the Philistines with an oxgoad, and he also saved Israel. (Judges 3:31)

> "In the days of Shamgar, son of Anath,
>   in the days of Jael, the highways were abandoned,
>   and travelers kept to the byways." (Judges 5:6)

An oxgoad was a pole six or seven feet long, about two inches in diameter, pointed on one end and shaped as a spade on the other end. Thus, an individual could use it to dig (and plant) with, and as a cattle prod. Given his skill in handling an oxgoad, Shamgar must have been a farmer or shepherd. Evidently the Philistines controlled the main roads, causing the Israelites to have to use the longer, safer back roads to travel, take goods to market, and communicate with other Israelites, etc., thus hampering life in general. All for fear of being attacked by the Philistines.

We can imagine Shamgar accompanying fellow Israelites on the road and protecting them with his oxgoad. He likely did not kill six hundred Philistines in one battle, but over years of time as he lived his life carrying out this protective role. But notice scripture says, "he also saved Israel." What an awesome statement to be said of anyone tucked in this passage. So the sum of Shamgar's contribution to Israel must have been significant. Trip by trip, one event at a time, his consistent availability and his ongoing bravery made this farmer and shepherd and warrior a noteworthy addition to scripture for us all to imitate.

It has been said of Shamgar that he was so effective because he

1. started where he was,
2. used what he had,
3. and did what he could.

Three truly profound characteristics we should follow in our lives as we, too, seek to promote kingdom work.

HEBREWS 9:27–28

The author of the book of Hebrews is unknown, but was obviously inspired by the Holy Spirit for the book discusses subjects and principles only God could have known and provided. The truths in this passage provide us information concerning judgment at the end of time, and how Christ will return to save those who believe in Him and eagerly wait for Him. Notice then, the eternal hope believers have:

> And just as it is appointed for man to die once, and after that comes judgment, so Christ, having been offered once to bear the sins of many, will appear a second time, not to deal with sin but to save those who are eagerly waiting for him. (Hebrews 9:27–28)

As everyone realizes, all mankind will die once, an earthly death. And after that will come a time of judgment. Christ will be that judge and He will (perfectly) evaluate everything we have done, thought, and said. This passage communicates a huge truth without directly stating it. That is, that all mankind will have one chance only to make their decision for Christ, that being while they are alive on earth. Man is appointed "to die once, and after that comes judgment." There will be no second chance after death to change their eternal destiny. That destiny is offered freely by Christ to be heaven spent with Him via God's grace through faith.

That judgment is specifically identified in Ecclesiastes, too, attributed to King Solomon. See this passage which clearly makes the point everyone will be judged and judged completely: "The end of the matter; all has been heard. Fear God and keep his commandments, for this is the whole duty of man. For God will bring every deed into judgment, with every secret thing, whether good or evil" (Ecclesiastes 12:13–14).

The Hebrews passage describes Christ's first appearance on earth and His sacrificial death on the cross to bear the sins of many, that is, those who believe in Christ. And Christ will also at some point appear on earth a second time; this time not to deal with sin (He already did that on the cross) but to save those waiting for Him. Notice several important points: those people waiting on Christ are eager for His return. They know they are saved, they know they are going to spend eternity in heaven with Christ, and they know the joy of their salvation indicates heaven will be wonderful and beyond imagination. So, believers can have that joy now, here on earth. They can be so sure they are heaven-bound that they can live here, now, knowing their eternal life has already begun. **True faith enables believers to experience that kind of life now.**

The time is now to deal with our relationship to Christ. The sooner the better, not just to ensure an eternity in heaven, but to enjoy that relationship with Christ in all our earthly situations, and to better enable us to share this wonderful news with those we care most about so they, too, will come to know Christ as Savior and Lord.

Saved people and unsaved people will live about the same length of time on earth. But think of the difference a relationship with Christ can make in those same years. If, through the presence of the Holy Spirit in our lives, believers can influence even just one other person to receive Christ's free gift of eternal life, that person will live forever in harmony with Christ, knowing untold joy and peace.

MATTHEW 24:14

Our heavenly Father sent His Son, Jesus Christ, into the world for a specific reason, to save us from our sins. And He spent most of His earthly ministry training twelve disciples to go and make other disciples. And in their role as disciple makers, they were to spread the gospel, the good news of Jesus Christ. That gospel, or "good news," defines the way to eternal life via God's grace and our faith in Jesus as Savior and Lord. Jesus put it this way: "I am the way, and the truth, and the life. No one comes to the Father except through me" (John 14:6). At one point Jesus spoke to His disciples of the time of His return to earth to gather all believers to Himself, and when He would establish His kingdom. And Jesus' disciples asked Him when this would happen. Believers today ask that same question. Here is Jesus' answer to us all.

> And this gospel of the kingdom will be proclaimed throughout the whole world as a testimony to all nations, and then the end will come. (Matthew 24:14)

God obviously has a plan. The gospel is to be spread throughout the whole world. Every nation then will hear and have opportunity to believe the truth concerning Jesus' sacrificial death on the cross to pay the sin debt of all who will believe. At this time the gospel has simply not yet been carried to every nation. Many millions of people have never even heard the name of Jesus, much less heard of the only way to eternal life He provides. And notice the passage assures us an end is coming. So the message we get rings with a sense of urgency for us all to act now.

Therefore, Jesus' general command to all believers to "go and make disciples" describes the way Jesus would have the gospel spread to the whole world. His is a one-on-one approach. Believers today call this command to "go and make disciples" the Great Commission, and all believers are commanded to participate. Notice the prophecy speaks of the gospel of God's kingdom being spread to every nation, but not that every person in every nation will hear and believe. Some will hear and still deny Christ to be who He claimed to be, Son of God, the prophesied Messiah.

But the fact remains, believers are to share what they know is true concerning Jesus. That does not guarantee that those they share with will all believe. The believer's assignment is to spread this good news (wherever they go). God's Holy Spirit determines the response from those who hear. Thus, every witness effort a believer makes in Jesus' name is a successful effort regardless of the seeming result.

Given the significance of what Christians know of Jesus and His love for us, there should be no hesitation on a believer's part to participate. What better information could one individual provide for another individual than to show them the way to eternal life? How better could anyone show their love for someone else than to introduce them to the Savior of the world? What greater joy could any person feel than that joy that comes with the establishment of a saving relationship with Jesus Christ?

So yes, the future is secure for those who believe, but what of those who have never heard? We have a privilege and a responsibility to share what we know.

ROMANS 5:1

The title of Romans 5 is "Peace with God Through Faith." God knows better than we do how important peace with Him is. We don't often enough consciously consider the subject of peace with God, but consciously or subconsciously that is what we want and need, for there is nothing more satisfying than God's peace; more than anything this world can offer. See how the Holy Spirit has Paul word this blessing God provides:

> Therefore, since we have been justified by faith, we have peace with God through our Lord Jesus Christ. (Romans 5:1)

Paul has been talking in chapter 4 about Abraham, and how Abraham was not justified by works, but because he "believed God, and it was counted to him as righteousness" (Romans 4:3). So it was his faith that led him to obey God and follow Him. And we are saved the same way, by God's grace and our faith. Put very simply, we are all born sinners, so our basic need is to either not ever sin, or to have all our sins somehow completely atoned for (forever). Given our tendencies to sin and God's just nature, it would require a perfect sacrifice to atone for our sins and justify us. That sacrifice was Jesus Christ and His death on the cross for our sins. Jesus thus became our propitiation, that is, He was not just "a" sacrifice, but the only sacrifice that could satisfy the wrath of God generated by our sin. Thus, we are justified, meaning acquitted or found not guilty of our sin, by our faith in Jesus' sacrificial death in our place.

And praise the Lord, see from the verse what accrues to us via God's love for us (His grace) and our faith: peace with God. And the verse tells us it came to us through our Lord Jesus Christ. The fact of our salvation and our being then filled with the Holy

Spirit provides us the assurance and inherent certainty of eternal life with God that give us that rest, that hope, that confidence, and that excitement we call peace with God. You can't think very much about peace with God for an eternity without the word *joy* coming to mind. See Psalm 51:12 where King David prays for that kind of joy. We should too.

1 PETER 4:7-11

The Holy Spirit has Peter make clear to his readers exactly what kind of lifestyles they are to live. His words apply to us in our day too. God has prepared the way for eternal salvation for any who will believe. At this point of Peter's writing, all of God's salvation plan has been accomplished. He has sent Christ into the world to live, be crucified (in our place), to rise again on the third day, and to ascend to heaven forty days later, and even to send the Holy Spirit to indwell believers to guide and protect them throughout their earthly lives. See how now Peter is led to remind believers everywhere how to best glorify the Father until Christ returns:

> The end of all things is at hand; therefore be self-controlled and sober-minded for the sake of your prayers. Above all, keep loving one another earnestly, since love covers a multitude of sins. Show hospitality to one another without grumbling. As each has received a gift, use it to serve one another, as good stewards of God's varied grace: whoever speaks, as one who speaks oracles of God; whoever serves, as one who serves by the strength God supplies—in order that in everything God may be glorified through Jesus Christ. To him be glory and dominion forever and ever. Amen. (1 Peter 4:7–11)

As we read this passage, we cannot help but be impressed how in one short paragraph God has had Peter outline a proper lifestyle for people to live in any time era. God's plan works in any society, with any level of sophistication. Notice the whole point of our living is for God's glory. And we are to do this through commitment to Christ, and by imitating His lifestyle.

The phrase, "the end of all things is at hand," does not imply that Christ is due to return any minute, but that God has accomplished already all the major events in His salvation plan. Christ has come to earth, proved His divinity through His miracles and by living a perfect life, died a sinner's death on the cross, and conquered death by His resurrection. And if He rose again we can be sure we believers will, too, in like manner. Thus, our instructions are clear: though our good deeds don't save us (we are saved by God's grace through faith), we are to live out our lives in imitation of Christ's life, loving God with all our hearts, souls, and minds, and our neighbors as ourselves (Matthew 22:37–40).

Such lifestyles will bring us into a Christlikeness that will be evident to those around us, and God the Father will thus be glorified, for everything Christ said and did glorifies the Father. Notice how Peter speaks to us of what we are to make a priority in our lives. He tells us to "above all, keep loving one another earnestly." More than anything else then, we are to express a "lived out" love for each other. Surely then, that one principle will guide all our words and deeds (and our motivations for them).

Obviously, such lives will be led by our prayers. It's not so much that we have an effective prayer life, but that we live a "praying" life. The concept that we constantly stay in touch with the Father, in every part of what we do and who we are, is critical for us. To be governed by our allegiance to God the Father is thus to dictate everything about us. Our one desire should be to obey and please Him. Peter commends it, and Jesus commands it.

ROMANS 11:30-32

That God would have all be saved is clearly pointed out in scripture. See 1 Timothy 2:3–4: "This is good, and it is pleasing in the sight of God our Savior, who desires all people to be saved and to come to the knowledge of the truth."

We see in Romans 11:30–32 a further explanation of this same truth:

> For just as you were at one time disobedient to God but now have received mercy because of their disobedience, so they too now have been disobedient in order that by the mercy shown to you they may also now receive mercy. For God has consigned all to disobedience, that he may have mercy on all.

God's mercy in regard to salvation is emphasized all through scripture. After all, we might well have thought He would only save Jews, His chosen people, yet He has made provision for Gentiles too. It is important to note this letter is written to the church in Rome which contains both Jewish and Gentile Christians. So lest there be conflict among them, both groups are reminded to be grateful for God's mercy that any individual of either group is saved. **Clearly that thought is to carry over to our day. All believers are thus to be grateful to God for the grace He has shown in saving us.**

Note the use of the word *consigned* when referring to the disobedient character of us all, both Jew and Gentile. To consign means to commit to a final fate. Thus, someone must do the consigning, and God has done that. And He has a reason for doing it, so that He may show mercy, else we would all be condemned to the fate our disobedience earns us.

We are to beware of taking this passage as a basis for belief that all Jews or Gentiles will be saved. This passage does not teach that. Many from both groups will be saved the same way, by God's grace through faith. Scripture does teach that. So the concept of God's love is behind the whole process, leading to His mercy and appropriately then our grateful thanksgiving for our undeserved salvation.

There then is a key lesson for us to learn from this passage. God merits our undying love and obedience for the supreme love He has provided us through the gift of His Son at Calvary for our sins. Certainly, there is no way for us to overstate the significance of the eternal life God's love has provided us believers. What a source of peace and joy we've been given. What a privilege (and responsibility) we have to share this truth with a lost world. Our perspective concerning all we experience in life, both good and bad, is to be colored by God's presence, His will, and His provisions for us. Hallelujah! What a great God we have.

JOHN 3:2-3

Perhaps the most important question any person ever addresses is, "How do I acquire eternal life?" or "What is the way to eternal life?" If there is anything after death, then certainly this concept is worth considering. Many people, whether due to ignorance or pride, never consider their eternal destiny; others do but come to the wrong conclusion. This question has always been one thinking people would wonder about. When you think about it, this is the question we should want to answer correctly. And so it was just as important in Jesus' day as it is now.

There was a man named Nicodemus who came to Jesus (by night) with questions about this subject. He was a ruler of the Jews, that is, he was a man of influence within the Jewish government called the Sanhedrin. He recognized Jesus as having come from God, given His ability to perform miracles. Notice how his conversation with Jesus went:

> "Rabbi, we know that you are a teacher come from God, for no one can do these signs that you do unless God is with him." Jesus answered him, "Truly, truly, I say to you, unless one is born again he cannot see the kingdom of God." (John 3:2–3)

Notice Nicodemus had not exactly asked the key question yet, but Jesus being who He is, anticipated his concerns and provided the answer. In the first place, when we realize the Greek word for "again" can also mean "from above," we get a huge clue as to Jesus' meaning. Thus, Jesus was saying there is another or additional or new birth in the eternal life equation that involves God. This heavenly or spiritual rebirth comes from an earlier point John had made concerning Jesus: "But to all who did receive him, who believed in his name, he gave the right to become children of God, who were born, not of blood nor of the will of the flesh nor of the will of man, but of God" (John 1:12–13).

Thus, the concept of belief or faith is introduced in the discussion. Notice two more elements are conspicuous by their absence: good works are not required, and the phrase "eternal life" is not mentioned. Good works come later as a result of one's salvation (and are not the reason for it), and the words *kingdom of God* are equivalent to eternal life. Notice, too, the reference to children of God is used to indicate that those who are born again are those who have eternal life.

While baptism is not required for salvation, it is symbolic of the transformation a new believer has experienced. The one doing the baptism often quotes from Romans 6:4 referencing this same "born again" concept: buried with Christ in baptism, raised to walk in newness of life.

Thus, yes, we must be born again to obtain eternal life. The phrase describes in essence what has happened; that is, a spiritual renewal to a new life in Christ our Lord and Savior. And this was brought about by the whole of God's involvement, His grace (the unmerited favor we have from God) which initiates the process, and our repentance of our sin by faith in Jesus' substitutionary death in our place (which God also provides) as full atonement for that sin. If at all possible, we celebrate this transformation by baptism. Once again, our great God has made all the necessary provisions.

MATTHEW 15:30-31

Jesus healed a lot of people during His ministry on earth. And there was a reason for this. It was to show that the God of Israel was the only God of the universe, and thus, to bring honor and glory to Him. See this passage that shows how what He did led to such worship:

> And great crowds came to him, bringing with them the lame, the blind, the crippled, the mute, and many others, and they put them at his feet, and he healed them, so that the crowds wondered, when they saw the mute speaking, the crippled healthy, the lame walking, and the blind seeing. And they glorified the God of Israel. (Matthew 15:30–31)

This passage speaks of a time when Jesus had separated Himself from the populated areas of Galilee and gone around the Sea of Galilee to the eastern side where Gentiles lived. Even in this sparsely populated area crowds gathered before Him. And it is thus likely many of those Jesus healed were Gentiles. This is very significant, indicating God's love for and involvement not with just the Jews (descendants of Abraham), but the whole world.

Interestingly, nothing is specifically mentioned of faith on the part of those healed, or their loved ones who brought them to Jesus. Although such faith is implied in that they have come to a remote place specifically to meet with Jesus. See some key points we can draw from this passage:

1. Jesus was able to heal any malady that was presented to Him. This is still true.
2. At no point in scripture do we read of Jesus coming upon a need that He cannot heal.

3. Severe physical and mental needs will lead people to go to great lengths to bring their sick to a place and before a person they feel may heal them.
4. Love drives such efforts.
5. When people see obvious miracles performed before them, they will give credit to God, and acknowledge His involvement (though after a time they may lose their enthusiasm).
6. All these characteristics and tendencies are true in our day too (for human nature has not changed).
7. Notice Jesus did not seek His own glory, but that of His Father.

In a very real way, we have a unique opportunity to believe in Christ. Jesus spoke some revealing words to "doubting Thomas" after he maintained he would not believe Christ had risen unless he could put his hand in Jesus' pierced side. "Jesus said to him, 'Have you believed because you have seen me? Blessed are those who have not seen and yet have believed'" (John 20:29).

We believe and "have not seen." And Jesus calls us blessed. Jesus proved His deity and love many times, as related to us in scripture, particularity with regard to His death in our place and His resurrection. Let us then exhibit a "lived out" faith in what we have not seen, but know to be true.

JOHN 20:19

On the third day after His crucifixion, Jesus rose from the dead, thereby proving His deity conclusively. Picture the darkness of His tomb and Him lying there, and suddenly He begins to breathe. His chest begins to rise and fall, and His lungs that had been empty begin to draw in air and He wakes up. **He had been dead, but now He is alive.** We've heard about this all our lives but only by faith can we come close to really grasping its significance. See this verse describing His first appearance to His disciples:

> On the evening of that day, the first day of the week, the doors being locked where the disciples were for fear of the Jews, Jesus came and stood among them and said to them, "Peace be with you." (John 20:19)

We can only imagine the shock, the confusion, the fear, and the anxiety that filled the disciples. It is the evening of that first day of the week, and with many questions and no answers, the disciples were gathered in fear of the Jews. Just a few days earlier they had seen the Jewish leaders inciting the crowd before Pilate to cry out for Jesus' crucifixion, and they had seen it happen. That morning, some of them had seen the empty tomb, and several of the women had told them they had seen angels at the tomb. And one even said she saw Jesus alive.

And now, suddenly, somehow, Jesus appears among them. Notice the first thing Jesus says to them: "Peace be with you." Leave it to Jesus to always say exactly the right thing. If there was anything the disciples needed at that point it was peace. They needed to calm down and realize what had happened. They needed to recognize that this was truly Jesus in front of them and that per

His prophecy to them earlier He had risen from the grave. **This was their risen Lord there with them.**

And we, too, need to recognize this was really Jesus standing there. Our heavenly Father had sent Jesus to earth to save us from our sins. Part of that mission involved Jesus' sacrificial death on the cross to pay our sin debt. And additionally, Jesus was to rise from the dead, proving that we who believe in Him will also rise again to be with Him eternally.

So right here on earth, in the middle of our busy lives, where we face everyday pressures to conform to Satan's world, we need to calm down and acknowledge Jesus' resurrection, His lordship, and His power to save. We believers need to take joy in our salvation, share the truth of His resurrection, and live out the good news of Jesus.

Over the next short period of time, Jesus would meet with the disciples on several occasions, explaining and reminding them again of His plans for them. Our assignment is not unlike that Jesus gave to the disciples: go and make disciples and tell others about God's love for them.

And why not? We believers have been the recipients of the greatest gift anyone can ever receive, the gift of eternal life. What of this world could be more significant? What better news could we give anyone?

Psalm 33:8–9

While its author is unknown, it is plain the purpose of this Psalm is to teach us to praise Jehovah God, for He alone is worthy. The psalmist would have every single occupant of this planet praise the Lord, not Jews alone, but Gentiles too. If God has seen fit to inspire this written word, and He did, then there must be a reason for it. Since God loves the whole world, it must follow that God knows there is benefit available for each individual to humble themselves before Him in praise and prayer. See these two verses:

> Let all the earth fear the LORD;
>> let all the inhabitants of the world stand in awe of him!
> For he spoke, and it came to be;
>> he commanded, and it stood firm. (Psalm 33:8–9)

People were busy in David's day just as we are today. Yet God has the psalmist call them and us aside from our daily tasks on a regular basis to honor Him, to regulate our lives around Him, and to express our love for Him. The word *fear* does not imply fear as in afraid, but fear as in respect, as in awe, and as in honor. Such is to be our relationship to God for He is God and we are not. Just as a wise woodcutter delays going into the forest until he has sharpened his ax. He knows the time spent preparing his ax will be well spent, resulting in more wood harvested by the end of the day. Just so we are to spend time daily in praise and worship of holy God so that the spiritual results of our day in kingdom labor will be greater for God's glory.

Notice how the psalmist educates us on why and how God is worthy of all our praise. God is worthy because by His power and influence He created the universe. He actually spoke and all that was created came to be. He commanded and everything that is, was there permanently. Further, the Lord maintains all He created, keeping each part properly in place, functioning as He sees fit.

Obviously, God has a plan, and praise the Lord, we are part of it, the best part of it. Just imagine, this God of ours who created the most distant stars (and named each one) also counts every grain of sand on the seashore, and accounts for every hair on our heads at the same time. And best of all He loves each of us with a steadfast love and has made provision for our eternal life with Him in heaven. How wise we are to recognize our need for Him, and not be blind to His presence in our lives, to believe He sent His Son Jesus to save us from our sins, and to "love Him back" because He first loved us.

ROMANS 2:6–8

God is completely just and evenhanded in His judgment of us and our lives. We readily acknowledge God knows our hearts—what we want, what we are thinking, and our every deed and their motivations. Yet we often find ourselves going in a direction that if we ever stopped to think about it, we would have to admit was the wrong direction, and not in accord with God's will at all. Look at this passage for confirmation of God's position relative to our works:

> He will render to each one according to his works: to those who by patience in well doing seek for glory and honor and immortality, He will give eternal life; but for those who are self-seeking and do not obey the truth, but obey unrighteousness, there will be wrath and fury. (Romans 2:6–8)

In one long sentence God has Paul lay out how He will deal with us in judgment. It's clear God wants us to be "doers" of His word and not "hearers only" (James 1:22). In the first place, Paul points out there will, in fact, be a judgment. There will thus surely be a godly assessment of our lives. Paul tells us God will "render to each one according to his works." Notice, secondly, the concept of consistency and perseverance in our walk is huge in God's decision-making process. The passage tells us we are to be patient in our well doing, implying our actions are to be "thought about," ongoing, precise, and focused on well doing (for others). Thirdly, we are to seek glory (the manifestation of God Himself), honor (God's approval), and immortality (an eternity in God's presence). **Those last are not selfish goals, they are worthy goals, already promised by God as an inheritance for His children. The reward**

for such seekers is eternal life. If ever a huge Hallelujah from our hearts is in order, those facts demand it.

Conversely, those "self-seekers" who not only fail to obey the truth, but obey unrighteousness instead, will face God's wrath and fury. Webster defines these as "strong vengeful anger," and "intense, destructive rage." Picture facing those from almighty God **for an eternity.**

So periodic reordering of our priorities and actions would surely be required of us all. Thus, it is not what we know to do, plan on doing, or would like to do that truly counts; it's what we do (and why). We can, and should, thank God for this insightful passage given us because He loves us.

1 CHRONICLES 22:19

David, King of Israel, had in mind to build a temple for the worship of the Lord, but God denied his request, saying that his son Solomon would build the temple. In this verse David is speaking to all the leaders of Israel, telling them to help Solomon in this project. Notice before anyone does anything, they are to seek the Lord. That's a great rule for us to follow too. See the wording in this verse concerning our commitment to the Lord:

> Now set your mind and heart to seek the LORD your God. (1 Chronicles 22:19)

See the first word, *now*. When it comes to seeking the Lord, *now* is always the proper time to begin. There is an urgency, a level of importance, and the idea of first priority about seeking the Lord. This was true in David's time, three thousand years ago, and it's still true in our day. Notice, too, that each individual is to set their own mind and heart to the task of seeking the Lord. That obviously means doing so is within our capacity to accomplish. God will never assign us something that with His help we cannot complete. In fact, with His help we can accomplish great things. And since we never know the total ramifications of anything we do in God's name, then even small (by our definition, not God's) things are to be given our total attention. See the classic example of this in Matthew 10:42: "And whoever gives one of these little ones even a cup of cold water because he is a disciple, truly, I say to you, he will by no means lose his reward."

See how complete our focus is to be: we are to put our minds and our hearts into seeking the Lord. In short, we are not to hold back anything in the effort to know God, and in determining His will for our lives. Not stated here, but surely implied, is the fact that the Lord will assist us in this assignment if we are obedient. David winds up gathering the material together for the temple, enabling Solomon to complete the building task in only seven years; this, after David's death. So David did play an important role in the temple project.

So what can we learn from this episode in David and Solomon's lives? We can learn mainly that we are to be praying and thinking servants of God. Every person's circumstance is unique. God has a plan for all of us to be enacted where we are, doing what lies in front of us for His glory. Thus, accompanying our prayers we are to live with our eyes and minds open to the needs around us, looking for (and expecting) the direction of the Holy Spirit.

We may tend to conclude we don't know (and cannot find) God's will for our lives, and wish we had a simplified way to do so. This verse gives us that approach. The point made in this verse is we are to decide we really want to know God's will and take proactive steps consistently to know Him.

1 JOHN 4:10–17

Here is a passage under the heading "God Is Love," one of the most profound subjects we can ever consider. So here we read of the concept that (1) God loves us, and that (2) God Himself is the essence of love itself. God is love. Thus, John the apostle is telling us here about how we are to take these two facts and live them out in the world, and that as we do, we illustrate to the world that we love God back for the love He has shown us. God's love for us is personified in Jesus Christ's arrival in this world; to live a perfect life and die a sinner's death on the cross (in our place) to pay our sin debt. So, we believers have a love relationship with both the Father and the Son. See what John tells us about these concepts.

> In this is love, not that we have loved God but that he loved us and sent his Son to be the propitiation for our sins. Beloved, if God so loved us, we also ought to love one another. No one has ever seen God; if we love one another, God abides in us and his love is perfected in us.
>
> By this we know that we abide in him and he in us, because he has given us of his Spirit. And we have seen and testify that the Father has sent his Son to be the Savior of the world. Whoever confesses that Jesus is the Son of God, God abides in him, and he in God. So we have come to know and to believe the love that God has for us. God is love, and whoever abides in love abides in God, and God abides in him. By this is love perfected with us, so that we may have confidence for the day of judgment, because as he is so also are we in this world. (1 John 4:10–17)

The most amazing thing about God's love is not that He loved us when we were not worthy of His love, but that He loved us first, before we realized it; in fact, God loved us before the world was formed. And He proved His love by sending His Son Jesus Christ to earth (at the proper time) to be the propitiation for our sins. Propitiation means the sacrifice Jesus made when He gave His life on the cross in our place to satisfy God's wrath for our sins. So that's what Jesus' death provided, payment for our sins. We don't realize the significance of our sins or the significance of Jesus' (as Son of God) substitutionary death in our place. Yet it happened one day on a hill outside Jerusalem.

John's main lesson for us in this passage is that we are to love one another as God loved us. And if we do, we are reflecting the love of God before the world, and that love grows more perfect over time. And God has gifted His Holy Spirit to us believers so that we might recognize God abides in us through His Spirit. And so, the apostles in the first century and we now are to live out our faith in Christ before a world that for the most part does not know God.

John was there, as an eyewitness to Jesus' ministry on earth. He saw and heard Jesus' testimony of His deity, He was present to witness many miracles, he heard Jesus preach the gospel of His birth and soon-to-be death on the cross, He felt the wind die down when Jesus called out to the storm, "Cease, be still," and He experienced Jesus' resurrection from the grave on the third day after His crucifixion. So, yes, John knew what he was talking about. He knew what he was saying was true when he said, "Jesus is the Son of God and God abides in him and he in God."

And just as true is the confidence we can have in our eternal destiny with this wonderful Savior of ours.

PHILIPPIANS 3:17, 20–4:1

If we are to be the witness the Lord would have us be, then our lives should truly reflect our beliefs and the verbal witness we promote. Paul was that kind of witness and he worked at it, claiming that truth and urging his readers to imitate him. We have to be very confident in our faith to put in writing the request that other people use us as their examples. Our doctrines must be sound, correct, and in keeping with our lifestyle. If they are not, we are the biggest of hypocrites and we make a mockery of the gospel in the eyes of those we are witnessing to. Notice Paul's wording of these truths:

> Brothers, join in imitating me, and keep your eyes on those who walk according to the example you have in us . . . Our citizenship is in heaven, and from it we await a Savior, the Lord Jesus Christ, who will transform our lowly body to be like his glorious body, by the power that enables him even to subject all things to himself. Therefore, my brothers, whom I love and long for, my joy and crown, stand firm thus in the Lord, my beloved. (Philippians 3:17, 20–4:1)

Paul does not claim perfection but he is confident in what he knows he knows. For what he knows and promotes (and lives out) is in accord with all doctrine, his and that of other biblical writers. Paul even urges his readers to follow the example of others whom he knows are already following his example, such as Timothy.

It's one thing to claim citizenship in heaven, it's quite another to make one's earthly lifestyle heavenly in nature. Paul's mind seems to be on heavenly matters a lot more than ours. And he voices those heavenly thoughts more than we do. And his earthly perspectives reflect those heavenly thoughts. Paul's faith is a step ahead of most of ours. We are not likely to be so bold with our witness. He is looking forward to his heavenly body (to be like Jesus') that Jesus will provide him one day. And he well knows that only Jesus has the power and will to provide such a future existence for him.

So, Paul comes back to the bottom line of the gospel, Jesus Christ is Lord, was and is and will always be Lord. Jesus is the key to eternal life. He, only, paid the total sin debt we owed. Thus, Paul tells his readers (and us) to make and keep Jesus as their focus. He tells them to stand firm in Him. To stand firm means to never doubt. It means not only to never doubt, but that doubting never occurs to you, doubting never shows up in your words, your decisions, or your influence. Never even considering doubting leads to the firmest of decisions, clearly made, and fully executed. We make moves now toward obedience to the Lord because we know the Lord is in those decisions. We don't waiver, we know the conditions around us are urgent. We, too, need to take that advice and live it out. Once we turn that corner into a "sold out to Jesus" direction, our whole perspective on life is different. No longer are we self-focused, no longer are we self-willed, and no longer are we self-motivated.

Whether we are in a full-time ministry, or being a "sold out" witness on our day job, God can and will use us every day to accomplish His will. And if He wants a change, then He will bring about the change conditions. But one thing we can be sure of, God does not waste time, nor does He want us to waste time. He knows better than we do the degree of the worldwide sin problem. And He knows better than we do the urgency of the worldwide needs. The next move is ours to make under the Lord's direction.

MATTHEW 5:7

Jesus once spoke to crowds from the hillside around the Sea of Galilee. This sermon became known as His Sermon on the Mount. He began that sermon with a listing of blessings that come to believers as they follow Jesus in obedience. Jesus simply lists blessings that accrue when we believers are obedient in certain ways. The list forms the outline of the whole sermon. One of those blessing promises has to do with our being merciful. Notice how applicable it is to us:

> "Blessed are the merciful, for they shall receive mercy." (Matthew 5:7)

This listing of blessings is called the "Beatitudes," from the Latin word *beatus*, meaning blessed or happy. So, clearly, we see Jesus encouraging His listeners, and us, to be merciful. As used here by Jesus, merciful implies compassion that forgoes punishment even when justice demands it. So that's the kind of mercy Jesus is telling us to live out in our lives if we want to obtain mercy for ourselves.

Notice there is no "probability" about our receiving mercy when we are merciful. **Those who are merciful will obtain mercy.** As always Jesus is specific, and His promises contain no exceptions. This would imply consistency in our lifestyles. We cannot live without interacting with other people, and from time to time we will absolutely have opportunities to be merciful. And we will also face times when we want others to be merciful to us. That has always been the case.

God does this for believers through His grace. Grace is love we receive from God in spite of our unloveliness. We are not worthy of His love, yet He loves with a steadfast love to the point He sent His sinless Son Jesus Christ to the cross to die, paying our sin debt. Notice the verse implies God is involved in a monitoring process for us all. He knows not only of everything we do but also why we do it. Thus, He is able to make perfect judgments.

Jesus told a story once about a king who was owed millions of dollars by one of his subjects. He called the man in and when he found he could not repay the debt, the king sentenced him and his family to prison. The man fell on his knees before the king, pleading for forgiveness, promising to repay the debt. Knowing the man could never repay the debt, the king still had pity on the man and forgave the entire debt. Shortly thereafter, that same man went to a fellow servant who owed him a few hundred dollars and had him thrown into prison when he could not repay the debt. Some other servants, seeing this, went to the king and related what had happened. The king then called in his debtor and reminded him of the mercy he had been shown, saying he surely should have been merciful to his debtor, and had him thrown into prison. Jesus closed his story saying, "So also my heavenly Father will do to every one of you, if you do not forgive your brother from your heart" (Matthew 18:35). Surely that principle applies to all of us.

Other Beatitudes address subjects such as being poor in spirit (humble), our being meek, pure in heart, and peacemakers. The early verses of Matthew 5 contain them all and is worthy of our study and obedience.

REVELATION 22:6–7

John the apostle is an old man, living in exile on the Isle of Patmos late in the first century when he writes this book of Revelation. God has given him a vision of heaven describing what is to come there and on earth in the end times. John is to write what he has been told and what he has seen. Here, near the end of the book, he quotes Jesus as He affirms the truth of what has been written. We, about two thousand years later, can be sure these words are true:

> And he said to me, "These words are trustworthy and true. And the Lord, the God of the spirits of the prophets, has sent his angel to show his servants what must soon take place."
> "And behold, I am coming soon. Blessed is the one who keeps the words of the prophecy of this book." (Revelation 22:6–7)

So, John quotes the angel Jesus sent and Jesus Himself. The angel has been showing John future events and here assures him what he has seen and heard will take place. For twenty-one chapters of the book, John has faithfully recorded what he was told, and like John we are blown away with the majesty and glory of what he describes. From the establishment of a new heaven and a new earth for believers to inhabit, to how God will deal with Satan are described in detail. On the other hand, if we are looking for a specific date when all this will take place, we won't find it in Revelation. God has given us what He wants us to know, and what we need to know. Thus, believers in every era can rest easy; God has everything under control and surely the best is yet to come for us.

God has been behind it all from the beginning, even this time and vision John has spent with his guiding angel. God knows human nature well and knew we would make up erroneous scenarios of our own if He did not put His truth before us this way. Thus, He assigned John to record these visions. Notice the angel advises John these events will soon take place, soon as per God's timetable, not man's.

And then we see Jesus' comments. "Behold, I am coming soon. Blessed is the one who keeps the words of the prophesy of this book." The Greek word for "soon" can also mean "quickly" and/or suddenly. So, there is no clue here as to when we might expect Jesus' return. But return, He will. The fact of His return is clear and the fact of future blessings for believers is clear.

And what must we do to receive these blessings? (1) Get familiar with God's Word, scripture. And (2) do not just get familiar with scripture, but believe it, and keep it, that is, obey it, live it out, and share it with others. And there is an implied purpose for our obedience to scripture, and that is to glorify God. The "why" of our obedience, and the purpose we give to our very lives is important to God. He sees our hearts and knows our innermost thoughts. God requires sincerity on our part, not the hypocrisy of our living a false narrative, not really believing the principles we promote. And we benefit when we live an honest Christian doctrine. Consciously or subconsciously we know if we truly believe the way we live is God's will for us and whether His will is important to us.

Inherent, too, in this verse is the requirement we share this truth with others. We can hardly be sincere in our witness if we are not both verbalizing our beliefs (especially to those who mean the most to us) and living out our "words."

PSALM 145:4-7

Surely the Holy Spirit had filled David's heart as he was led to draft this Song of Praise to God. What an awesome description of God's glory and majesty we have been given in this passage. Let us read it with humility, seeking to gain more insight into His nature and sovereignty so we can better worship Him:

> One generation shall commend your works to another,
>   and shall declare your mighty acts.
> On the glorious splendor of your majesty,
>   and on your wondrous works, I will meditate.
> They shall speak of the might of your awesome deeds,
>   and I will declare your greatness.
> They shall pour forth the fame of your abundant goodness
>   and shall sing aloud of your righteousness. (Psalm 145:4–7)

Just look at the list of construction projects God has completed to protect us, to inform us, and guide us: His works, His mighty acts, His wondrous works, and His awesome deeds. And notice the reaction such work on His part is to foster in us; commending Him to the next generation, declaring His acts to the world, leading us to meditate on His love, speaking of His might to all we meet, and declaring His greatness to those who have never heard. Finally, David tells us the result of our efforts: the fame of God's abundant goodness will pour forth, and the works themselves will "sing aloud" of God's righteousness. All this so that the whole world can see, and hear, and know of this almighty God whose love, and power, and purity can transform any heart willing to respond.

It is no small thing for us to recognize that we have been given the privilege and assigned the task of communicating this information to the nations. And God has given us the approach to take, informing the next generation. That would imply teaching individuals as children, our own and others. Children hear, and learn, and remember and are influenced. And nations are transformed as a result.

For God so loved the world He made all these provisions, culminating in the giving of His only Son that whoever believes in Him should not perish but have eternal life. His love is ongoing, steadfast in every respect. We are to love also: God with all our hearts, souls, and minds, and our neighbors as ourselves.

Our assignment is clear, our responsibility is evident, and our privilege is great. Let us begin.

ROMANS 5:2–5

The book of Romans is heavy with truth, with vital, life-changing doctrine and wisdom that God had Paul write for our benefit. This passage is especially so. Let us consider it carefully and with strict attention, for it provides information on what possession of the Holy Spirit really means to believers:

> Through him we have also obtained access by faith into this grace in which we stand, and we rejoice in hope of the glory of God. Not only that, but we rejoice in our sufferings, knowing that suffering produces endurance, and endurance produces character, and character produces hope, and hope does not put us to shame, because God's love has been poured into our hearts through the Holy Spirit who has been given to us. (Romans 5:2–5)

Believers are secure in their position as saved individuals (via God's grace and their faith) because of their justification (having had all their sins forgiven and having been declared not guilty). Thus, we can rejoice knowing one day (upon Jesus' return) we will be completely cleansed (of the effects of sin) and glorified, preparing us for heaven. At that point we will experience the glory of God forever which defies description, although we can be sure it will be wonderful.

Additionally, though we can expect trials in this life, we can rejoice in those sufferings because of what they provide: endurance, character, and hope. Notice this kind of God-based hope will not put us to shame, that is, IT WILL NOT DISAPPOINT. Just think about that truth: our tough times, fearful and painful though they may be, will be worth it all for what they lead to, our becoming more like Christ. **And that has been the plan God (who loves us**

supremely) had all along. Proof of God's love and the knowledge of God's love has been poured into our hearts by the Holy Spirit (what a neat way to describe how we become aware of God's love and provisions).

Notice, too, how we acquire the Holy Spirit: it has been given to us (by God). God has simply thought of everything for His chosen believers. We are born in sin, but He loves us anyway (describing His grace). Because of His great love, He sent His Son Jesus Christ to earth to save us from our sin by paying our sin debt on the cross (see John 3:16). He instills faith in us to believe and raised Jesus from the grave to signify that His sacrificial death was sufficient to atone for all our sin. Further, over time He matures us in our faith as described in this passage through the sufferings we experience. And praise the Lord, one day Jesus will return to bring us home to glory with Him.

How could we not shout "Hallelujah!" at the thought of what lies ahead (no matter what we face now).

MATTHEW 16:26

To have a proper perspective concerning God and our eternity with Him, and with Jesus Christ and our relationship with Him, and with the Holy Spirit and His dwelling within us, are all part of what comes to a believer who has trusted Jesus Christ as Savior and Lord. Such an existence offers the only route to heaven, to eternal life, and to the joy and peace that God freely gives to His children. See this verse that describes that eternal trade-off God has made available to those who believe in His Son:

> For what will it profit a man if he gains the whole world and forfeits his soul? Or what shall a man give in return for his soul? (Matthew 16:26)

Our soul is defined as the spiritual principle embodied in human beings, or our total self. So it is our real and complete being that scripture describes here as being potentially traded for some measure of worldly treasure. No rational person would seemingly ever trade seventy or eighty years of worldly pleasure (even if that could be guaranteed, and it can never be guaranteed) for an eternity of joy and bliss in heaven with almighty God (which God does guarantee). And yet in actuality people everywhere consciously or subconsciously live out that exact same reality every day. And they do this either in ignorance of the provisions for eternal life God has made, or in stubborn resistance to or unbelief in those same provisions God has made. Thus, the witness of every believer is important.

So in His infinite love God has provided scriptural counsel such as this verse describes, and many other biblical warnings to mankind relative to our eternal destiny. Not covered in this verse, but covered in many other scriptural passages, is the fact that choosing allegiance to Christ rather than the world leads to true joy and peace even here on earth. Our eternal life then begins here on earth the moment we receive Christ's free gift of salvation through God's grace and our faith, though it is only a taste of what lies ahead for believers with God in heaven.

Jesus set the example for us when He was tempted by Satan. He turned down the whole world rather than worship Satan (Matthew 4:8–11). So there is no comparison between what Satan lies about and what God guarantees. Therefore, let us beware of the daily trades Satan sneaks into our decision making. It's no wonder Jesus included the phrase "lead us not into temptation" in His model prayer, for that is a daily occurrence for us all, once again advising us to stay "prayed up." Surely it is clearly implied from this passage that we are to live out this truth by putting the time, talent, and energy we have into it and verbally sharing it with those we influence.

MATTHEW 7:1–2

Webster says to judge means to "form an opinion about through careful weighing of evidence and testing of premises." That sounds all well and good, but scripture advises us to beware of judging. For most of the time we are not in a position to judge, or qualified to judge, or do not have all the facts to judge properly. In fact, scripture tells us not to judge, and implies we are not to judge even if we are correct in our evaluation. See how Jesus words this command in Matthew:

> Judge not, that you be not judged. For with the judgment you pronounce you will be judged, and with the measure you use it will be measured to you. (Matthew 7:1–2)

Judging then is obviously a role God does not want us to play. God loves us and He knows judging is too dangerous for us. It's sort of like playing with matches; we are liable to burn ourselves or do far more damage around us than the satisfaction we get is worth. And besides, the worst thing about it is the sense of superiority it expresses. Who are we, as sinful as we are, to pretend to be superior to anyone? God will handle all judging matters in His way and in His timing.

As believers we are likely most tempted to judge. After all, we know right from wrong, for we often read what God commands in His word and then see such terrible things going on in the world. And especially are we tempted to judge when some of those terribly wrong things are being done to us. And how are we supposed to stay in right relationship to God if we live with a critical mindset given all we experience and see around us? So the lesson is clear, run from judging.

And notice how God deals with those who do judge. He judges them in like manner. Romans 2 provides practical prohibitions against living one way and proclaiming (even teaching) another way. The hypocrisy of it all is staggering. And it is such pride that Jesus is speaking against in Matthew. On this judging subject, Oswald Chambers points out, "God looks not only at the act, He looks at the possibility." Now that's a scary thought. We would not recognize the sin and hypocrisy in others if it were not potentially available in our hearts. Again we can only conclude, do not judge.

But praise the Lord, believers will not be judged as we are tempted to judge others. Jesus' sacrificial act of atonement on the cross paid all the sin debt we will ever owe. That's a message we are to share.

LUKE 6:17–19

Things were progressing in Jesus' earthly ministry by the time we get to this passage. Just before this we read that Jesus went out to the mountain to pray. And after praying all night, in the morning He selected His twelve disciples. Thus, Messiah, the Son of God, sought His Father's counsel in prayer before this momentous decision as to who would be His closest associates. Look what happened then:

> And he came down with them and stood on a level place, with a great crowd of his disciples and a great multitude of people from all Judea and Jerusalem and the seacoast of Tyre and Sidon, who came to hear him and to be healed of their diseases. And those who were troubled with unclean spirits were cured. And all the crowd sought to touch him, for power came out from him and healed them all. (Luke 6:17–19)

Notice the three groups described who were there that day: His newly selected disciples, a great crowd of His (other) disciples, and a great multitude of people from distant places. This would obviously include a mix of believers, unbelievers, Jews and Gentiles. So a large cross-section of the general population was present to hear Him and to be healed of their diseases. The several references to the size of the group are indicative of Jesus' growing popularity. The point is, Jesus healed anyone of any disease, and much of it involved only their touching Him. And no limit was placed on the number of "patients." That same concept is true today. Jesus' healing power and His saving grace are available to the whole world. People anywhere, of any age group, and in any condition can find salvation and relief in Him.

That last sentence is one of the amazing things about God's provision for mankind. He loves us, and He does not start out loving us as innocent babies and then at some point, because we get sick or commit many sins, stop loving us. He would have us come to Him as we are, and from right where we are, no matter our circumstances. Notice the separate mention of Jesus' healing of people with unclean spirits. In those days as in our day, such problems are among the most difficult to understand and to deal with. As challenging and as debilitating as some physical disorders are, they are more tangible than mental diseases. But, hallelujah, Jesus was and is able to deal with them all.

So, what can we conclude from this passage? First, we can be sure God is all-powerful. He did, in fact, create all that is. Thus, He can fix any problem, spiritual, mental, physical, or relational. Second, He loves us with a steadfast love. Thus, He would have all come to Him in faith, to receive His free gift of eternal life. Third, He has made all necessary provisions for our healing physically or spiritually. "By grace you have been saved through faith. And this is not your own doing; it is the gift of God" (Ephesians 2:8).

There is a line from the song "Holy, Holy, Holy" that says it all, where it speaks of almighty God: "For you are perfect in power, perfect in love, and perfect in purity."

That's the kind of God we have. I love you and pray for you every day.

EXODUS 22:29; 23:19

God provided a lot of commands to the children of Israel as they traveled through the wilderness on their way to the promised land of Canaan. Every one of them is important. And He saw fit to have them recorded in scripture, and He did this for a reason. He wanted us to hear and obey those same commands. These two verses speak to how we are to handle the financial blessings that God has provided us. See these two important verses given to the Israelites and us.

> You shall not delay to offer from the fullness of your harvest, and from the outflow of your presses. (Exodus 22:29)

> The best of the firstfruits of your ground you shall bring into the house of the LORD your God. (Exodus 23:19)

God does not mince words here. Clearly, He is commanding us (not just suggesting) that we are to give of our financial income to His kingdom work here on earth. And the implication is we are to do this regularly, immediately after "our harvest," and to do so gladly and with thankful hearts. **But the most meaningful thought about this command is that God requires it because He loves us.** He KNOWS better than we do, that if we are obedient in doing this long-term, we come out ahead. We prosper if we do what we clearly know already He wants us to do. God will bless us in ways far beyond our ability to foresee, and in ways far more significant than our "simply keeping more of the money HE enabled us to make."

And we are not the only beneficiary of blessings if we are obedient in bringing our tithes to God's storehouse, the church. Needy people are blessed, kingdom "work" gets accomplished, mission efforts are completed, **and most important of all,** God gets glorified. And God being glorified, His being honored, His being praised, His being worshipped, is the reason we were born. So none of us need ever wonder what God's will is for our lives, He has plainly told us; it's to glorify Him. AND we are to do things that lead other people to feel the same way about glorifying Him (like, for example, giving of our resources to help them when they need help).

And further, we are not to stop with the giving of our financial resources. We are to give more deeply; we are to give of ourselves: our time, our interest, our abilities, our very hearts. That's the kind of example Jesus set for us. And we are to imitate Him in every way we can.

JOHN 11:25-26

This passage finds Jesus speaking to Martha, a friend of His, on the occasion of the death of her brother Lazarus. His words are to encourage her concerning the relationship of death and life for those who believe in Him. She is naturally saddened at her brother's death, but Jesus knows He is about to raise him from the grave, and so He says these words to prepare her for this coming miracle. Shortly after speaking to Martha, Jesus does, in fact, call Lazarus forth from the grave. See Jesus' words to Martha:

> Jesus said to her, "I am the resurrection and the life. Whoever believes in me, though he die, yet shall he live, and everyone who lives and believes in me shall never die."

What an awesome promise Jesus makes! This amazing statement is meant to tie belief in Jesus to the eternal life of that one who believes in Him. Notice again the simplicity of Jesus' statement, but the huge significance of that statement. "Whoever" obviously means this truth is applicable to any person; that's any person in Jesus' day or at any other time, including us in our day. And the requirement for eternal life is simple, that is, belief in Jesus. But what does belief in Jesus really mean? That kind of belief has to do with knowledge of and trust in Jesus as Son of God, who came from heaven to earth to save us from our sins through His sacrificial death on the cross to pay our sin debt.

Notice how Jesus identifies Himself as "the resurrection and the life." He thus claims that He and He only can and does provide the way to eternal life for mankind. He refers to Himself as the way to resurrection from the dead for anyone who believes in Him. Believers then, do die, once, physically, but are raised to new life in Christ to live with Him in heaven for eternity. Jesus words this effectively and clearly, "whoever believes in me, though he die, yet shall he live." And that new life is eternal in scope. And praise the Lord, He also assures us that after their new birth, those believers shall never die.

No man, other than Jesus, can then or now truthfully claim such power and position. And for Him to make such a statement would have to mean one of three things: either He is lying, or He is demented, or His statement is true. Jesus went about healing the sick, casting out demons, and raising the dead to prove He is not lying or demented when He claims to be Son of God. What other conclusion could those people then or we now draw as to His identity other than that He is truly God?

So, our mandate is clear. We are to believe ourselves, and then consistently be about the business of sharing what we know to be true concerning the gospel: that Jesus Christ truly is Lord. And that by God's grace and through faith believers are freely given eternal life. And how could Jesus more effectively have proved His deity than to Himself rise from the grave after His crucifixion.

So the news we have to share is better than good, it is "earth-shaking." Nothing anyone could hear has more important implication for their lives than that eternal life is available for them. Let us go and share what we know about the most important subject in the world.

PSALM 121:1–4

Here is a Psalm titled "My Help Comes from the LORD." It pictures pilgrims making the annual journey back up the hills to Jerusalem to worship. Their take on this journey can be seen as an image of their whole lives, and God's role in their ongoing protection and guidance. So this Psalm is a reminder to them and us of God's love for us all and His provisions for our lives. See how the psalmist conveys the idea that God's care for us is completely seamless, with there being no time or circumstance when He is not in place guarding and guiding us as required.

> I lift up my eyes to the hills.
> From where does my help come?
> My help comes from the LORD,
> who made heaven and earth.
> He will not let your foot be moved;
> he who keeps you will not slumber.
> Behold, he who keeps Israel
> will neither slumber nor sleep. (Psalm 121:1–4)

It may well often seem sometimes as if God is absent from our lives. Troubles and stress pile up on us continually, with no end in sight. Thus did the journey back to Jerusalem seem long and uphill all the way. So we can picture the analogy the psalmist is making. Like the psalmist we can be confident God knows our situations and is ever ready to be of appropriate help, in small things and large. And though God is there for us in small ways, no problem is too large, for our Lord made heaven and earth.

The key point in the psalmist's message is **he recognizes his help comes from the Lord, and he goes to Him for help.** When Jesus gave us His model prayer, He started it with the sentence,

"Our Father in heaven, hallowed be your name." From the outset Jesus orients us to the proper source of our help. Just so the psalmist also sends us to the Lord for help. The old-time hymn writer got it right when he wrote "What a Friend We Have in Jesus," saying, "O what peace we often forfeit, O what needless pain we bear, all because we do not carry, everything to God in prayer."

So the psalmist has good news for us, his readers. As believers and children of God, we (spiritual Israel) do not lack for God's full-time, detailed attention. And His attention comes with the love and power necessary to tend to our needs completely. How foolish are we if we fail to seek His help and direction in all things?

1 Peter 3:10–12

In this passage Peter is writing to believers, encouraging them to persevere in their faith. All believers in every era need such encouragement, for all believers suffer for their faith. The Holy Spirit led Peter to draw from Psalm 34 (written by King David) for an example of how God delivers righteous believers in the midst of their suffering. And God still delivers believers:

> Whoever desires to love life
>> and see good days,
> let him keep his tongue from evil
>> and his lips from speaking deceit;
> let him turn away from evil and do good;
>> let him seek peace and pursue it.
> For the eyes of the Lord are on the righteous,
>> and his ears are open to their prayer.
> But the face of the Lord is against those who do evil. (1 Peter 3:10–13)

All of us desire to love life and see good days. And Peter gives us the godly wisdom to achieve that. Obedience then is inherently required for us to experience God's blessings. Notice what is required of us. We are to keep our tongues from evil and our lips from speaking deceit. Thus, our association with other people and the how and why of it are key markers for us to measure by. Evil and deceit both come in many forms, all of which are prohibited. Yet such sinful speech doesn't come forth unless our thoughts our evil and deceitful.

And not only are we to stop evil thinking and deeds; we are to start positive and good thinking and deeds. We, therefore, are to be proactive in our thoughts and actions. Simply put, we are to turn away from evil and do good, two thought processes, two decisions, and two actions.

And apparently peace should be more desirable than it is for most of us. Notice we are to both seek peace and pursue it. When we seek something the implication is we don't know where (or what) it is. When we pursue something the concept indicates we have defined it, and maybe we can even see it, but it is not yet within reach. **So we have to define (God's) peace and then we have to locate its source.**

And the reason we have to guard our thoughts, and our speech, and our actions is God has His eyes on us, and His ears are open to our prayers. Remember Peter is writing to believers, like us, who are theoretically righteous individuals. So, the lesson for us is, even saved individuals experience confusion, fear, doubt, and sin, and God knows that. Thus, He has provided for those conditions within our lives. His provisions involve (1) His Word, scripture designed to provide God's revelation of Himself and His love, (2) His Holy Spirit, who is available to both educate us on the truth of scripture and guide us as to our thoughts, words, and actions, and (3) prayer, that line of communication between God and man He has made possible at any time and from anywhere.

And yet even with the power, wisdom, and love God saturates us with, there are those who don't believe, those who deny the truth they've heard, those who refuse to obey, and those who don't understand that consistent obedience is the real evidence of belief. See how God's relationship with them is described: "The face of the Lord is against those who do evil." We don't have a complete feel for the significance of having the face of the Lord against us, but we do know we don't want any part of that. And we don't have to have any part of it, for Christ's death paid all our sin debt, in and for all time.

ROMANS 10:14-15

The gospel of Jesus has been designed by almighty God to acquaint the whole world with His steadfast love. This gospel relates a chain of events concerning how it is that a person is saved. For a person to be saved means for them to be transformed (while in this world) in such a way that their eternal destiny becomes one of an eternity with God rather than an eternity separated from God. This comes about when someone establishes a saving relationship with Jesus Christ. The gospel then is a truth or set of truths that God wants communicated to the world. See how God has led Paul, the author of Romans, to describe this (only) way to eternal life.

> How then will they call on him in whom they have not believed? And how are they to believe in him of whom they have never heard? And how are they to hear without someone preaching? And how are they to preach unless they are sent? (Romans 10:14–15)

Notice how Paul brings this most important truth the world has ever heard down to a series of four statements:

1. People will call on Jesus to save them only if they believe He can do so.
2. Belief in Jesus cannot exist without knowledge about Him.
3. People hear about Jesus only when someone, somehow, proclaims the gospel message.
4. The message about Jesus will not be proclaimed unless someone is sent by God to do so.

So it is belief in Jesus that makes the difference. But it is real belief we are talking about, sincere belief that leads to life-changing commitments to Him, and a heartfelt relationship with Him. Our response then to someone coming and sharing the gospel of Jesus with us, is to be one of trust and faith in Jesus as our Savior and Lord.

Jesus is real. The gospel is not a fairy tale. Jesus' death on the cross in our place happened. God's provision for the forgiveness of our sins required the satisfaction of His wrath (over our sin). And that satisfaction involved a perfect sacrifice; and there was only one perfect sacrifice, God's Son, Jesus Christ. It's no wonder Jesus is referred to as the "Lamb of God."

So per the passage above someone must be sent to share the gospel. And someone must go. Jesus' last words on earth before He ascended to heaven involve Him sending you and me, and His telling you and me to go. God's method of getting the good news of Jesus to the world involves individuals talking to other individuals. Every believer is assigned that task. To begin, decide who you most care about in this world and talk to them about their relationship with Jesus. You could not show your love in a better way. That's why I'm writing to you.

1 THESSALONIANS 5:19–22

Paul is writing to the Christians in the church at Thessalonica with counsel on how to live according to God's Word. So, he lists key habits for them to form and what to do with the truth they find in scripture. The Bible provides us eternal truth, good in the first century and good today. Nothing of the truth of scripture has changed through the years. We are wise not to try to apply modern-day logic and standards to what we see in scripture. Our society needs God's original truth just as much as the society of Paul's day. Look at his words:

> Do not quench the Spirit. Do not despise prophecies, but test everything; hold fast what is good. Abstain from every form of evil. (1 Thessalonians 5:19–22)

"Do not quench the Spirit" is a scary thought. To quench the Spirit is to ignore the Spirit's counsel and direction. It means an individual knows the will of the Spirit and deliberately ignores it. And it means not to just ignore the Spirit but to work against the Spirit's teachings, trying to extinguish it. Surely no one with any knowledge of scripture at all will purposefully try to quench the Spirit. Those who do are Satan inspired, for it is his goal to eliminate all scriptural instructions.

And we are not to "despise prophecies." Certain believers are given the gift of prophecy, but not unbelievers. And we are to listen to those believers else we miss information God would have us hear. To despise prophecy is to deny it, to not regard it as truth, and to ignore its warnings. To hear prophecy certainly means we are with other believers and that we are open to hearing God's word from them. The only way we can be with other believers is to associate with them, to gather with them periodically, and to give credence to what we hear from them.

But notice the next instruction. We are to test what we hear from prophets. That means we must have some standard to lay down beside what we hear to measure its authenticity. That standard can only be the Word of God. It does no good to judge one individual's words, or even our own words, by comparing them with another individual's words, for neither one can be considered the ultimate truth. And we deceive ourselves when we do that. Only God's Word can be considered valid and worthy of our belief and obedience. Thus, the Bible (all of it) must be our standard and source of instruction.

Paul does not stop even here. He goes further to make his point. He urges all believers not only to listen to prophets, but to test their words, and after testing to hold fast to what is good. That is, hold on to those words that pass the scriptural test. And surely, "hold fast to what is good" implies we live out those principles in our daily lives.

And Paul sums up his instructions in the last verse. We are to abstain from every form of evil. As we live in accord with the Holy Spirit's direction, listening to other God-fearing believers, measuring their words by God's Word, holding on to what we hear that is in accord with scripture, we turn back from all forms of evil. In its very essence that is how Jesus lived. Thus, Paul is leading us toward Christlikeness. And in its purest form Christlikeness glorifies our heavenly Father and that's why we were born.

1 JOHN 3:16–18

This passage discusses how believers are to love one another. Such a concept is to be taken as a given for Christians, but to live out that approach to life is often difficult. Some people are simply hard to love, but this passage covers them too. Jesus did not differentiate among people as to whom He chose to love, nor should we. John points out Jesus as that example for us to follow, and how He lived such that His life spoke of His love as much as did His words. That is to be our goal too.

> By this we know love, that he laid down his life for us, and we ought to lay down our lives for the brothers. But if anyone has the world's goods and sees his brother in need, yet closes his heart against him, how does God's love abide in him? Little children, let us not love in word or talk but in deed and in truth. (1 John 3:16–18)

John's first point here is a critical one: "by this we know love." What follows is proof that Christ did, in fact, truly love us. "He laid down his life for us." And thus, we can know that. We are not to question it, or doubt it, or forget it, or take it for granted. We can know Christ loves us. We can be confident of that, we can base our life (and our eternity) on that fact, and we can, with integrity, share that truth with others. Scripture assures us of the validity of the fact that sacrificial death in our place is the ultimate proof of love. See John 15:13: "Greater love has no one than this, that someone lay down his life for his friends."

And Jesus did that gladly under the most horrendous of conditions. John provides us the proper conclusion to draw from these facts: we ought to lay down our lives for the brothers. It's an obvious conclusion, but a difficult one to execute. Sometimes it might even be more difficult to live for our friends than to die for them. John adds an example of living for others, the giving of material goods to meet physical needs of the "brothers" (other believers). We are thus to live with our eyes open and our hearts sensitive to the needs of those around us.

Thoughtlessly ignoring the needs of people around us (that we could easily provide) is the ultimate example of our attempting to deny them the love of God. God does love them and if we don't avail ourselves of the opportunity to express God's love to them, He will use other people to help them and we miss the opportunity to exhibit Christlikeness.

It's interesting that John refers to his readers as "little children." That has to be a "love" expression that he feels for them. No doubt they are often in his prayers and on his heart. It's good for any of us to feel that way for other people. It's indicative of a kinship in Christ that will only get closer in heaven.

We think and we say we love others and John reminds his readers and us to put that love in motion. God would have us be His hands and feet in this world showing His love to the world. It is so easy to get caught up in the rush of our own world and forget or not notice those around us and their needs. God notices our needs and we need to be open to fulfilling His love for others by acting as His ministers.

HEBREWS 13:15–16

In the letter to the Hebrews we find a beautiful description of Jesus Christ as Messiah, Savior, Son of God and King of Kings. The unknown author surely knew Jesus as who He is. The Holy Spirit used him to encourage Jewish believers in their faith to better enable them to face the challenges of their times in ways that glorified their heavenly Father. We need such encouragement as well. See how the Holy Spirit words His message to us:

> Through him then let us continually offer up a sacrifice of praise to God, that is, the fruit of lips that acknowledge his name. Do not neglect to do good and to share what you have, for such sacrifices are pleasing to God. (Hebrews 13:15–16)

Through Jesus Christ, and because of what He has done for us, we are to lift up verbal praises to God. In the first century people worshipped God by bringing animals to the priests to sacrifice to God, thereby receiving forgiveness for their sins. We are told in our day to bring verbal sacrifices of praise to God. Jesus' model prayer begins by teaching us to do the same thing. "Our Father in heaven, hallowed be your name" (Matthew 6:9).

Think about those words. No matter what we do we surely cannot make God's name (or Him) any more hallowed than He already is. What we can do, and are told to do in Jesus' prayer and in this passage from Hebrews, is to acknowledge how hallowed God is. We do that by actually considering, praying, and saying praise words aloud. Thus, the fruit of our lips begins to over time reflect our relationship to God and gradually bring us to know and love Him more. Certainly if we begin to truly see God in this manner, we will take His Word to heart and become more obedient to His commands.

So, it is not a coincidence that we are first told to praise God and then told to do good, which would naturally follow our thinking more accurately and more often about God and His nature. So our act of praising God is a lot more profound than we might think, and by definition is bound to affect how we see and treat those around us. One obvious way to do good is to share what we have. When we truly realize Who has provided what we have, then such sharing commands are easier to obey. After all, if God loves those around us (as He loves us) does it not follow that we should be sensitive to their needs?

And amazingly, we are told such sacrifices are pleasing to God. We see two obvious facts from that condition; first, God must be somehow monitoring everything we do and why. And second, apparently, we can do things that God enjoys. Imagine God being so sensitive to the thoughts and actions of everyone who has ever lived and that each one of us has the potential even in our small ways to bring joy to almighty God.

When you think about it, we are given some huge opportunities and responsibilities. The chance to bring help to other people is pretty awesome itself, but to realize how such actions bring joy to God is "off the chart" wonderful.

2 CORINTHIANS 2:14–17

As traveling missionaries, Paul and Timothy made their way throughout the known world of the first century. They particularly covered the areas including present-day Turkey, Greece, and Italy. Preaching the gospel of Jesus Christ wherever they went, and as led by the Holy Spirit, they established churches in a number of major cities, Corinth, Greece being one. Paul often felt led to later write letters to some of these churches answering questions they had and encouraging them to stay strong in their faith. In this letter to the church at Corinth Paul covers the subject of suffering for Christ's sake. See Paul's take on his own ministry and how it might well be applied in our ministries today:

> But thanks be to God, who in Christ always leads us in triumphal procession, and through us spreads the fragrance of the knowledge of him everywhere. For we are the aroma of Christ to God among those who are being saved and those who are perishing, to one a fragrance from death to death, to the other a fragrance from life to life. Who is sufficient for those things? For we are not, like so many peddlers of God's word, but as men of sincerity, as commissioned by God, in the sight of God we speak in Christ. (2 Corinthians 2:14–17)

Believe it or not, one of the criticisms against Paul by his opponents is that he had suffered too much during his ministry to be considered a true servant of the Lord. This, as if God would not allow a true servant to suffer so. Paul admitted his suffering, but took that as God's way to encourage other believers, who were also suffering, to stay the course of faith in Christ. Paul saw the gospel of Jesus he and Timothy taught as a "fragrance" of truth that was believed by some and thus led them from life (here on earth) to life (eternal, in heaven with the Lord). Others, having heard the same truths, rejected that fragrance (truth) and went from physical death on earth to eternal death (separation from God).

Paul admitted to not understanding all of God's purposes, but he thanked God for the success he had seen. He did point out that he did not require payment for their ministry as some of his opponents did. He saw his ministry and Timothy's as a sincere reflection of their commission from God to take the gospel to nations. And that is the Great Commission we have too.

So, what about us and our expenditures of time, energy, money, and "heart" in kingdom work? What are we to expect, and how are we to consistently respond to successes and failures (however those may play out in our lives)? Notice Paul thanks God for always leading us in triumphal procession. If we consistently live our lives as the aroma of Christ as Paul and Timothy did, apparently there is no such thing as eternal failure. We may not see and think of our lives as one long string of successful Christian experiences, but then we don't know the full, long-term effect of our influence. God controls the results of our lives. What He wants from us is ongoing, sincere belief and obedience to what we know already to be His will. And that shows up in our lives as love for the Lord and love for others. If we get our love priorities in order, God can and will work out the triumphal processions we experience.

We already have the necessary knowledge Paul talks about. We can spread it everywhere as He did. Paul and Timothy had to pretty much walk wherever they went. We have cars, planes, email, the Postal Service, and telephones, etc., to spread the same "fragrance of the knowledge of Jesus" Paul was preaching. Let us take to heart the commission we've been given as he and Timothy did.

PROVERBS 2:20-22

This passage is part of the section in Proverbs 2 covering "The Value of Wisdom," and describes the destiny of believers by depicting the ultimate outcome of obedience. So think eternally when you read these verses, think not just of this present life, but heaven beyond for believers.

> So you will walk in the way of the good
>> and keep to the paths of the righteous.
> For the upright will inhabit the land,
>> and those with integrity will remain in it,
> but the wicked will be cut off from the land,
>> and the treacherous will be rooted out of it. (Proverbs 2:20–22)

"The way of the good" and "the path of the righteous" refer to the same thing: the lifestyles of obedient believers. They are truly good and always righteous. They consistently seek and live per God's will and for His glory. God's wisdom has already taught them the "why" of such living (to gain goodness and righteousness), but also the benefits of it. So how do we achieve real goodness and true righteousness?

In the first place we need to remember God loves us with a steadfast (eternal) love. And because He does, we can be sure He will lead believers toward all the good and righteousness of His kingdom because He always wants the best for us. "Good" refers to praiseworthy character conforming to God's moral order for the world, and "righteous" describes those who live according to God's laws. Thus, as we live per God's wisdom, He rewards us with His goodness and His righteousness that the world will recognize as coming from Him. The author (probably King David) titles those people as "upright" and "those who walk with integrity." Notice their destiny is prophesied as "inhabiting the land (heaven)" and "remaining in it." Hallelujah!

On the other hand, the "wicked" (both a noun and an adjective, reflecting a person who causes or is likely to cause harm, distress, or trouble) and the "treacherous" (those characterized as likely to violate allegiance, faith, or confidence) will be cut off from heaven. It's one thing to think that this is as it should be, that is, the obedient rewarded, and the disobedient condemned. But it is quite another to dwell on the significance of those conclusions. Heaven will be infinitely wonderful (eternally), and to be condemned will be the complete opposite (also eternally).

So for both reasons our assignments are critical. When Jesus tells us to go and make disciples, we need to consider He knows these two eternal consequences are mankind's only options. **And the world needs to know that.** Having been given God's free gift of salvation we are privileged and commanded to go and tell others.

NUMBERS 22

God gets involved with things in this world when He needs to accomplish His will. That's what happened in this story in the Bible book called Numbers. This is a true story about two men, one named King Balak, king of the country of Moab, and the other man's name was Balaam. Balaam was a prophet, which means that from time to time, God used him to teach other people lessons He wanted them to learn.

God had decided to bless a group of people called Israelites as His favored nation. They still exist today as the nation of Israel. At the time of this story God had directed the Israelites to move to a new land that He had provided for them. There were about two million of them, so it was a very big deal for them to pack up and move families, livestock, and everything they owned to the new land about five hundred miles away. It took over forty years for them to travel that far. That many people slowly making their way over hills and valleys attracted the attention of other nations who lived along their path.

Some of these other nations tried to stop them from passing through their territory and they had many small battles along the way. One of those countries that objected to them going through their country was the country of Moab. The king of Moab, Balak, was afraid of the Israelites, and decided to get Balaam to come and put a curse on the Israelites. Balak knew that Balaam was close to God and wanted him to ask God to call down a curse on the Israelites to keep them from passing through His kingdom because he knew his small army was not strong enough to stop them. So he sent some men to fetch Balaam and get him to come and see the Israelites for himself and place that curse on them.

As Balaam got ready to travel, he saddled his favorite donkey and with a few servants started out on the journey to meet Balak.

But Israel was a chosen nation of God, and He did not want Balaam to put a curse on them. So God sent an angel of the Lord to stand in the road ahead of them with a sword in his hand. The donkey could see the angel, but Balaam could not. So the donkey was afraid of the angel and turned off the road into the fields, and that made Balaam mad. He had a rod and began to beat the donkey, and made him get back on the road. Then the donkey saw the angel again and got over to one side of the road as far as he could against a wall and mashed Balaam's leg against the wall. This really made Balaam mad, and he began to beat the donkey again. As the donkey began to move forward again, he saw the angel for the third time and just laid down in the middle of the road. As you can imagine Balaam still could not see the angel and he began to beat the donkey again.

This time God performed a miracle and gave the donkey a voice. He could talk. So the donkey asked Balaam why he was beating him. Balaam said, "Because you won't obey me." And then the donkey told Balaam, "I have been your donkey for years and have never disobeyed you before, have I?" And Balaam answered, "No." **Then God opened Balaam's eyes and he could see the angel, and he bowed down before the angel. And he said, "I have sinned and done wrong to beat the donkey. I will turn back and not go put a curse on the Israelites."**

But the angel told Balaam, "No, go ahead and see King Balak, but do not curse the Israelites, but bless them for they are my chosen people and I have many plans for them." So that's what Balaam did.

God has plans for us, too, and sometimes we make mistakes as to what those are. That's why we need to read the Bible and pray often to better understand exactly what God wants us to do.

REVELATION 5:11–14

John the apostle is writing to churches within Asia (present-day Turkey), describing heaven to his readers. This particular passage reflects the scene around the throne of God and the worship that happens there. Our heavenly Father is described as He "who sits on the throne," and Jesus as "the Lamb who was slain." John had been told to write down what he saw, and this book of Revelation is the result. We cannot truly grasp the significance of this scene, but we do get a clear picture of the worshipful atmosphere around the throne. Maybe that's what God wants us to picture heaven will be like.

> Then I looked, and I heard around the throne and the living creatures and the elders the voice of many angels, numbering myriads of myriads and thousands of thousands, saying with a loud voice,
>
> "Worthy is the Lamb who was slain,
> to receive power and wealth and wisdom and might
> and honor and glory and blessing!"
>
> And I heard every creature in heaven and on earth and under the earth and in the sea, and all that is in them, saying,
>
> "To him who sits on the throne and to the Lamb be blessing and honor and glory and might forever and ever!"
>
> And the four living creatures said, "Amen!" and the elders fell down and worshiped. (Revelation 5:11–14)

John had been told to take notice of what was happening, and he does. Imagine what hearing and seeing myriads of myriads and thousands of thousands of angels are saying will be like. Myriad has the connotation of numberless, but very large. In our minds the message should be hundreds of millions and/or without number. Notice they are all saying the same thing, "Worthy is the Lamb who was slain, to receive power and wealth and wisdom and might and honor glory, and blessing!" A sevenfold tribute (seven being the perfect number).

And it's not just the angels that John hears. Every creature that has ever been born (anywhere) recognizes the Father and Jesus Christ as the appropriate and only two worthy of such praise. This group is heard proclaiming that the Father and Jesus are to receive blessing, honor, glory, and might forever and ever. So, it's all of God's creation that is "sold out" to Him and Jesus in worship. If we just consider humans, we know there are about eight billion people alive today in the world, thus, at least several multiples of eight billion have been born. So, the scene John is describing is enormous, and really beyond our imagination. **The point is that the Father and Jesus have always existed, and always will exist and they do and always will merit our praise and worship.**

Are these figures and this description to be taken literally or are they simply symbolic of the magnitude and all-encompassing nature of the Father and Jesus' worthiness of all our adoration, obedience, and praise? We cannot be sure, but we can know if they are not to be taken literally and are symbolic, they are symbolic of something truly magnificent and far beyond our imagination. And we can be sure that as we believers participate in such worship (here on earth and later eternally in heaven) we are blessed and favored indeed.

Thus, the Holy Spirit did not show John every detail of heaven, nor give us enough information to answer all our questions. But He did clearly indicate the Father and Jesus are worthy of all our love, obedience, and worship. That's the message we are to both remember and to share with others.

HEBREWS 6:13–18

When we read of God's promises in scripture, we can be absolutely sure He will fulfill them. If that were not true, then nothing God says to us in scripture would be worth reading. But since it is all true, we believers are assured of eternal salvation, and we are therefore well advised to trust our whole lives to Him. A classic example of these promises is God's promise to Abraham that He would make of him a great nation (Genesis 12:1–3). **This passage in Hebrews reflects the basis upon which we can be sure of our salvation.**

> For when God made a promise to Abraham, since he had no one greater by whom to swear, he swore by himself, saying, "Surely I will bless you and multiply you." And thus Abraham, having patiently waited, obtained the promise. For people swear by something greater than themselves, and in all their disputes an oath is final for confirmation. So when God desired to show more convincingly to the heirs of the promise the unchangeable character of His purpose, He guaranteed it with an oath, so that by two unchangeable things, in which it is impossible for God to lie, we who have fled for refuge might have strong encouragement to hold fast to the hope set before us. (Hebrews 6:13–18)

The two unchangeable things referred to (that we can count on as being rock-solid truths) are God's promise (He cannot lie), and His oath (nothing is greater than He is to swear by). So when we "flee to God for refuge" we have strong encouragement to "hold fast" to the faith we have concerning Jesus' substitutionary death on our behalf. Everything that has been said of Him in scripture is true and worthy of our belief and commitment.

So we can clearly see how our salvation comes down, not to any deeds on our part (many good ones, and no bad ones), but to our faith in the truth of God's Word. Are His promises and His oath valid? Is Jesus Christ who scripture says He is, and did He do and say all scripture describes?

No matter our level of education and sophistication, no matter our good intentions, and no matter the status of those around us, the "bottom line" question for each of us is, have we truly fled to Jesus Christ for our eternal refuge? Have we acknowledged we are sinners in need of a Savior? Have we trusted Jesus' sacrificial death on the cross as payment of our sin debt? Do our lives reflect these commitments?

Abraham was childless at the time God made His promises to him. And he did not live long enough to see them fulfilled. Yet he, by faith, was obedient to God, and we know God did fulfill His promise to him. As believers we may or we may not live long peaceful lives. We may or may not live out our faith seeing evidence of God's involvement every day. And we may or we may not experience great worldly success. But as obedient believers, if, like Abraham, we patiently wait, we will obtain the promise. God will bless and multiply us by His definition of blessing and multiplication. **And we can hold fast to the hope set before us.**

2 Corinthians 5:10

Our God is a just God, He is also a loving God, a merciful, and forgiving God; all these in abundance. The fact that we cannot completely grasp all of God's characteristics, or how they all, taken together, make up His nature, does not lessen their extent or their impact on us and the world. In this verse Paul is calling attention to the final judgment that everyone will face. So, no matter our talents, circumstances, or location, God would have us glorify Him in all we do. We don't do that naturally, it's a committed lifestyle we take on by faith when we come to know Jesus Christ as Savior and Lord. Paul is writing to the church at Corinth, Greece, whose members were a lot like us, often not living up to the standards they know they should. See Paul's description of that final judgment:

> For we must all appear before the judgment seat of Christ, so that each one may receive what is due for what he has done in the body, whether good or evil. (2 Corinthians 5:10)

Notice we must appear before the judgment seat of Christ. We have no choice in the matter. That judging process could take the equivalent of five minutes, or five years, or more, but we can be sure it will be thorough. And Jesus himself will be our judge. John 5:22–23 clearly points that out: "The Father judges no one, but has given all judgment to the Son, that all may honor the Son, just as they honor the Father."

Certainly, the implication in 2 Corinthians 5:10 is that everything we have done will be evaluated. Nothing will be left out, and that evaluation will be perfect. Jesus' judgment will not just be of everything we've done, but also of the "why" of our actions or omissions. God's justice will see to that. We won't be able to claim God does not love us or was not merciful. How could anyone make such claims in light of God's action as He sent His Son Jesus to die in our place, thereby making atonement for all our sins available if we but believe?

Thus, heaven is ours to lose. God's love is such that He provided everything possible for us to spend eternity there with Him. He sent His Holy Spirit to indwell us to remind us of all Jesus said and did, and even had it all recorded in His Word for us to read and obey.

We won't be witnessing to people in heaven trying to convince them of Jesus' identity and love. No one will be there who doesn't already know that. Heaven for us then will be living out the relationship with Christ we established while we were alive on earth. Thus, there are long-term consequences for what we do (or don't do) here on earth, and our choice of eternity is defined when we die an earthly death. There are only two choices of eternal destinies available for everyone: to be with Christ in heaven, or to be separated from Him. The judgment discussed in this passage has to do with the rewards due believers that will be experienced for eternity. Details of how that will play out are not provided us in this life. This because, God would rather we "walk by faith and not by sight" (2 Corinthians 5:7). Who among us could possibly doubt that what the Father and Jesus are preparing for us in heaven will be anything but glorious beyond our imagination?

REVELATION 14:9–13

Here, John the apostle is following God's instructions and recording the visions of heaven that he has been given. This particular passage contrasts the eternal destiny of unbelievers with that destiny in store for believers. These descriptions are likely symbolic, but are still accurate pictures of the torment due unbelievers (forever) and the blessings that believers will receive (also forever). Thus, we in our day are wise to see these as warnings for us. See the two destinies spelled out:

> "If anyone worships the beast and its image and receives a mark on his forehead or on his hand, he also will drink the wine of God's wrath, poured full strength into the cup of his anger, and he will be tormented with fire and sulfur in the presence of the holy angels and in the presence of the Lamb. And the smoke of their torment goes up forever and ever, and they have no rest, day or night, these worshipers of the beast and its image, and whoever receives the mark of its name." Here is a call for the endurance of the saints, those who keep the commandments of God and their faith in Jesus.
>
> And I heard a voice from heaven saying, "Write this: Blessed, are the dead who die in the Lord from now on." "Blessed indeed," says the Spirit, "that they may rest from their labors, for their deeds follow them!" (Revelation 14:9–13)

Notice how vivid the description is of the punishment of unbelievers who worship the beast (representative of Satan). "They will drink the wine of God's wrath, poured full strength into the cup of God's anger." That punishment is not clear, but what is clear is that we don't want any part of that. And what could the words "and the smoke of their torment goes up forever and ever" mean but that their torment with fire will go on forever as the angels and the Lamb (Jesus Christ) watch. "And they will have no rest, day or night." Thus, their suffering will never stop.

Then John gives us a description of the destiny of believers. They are urged to endure and keep God's commandments and their faith in Jesus (the Lamb). The voice from heaven mentioned has to be the Lord speaking to John. That voice ensures believers they will be blessed and find rest. Again John leaves the definition of some words to our imagination. We don't know exactly what "blessed" and "rest" in the Lord entails, but we can be sure that it will be wonderful. A believer's obedience will be rewarded per God's definition of rewards; again, beyond what we can imagine.

In short, our God loves us enough to provide clear instructions as to how He wants us to live. And He lists both the punishments and rewards due us given the choices we make. How foolish we are to deny God's Word, not believing the warnings and promises He has provided.

Unfortunately, there are many in this world who have never heard these warnings. And that's where we come in. God loves us and those who have never heard the gospel. And He has assigned us to go and make disciples of those who have not yet been blessed with knowledge as we have. And those people are everywhere. Yes, some are in other countries, but some live next door. Thus, the options to share what we know lie before us. God would have us "go and tell."

COLOSSIANS 3:12-14

Here Paul is describing what a Christian looks like to the world as they "put on" Christlike characteristics. Believers now have a new heavenly home, but they still exist first in this world, and are to live such that other people see Christ in them. The Colossian readers (and we believers now) are to live holy lifestyles consistent with our new relationship with Christ. The whole of Christianity is built around Jesus Christ, His deity, His perfection, His righteousness, and His love for us reflected in His atoning sacrifice on the cross. See this passage for standards for us to take on as we glorify God here on earth:

> Put on then, as God's chosen ones, holy and beloved, compassionate hearts, kindness, humility, meekness, and patience, bearing with one another and, if one has a complaint against another, forgiving each other; as the Lord has forgiven you, so you must also forgive. And above all these put on love, which binds everything together in perfect harmony. (Colossians 3:12–14)

Because we believers have been chosen by God we have been judged to be holy and beloved, and given other characteristics such as compassionate hearts, kindness, humility, meekness, and patience. We live these out by bearing with one another, forgiving one another, and above all, loving one another. Thus, Paul's point is, if Christ is really our Savior and Lord, and if we are truly given over to His will for our lives, then we will strive for Christlikeness in all we do, say, and are.

After all, it is God almighty who has eternally chosen us. The One Who created all that is and Who will come again to take us to heaven to live with Him eternally. Just imagine, as believers, **God**

has selected us, made us holy, and loves us already with a steadfast love. So, we are to take off our old self, put on His likeness, and live out His commands as we make disciples for His glory.

Notice the mandate in this passage to forgive others. How could we not forgive others who offend us, given the extent to which God has forgiven us? Our perspective on our old self has to include the realistic awareness of how unworthy we were of God's grace, that love God has for us that we don't deserve. And yet God loved us anyway from the beginning, knowing we would still keep on sinning after conversion.

It is amazing how consistent scripture is. Over and over again, God has the biblical authors (who lived hundreds of years apart) hammer home the principle of love. We see it emphasized here and in many other passages. For example, see John 13:34–35: "A new commandment I give to you, that you love one another: just as I have loved you, you also are to love one another. By this all people will know that you are my disciples, if you have love for one another."

Don't we want the title of a disciple of Christ? Don't we want other people to recognize us as Christ followers? **Here is the way to achieve that reputation: love one another and live out that love. People will take notice and God will be glorified.** So, let us live as Paul urges the Colossians, with compassionate hearts, kindly, and humble before and with all others, and with meekness and patience, forgiving others as we have been forgiven. Note: God loves us enough to tell us how to be what He wants us to be.

MARK 8:38

Believers have a responsibility (and a privilege) to live out their faith now, in this world, in their lives daily, in whatever they are involved in, and wherever they go. No place, no time, and no circumstance is excluded. In Matthew 28:20 we read where Jesus tells us, "Behold, I am with you always, to the end of the age." We usually take that to mean Jesus is always available to protect and assist us wherever we are. And that is very true. Just as true is the concept that Jesus is always with us in a monitoring role. He knows where we are, what we are experiencing, and what we are thinking and doing at all times. And He also knows "why" we do everything we do. Thus, Jesus is always there seeing our mistakes, our failures, and our sins. Notice Jesus' comments relative to our activities:

> For whoever is ashamed of me and my words in this adulterous and sinful generation, of him will the Son of Man also be ashamed when he comes in the glory of his Father with the holy angels. (Mark 8:38)

Jesus has all authority and will be judge and jury one day as He evaluates all our lives. Clearly the passage tells us one day Jesus will return with every bit of the glory of the Father accompanied by the holy angels. We are not sure what that looks like, but we can be sure it will be the most noteworthy event mankind ever experiences, for it involves every human being, and has eternal implications. It precedes that final judgment where Jesus judges us per Ecclesiastes 12:14: "For God will bring every deed into judgment, with every secret thing, whether good or evil."

Notice in Mark 8:38 Jesus discusses the concept of how we interact with the world with regard to our allegiance to Him.

Notice, too, worldly interaction on our part governs how God will judge us. And it's "like for like"; if we are ashamed of Him, He will be ashamed of us. It's scary to go very far in considering what God being ashamed of us involves. But let us go back some. We need not worry about the definition of "God being ashamed of us," if we are not ever ashamed of Him.

Therefore, the key question for us is, "What does our not being ashamed of Jesus in this world involve?" First and foremost, it involves our being led by the Holy Spirit. If we are so led, we will not ever be ashamed of God before the world. In fact, quite the opposite is true. True believers live looking for witness and service opportunities.

How did God know our generation would be adulterous and sinful? One, He is God, and two, every generation is adulterous and sinful. So in our adulterous and sinful generation we are to live with Jesus on display. It's like we put a "Jesus is Lord" sign around our neck every day for all the world to see. Wouldn't that be something? Think of the potential results such a bold act would create. We get the idea. We are to live "sold out," "all in" lives before God and the world with the Holy Spirit guiding.

JOHN 3:31-34

John 3 is a very significant chapter of the Bible. Within it are a number of references to God's love for the world resulting in His sending His Son, Jesus Christ, into the world to save us from our sins. What better or more significant news could we receive than that? Eternal life originates with God, and **He has provided it.** The whole world now has direct access to heaven and eternal existence there with God. This, via Jesus' sacrificial death on the cross in our place. See how the Holy Spirit has led John the apostle to describe this to us:

> He who comes from above is above all. He who is of the earth belongs to the earth and speaks in an earthly way. He who comes from heaven is above all. He bears witness to what he has seen and heard, yet no one receives his testimony. Whoever receives his testimony sets his seal to this, that God is true. For he whom God has sent utters the words of God, for he gives the Spirit without measure. (John 3:31–34)

"He who comes from above is above all." That can only be a reference to Jesus Christ and His position relative to us. He resided in heaven and at the appointed time came from there down to earth. And when He arrived His words and life reflected His heavenly identify and background. Only He could define heaven for only He had been there and come to earth. And only He could describe, illustrate, and provide our route to heaven.

Notice though, the verse says, "yet no one receives His testimony." This is a reference to the fact that of the many people who experienced Jesus on earth, only a very few believed in Him. Many saw Him, heard His teachings, witnessed His miracles, watched Him die, and later saw Him resurrected, all without trusting Him as Son of God and Messiah. We wonder how this could be. We say, "How blind could those people be?" And yet we, who know the end of the story, still do not have the faith we should have, we are not out and about sharing this gospel of Jesus to a lost world as we should be.

The passage tells us, however, that those who do receive Jesus' testimony "set their seal to this, that God is true." That is, those who believe in Christ do authenticate His identity as Son of God by their lifestyles. They demonstrate their faith by their priorities, they show their love for Him by their love for others, and they obey Christ by making disciples wherever they go.

And why would we not do the same thing? Jesus came from God and utters the words of God, and God has provided Him "His Spirit without measure." Thus, Jesus came and lived on earth totally in sync with the Father and the Spirit, showing us the Father, and illustrating the way to eternal life. And in the end, Jesus went to the cross to die in our place, thereby paying our sin debt and providing us access to God's free gift, life eternal in heaven with Him. There is no greater gift He could provide.

TITUS 2:11–14

This letter from the apostle Paul to his disciple Titus was written during the mid-sixties AD to encourage him in his faith. The emphasis in the letter is the connection between our faith and our lifestyles, our beliefs and our behavior. Certainly, what we believe is best reflected in how we live. If Jesus Christ is truly Lord of our lives that fact will be apparent to those who know us. Thus, this letter is as relevant in our day as it was in the first century. Paul had left Titus in Crete to minister to the church there. The good news of the gospel of Christ remains unchanged from then until now. So, Paul's instructions to Titus for the Crete church are appropriate for us too:

> For the grace of God has appeared, bringing salvation for all people, training us to renounce ungodliness and worldly passions, and to live self-controlled, upright, and godly lives in the present age, waiting for our blessed hope, the appearing of the glory of our great God and Savior Jesus Christ, who gave himself for us to redeem us from all lawlessness and to purify for himself a people for his own possession who are zealous for good works. (Titus 2:11–14)

This passage does not teach that all people will be saved, but that salvation **is available to everyone who will believe in Christ.** So, anyone, at any time, can turn to Christ in sincere repentance of their sins and receive forgiveness of their sins and be given the free gift of eternal life. Notice the difference accepting Christ makes in someone's life. They renounce worldly passions and live self-controlled, upright, and godly lives right where they are.

And they live such lives patiently waiting for the return of Jesus. Paul even includes the qualifications Jesus has that make only

Him the appropriate sacrifice to pay our sin debt. He is described as our blessed hope and the glory of our great God and Savior. Thus, His sacrificial death redeemed us from all lawlessness and purified us as His personal possession. And that new relationship all believers have as children of God provides them zealousness for good works. We will, therefore, want to obey God, we will want other people to see Jesus Christ in us, and we will feel the need to share the truth of the gospel with them knowing that is the only way to eternal life. So, the transformation from an unbelieving and lost individual to a believing, saved saint is complete. A saved believer's whole life perspective will change when they recognize Jesus for who He really is; that is, God come to earth to save us from our sins. Such knowledge is impossible to withhold. Believers gladly share the truth of the gospel, especially with those they care about the most.

Interestingly, the Greek word for waiting also carries with it the idea of waiting eagerly. And, of course, that is true. Believers do eagerly await the return of Christ and the hope of glory that will bring. And they eagerly await the eternity in heaven with Christ that we anticipate. Thus, the phrase "joy-filled" comes to mind as the description of the lifestyle of those believers. Happiness depends on "happenings," but joy is not dependent on our physical circumstances.

Therefore, believers also live godly lives. By definition, the lives of truly saved individuals give evidence of their redemption by their values, their perspectives, and their good deeds.

MATTHEW 16:27

In this verse we find Jesus teaching His disciples (and us) lessons concerning the end time, promising to return and repay (reward) each person according to what they have done. What an awesome concept! He is Messiah, Lord, King of Kings, and Redeemer, and is standing on earth when He speaks of coming (again) to judge and reward each person (who has ever lived). See this emphatic verse and the clear definition of a coming judgment day:

> For the Son of Man is going to come with his angels in the glory of his Father, and then he will repay each person according to what he has done. (Matthew 16:27)

Jesus is already on earth and yet speaks of returning, so He must be planning to leave for a time. And so before He leaves, He provides both a promise and a warning for all mankind. Whether this verse is a promise or a warning depends on our reaction to it. Will we believe He is who He says He is, and by faith receive His free gift of eternal life, or will we choose to go our own way seeking self-gratification and fulfillment by our own hand?

This verse is much like one in the Old Testament from Ecclesiastes 12:13–14: "The end of the matter, all has been heard. Fear God and keep his commandments, for this is the whole duty of man. For God will bring every deed into judgment, with every secret thing, whether good or evil."

How many times does God have to tell us there will be a perfect accounting of our lives at some point? What does it take to convince us of the truth of His sovereignty, and that He has a plan for each of us? One thing is for sure, from this description of Christ's Second Coming we can and should generate a more accurate perspective concerning what is required of us in this life.

God's Word provides all the guidelines we need, and all of it is appropriate for our "consumption and obedience," not just bits and pieces. All of it is needed and nothing is left out that we do need.

Some of us have been more blessed than others with access to God's truth. That's the good news; the bad news is we will be held responsible for that plentiful access and what we did with those opportunities. Time is of the essence, people are "dying lost" every day, and we have information they need. And God has commissioned us to share what we know.

PROVERBS 4:5–7

God loves you, and because He loves you, He wants the very best for you. And the very best for you is a proper relationship with Him and His wisdom and insight. The book of Proverbs in the Bible is basically a wisdom book, with wise sayings and information about many aspects of life. It would be worth anyone's time to read all of Proverbs. It's the kind of book that will enhance your ability to define yourself. See the fundamental truth in these three verses.

> Get wisdom; get insight;
>> do not forget, and do not turn away from the words of my mouth.
> Do not forsake her, and she will keep you;
>> love her, and she will guard you.
> The beginning of wisdom is this: Get wisdom,
>> and whatever you get, get insight. (Proverbs 4:5–7)

Wisdom is defined as the ability to discern inner qualities and relationships. Insight is similar; the act or result of apprehending the inner nature of things or of seeing intuitively. Thus, wisdom seems to be more of a gift, and insight more something we work at and get better at over time. And both are kin to knowledge. Each of them supports and extends the others, and so they all are very important and well worth praying to God about.

God clearly says here that we are to seek these characteristics, **and that He is their source.** In fact, in Proverbs 1:7 we see God saying, "The fear of the Lord is the beginning of knowledge." **In other words, the first thing we are to understand is that our "fear" of the Lord (not as in afraid, but as in respect and reverence) is step one in this process of obtaining both wisdom and insight.**

Notice God clearly tells us He is giving us truth, and that we are not to turn away (ever) from that truth. God has the author of Proverbs, King Solomon, liken wisdom to a female (caretaker) who will stay with us, and protect us all lifelong. Thus, we can conclude God's wisdom is appropriate and relevant all lifelong, for everyone, everywhere, and in all kinds of situations.

If God is the source of both wisdom and insight, how do we access them? God makes access to Him very simple, via prayer and His Word, the Bible. Sincere prayer (and you know when you are praying sincerely, and God knows, too, when you are praying sincerely) is that access. Regular prayer times will lead to spiritual maturity, and thus, a better approach to the decisions we all make in life. God knows that, and this is just one scripture passage of many that points up the benefits of depending on God for our growth spiritually. As for other parts of God's Word I can only recommend you begin the habit of reading scripture daily. It will be a fascinating experience for you. **Anything almighty God has originated will have that effect on us.**

MATTHEW 26:56

The night before His crucifixion, Jesus and His disciples went to the Garden of Gethsemane to pray. It was there that the traitor, Judas, brought the temple guards to arrest Him. There was a crowd of people with them. So, there in the dark of night, carrying torches, the guards seized Jesus and carried Him away to Caiaphas the high priest for trial. Notice Jesus' comments at this moment of stress:

> "But all this has taken place that the Scriptures of the prophets might be fulfilled." Then all the disciples left him and fled. (Matthew 26:56)

No doubt these temple guards who arrested Jesus were not listening to Him when He spoke of His arrest and trials being foretold by the prophets. But Matthew heard Him, and was later led by the Holy Spirit to record this reminder for us who are reading this now, that this was all part of God's plan. Isaiah 53 records more of what God led Isaiah to write about how Jesus would suffer for our sake. And Isaiah wrote his letter about seven hundred years before Jesus came to earth. So, yes, this was all part of God's long-term plan to send His only Son to earth to be arrested, tried, and to die a sinner's death on the cross to pay our sin debt. And praise the Lord, God's plan also included Jesus rising from the dead on the third day.

Notice the disciples all left Him and fled at this crucial moment. They had been with Jesus three years. They had heard Him speak many times and seemingly were convinced of His deity. They had seen Him perform multiple miracles, that without question were proof He was the Son of God. Only a few hours earlier at the Last Supper, they had heard Jesus speak of His coming death, and they had all pledged loyalty to Him, no matter what happened. See that described in Matthew 26:35: "Peter said to him, 'Even if I must die with you, I will not deny you!' And all the disciples said the same."

And still they fled. Why was that? Why did the disciples who had committed so vehemently to follow Jesus, flee at this first sign of opposition? It was because they were human. Like us, when the future is unknown, but likely dangerous, we tend to stop, or turn away, or even run in the opposite direction. Think about the scene. It was dark, it was about midnight or later, and they were tired, and the temple guards were there giving some semblance of authority to the arrest. The crowds were there, too, likely noisy and rowdy, and definitely supporting the guards. They had heard Jesus talk about being crucified, but that thought had not taken root in their minds. And they had certainly not thought ahead about what Jesus being arrested would look and feel like to them. And they just did not know what to do. And so they fled. Can we say with all honesty that we would not have fled? Would we have taken what looked like it might be a life-or-death stand right there, right then?

What would we do nowadays in some sort of equivalent situation? Do we take a stand for Jesus today even when our lives are not at stake, but what people will think of us is at stake? Consider what the next several days had in store for the disciples. They saw Jesus die on the cross, watched Him be buried in a borrowed tomb. On the third day they heard He had risen. That night He miraculously appeared to them, and several times over the next forty days they saw and heard Him. And then just before He left them to return to heaven, He reminded them to go and make disciples, and that He would always be with them while they did so. We know all this was done for our benefit. What a story we have to tell!

2 PETER 1:5–8

Believers in the first century and in our day are urged to make their calling and election sure. Thus, their designation and selection as children of God will show in their lifestyles. Peter is not teaching a "works salvation," but preaching the point that an individual's true salvation will lead to a pattern of life as described in this passage. Note the sequence of spiritual growth that Peter describes, beginning with faith, and ending with love.

> Make every effort to supplement your faith with virtue, and virtue with knowledge, and knowledge with self-control, and self-control with steadfastness, and steadfastness with godliness, and godliness with brotherly affection, and brotherly affection with love. For if these qualities are yours and are increasing, they keep you from being ineffective or unfruitful in the knowledge of our Lord Jesus Christ. (2 Peter 1:5–8)

Our Christianity is not a static condition. We begin our Christian journey at the point of our salvation as babes in Christ, and over time grow (our sanctification) toward our glorification (that point when we reach full spiritual maturity in Christ) in heaven. Notice every effort is required, effort of all types, and we are to use them all. We see eight characteristics listed, each built on the one before. This spiritual maturing process will not happen without our putting in the effort. We will not grow spiritually without making that process our primary goal in life. And we will not properly achieve that final state of love without the intervening stages being completed.

Love being the final step listed here fits perfectly with the priorities Jesus described to the lawyer in Matthew 22:35. When asked what the greatest commandment was, Jesus' answer was "to love the Lord your God with all your heart, all your soul, and all your mind," and further "to love your neighbor as yourself." Love then clearly is the chief orientation we must have to be effective and fruitful disciples of Christ. Love is to be the driving force behind all we do, providing never-ending effort and an ongoing heartfelt attitude of concern and care for those around us.

The fact that the Holy Spirit had Peter break down the sanctification process into eight separate steps speaks volumes as to the importance such stepped spiritual growth has for believers, and of the degree of thoroughness of God's overall salvation plan for every believer. God would not have any of us believers be ineffective witnesses, or unfruitful. Notice, too, our spiritual growth is to be an increasing process, and thus, never ending.

So, yes, we are to make our calling and election sure. There is to be no doubt in our mind, or the minds of those who know us, as to our eternal destiny. But this side of heaven, we won't ever reach the state of "having arrived," that is being fully, completely in sync with God's will for our lives. But we can and should never stop that ongoing effort to glorify our heavenly Father.

And why not? God is love. He is the very essence of what this passage urges us to live out before the world. We owe Him all we have and are, and He only is worthy of all our praise, honor, glory, and love.

REVELATION 22:6–7

This last section of the Bible is titled "Jesus Is Coming." What an appropriate way to end scripture. His promised return extends our faith until His arrival. An angel has been speaking to John and sharing God's message with him and us. And now he presents the Lord's concluding statements:

> And he said to me, "These words are trustworthy and true. And the Lord, the God of the spirits of the prophets, has sent his angel to show his servants what must soon take place."
>
> "And behold, I am coming soon. Blessed is the one who keeps the words of the prophets of this book." (Revelation 22:6–7)

We are assured what we have read is trustworthy and true, even in our time. God has seen fit to send an angel to communicate His message to John to relay on to us. And that is the same God that inspired the earlier prophets to also communicate His message. This, because God wants His servants to understand what is about to happen. And notice what that message is: "**I am coming soon**." That the Lord is returning is confirmed, as well as His timetable. What a comforting message for all God's children. Thus, when all seems lost to us in turbulent times, we can be assured Jesus is aware of it all, and still in control. His words are still the same as they have always been, trustworthy and true. God means for us to believe that and take comfort in them.

We might ask, What is the significance of the Lord's soon coming? It will mean the end of all that is counter to what our Lord is and stands for. It means the beginning of His kingdom on earth. And it means what He has been preparing for those who believe is finished, and now theirs to enjoy. But how soon is soon?

Jesus came and lived on earth for a while two thousand years ago and still He has not returned. Do we have cause to justify doubt? The answer to that is a resounding NO. What almighty God has planned and said will prevail per His timetable and His definition of "soon." What we can and should do is thank God for the time He has provided for our sharing His plan of salvation with the world, even those we love the most. God never makes mistakes nor is He slow in providing for us. His timing and reasoning are always perfect. Thus, the question we should address is how should we utilize the time and opportunities He provides?

Notice, too, the Lord's promise in this passage. Those who keep the words of the prophets in this book will be blessed. That is not just good news, it is the best news the world has ever heard. Almighty God has provided eternal life for those who believe and had the route to His salvation recorded for our edification. We are therefore without excuse if we miss heaven. Shallow-minded individuals might question the value and validity of God's blessings. By definition, God's words are trustworthy and true. When God promises blessings, He blesses indeed. We cannot conceive of the extent and worthiness of God's blessings. Infinite in length and eternal in scope, God's blessings are the Alpha and Omega of joy, peace, bliss, and rest. Do not doubt that.

So, what we do know for sure from this passage? We know almighty God loves us with an infinite love and has made provision for eternal life for those who believe. And God has a plan for the fulfillment of His plan of salvation and active believers will be the beneficiaries of His infinite blessings. Who do you know that needs to hear these truths?

ROMANS 2:13-16

Paul is writing to the churches in Rome, giving them instructions concerning their responsibilities with respect to obedience to the law. Paul assumes his readers are believers already, but not perfect (yet) in their obedience. And they live among and deal with unbelieving Gentiles every day (as we do). So those relationships and responsibilities are also part of what Paul is discussing. See some basic concepts Paul is teaching (that are readily applicable in our lives too):

> For it is not the hearers of the law who are righteous before God, but the doers of the law who will be justified. (Romans 2:13)

That seems clear enough, and quite logical. At the point of conversation, the Holy Spirit opens our heart to the fact of our sinful condition and need of a Savior, and to the truth of the gospel. And by God's grace and our faith we believe, and are gifted with eternal life. Then, if our faith is real, if it is legitimate, if it is true, we will work to live it out based on the gospel. As a result, other people will see Jesus Christ in us. So being "doers of the law" gives evidence of our conversion.

But what about the Gentiles who don't have or know of the law as the Jews do? Paul quite logically addresses that question, too, for it is an everyday thought and concern among his readers.

> For when Gentiles, who do not have the law, by nature do what the law requires, they are a law to themselves, even though they do not have the law. They show that the work of the law is written on their hearts, while their conscience also bears witness, and their conflicting thoughts accuse or even excuse

them on that day when according to my gospel, God judges the secrets of men by Christ Jesus. (Romans 2:14–16)

The concept of the universal knowledge of God's law is what Paul presents here. **So praise the Lord, here is scriptural confirmation that those Gentiles in Paul's day and we Gentiles now also have access to the saving knowledge of the gospel.** Thus, not only will selected Jews come to salvation in Christ, so will be those Gentiles who are chosen. Notice three key elements of the judgment process:

1. God judges the secrets of all men; their hearts, every sin completely, and with perfect justice.
2. God's judgment will take place through Jesus Christ. **Our judge will be our Savior. Hallelujah!**
3. God's salvation includes deliverance from our guilt and sin, and rescue from God's wrath.

Our God has made every provision necessary for the salvation of both Jews and Gentiles, and here we see that confirmed. What a great, great God we have.

ROMANS 12:1–2

In this passage Paul describes the commitment we as believers are to make to God, calling the process "A Living Sacrifice." Inherent in that title is the idea of a total, ongoing, and consistent lifestyle given over to praise, honor, and glory to God. Thus, every motive, purpose, and desire of ours is to be focused on our being holy and acceptable to God. See how the Holy Spirit has Paul word these thoughts:

> I appeal to you therefore, brothers, by the mercies of God, to present your bodies as a living sacrifice, holy and acceptable to God, which is your spiritual worship. Do not be conformed to this world, but be transformed by the renewal of your mind, that by testing you may discern what is the will of God, what is good and acceptable and perfect. (Romans 12:1–2)

Paul has something important to relate to his readers, and it is his prayer (by the mercies of God) that we all understand that. The Old Testament laid out God's sacrificial system whereby man's sins were pardoned using the blood (that is, lives) of animals. But in this letter Paul (Romans 6:1–14) describes the forgiveness of sin Christians have now coming via trust in Jesus' sacrificial death on the cross in their place. Saved individuals (then and now) are dead to sin and transformed into new creatures (2 Corinthians 5:17), now raised (from baptismal waters) to walk in newness of life (see Romans 6:4).

Notice Paul says we are to "present our bodies as a living sacrifice." Thinking of our commitment that way implies a completely "sold out" effort. He is thus saying, with God's help, it is doable. We can do it. It is possible for us to be holy and acceptable to God. God's Holy Spirit works within believers to save them and enable them to not be conformed (a slave) to this world, focused on its standards and value system.

We are, thus, to continually seek God's will (which will always be "good and acceptable and perfect"). Paul urges his readers then and us now to test his proposal. We often find out what some idea is worth by putting it into practice, and Paul is confident that will be true here. So we are to make use of what we already know is God's way to communicate to us, His Word and prayer. As we go to God's Word and as we pray, we are to expect God to respond; we are to look for His involvement in our lives.

Such a commitment and such an effort begins with the realization this is almighty God's will for us all. Once we truly recognize that our Savior and Lord Jesus Christ died to save us eternally, our perspective will be changed concerning what we might be called to do or give up. Jesus is Lord and worthy of all our love and commitment.

PSALM 119:105, 130, 165

Those unfamiliar with scripture might wonder why Christians spend time reading and studying the Bible. They probably ask, "How could anything written thousands of years ago be consistently relevant in our modern society?" The basic reason for scripture's ongoing relevance is its author. If we accept the concept of one holy, all-powerful creator God, then it's only a small step to see Him involved in explaining Himself and His work to His creation. And for those who do not accept the concept of one holy, all-powerful creator God, time spent in God's Word is still worthwhile if they ever seek the true meaning of life and its purpose. See how the psalmist addresses this subject:

> Your word is a lamp to my feet
>   and a light to my path . . .
> The unfolding of your words gives light ..
> Great peace have those who love your law;
>   nothing can make them stumble. (Psalm 119:105, 130, 165)

Looking at the last verse first, we notice not only peace, but great peace is in store for those who love God's law. Thinking in terms of the analogy of our lives being described as walking, then the word *stumble* becomes clear. Loving God's law, that is, appreciating it, being drawn to it, and seeing its significance, leads to walking (or living) well or per God's will. Notice, too, nothing this world generates can dislodge those who love God's law from their path. But is peace, even great peace, worth loving God's law to the point of living it out? And if so, how does one come to love God's law?

If ever there was an illustration of the concept "seeing is believing," this is it. The idea of "trying it" comes to mind. To step into God's throne room via studying His Word brings with it understanding and acceptance of the love inherent in the truths presented in scripture. There is absolute power in God's Word, power residing in His steadfast love. And thus, it is no accident that the love of God described in the Bible, and exampled by God's gift of His Son, can and does transforms hearts.

The first two verses listed above describe how and why this transformation takes place. God's Word is a lamp, it does provide light (the way to eternal life). Such revelation becomes evident through the work of God's Holy Spirit acting per His will in a reader's heart. So God not only provides eternal life, He has recorded in scripture how to find it for us to reference. See one example in John 3:16: "For God so loved the world, that he gave his only Son, that whoever believes in him should not perish but have eternal life." A verse so simple the weakest intellect can understand it, and so profound the greatest intellect cannot "mine out" all the significance of it.

MATTHEW 13:12-13

Jesus often taught in parables, illustrating godly truths to His disciples through everyday kinds of common situations. By telling stories about people, animals, crops, nature, etc., He managed to communicate the biblical principles He wanted His disciples to learn. Many times there were unbelievers in the crowds who heard the same parable, but obviously did not understand Jesus' truth in what they heard. Sometimes, even the disciples did not understand either. So, His disciples asked Jesus why He taught that way. See Jesus' response:

> For to the one who has, more will be given, and he will have in abundance, but from the one who has not, even what he has will be taken away. This is why I speak to them in parables, because seeing they do not see, hearing they do not hear, nor do they understand. (Matthew 13:12–13)

The concept Jesus is talking about has to do with the sensitivity people have to His message. Some people are open to it and others are not. In the secular world two people can see and hear the same thing and come away with two entirely different perspectives concerning what they experienced. And that is especially true when spiritual truths are involved.

Here, Jesus is telling us that the more open we are to His gospel, the more we will be able to understand its implications in our lives and in the world. And the reverse is also true. The more deadened we are to the good news of Jesus' coming, the farther away we grow from belief in Him as Son of God, come to save us from our sins. This truth sort of screams at us to pray long and hard for the Lord to give us ever-increasing insight into the truth of His word and the purpose of His coming. In Jesus' day the

Pharisees heard Jesus speak multiple times, and witnessed His miracles, and still refused to accept Him as who He is, Messiah come to earth as promised in scripture, and Son of God, creator of all that has been created. They did not want to know the truth of His identity. They wanted only to reduce His influence with the people and to keep the power they had. To that end they saw to His crucifixion.

We tend to think if we had seen and heard all the Pharisees saw and heard we would not have been so blind to Jesus' Lordship. And yet we have scripture to tell us the complete story, from Jesus' birth through His life, death, and resurrection. And best of all, scripture advises us of the eternal destiny believers have in heaven with the Lord. And with all this confirmation many still will not believe. They do not see themselves as lost sinners in need of a Savior, and do not accept the concept of Jesus' death paying their sin debt.

In a very real way we deny ourselves the opportunity to believe and gain God's free gift of eternal life. Whether it be pride, ignorance, or the world's attractions that cause it, we turn deaf ears to Jesus' words of life. There are many in the world who have not heard the gospel, but not us. We know the truth. We are without excuse. In fact, we ought to be out and about more than we are sharing what we know with the ignorant in the world.

Let us pray for the Lord's help and guidance to be the witnesses, servants, shepherds, ambassadors, disciples, and disciple makers God would have us be. That's God's will for us.

JOHN 11:41-44

When Jesus came to earth, His power was limitless. There was nothing He could not accomplish or make happen. For He is God and had been involved in the creation of the universe from the beginning. At this point in scripture Jesus was returning to Jerusalem for the last time before His crucifixion there. As it happened, His friend Lazarus had died and been buried four days earlier. Lazarus' friends and family were still in mourning when Jesus arrived with His disciples. When He came to Lazarus' tomb (a cave), He asked that the stone at the cave opening be rolled away. See what happened then:

> And Jesus lifted up his eyes and said, "Father, I thank you that you have heard me. I knew that you always hear me, but I said this on account of the people standing around, that they may believe that you sent me." When he had said these things, he cried out with a loud voice, "Lazarus, come out." The man who had died came out, his hands and feet bound with linen strips, and his face wrapped with a cloth. Jesus said to them, "Unbind him, and let him go." (John 11:41–44)

Here, only a few days before His crucifixion, Jesus performs an amazing miracle before the eyes of many. And He even tells us why He did it: that those people seeing it would know God the Father had sent Him into the world; in other words, to prove (once again) He is divine. We can only imagine the scene; people, who minutes before had been weeping over the death of Lazarus, see him walk out of his tomb, alive once again.

Many of those who witnessed this miracle believed in Jesus. That is not surprising. Of course witnessing such a miracle would stir people's hearts. What is surprising is that not everyone who witnessed this miracle believed in Him. Some went quickly to the Jewish religious leaders to tell them what Jesus had done. Their reaction was to become even more convinced they needed to protect their authority by getting rid of Jesus. In our day, too, some people are blind to God's obvious presence.

What is interesting is that scripture does not record any reaction from Lazarus to this miracle. Scripture's focus is on Jesus and communicating who He is. That is where our focus should be too.

Jesus had been ministering for about three years at this point. And in a few days, His ministry would climax with His arrest, trial, crucifixion, and resurrection. His earthly ministry would be finished. God's provision for eternal life for believers would be complete. Our earthly ministry was beginning.

So where does all this leave us? We know of God's love for us, and we know all that love led Him to provide. We know the truth of the significance of Jesus' sacrificial death on the cross to pay our sin debt. We know we receive salvation only by God's grace through faith. And we know we have been commanded to go and tell the world the good news of Jesus' coming. In short, we know everything we need to know. Now let us be about obedience to all we know.

1 Peter 3:13–15

We recognize readily there is much suffering in this world, a great deal of it coming to us believers. The subject of suffering for righteousness' sake, therefore, is always fresh on our minds. And it has always been that way. It's no wonder God saw fit to have this subject covered in His word for our benefit. See this passage for encouragement when suffering comes to us:

> Now who is there to harm you if you are zealous for what is good? But even if you should suffer for righteousness' sake, you will be blessed. Have no fear of them, nor be troubled, but in your hearts honor Christ the Lord as holy, always being prepared to make a defense to anyone who asks you for a reason for the hope that is in you. (1 Peter 3:13–15)

Peter was probably writing from Rome during the reign of Nero (AD 54–68). He wrote to believers in Asia Minor (modern-day Turkey) to encourage them in the suffering environment they lived in under the Romans. So, his readers knew about suffering. They understood what it was like to be persecuted for their faith. Now if there was one message Peter wanted to communicate to his readers and to us, it was that God was aware of their plight. And he promoted the long-term approach to their discipleship.

His point was that there was no one who could harm them eternally if they were in Christ, and his readers should keep that in mind. Suffering on this earth for their faith would lead to blessings in the world to come. Thus, believers should not fear, nor be troubled about their present circumstances. They were to honor Christ as holy; that is, Lord of the universe, and that one who would be the final judge of all people. Solomon, in writing Ecclesiastes, gives us a stark picture of the final judge and judgment:

> The end of the matter; all has been heard. Fear God and keep his commandments, for this is the whole duty of man. For God will bring every deed into judgment, with every secret thing, whether good or evil. (Ecclesiastes 12:13–14)

Therefore, they should be about the business of doing good, even "zealous" in doing good. That is, they, and we, should be proactive in doing good, plan on doing good, look for ways to do good, and for people they can help. Even a worldly society will recognize such a person as "sold out" to something beyond this world. It's those kinds of people who live out their faith, who will have credibility when they give their Christian testimony to a lost world who wonders about why they are so different.

The same principle applies in our day. Societies change, but human nature does not change. We are all born sinners, but when we take on Christ's righteousness at salvation we are born again with new priorities and goals, a new focus to our lifestyles, and a new home to look forward to. And those new perspectives will show in our lives. So yes, like those readers in Peter's day we need to be prepared ahead of time to make a defense for our faith, to explain the reason for the hope that is in us.

All of us have some level of influence on someone in our lives. That fact builds in a degree of opportunity and responsibility for believers to share God's truth, what Peter calls "the hope that is in you." God has built in a one-on-one plan of salvation where individual believers can and should expose Christ to others with their words and their lifestyles. Jesus is worth talking about. He is the best and only hope the world has for eternal life.

JOHN 15:16–17

God would have us love one another. Such a profound concept is far reaching in its scope for our lives. It should inhabit every aspect of what we do and say and who we are. Toward this end God makes it known to us that He has a plan for our lives that when executed will enable each of us to be the witnesses, the servants, the shepherds, the ambassadors, the disciples and the disciple makers He wants us to be. All these roles involve our loving one another. See this passage wherein God assures us of His ongoing participation with us:

> You did not choose me, but I chose you and appointed you that you should go and bear fruit and that your fruit should abide, so that whatever you ask the Father in my name, he may give it to you. These things I command you, so that you will love one another. (John 15:16–17)

Notice how God has worked in our lives apart from our realization of His involvement, choosing us to bear fruit. Just imagine what our bearing fruit consists of. Our simply living and thus having influence on other people is to be in accord with God's plan for us. Our bearing fruit then would imply our influence would be a good and permanent influence, causing changes and leading to results in other people's lives that bring glory to the Father. He has appointed us for assignments specific to us, that He has not assigned to anyone else. This whole "fruit-bearing" concept absolutely gives meaning to every day, every act, and every word of our lives. And it goes further, even determining the motives we have for what we do.

Interestingly, this passage indicates that as we go about bearing fruit we will be led to ask various things of the Father in Jesus' name. And that's only logical. As we submit to God's will for our lives, we will naturally gravitate to the habit of seeking His guidance and direction in prayer, for pleasing Him will come to be our major goal. And Jesus advises us ahead of time, the Father will hear our prayers and provide what we have requested. We can be assured God will certainly do His part to help us be obedient to Him.

The concept of our bearing fruit and our seeking the Father's direction in doing so are commands, not suggestions. Notice from the passage Jesus gives us these commands so that we will love one another. **Because Jesus loves us, He wants the best for us. Thus, evidently our loving one another results in benefit to us. Could it be that this idea of love abounding in all areas of our lives has been God's plan all along? I believe so.** If we love someone, we will naturally care for and help them any way we can. If they love us, they will be appreciative of that help and love us (and others) back and reciprocate with loving acts. Imagine the whole world involved in such fruit-bearing. If you can you are picturing what heaven will be like. After all, God is love (1 John 4:8) and we are made in His image. Let us begin loving others as God loves us.

MICAH 4:2–3

Micah lived and prophesied about 700 BC. His words, given to him by God, were particularly for the people of Judah describing what was ahead for them. They had fallen into idolatry and at that time were oppressed by the country of Babylon. Micah spoke of an eventual better time, when the peaceful leadership of the whole world would come forth from Zion and Jerusalem and there would be no more wars. See the message God has given Micah to speak then that we need to know about too:

> For out of Zion shall go forth the law, and the word of the LORD from Jerusalem. He shall judge between many peoples, and shall decide for strong nations far away; and they shall beat their swords into plowshares, and their spears into pruning hooks; nation shall not lift up sword against nation, neither shall they learn war anymore. (Micah 4:2–3)

No timetable is provided, but clearly Micah speaks of a time in the "latter days" when the Lord will reign from Jerusalem directing "strong nations far away." During the Lord's reign there will no longer be any need for armies or weapons to protect nations against the potential for war with other nations. The whole world will be at peace. Micah's message is that the God of Israel (our God) is the one and only almighty God whose power reigns supreme, and He will direct a society of peace. People of Micah's day and our day can all take comfort in that truth.

When we look around us in our day it is hard to visualize this happening. It was hard for the people of Micah's day to visualize it, too, at that time. Twenty-seven hundred years have passed, and it hasn't happened yet, and so our perspective concerning God's direct action in the world is apt to be focused on the here and now and not the "latter days." It's not that we don't believe scripture, we just don't think about it enough. We are too tied up with what is happening to us and things we want to do.

And therein lies our problem. Inward focus limits our ability to see God acting in the world around us. God has not waited twenty-seven hundred years to do anything. Whether we realize it or not, He is active every day, protecting us, guiding us, teaching us, and giving us serving and learning opportunities. **He wants us to live as if His kingdom is coming today. He wants us to be aware of His "everyday" involvement in our lives.** Jesus even told us to pray for it to come in His model prayer: "Your kingdom come, your will be done, on earth as it is in heaven" (Matthew 6:10).

If we are sincerely praying this simple, but profound, prayer every day, we are much more likely to be a part of God's kingdom work. We miss so much when we leave God out of our lives. He loves us and did not intend for us to live that way. **He knows we live much happier, productive lives, if we give Him first place.** We do this by daily prayer and Bible study, and by associating with other believers who are doing that same thing. We do this by expecting to see Him working in our lives as we open ourselves to lives of service for others, being sensitive to how we can show God's love to others (those inside our family and those outside). So let us establish and work at our relationship with God, and make glorifying Him the goal of our lives.

MATTHEW 6:34;
2 THESSALONIANS 3:12

We sometimes find scripture that is hard to understand completely. Praise the Lord, He knew this was going to happen to us, and He did several things to help us deal with such situations. One was to put other scripture in place that deals with the same subject, and another was to give wisdom to some people to enable them to interpret the meanings for us. This, to help us with our understanding and obedience. The two passages above are examples of such a principle. They have to do with our focusing on God's will for our lives and not worldly ambitions or goals.

> Therefore, do not be anxious about tomorrow, for tomorrow will be anxious for itself. Sufficient for the day is its own trouble. (Matthew 6:34)

> Now such persons we command and encourage in the Lord Jesus Christ to do their work quietly and to earn their own living. (2 Thessalonians 3:12)

Apparently, Matthew was writing to some Christians who were so concerned about their own daily needs and desires, they gave themselves over to working their jobs with the result they gave little (or no) attention to "kingdom service" in their communities. Matthew was led to tell them to refocus on the Lord's will, to give more emphasis and priority to the needs of others than they were doing. Paul though was addressing the problem of some people not working at all, depending on other believers to meet their daily needs while they proposed they spent all their time serving in the community. And apparently, they were not doing that very well.

Certainly, both these concepts fall short of God's will. Matthew tells his addressees (and us) not to give primary focus in their lives to material things, for God knows what our needs are and will take care of us, His children, as He does birds and lilies of the field. Matthew words this well when he says, "Seek first the kingdom of God and his righteousness, and all these things will be added to you" (Matthew 6:33). Paul tells his readers that believers are to care for themselves, meeting their own needs, while they "quietly" earn their own living. And he set that example, working as a tentmaker (Acts 18:3; 20:34) while he also ministered in the community. Theologian David Guzik, interprets the balance between the two concepts above this way: "God wants us to remember the past, plan for the future, but live in the present."

It is possible to obey the "spirit" of both these passages. We can and should earn our own way, we can and should go and make disciples (wherever and whenever we go). If our hearts are truly open to God's will He will lead us to "fruit-filled" lives as we live out both passages.

ISAIAH 2:17, 20

Isaiah was a prophet. And a prophet is a man blessed by God with special knowledge and leadership abilities who God intends should go forth to proclaim God's sovereignty and judgment to the society around them. Isaiah lived around 700 BC in Judah, a small country bordering the Mediterranean Sea. That's twenty-seven hundred years ago. And if we are not careful, we will let the fact that Isaiah spoke so long ago cause us to think that his words have no application or credibility in today's world. Not so. Isaiah was led by almighty God to write what he wrote, and thus, we can consider these words from God Himself and designed especially for us, because they are. See what God is telling us via Isaiah:

> And the haughtiness of man shall be humbled,
>   and the lofty pride of man shall be brought low,
>   and the LORD alone will be exalted in that day . . .
> In that day mankind will cast away
>   their idols of silver and their idols of gold,
> which they made for themselves to worship. (Isaiah 2:17, 20)

There will come a time of reckoning, when God judges all mankind. Isaiah refers to that time as "that day," or the Day of the Lord. And at that judgment each of us will give an account to God of all that we have done, and why we did it. God has given everyone a given degree of knowledge and abilities. And He knows exactly what our circumstances are and how we can use what He has given us for His glory. And He would have us use them for His glory consistently all lifelong. This is not a situation where we can think, "I will begin living life God's way later on, when my circumstances change." **God does not make mistakes. He would have us live**

per His will and for His glory now, right where we are and as we are. And the very good news is, we are so, so blessed when we do.

Put very simply, living for God's glory means we live such that those who know us or who we influence think better of God for having known us. It means our priorities are such that we use what God has given us to help others, it means that we stop thinking of self and focus on others, and it means that we consistently do the best we can to take advantages of every chance we have to use the talents God has given us and to sharpen those talents through study, education, and hard work so that as God brings us opportunities for service for others we will be ready. **All this is part of glorifying God. And the more we engage this kind of attitude in our lives, the more God WILL use us FOR HIS GLORY.**

Notice the decided emphasis in the passage above on haughtiness and pride. Most of us don't think of ourselves as haughty or prideful. But everything we do and every decision we make that is contrary to God's will for us is an expression of our willful pride and independence. It reflects us not trusting God with our lives, and thinking we need to do this or that with no concern given as to whether what we are considering is God's will for us or not. He made us the way we are, and put us in the place we are, and with the family we have, and with the talents we have all for a reason. And He knows best. Trusting God is what God wants from us. Think about it, such trust reflects our dependence on God to be exactly what He is, almighty God who loves us and sent His Son to earth to pay our sin debt so we could spend an eternity with Him in heaven. What more could God do to prove His love for us?

Too many people in Isaiah's day gave emphasis to self, things, and their own well-being, That's true in our day too. Let us live honoring God so we can look forward to the Day of the Lord, not dread it.

2 TIMOTHY 3:16–17

God's Word, the Bible, is often quoted as the authentic word of God. Some people, though, doubt that to be true. Only true believers would dare to claim the whole Bible to be true, and to be God's only revelation of Himself to mankind. And they have done so by faith. The fact is, the Bible makes its own claims as to its authenticity. God has a way of moving in the heart of those who read His word with an open mind, ready to receive His message. His word, to them, is sharp, relevant, and personal. Thus, they see it as powerful, wise, true, and appropriate for people in every society. In this passage God has led the apostle Paul to write to his young disciple, Timothy, concerning the power of His word, and the relevance it has to every person. Notice the scope of the application of God's Word:

> All Scripture is breathed out by God and profitable for teaching, for reproof, for correction, and for training in righteousness, that the man of God may be competent, equipped for every good work. (2 Timothy 3:16–17)

The Bible consists of sixty-six books, thirty-seven in the Old Testament, and twenty-nine in the New Testament, all recorded by a total of approximately forty authors (under the leadership of God's Holy Spirit) over a period of about fifteen hundred years (from 1500 BC to toward the end of the first century AD). The first four words in Genesis 1 are "In the beginning, God . . ." announcing God's role and His authority in all that follows. The last thought presented at the end of the book of Revelation has to do with the grace of the Lord Jesus being with us all. He is the only source of relief from the trials of this world, and the only leader providing access to the eternal heaven beyond.

Notice the wide range of application of God's word: teaching, reproof, correction, and for training in righteousness. These God-inspired truths are said to be "breathed out" by God. What a great way to picture measuring the significance of God's truths, as coming from within His very heart, potentially to come to rest in the hearts of all who would believe. And His thoughts are profitable. How so, we might ask? God's scripture is profitable because acquisition of His truths, and the application of His principles lead believers to an eternal relationship with Him that merits our total lives as participants.

As for the teaching benefits from scripture, there is both an intellectual and a spiritual aspect to the teaching referred to here. Scripture then presents a certain amount of factual data concerning God with regard to time, date, and place, and other factual information that must be taken on faith. God then, without apology, tests our faith to believe His miraculous intervention in world affairs.

Scripture is also appropriate for reproof, that is, for criticizing our sinful orientation, to thus give us a measuring stick to judge ourselves by. And if we do wrong, there must be a better path; and scripture provides that, too, adding corrective measures we can use to reorient our perspectives toward God's way. And then note, scripture presents training principles and practices we may use to implement the corrective courses it introduces. **Then, notice how we are to use scripture to train us, and what we are to learn to be. In one word, it's righteousness that we are to acquire. There must be something especially worthwhile in our becoming righteous. And there is. It exemplifies Christlikeness, and that is to be our goal as we use that orientation to live, glorifying our heavenly Father.**

REVELATION 21:5–7

Within the book of Revelation is the prophecy of the end time, and a description of the future hope of those who conquer, that is, those who persevere in their faith. God saw fit to have John the apostle write this down for us. This, to provide us direction, protection, and hope given the trials this world provides us all. Notice how personal the Holy Spirit makes His instructions to John (and thus to us too):

> And he who was seated on the throne said, "Behold, I am making all things new." Also he said, "'Write this down, for these words are trustworthy and true." And he said to me, "It is done! I am the Alpha and the Omega, the beginning and the end. To the thirsty I will give from the spring of the water of life without payment. The one who conquers will have this heritage, and I will be his God and he will be my son." (Revelation 21:5–7)

John gets a word from God to pass on to us. He is saying, "Understand me, don't forget what you hear, and take to heart what I've said." That's for John's ears and his to pass on to us. So we are to be as attentive as John, and as obedient. Anything and everything that God says is trustworthy and true, and for Him (who created all that is) to tell us what He is about to say is trustworthy and true assures us that what comes next is significant indeed.

And then God said, "It is done." What is done? What is He referring to? **He is talking about what His providing His Son as a sacrifice for payment of our sin debt accomplishes. It satisfies the wrath of God.** Jesus' death on the cross, and nothing else, could have satisfied God's righteous wrath. We humans have little understanding of the significance of our sin and how abhorrent it is to God. So when it comes to dealing with sin, He who comes before the Alpha (the beginning of everything) and extends after the Omega (the finish of it all) has both spoken and acted. He has made the complete provision for all sin.

And for those who are thirsty, that is, those who search for and find the peace of God's salvation through His grace and the faith He provides us, God promises the spring of the water of life. What could the spring of the water of life be but eternal life, the free gift God provides those who persevere. It cannot be bought, but comes from God's mercy-filled heart.

Notice what the reward is for those who are thirsty, **a heritage provided by God.** And what is a heritage, but something provided by a predecessor, and hallelujah, Jesus Christ is our predecessor who provided payment of our debt by the only way possible, His death on the cross in our place. And what comes with that heritage? Our being a joint heir with Jesus as children of God. God told John plainly, He will be the believer's God, and the believer will be His son. WOW! What a great God we have and what a great heritage we have in Jesus. Who do you know that needs to hear what Jesus has done for them?

LUKE 5:27-32

Jesus' call is always a call to leave everything and follow Him. It was so during those days of His ministry on earth, and it still is today in our society. Tax collectors then were considered evil men, who had left their Jewish heritage and joined with the Romans to rule over the Jews. They had the power of the Roman army behind them as they collected taxes, and often collected more than was due, and kept the difference for themselves. Thus, it was no wonder they were hated by the Jews. See this story of how one of those hated tax collectors comes to a saving knowledge of Christ:

> After this he went out and saw a tax collector named Levi, sitting at the tax booth. And he said to him, "Follow me." And leaving everything, he rose and followed him.
> And Levi made him a great feast in his house, and there was a large company of tax collectors and others reclining at table with them. And the Pharisees and their scribes grumbled at his disciples, saying, "Why do you eat and drink with tax collectors and sinners?" And Jesus answered them, "Those who are well have no need for a physician, but those who are sick. I have not come to call the righteous but sinners to repentance." (Luke 5:27–32)

WOW! What a great answer by Jesus. What a profound truth for us to remember too. Notice Levi's response to Jesus' call. He left everything immediately, and followed Jesus. And he left what would be considered "a lot" in those days. As a tax collector, he had it made financially. He did not know where Jesus was going, or what lay ahead for Jesus or him. But acting on faith alone he followed Jesus. Thus, Jesus' calling him, and his commitment to follow Jesus was indicative of his being forgiven of all the sins the Jews thought a tax collector was guilty of. The lesson Jesus taught that day was, if He could forgive a tax collector and accept him as a disciple, then salvation was available to anyone. What a great concept for us to consider in our day.

And then, of all things. Jesus accepted an invitation to a luncheon at Levi's house, where there were lots of tax collectors present. We cannot help but wonder what those tax collectors (and sinners) thought of Jesus when they saw Him at Levi's house. We can imagine Levi even announcing there the fact that he was leaving the tax collection business to follow Jesus.

Jesus' association with Levi, and His eating and drinking with a lot of tax collectors did not "compute" with the Pharisees. They saw this as a great sin, thus indicating they thought there no chance for a Jewish tax collector to ever come to (what the Pharisees saw as) a proper relationship to God. Too many Christians today seemingly have that same attitude concerning certain groups, for conspicuous by its absence is any visible concern for that group's eternal destiny. That kind of attitude is why today there are still over six thousand unreached people groups in the world two thousand years after Jesus came and talked to the Pharisees that day.

Surely, there is a role for us all to play in reaching those who have never heard of Jesus. That's what the Great Commission is all about. See Matthew 28:19–20.

1 Peter 1:3–5

Believers can be said to be "born again to a living hope." That kind of hope is sure, firm, and everlasting. There is no "might be" about it. God, through Christ's death on the cross, established this hope once and for all time. So, Peter is writing to affirm this fact for readers of that day, and for us in our day. He refers to this provision from God as hope in verse 3, inheritance in verse 4, and salvation in verse 5. See how Peter words this important concept for us:

> Blessed be the God and Father of our Lord Jesus Christ! According to his great mercy, he has caused us to be born again to a living hope through the resurrection of Jesus Christ from the dead, to an inheritance that is imperishable, undefiled, and unfading, kept in heaven for you, who by God's power are being guarded through faith for a salvation ready to be revealed in the last time. (1 Peter 1:3–5)

As we read this passage, we can't help but wonder what it meant to the first-century readers. There in the midst of Roman oppression, disbelieving neighbors, the trials of just putting food on the table, the complaints from fellow believers, etc., what encouragement did they find? The source and truth of encouragement is there. Were they able to take it in and apply it to their lives? Are we? What a powerful description of the joy that will come to born-again believers. What a source of strength and stamina in the face of trials, and what a vivid reflection of the love God has for us! Surely, we won't miss this display of wisdom as we attempt to apply God's truth to our lives.

At the outset of this beautiful passage Peter rightfully gives praise, honor, and glory to God the Father for His provision of the gift of eternal life for believers. As he does, he is reminding all readers, then and now, to keep a proper perspective concerning where that free gift originates. Only with a right perspective concerning our eternal life will we be prepared to live out our faith daily. For it is for the glory of God that we even exist.

Notice why and how God brings about our new birth. The passage makes clear it's through His great mercy. In our day we refer to that characteristic as God's grace, the amazing love God has for us, as undeserving and unlovable as we are. And it was reflected in Jesus' resurrection from the dead. We believers then, live our lives filled with this firm hope of a future resurrection like Jesus'. Such a conviction of an inheritance like Jesus' is sufficient to comfort us through any and all manner of trials in this world. Peter describes it as imperishable, undefiled, and unfading. Thus, our unchanging, perfect, and eternal heavenly inheritance is preserved in heaven for us. What could be a safer place?

As a born-again Christian, visualize the living hope that is available to you. As a believer, picture a home reserved for you in heaven guarded by God's power. As a child of God, imagine if you can, a salvation more complete and more permanent than what God has prepared for you. You cannot; no one can. And all this via God's grace and our faith that one day it all will be revealed by the God and Father of our Lord Jesus Christ that Peter describes.

Talk about good news! Talk about a time for hallelujahs! Talk about a God who is worthy of all our praise, honor, and glory! This passage gives every believer, in every era, cause to shout for joy, to run next door, and tell somebody about the great God they have.

REVELATION 22:12-13

In this passage, John the apostle is finishing his letter to seven churches in Asia. It is his goal to record the visions of the end times God has given him, and to provide encouragement and endurance in their faith to believers of that day (late in the first century) and now. What better way to do that than to quote Jesus Christ's final comments to his readers? Certainly, these words are applicable to us in our day as well.

> Behold, I am coming soon, bringing my recompense with me, to repay each one for what he has done. I am the Alpha and the Omega, the first and the last, the beginning and the end. (Revelation 22:12–13)

"Behold" means wake up, be aware, and take notice. Thus, Jesus advises John's readers He is coming soon, and suddenly, with no more advance warning as to when than this notice. Jesus' words should be sufficient to trigger belief and obedience in believers in that day and ours. When you think about it, who could speak, or what event could happen, that would be of more significance and of greater importance than a commitment to return to earth from the creator of the universe? How could we doubt His words or the love they reflect?

And Jesus goes further. He tells us why He is coming: "to repay each one for what they have done." That statement presumes some sort of evaluation or judgment will have taken place as to what we have earned. And that is true, Jesus being the just judge. Jesus will be bringing His recompense with Him. Recompense is that compensation someone receives for services rendered or damage done. Thus, it involves either reward or punishment dispensed fairly by an appropriate authority. And that perfectly describes

347

what Jesus will do as our final authority. Think about it, all that has ever happened will be reviewed with a perfect assessment of the total consequences and who is responsible (for the good or bad results).

Jesus clearly tells us He will do the judging, and He even describes His qualifying credentials for such a role. He is "the Alpha and the Omega, the first and the last, and the beginning and the end." Here are three different phrases reflecting the completeness, thoroughness, total, and all-encompassing power and authority Jesus has to accomplish this assessment.

Notice, too, no one escapes this judging process. Jesus will properly repay everyone. He could only do that if He has all knowledge and all power, which He has always had. That is true, and it is also as it should be. Only He, with the perfections He has in love, mercy, and truth, is qualified to do this work.

Thus, we see the day will come when "all will be made right," when God will reveal all we have done and deliver us to our final destiny. Ecclesiastes 12:13–14 says it well: "The end of the matter; all has been heard. Fear God and keep His commandments, for this is the whole duty of man. For God will bring every deed into judgment with every secret thing, whether good or evil."

JOHN 14:27

People seek peace, real peace. We may not use the word *peace*, but we do seek freedom from worry and stress. And we do all kinds of things trying to find peace. The older we get the more we realize the world does not bring true satisfaction. This was true in Jesus' day also. During His time with the disciples at the Last Supper Jesus spoke to them of lasting peace. And God saw fit to have this principle recorded in scripture for our benefit. See this truth and how it applies to our lives:

> Peace I leave with you; my peace I give to you. Not as the world gives do I give to you. Let not your hearts be troubled, neither, let them be afraid. (John 14:27)

The word used for peace here does not just indicate the absence of turmoil, but also the blessing of a right relationship with God. We need to recognize what was going on in the disciples' lives at that moment in time. Jesus, and they, were under tremendous pressure from the Pharisees. They were being followed, challenged, and threatened, wherever they went. So here in the crowded streets of Jerusalem during Passover, the tension was building. And now Jesus is speaking of leaving. So naturally the questions of where is He going and what would happen to them were uppermost in their minds. So Jesus advises them that He understands their feelings, and has made and is making provisions for them. In our day, we would probably use the familiar phrase "everything is going to be all right" to describe what Jesus is telling them. We can certainly take Jesus' words as applicable to our lives in times of stress too.

So Jesus makes clear it is not the world's kind of peace He is talking about. And He goes on to give them a description of His kind of peace. Jesus' peace is free from trouble and fear. He says to them and us, "You can be afraid, and let your troubles get you down, **but you don't have to live that way.**" Jesus is assuring us all He provides eternal freedom, and an everlasting worldview that reorients our perspective concerning events and experiences that would normally really bother us.

Notice Jesus tells the disciples to address the condition of their hearts. That innermost part of their being is representative of where the worry and hurt are happening. He tells the disciples "let not your hearts be troubled." That would indicate they have power to change things within their hearts. Surely that means they (already) have access to relief from troubles and fear if they would just take advantage of the resources Jesus has and can make available.

We have those same options. God is eternal in both His love and in His power. **Key to our finding Jesus' peace is our relationship with Him.** If we have settled the matter of His Lordship, and already determined this world is not our home, we have a whole new perspective on both the "good and bad news" that comes into our lives. And the principles we have always heard about (God's grace, our faith, and His love) all displayed via the cross are (still) the (only) route to salvation and His peace.

1 JOHN 4:9

It's one thing to believe that God loves you, and it's even more real when you see evidence of it. That's the way God treats us. He tells us of His love and His provisions, and then He proves it specifically. The absolute ultimate example of God's love for us was His provision of His Son Jesus Christ as the atonement for our sins. Without question we are born sinners, and without question the wages of our sin is death. Thus, either we do the dying for our sins, or the payment for our sin debt is made some other way. Someone else has to die in our place. And that's the approach God chose. To make it even more astounding is the fact that Jesus came to earth as man and lived a perfect life. He who lived without sinning died for our sin. Not only that. He lived among us for about thirty-three years exampling a sinless life while He taught us His two key principles: love the Lord your God with all your heart, soul, and mind, and love your neighbors as you love yourself (Matthew 22:37–38). See this verse in 1 John outlining the purpose of Jesus' earthly ministry:

> The love of God was made manifest among us, that God sent his only Son into the world, so that we might live through him. (1 John 4:9)

God had a plan. He knew and knows the full of extent of the power and capacity of love and wants us to grasp those concepts too. So by His grace He provided us the necessary love to justify (that is, to acquit) us of our sin. God's grace then describes the love He has for us that we don't deserve. Even before we were born God knew of us and loved us even knowing we would be born in sin, not worthy of His love. We are thus, born sinners and can never accomplish enough good deeds in our own strength to make amends for our sinful condition.

The second huge provision God made was also through His grace when He enabled us to "faith" our way to belief in Jesus' sacrificial death on the cross in our place. Our God-provided faith then enables us to believe in Christ and His life, death, and resurrection even though we were not there to witness His sacrifice. But through our faith that God provided us He made a way to eternal life for us.

The verse in 1 John tells us we may live through him. The implied truth here is that Christ is the only way to life, that is, eternal life. All the provisions God made were for that one purpose, that we sinners can, by faith, believe, and be given God's free gift of eternal life. We don't have to live a perfect life, we don't have to do anything other than believe. As it happens though, when we do sincerely believe, we come into a relationship with Christ that leads to our loving Him for His having loved us first. Thus, by definition, we want to please Him, we want to obey Him, and we naturally want to share the good news of His salvation with others, especially those we are closest to. While we strive for perfection, when we do sin, we feel it, and can and should repent and seek forgiveness for those sins. God has promised to forgive those who sincerely repent. The sense of remorse and need for forgiveness we feel is proof of our love for God.

One of the most encouraging verses in all of scripture is Matthew 28:20, where Jesus makes the ultimate promise to us. "Behold, I am with you always, to the end of the age." We can take that thought with us.

JAMES 1:16–18

We can be sure God knows everything about us and what is going on in our lives. Add His love to His knowledge of us, and the power to bring about any outcome in our lives due to circumstance, and we realize how fortunate we are to have the God we have. James' readers were subject to the oppression of the Romans on top of their daily requirement to supply food and shelter for their families. Thus, they needed the encouragement this letter brought. The concept then of eternal life in heaven with God was something all believers then and now could use to adjust their perspectives concerning what should be most important in their lives. See the wisdom James provides for any believer in any society:

> Do not be deceived, my beloved brothers. Every good gift and every perfect gift is from above, coming down from the Father of lights, with whom there is no variation or shadow due to change. Of his own will he brought us forth by the word of truth, that we should be a kind of firstfruits of his creatures. (James 1:16–18)

James urges all his readers to keep (correctly) in mind where all their blessings originate, and that would be from above, that is, with our heavenly Father. When you think about it, it truly is important that we keep in mind what our blessings are and who supplies them. How better to relate to our heavenly Father than with ongoing gratitude for all His love and provisions.

Notice James' reference to God as the Father of lights, that is, the creator of all that is displayed in the heavens. See Psalm 74:16: "Yours is the day, yours also the night; you have established the heavenly lights and the sun." What an example of God's infinite power and concern for us, His children. How dull are we to ignore heaven's splendor and take for granted the stars and their function. And all this comes to us constantly, consistently, and without change or variation. This then is God's nature: **to always be the loving creator and redeemer He is.**

And this very God, this unchanging Master and Creator of the universe knows our names, loves us individually with an infinite love, and has provided us a way to spend eternity with Him. He made the decisions to love us and provide His only Son as the way, the truth, and the life for all who believe. Why would God do this? James gives us that answer, that his readers might be the firstfruits of God's creation. James was a Jew writing to Jews telling them of their blessed selection as God's chosen people. But God would not stop there. His message, through James, implies the gospel is for all the nations. These readers were to go and make (other) disciples throughout the world. And now as Gentiles we have heard the word of truth, too, and have the same assignment, to take the gospel to the nations.

What are firstfruits? They are that portion of the harvest that comes before the rest, and reflect therefore, the kind of fruit (harvest) that will be forthcoming later in abundance. That's exactly what we are to be. We are the firstfruit believers for someone or some group. We are the ones who had the seed of the good news of the gospel planted in our hearts and it grew to full faith and belief. And now as full-grown believers we are to reflect what God has done in our hearts and thus, what is available to others who believe. What does God then want from us, but for us to be firstfruits. What a privilege, and what a responsibility.

JOHN 15:12–14

Love for one another is a hallmark message within scripture. In this passage Jesus explains that principle to the world and indicates the depth that love is to take, that is, to the point of one giving their life for another. That is the greatest example of love. It's what Jesus showed in going to the cross in our place to pay our sin debt, and thus, make eternal life available to us. See how the Holy Spirit has John word this:

> This is my commandment, that you love one another as I have loved you. Greater love has no one than this, that someone lay down his life for his friends. You are my friends if you do what I command you. (John 15:12–14)

So clearly God would have us love each other. What this passage adds to that concept is (1) that Jesus has set the example for this kind of love, (2) that laying down one's life for their friends is the greatest way to exhibit this kind of love, and (3) that we are friends of Jesus if we do so.

The most effective way for us to teach a life principle to another person is to live it out in our own life. Then that other person sees how that principle applies in everyday life, and they see the result of such action. Seeing the result of the application of a principle is what truly cements the principle in our minds. Second, Jesus is teaching that nothing we have to give, or that we can do for another person exceeds our laying down our own life for them. And, of course, that is exactly what Jesus did for us on the cross. And third, we prove we are friends of Jesus if we do lay down our lives for Him.

We need to note, too, that Jesus is teaching this principle to His disciples (and us) during His last meeting with them at the

Last Supper, the night before His crucifixion. Surely, principles Jesus taught them then were of critical importance, and should be taken as especially significant in our day. So we are not to withhold the emotion of love in our relationships with others. **Notice Jesus reminds them that He loved them that way.**

Notice, too, Jesus brings up the subject of their being His friend if they obey His commands. The very idea of the friendship of God being available to us humans by any means is a mind-boggling concept. And yet here is "God come to earth" telling them this about twelve hours before He goes to the cross on their behalf. And praise the Lord, by extension this same privilege is available to all obedient believers.

The staggering part of this concept of loving one another is that Jesus loved us first, while we were lost in our sins, and very unworthy of His love. That's the absolute definition of grace; no wonder we think of it as God's Amazing Grace. See how scripture describes this:

> For by grace you have been saved through faith. And this is not your own doing, it is the gift of God. (Ephesians 2:8)

> But God shows his love for us in that while we were still sinners, Christ died for us. (Romans 5:8)

God has loved us so much, who are we not to love others?

JONAH 3:4–5

God works in mysterious ways, His wonders to perform. Those exact words are not in scripture, but the thought is. See Isaiah 55:8–9:

> For my thoughts are not your thoughts,
>   neither are your ways my ways, declares the LORD.
> For as the heavens are higher than the earth,
>   so are my ways higher than your ways,
>   and my thoughts than your thoughts.

God worked thought the prophet Jonah in just such a way. He sent him to Nineveh, the great city in Assyria, to "call out against it." We know the story. Jonah rebelled against God and did not go. He sailed in the opposite direction and wound up spending three days in the belly of large fish. The Lord spoke to the fish and He spit out Jonah upon dry land. Then Jonah obeyed God and went to Nineveh. See what happened when Jonah obeyed God: "Jonah began to go into the city, going a day's journey. And he called out, 'Yet forty days, and Nineveh shall be overthrown!' And the people believed God. They called for a fast and put on sackcloth, from the greatest of them to the least of them" (Jonah 3:4–5).

Jonah's message was eight words long; short, but effective: "Yet forty days and Nineveh shall be overthrown." God's words were clear, with the implication that if the people of Nineveh repented within forty days God would relent. Notice Jonah did not even tell the Ninevites that he was speaking a message from God. God saw to it that all the people of Nineveh got the message as to whom Jonah represented. See Jeremiah 18:7–8 for an ongoing word from God: "If at any time I declare concerning a nation or a kingdom, that I will pluck up and break down and destroy it, and if that nation, concerning which I have spoken, turns from its evil, I will relent of the disaster that I intended to do to it" (Jeremiah 18:7–8).

And that's what happened. Nineveh repented and God relented. God's ways and thoughts really are higher than ours. Could this still be true of nations today? Could it be true of individuals? God is immutable, unchanging, and so absolutely, yes, the same mercy God showed to Nineveh is available to countries today and individuals today.

Thus, those messages God gave Jeremiah and Jonah are the very same messages God has given to us today to take to people and places like Nineveh. We've got even more to tell them than Jeremiah and Jonah had. The whole gospel of Jesus Christ contains the "why" (God's love) and the "how" (Jesus Christ's sacrificial death to pay our sin debt) God has provided His forgiveness. We can go in the opposite direction as Jonah did, but God still holds us responsible for obedience to His commands. Some sort of equivalent to Jonah's experience with the large fish is apt to await us if we rebel as he did.

God provides us scripture experiences like Jonah had to illustrate His love for us and His direct involvement in world affairs. Let us not "run" in the opposite direction as Jonah did, but yield to His will. He knows who we are, where we are, and what we are experiencing. He will use us right where we are.

MATTHEW 21:12-13

This passage finds Jesus in Jerusalem early in Passion Week. He has only recently come to Jerusalem making what has come to be known as His Triumphal Entry, riding on a donkey as many of His followers sang and shouted praises to Him. When He came to the temple, He found it crowded with God-fearing people from all over the Roman Empire. They had come to worship, but the process had deteriorated into a money-making effort as Jewish religious leadership participated in the sale of overpriced sacrificial animals and the exchange of currencies from various countries. See Jesus' response:

> And Jesus entered the temple and drove out all who sold and bought in the temple, and he overturned the tables of the money-changers and the seats of those who sold pigeons. He said to them, "It is written, 'My house shall be called a house of prayer,' but you make it a den of robbers." (Matthew 21:12–13)

Jesus did not hesitate to act against the desecration of the temple by the Jewish leaders who took advantage of pilgrims in Jerusalem for the Passover Celebration. These visitors came to Jerusalem to worship and needed to purchase sacrificial animals which required they exchange their currencies into that common to Judea. Often that process resulted in overpriced animals and exorbitant exchange rates. Both practices violated the very spirit of worship God had in mind.

We can imagine the chaotic scene when Jesus began to disrupt the bartering for animals and turned over the exchange tables. Would we care enough to do something similar in our day? Are we that confident of our faith?

This section of the temple was the only place Gentiles were allowed to come and pray, and now certain select Jews were making it impossible for that to happen. Those who had been made God's chosen people were acting in opposition to anyone else coming to the Lord. Jesus accused the Jewish leadership of hiding behind the façade of temple worship for personal gain.

We may well not be guilty of such deceit, but are we consistently in "sold out to the Lord" mode in our daily lives? What purposes are behind our long-range plans? Would there be any doubt in the minds of those who know us as to where we stand with the Lord? How proactive are we in kingdom work?

Jesus had come to Jerusalem this last time knowing at the end of the week He would be crucified. With only a few days left on earth, He made it a point to cleanse the temple, reminding those who saw Him (and us) where to place their priorities. We likely have more than just a few more days to live. However, we cannot be positive of that. But we can be positive of the fact that time is fleeting, and that the task Jesus has given us (of making disciples) is urgent.

Isaiah had reminded his readers (even now) that foreigners who join themselves to the Lord as His servants would be blessed to worship in His house of prayer alongside His chosen people Israel (Isaiah 56:6–8). That's very good news for us Gentiles, for now all believers (Jews and Gentiles) are assured that Jesus cared enough for us to "cleanse the temple," preparing the way to eternal life for all who trust Him as Savior and Lord.

JUDE 18-21

Jude, earthly brother of James and Jesus, is writing to Christians in general (likely both Jews and Gentiles) to urge them to defend the true doctrines of their faith. At this time, probably about thirty years after Jesus' crucifixion and resurrection, many false teachers were out and about teaching error and thereby disrupting the solidarity of the church. He reminds his readers that such false teachers had been predicted by the apostles. We, today, are witnesses to the fact that false teachers are still prevalent in our society. Thus, it is imperative that we know truth, and that we promote truth lest we allow Satan's influence to reign. See Jude's message for our day.

> In the last times there will be scoffers, following their own ungodly passions. It is these who cause divisions, worldly people, devoid of the Spirit. But you, beloved, building yourself up in your most holy faith and praying in the Holy Spirit, keep yourselves in the love of God, waiting on the mercy of our Lord Jesus Christ that leads to eternal life. (Jude 1:18–21)

Jude warns against being influenced by scoffers, those who doubt God's Word as written, and have their own thoughts on what is truth. Not only do they doubt God's Word, they preach and teach error, confusing and disrupting the unity of God's church. Thus, they promote divisions within the congregations. Their focus is on this world and its priorities and reflect the absence of the Holy Spirit in their influence.

So, Jude's counsel is made of three principles for his readers: (1) Building themselves up in their faith. (2) Praying in the Holy Spirit. And (3) waiting on the mercy of Jesus Christ. All of us would likely agree we need stronger faith. But how do we accomplish that consistently? How do we grow from weak faith to stronger faith? The answer is by taking that first step, realizing that we cannot (and don't have to) do so in our own strength. The Holy Spirit stands ready to help us. Believers have the Holy Spirit within and thus He provides that inherent knowledge of what we ought to do in a given situation. So, our first step consists of listening for the Holy Spirit's leadership, acting on what we sense is His will and watching for His next directive.

"Praying for direction as we step out" goes without saying. God will answer such prayers and we can be assured of that simply because we know that it is God's will for us to follow the Holy Spirit's leadership. And thirdly, we are to wait on the mercy of Jesus. That involves our (by faith) accepting Jesus' promised free gift of eternal life to all those who trust His sacrificial death on the cross as full payment of their sin debt. And (Hallelujah) membership in the family of God comes with our salvation. So, reality is, Jude is writing to believers, and who are believers? By definition, they are children of God, heirs, just like Jesus is. That defines our relationship with God, our heavenly Father. We have been adopted permanently into God's family. That knowledge should be a faith builder for us.

Thus, when we are tested by being exposed to doctrinal error and confusion, we know we are to speak out for truth, and stand up for what we know to be the truth of God's Word. Therefore, our lifestyles are to consist of ongoing efforts to build up our faith, consistent prayer, and patience, eagerly waiting on direction from the Holy Spirit as we go forward displaying Christlikeness. That's how God gets glorified.

COLOSSIANS 4:5–6

We have a hard time understanding the situation Paul's readers were in. These believers were intimidated daily by Roman influence and urged to consider the Roman emperor as God. Paul is in prison as he writes, so he, too, is feeling the Roman pressure. We also face a certain amount of oppression in our day for our beliefs, though for the most part unbelievers we know have likely heard of Jesus, but give Him little consideration. Incredibly, many, many people today have simply not given any serious consideration as to where they will spend eternity. Paul is giving his readers (and us) some good counsel on how to deal with the indifference we sense in other people:

> Walk in wisdom toward outsiders, making the best use of the time. Let your speech always be gracious, seasoned with salt, so that you may know how you ought to answer each person. (Colossians 4:5–6)

To "walk in wisdom" would involve constant attention to what effect our words and deeds have on other people. We do influence others whether we know it or not, or like it or not. Thus there is, inherently, a responsibility believers have for those they touch daily. **We do have that responsibility. Jesus gave it to us.** The perspective believers have about everything in life is to be based on glorifying our heavenly Father. "Outsiders" are unbelievers. Thus, the question we are to ask ourselves (but fail to do so much of the time) is do other people see Jesus Christ in us. And consistency in that regard is so, so, important. We all know how one instance of failure to reflect Christ in some act or word can spoil a lifetime of Christian influence.

It's true, but too simplistic to say, "We have all the time there is." Paul is emphasizing that we are to make every moment (of life) count, to take full advantage of each opportunity to witness, and to consider the importance of all our words and our intent. All our speech and influence is to be gracious, that is, marked by kindness and courtesy. Notice our speech is to be seasoned with "salt." What a neat way to describe the fact that like salt, our speech is to have a positive "flavoring" effect on our relationship with others. Jesus told us we are to be "the salt of the earth" (Matthew 5:13). That has to mean as God's witnesses we are to be attractive and stimulating to others when they see and hear us, drawing them to the same Savior we have.

We picture the apostle Paul as always being ready to say a word of witness to anyone, no matter the situation, whether they were a beggar, a Roman soldier, or a king. Paul reminds us to take on that same kind of heart set. We realize, of course, everyone needs a Savior, but we just don't seem to use the same weights of measure in every circumstance.

Paul's words are straightforward and simple enough to understand. It is the consistent execution of his instruction that gives us problems. It seems clear our hearts must be in tune with the Holy Spirit to foster such an ongoing lifestyle. Surely the Holy Spirit is always available to us. It remains then for us to dedicate the time and effort in prayer and Bible study to develop sufficient spiritual maturity to accommodate these Christlike attitudes.

JAMES 5:7–8

The author of this letter is James, Jesus' earthly brother, writing to Jewish Christians of that day, likely in the mid-forties AD. His key theme is living out one's faith, especially in the midst of suffering. Perseverance such as this requires patience, particularly when the suffering persists with seemingly no letup in sight. In our world today we sometimes experience similar suffering over long periods of time that test our faith. Thus, James' letter is appropriate for us too:

> Be patient, therefore, brothers, until the coming of the Lord. See how the farmer waits for the precious fruit of the earth, being patient about it, until it receives the early and the later rains. You also, be patient. Establish your hearts, for the coming of the Lord is at hand. (James 5:7–8)

It's usually easier to talk about being patient, than to be patient; patience being the ability or willingness to bear pain or trials calmly without complaint. Most people have difficulty living under such stress for long periods of time (or at least we don't want to), and that hasn't changed through the centuries. Thus, James reminds his readers to persevere.

James was writing to believers, people who knew the Lord, and had high hopes for better days ahead. They then, and we now, tended to think that as believers, God would protect them from such trials. So, when they had to face things like sickness and disease, crop failures, Roman oppression, and the normal problems of day-to-day living they were subject to losing heart.

It's not a coincidence that God saw fit to have such counsel and encouragement included in scripture for our benefit, for we face similar trials. And being patient is not easy. James uses the example of farmers patiently waiting for the rains necessary for a successful harvest, and they do this year after year. Notice how James tells us we can cope with our situations. We are to establish our hearts. That is, we are to firm up our convictions concerning the Lord, we are to stabilize our faith in God such that it will not waver. What we are waiting for is not rain, but the coming of the Lord; Jesus' return to gather those who believe for their journey to heaven with Him. We (and the farmers) assume rain will come sooner or later, but Christ's return is inevitable, not a "might be" event, sooner or later. We can count on the certainty of Jesus keeping His promises. We need not be disheartened by the fact that two thousand years have passed since Jesus ascended to heaven, and still He has not returned to earth. That's simply indicative of His love for mankind and His provision for more and more believers to come to know Him.

If scripture says "the coming of the Lord is at hand," then that simply is true. It is nigh, it is coming, and it will be on a day no one expects. The wording of Jesus' promise of His coming is particularly specific in the way we should anticipate it. We are to be assured of it, expecting it, and are not to be surprised when it happens. And our daily lives should reflect that kind of joy, peace, assurance, and confidence.

In fact, the announcement found in this passage should be one we excitedly repeat often, primarily because of the significance of it. And that's true because the news is so good. Let us share the truth we know concerning the gospel before it's too late. Those who don't know Christ have opportunity to prepare for His return through faith. No event can compare with the arrival of almighty God, coming to collect those who have trusted His sacrifice on the cross for eternal life.

MATTHEW 5:14-16

This passage speaks to people who believe in God and who recognize the importance of their influence in the world. These people know the truth of God's love and His provision in Jesus Christ. God has in essence blessed them with that knowledge and expects them to share that knowledge with those they influence by their lifestyles and priorities, and their words. All of us have some degree of influence on those around us, at least with our friends and family. Here Jesus is speaking to a first-century crowd and us in our day:

> You are the light of the world. A city set on a hill cannot be hidden. Nor do people light a lamp and put it under a basket, but on a stand, and it gives light to all in the house. In the same way, let your light shine before others, so that they may see your good works and give glory to your Father who is in heaven. (Matthew 5:14–16)

So when we have knowledge, we are obligated by God to share it, especially knowledge of God's love and salvation in Jesus Christ. We would not think of turning on a lamp in our home and then putting that lamp under a box so that no light escapes. That would miss the point of the lamp's function, and not only that, our home would still be dark. Thus we, and all our family that we love, miss the value of the lamp's light. That's the analogy of our knowing God but keeping that knowledge to ourselves.

So, we are to "live out" in front of the world what we know to be God's will for our lives. And if we don't know what God's will is for our lives, God has provided ways to show us His will. The Bible, God's Word, is the first place to start. In this same Bible book, Matthew, Jesus speaks and advises us of the most important commandment He ever gave us: "You shall love the Lord your God with all your heart and with all your soul and with all your mind. This is the great and first commandment. And a second is like it: You shall love your neighbor as yourself. On these two commandments depend all the Law and the Prophets" (Matthew 22:37–40).

It's easy to understand that if we love God and our neighbors with our whole hearts that will change our perspective concerning every area of our lives. And yes, good works will result from such love. We will naturally involve ourselves in the lives of others in positive ways that they will appreciate and recognize as God's influence in our lives. Thus, God gets the glory for who we are. And that is exactly what He is demanding in Matthew 5:14–16.

God has many ways of blessing us for obedience to His commands. Thus, we are not to see obedience to God's laws as a burden that somehow deprives us of the pleasures of life. We truly find real and lasting pleasures when we obey Him. God loves us and knows better than we do what eternal blessings He has in store for those who believe in Jesus Christ and have made Him Lord and Savior of their lives.

Many people have heard this gospel of Jesus Christ and given passing belief to that truth. However, Jesus commands our ongoing belief. He really is "God come to earth" to save us from our sins. He really is worthy of all our love and loyalty. We really can trust Him with our eternity. In fact, He is the only one we truly can trust eternally.

1 JOHN 3:1-2

The apostle John wrote this letter (probably in the late sixties AD) from Ephesus to churches in the surrounding area which now make up western Turkey. These recipients were believers, but they needed ongoing encouragement in their faith. They lived in a society dominated by the Romans in which idolatry was rampant and in which the worship of Christ was treated with indifference by some and looked on as a pagan religion by others. As is true now, many people in those days could not accept the "love thy neighbor" concepts that the Christians promoted. See how John words his encouragement:

> See what kind of love the Father has given to us, that we should be called children of God; and so we are. The reason why the world does not know us is that it did not know him. Beloved, we are God's children now, and what we will be has not yet appeared; but we know that when he appears we shall be like him, because we shall see him as he is. (1 John 3:1–2)

Everyone understands the love parents have for their children. But when believers claimed to be children of God, having that kind of special relationship with God, many people then disagreed. They saw believers as humans, born of human parents as they were, and they certainly did not understand the difference faith made in their relationship with Christ. And John explains why that is true. It was because they did not know Christ. They did not recognize Christ as the Son of God, nor did most people then believe He rose from the dead. So, this difference of opinion made for built-in conflict between believers and nonbelievers. That is still the case, made more prevalent now since it has been so long since Jesus returned to heaven promising to come back at the appropriate time.

But John plainly states to his first-century readers "we are children of God now," and so are we believers today adopted into God's family at the point of our salvation, with the same privileges and responsibilities as other children. And because believers are adopted into God's family, it is easy to grasp the concept of believers being chosen as children of God. Notice the specific point John makes relative to the kind of bodies we will one day have in heaven. Those kinds of bodies have not yet been seen on earth other than Jesus' body after His resurrection. When we get to heaven, Christians will be without sin, immune from sickness, morally pure, alive forever, and filled with the Holy Spirit. Thus, while we will not be all-knowing and all-powerful as Jesus is (for He is both fully man and fully God), we will be like Him. For "what we will be has not yet appeared." **But when God looks at us here on earth now, He sees us not as what we are, but what we WILL be, not God, but as perfect as man can ever be.**

Wow! What a day that will be, when we are in heaven with Christ, and we will KNOW we will be there for eternity. **And the greatest news about this condition we will have in heaven is, Jesus also knows what our perfection there will be like. He knows about the perfection we will have there because He made us in His image, and He knows we will therefore be able to adjust to heaven and be able to enjoy it more completely because of our new perfection. And that's no accident. Jesus and the Father have planned that perfect condition for us because they love us and have made heaven to be the complete, absolute maximum place of joy, peace, and contentment. And it will be because our triune God will be there with us! Hallelujah!!**

1 JOHN 4:12

All thinking people, especially believers, have wondered what God is like; how He looks, what His voice sounds like, and really about why He does what He does, particularly as it applies to us. We think of Him as all-powerful, all-knowing, all-loving, and all-merciful. He has all those characteristics to an infinite degree. What's more, He has promised us He will abide in us. Just think of it, we can take on God's characteristics and nature. How we do this is explained in these passages:

> No one has ever seen God; the only God, who is at the Father's side, he has made him known. (John 1:18)

> No one has ever seen God; if we love one another, God abides in us and his love is perfected in us. (1 John 4:12)

John the apostle wrote both these letters. In them he refers both to God the Father and God the Son. And we know that now Jesus, the Son, is at the Father's right hand interceding for us. Taken together, these verses tell us if we have questions concerning God the Father, then we can look at God the Son, "He has made Him known." So, if we ever wonder what God the Father would do, say, or think in any given situation, then consider Jesus and what He would do, say, or think in that situation.

The truth of the matter goes even further. We can take on God's characteristics as Jesus did (perfectly). And the way we do that is by loving one another. We are not to love just in words, but in thoughts, deeds, and motivations. Somehow in our humble concerns and expectations of others, God comes into our hearts, and gives us His perspectives on all our situations, and all our thoughts about others. This new heart set changes how we think about everything.

As used in 1 John 4:12, the word *abide* has deep meaning. It refers not just to God's presence within our hearts, but our whole attitude about life. It includes how we give over control of our lives to Him, and how His will becomes what motivates us in all we do.

Notice what the end point of God's abiding in us is: God's love is perfected in us. That has got to mean we love like God loves, we care like God cares, and we do (as best we can) what God would do in any given situation (and with the same motives God has). It has always been true that God considers why we do what we do as important as what we do. And the proper "why" for all we do is to glorify God. And in this verse, we are clearly told it's God's love that should be in us motivating all we do and are. God's love acting within us is to always be our "why."

Jesus is so consistent with His message to us. Over and over He emphasizes love as being the core motive for our lives. See this passage in John 13:34–35: "A new commandment I give to you, that you love one another: just as I have loved you, you also are to love one another. By this all people will know that you are my disciples, if you have love for another."

Notice what happens when we love one another: **it shows**. Other people see that we are joined in love to God the Father and Jesus as disciples causing us to love each other. And when they question us about this, we can share these verses with them because they apply to everyone.

MATTHEW 6:12

Jesus wanted His disciples to pray to Him regularly, so He took the time to teach them to pray (and at the same time to teach us to pray also). This verse is part of that teaching and has to do with God forgiving us of our sins. It would seem logical, and it is logical, for us to recognize we are sinners and regret that fact to the point of requesting in prayer that God somehow wipe away all our sins. God's thought on that subject is very sound. He tells us in this verse that He will forgive us of our debts to Him if and as we forgive those who are in debt to us. See this verse, it was applicable in Jesus' day, and is nowadays as well:

> And forgive us our debts, as we also have forgiven our debtors. (Matthew 6:12)

In the first place when we pray this prayer, we are acknowledging we are sinners in need of forgiveness. That in itself is a sobering thought. All of us have done things not in accord with God's will. One day there will come a time for each of us for reconciling all those sin debts before God. Both of those facts are true, whether we know it or not, whether we believe it or not, or whether we care or not.

Ecclesiastes addresses this subject directly in the last two verses of the book: "The end of the matter; all has been heard. Fear God and keep his commandments, for this is the whole duty of man. For God will bring every deed into judgment, with every secret thing, whether good or evil" (Ecclesiastes 12:13–14).

For believers, that Judgment Day will be a time of celebration, for their debts have been paid forever by Jesus' substitutionary death on the cross in our place. Many people deny they are sinners and thus have no need for forgiveness. Others do know they need a Savior, but put off their decision for Christ, thinking there will always be time later for conversion. Others don't know God made provision on the cross of Jesus for their debt payment, and die ignorant of what might have been if someone had come to them and shared the gospel of Jesus Christ. That last group is the saddest of all, because if you or I had shared Christ's gospel with them, they might have accepted Christ and been given God's free gift of eternal life.

We had best not ignore the last part of Matthew 6:12, about our forgiving others of their debts to us. We won't live long in this world before we are sinned against. We live in a sinful world and every day we are exposed to Satan working in the lives of people in ways that often impact us in sinful ways. Sometimes this happens in a direct way, and other times in an indirect way. In either sense we are told we are to forgive those who sin against us. Whether it was some schoolyard incident in our childhood or some business slight we felt as an adult, God would have us let Him do the avenging and settling of accounts. That is often easier to talk about than to execute. But then we don't have to do it in our own strength; God's Holy Spirit is always there to help us.

So, in essence God would have us forgive others if we want Him to forgive us, and has made provision for us to accomplish that. Thus, being the loving God that He is, He has advised us of how we are to live and to help us to live that way. And the stakes could not be higher. These verses are talking about our eternal destiny and that of those we love the most.

REVELATION 3:19-21

At one point early in the book of Revelation, the author, John the apostle, included a section specifically dedicated to seven different churches, wherein he included a message for each one. This particular passage is addressed to the church at Laodicea (in present-day Turkey) and describes that church as lukewarm, whose works are neither hot nor cold, and thus distasteful in all respects. What a true descriptive phrase for too many churches and individuals today. People attend church, participate (somewhat), and even contribute financially, but there is no zeal for kingdom work, no real heart for the lost, and no love for the Lord on display. Notice what the Holy Spirit had John tell the Laodicean church and how valid those comments are for us.

> Those whom I love, I reprove and discipline, so be zealous and repent. Behold, I stand at the door and knock. If anyone hears my voice and opens the door, I will come in to him and eat with him, and he with me. The one who conquers, I will grant him to sit with me on my throne, as I also conquered and sat down with my Father on his throne. (Revelation 3:19–21)

Therefore, we can expect to be corrected and disciplined, and that's a good thing, for per this passage that indicates God loves us. So, we are to be zealous, and just plain excited about the role God has us play in His kingdom work. And yes, we are still sinners, prone to transgressions, and in need of repentant hearts. Yet notice how God still takes the initiative in fellowshipping with us; He knocks at the door of our hearts and seeks our attention. And if anyone hears God's voice and opens the door (that is, is receptive to listening and obeying God) God will enter (that heart) and establish an ongoing relationship with them.

And for those who conquer, that is, that believe to the point of receiving the free gift of eternal life, they will sit with Christ on His throne. That has to imply a joint rule-and-reign role with Christ for them. The precedent for that has been set as Christ conquered death and sits now at the Father's right hand interceding for us.

Notice that while Christ initiates the decision on our part when He "knocks" on our heart, it is we believers who hear and open the "door." And it is we believers who repent. And, hallelujah, it is Jesus who then keeps His promise to come in and eat with us. In those days, and even now (though more subconsciously in our day), there is something intimate about sharing a meal with someone. The act of sitting together where both parties participate in replenishing their physical bodies together, that bonds the two, and gives words passed between them more meaning and significance. It is no coincidence that much in the way of business transactions is done nowadays over a lunch or dinner. Thus, eating together is representative of times when long-term commitments are made and validated. And the "eat with him and he with me" phrasing even adds to the concept of both parties agreeing to and approving this bonding.

Important to the significance of this passage is the ongoing message for us that God continually monitors our lives, our hearts, and our motives. He does know what is going on in our lives and He does want (via His Holy Spirit) to guide us in favorable directions. God's totally love-driven agenda for us merits our attention, obedience, and cooperation. What a great God we have.

PROVERBS 23:12

All of us seek wisdom. Consciously or subconsciously we want to make good decisions, to be well thought of, and to live favorable, comfortable lives for having done so. And we generally feel wisdom is the key route to comfort. Yet it is as if, while we want those capacities, we seem to think they will come naturally, and that we don't have to make any sort of effort to acquire them. Scripture tells us otherwise. Wisdom originates with God, and in passages like these we are told how to acquire it:

> Apply your heart to instruction
> and your ear to words of knowledge. (Proverbs 23:12)

The first point made in this verse is good news: wisdom is available, and apparently available to everyone. However, we definitely get the idea it doesn't come all at once, or even quickly, but slowly, over time, by consistent effort. And so if we want wisdom, step one is to first put ourselves in a position to acquire it. Thus, we must decide what and where is that place or position we can go to be instructed in wisdom. And the thought is clear that we are to stay there, or at least go there consistently. While there, we are to occupy our hearts in the effort to acquire wisdom. Our hearts are definitely the most tender and malleable part of us. So we can correctly conclude that wisdom is so valuable that only our hearts are appropriately applied to the work of getting this kind of instruction.

We are also to apply our ears to words of knowledge if we want to be wise. Our ears are representative of our minds. We may hear wisdom, see it, or read of it, for it comes to us from an outward source. So our intellect is also in the equation for acquiring wisdom. It goes without saying we must want wisdom to acquire it, and we must be able to recognize it when it is presented. To want wisdom badly leads to consistent ongoing effort. Recognition of wisdom when we do come upon it may require a bit of trial and error, for experience also plays a role in acquiring wisdom.

There is a certain amount of humility required also if we are to acquire wisdom. We must first admit we don't have it. There is real sadness involved when "we don't know what we don't know," and thus, make no effort to correct that situation. Sensitiveness is also a word that comes to mind when we consider obtaining wisdom. Sensitiveness to the importance of wisdom leads to the openness and transparency that are so key to really absorbing wisdom, and having it, therefore, readily available whenever we need it. We can be sure if acquiring wisdom were not important God would not have spoken of it so much, nor been so consistent in urging us to pursue it with determination.

Most important of all, by recognizing wisdom originates with God, we are led to pray for it. He loves us with a steadfast love and gives wisdom liberally to those whom He knows will use it for His glory.

MATTHEW 21:1–5

This passage reflects the beginning of Jesus' last week before His crucifixion. He and his disciples have arrived in the village of Bethphage, only about one mile to the east of Jerusalem. As they prepared to enter Jerusalem, Jesus sent two of His disciples into the village to collect a colt for Him to ride into the city. This triumphal entry had been prophesied about five hundred years earlier by the prophet Zechariah (9:9).

> Now when they drew near to Jerusalem and came to Bethphage, to the Mount of Olives, then Jesus sent two disciples, saying to them, "Go into the village in front of you, and immediately you will find a donkey tied, and a colt with her. Untie them and bring them to me. If anyone says anything to you, you shall say, 'The Lord needs them,' and he will send them at once." This took place to fulfill what was spoken by the prophet saying,
>
> "Say to the daughter of Zion,
> Behold, your king is coming to you,
>   humble, and mounted on a donkey,
>   on a colt, the foal of a beast of burden." (Matthew 21:1–5)

God knew five hundred years ahead Jesus would need to make this kind of humble entry into Jerusalem. This, representing both the humility and the kingship of Jesus. He is King of Kings, soon to die on a cross to pay the sin debt of all who would believe in Him as Savior and Lord. But the general public did not realize the full extent of what was about to happen. They took off their cloaks and spread them on the road ahead of Jesus, and sang His praises as He rode into Jerusalem on the colt. Ironically, only a few days ahead many of those same people would be shouting, "Crucify Him" as Jesus stood before the Roman governor Pilate.

It was important that Jesus fulfill all prophesy concerning the coming Messiah to validate His complete identity. And He did. Matthew, one of Jesus' disciples, is writing this years later as he confirms Jesus' actions for coming generations. We are blessed to have this record to read, believe, live out, and share with others who have not heard the gospel. Thus, there is a huge responsibility placed on us to care enough for the world to take all appropriate steps necessary to acquaint unbelievers with the way to eternal life.

Notice Jesus needed a donkey. We see here a classic example of Jesus maintaining His sovereignty, yet took on a human nature that had needs. He could have snapped His fingers and created a white stallion to ride, and everyone would have been impressed. But He chose to borrow a common donkey that someone else owned. **As Lord of all the earth, He has the authority to require any of us to provide anything we have. But He wants us to believe and willingly offer all we are. And that belief and willingness on our part is what makes all the difference.**

Would we let Jesus borrow our car? Probably, but that's not what He wants from us. He wants obedience, so would we go and tell others about His love for them as He has commanded us? Would we spend time tending to the needs of someone else? Would we do these kinds of things gladly and consistently? Bottom line, do we give Him the praise, honor, and glory He merits?

PSALM 103:8–12

Here in Psalm 103 we see David in general blessing the Lord, and in this particular passage of the Psalm, he begins to list why. We often hear some politician or some other noteworthy person asking God to bless America. And that's a good thing. But here we see David, an individual like us, doing the reverse, blessing God. We can and should continually raise up appropriate praise and adoration to Him, and that's a very good thing too. Look at why the Lord is deserving of our worship, and the results of such worship.

> The LORD is merciful and gracious,
>   slow to anger and abounding in steadfast love.
> He will not always chide,
>   nor will he keep his anger forever.
> He does not deal with us according to our sins,
>   nor repay us according to our iniquities.
> For as high as the heavens are above the earth,
>   so great is his steadfast love toward those who fear him;
> as far as the east is from the west,
>   so far does he remove our transgressions from us.
>   (Psalm103:8–12)

Key to this passage is the first sentence where David lists God's characteristics: he is merciful, gracious, slow to anger, and abounding in steadfast love. We ought to be very, very thankful those characteristics describe our God. Notice the words *us* and *our* are both used three times in this passage emphasizing where God directs His characteristics. And notice, too, why God needs to direct those characteristics toward us. The reason is our sins, our iniquities, and our transgressions. And what is the result of God's application of His characteristics in our situations; **we are**

forgiven completely and forever of anything and everything we have ever done wrong.

What wonderful news this is! What a powerful, organized, and all-inclusive description of our needs and God's response to them David has presented here. We can be sure God's Holy Spirit was behind this superb reflection of God's love and overall plan of salvation for mankind. And what is our role? See the phrase, "those who fear Him." That's not "fear" as in afraid, but "fear" as in reverence, respect, and honor, leading to obedience and love. And further, God even blesses us with the openness we have to these truths, and provides His indwelling spirit to guide us into and through the salvation process. What a great, great God we have.

So pray for God's direction, His forgiveness, and His mercy. They are available to those who come to Him, all because He loved us first, and He proves it every day.

PROVERBS 27:18

Sometimes Christian efforts seem fruitless. We pray, we initiate good works, and we engage others in meaningful conversation having to do with their relationship to the Lord. All to seemingly no avail. Here then is the verse for us. This one is designed to encourage and sustain us, for God knows our feelings in such cases. See how practical God makes His instructions:

> Whoever tends a fig tree will eat its fruit,
>> and he who guards his master will be honored. (Proverbs 27:18)

It takes several years for a seedling fig tree to produce fruit. That seedling requires consistent care and nurturing to properly mature into a producing tree. But, if the farmer is diligent, and if he is patient, and if he is consistent with his care, then one day he will be rewarded with a fruit-bearing tree, only because God has provided the rain, and sun, and soil nutrients to complete the process. **God has put such a sequence in place**. Just so is our journey with the Lord. Just so will we be rewarded one day with kingdom fruit, if we are diligent as the farmer is diligent planting and nurturing God's truths in the soil of someone's heart. This, because God provides the heart transformations necessary to complement our efforts. **God put that sequence in place also.** In both cases God adds the necessary factors to our efforts to affect a fruitful result. And as the farmer will enjoy the figs so God's disciples enjoy the fruit of their kingdom labor. **It has been God's plan from the beginning to use His disciples to produce eternal fruit.**

Notice the second phrase. As used here, the word *guard* refers to our continued attention and regard for our master's interests. Our master resides in heaven and the Proverbs verse assures us that those who guard and keep His word now will one day be honored. The idea of consistency in our Christian walk is understood here. See Mark 13:33–35: "Be on guard, keep awake. For you do not know when the time will come. It is like a man going on a journey, when he leaves home and puts his servants in charge, each with his work, and commands the doorkeeper to stay awake. Therefore stay awake—for you do not know when the master of the house will come."

True believers understand they are to be about their master's business until He returns. The promise in Proverbs is clear, he who diligently obeys his master in His absence will be honored. What type of honor is not defined, but when God honors us, we can be sure we are honored indeed.

HEBREWS 6:9–12

The author of this letter is unknown, but he clearly was teaching about the superiority of Jesus Christ and the importance of faith in Him as Son of God, Savior, and Lord. He urged his Jewish Christian readers to persevere to the end in their faith in Jesus and to urge others within the church to do the same thing. See how the Holy Spirit led the author to word his message to the Jewish believers:

> Though we speak in this way, yet in your case, beloved, we feel sure of better things—things that belong to salvation. For God is not unjust so as to overlook your work and the love you have shown for his name in serving the saints, as you still do. And we desire each one of you to show the same earnestness to have the full assurance of hope until the end, so that you may not be sluggish, but imitators of those who through faith and patience inherit the promises. (Hebrews 6:9–12)

At first the author warns of faithless people who claim the salvation of Christ, but have fallen away from their faith and deserve their final separation from God. But in the case of those he addresses here, the author is confident of better things, including eternal life with the Lord. He has observed their work and their love of the Lord, and if he has, certainly the Lord has. Thus, he is writing to encourage them to persevere in their faith to the end.

He mentions that they should not be sluggish, that is, that they not be adverse to activity or exertion. That certainly implies they are to be proactive in their faith, always seeking the well-being of others and how they can best be about the business of making disciples of Jesus Christ. The author's point is, when a person truly senses the love of God as displayed in Jesus' life, sacrificial death, and resurrection, they will naturally gravitate to obedience to Christ and a bent to sharing the gospel of Christ wherever they go. So, true believers cannot help but stick out in this world as they imitate the love of Christ.

Notice the key factors that will be visible in the lives of Christians in that first century, and even today: faith and patience. And through exhibiting those traits they inherit the promises of God. We understand the general definition of those promises, eternal life in heaven with the Lord. Scripture does not give us many specifics of life in heaven, but some examples are given that should excite us:

> Rejoice and be glad, for your reward is great in heaven. (Matthew 5:12)

> What no eye has seen, nor ear heard,
>   nor the heart of man imagined,
> what God has prepared for those who love him. (1 Corinthians 2:9)

Just consider what these passages tell us: Our reward in heaven is great (using God's definition of *great*), and we cannot in our wildest dreams imagine what God has prepared for those who love Him.

The passage above describes what is coming to believers in heaven as better things, leaving specifics to God, which should be fine with us. No question about it, we believers have incredible futures ahead.

PSALM 145:8–9

We see in these two verses a description of God's character, furthering our understanding of His goodness, and assuring us of His ongoing provisions for us. See how the psalmist, probably King David, lays this out for us:

> The LORD is gracious and merciful,
>   slow to anger and abounding in steadfast love.
> The LORD is good to all, and his mercy is over all that he has
>   made. (Psalm 145:8–9)

See the characteristics of God's nature listed: He is gracious, merciful, slow to anger, and abounding in steadfast love. See these defined:

Gracious: marked by kindness and courtesy, compassionate, characterized by charm, good taste, and generosity of spirit, easily approachable, and ready to respond pleasantly

Merciful: full of mercy, that is, with an abundance of charity and grace, stressing benevolence and goodwill shown in broad understanding and tolerance of others

Slow to anger: patient, kind, willing to consider forgiving and being merciful to others when faced with their unkindness, disobedience, and sin

Steadfast love: ongoing, unrelenting, never-failing love, often in spite of unloveliness shown by others

Picture these definitions "times a million," and you are beginning to grasp God's character.

Then notice to whom God applies His character: to all and over all that He has made. That has to include us. We are somewhere within "all," weak as we are, shortsighted as we are, inconsistent and failing as we are. Praise the Lord, for the kind of God we have.

So what should our response be to this revelation the Holy Spirit, using King David, has provided? Does it not follow that God would have us imitate those characteristics? Should we not pray consistently to the Lord to help us in this regard? Would not "our world" and "the world" be a better place if we and everyone else sought to live this way? Can we doubt that this is God's will?

Given that our reason for living is to glorify our heavenly Father, we quickly conclude here is how we do that. Isn't it just like God to give us clear directions as to how we should live? He surely loves us.

Luke 5:12-16

Everything Jesus said and did was worthy of the Father, and worthy of our noting and obeying. This passage describes one more instance of His love and power, and one more instance of His reliance on prayer. See how this plays out:

> While he was in one of the cities, there came a man full of leprosy. And when he saw Jesus, he fell on his face and begged him, "Lord, if you will, you can make me clean." And Jesus stretched out his hand and touched him, saying, "I will, be clean." And immediately the leprosy left him. And he charged him to tell no one, but "go and show yourself to the priest, and make an offering for your cleansing, as Moses commanded, for a proof to them." But now even more the report about him went abroad, and great crowds gathered to hear him and to be healed of their infirmities. But he would withdraw to desolate places and pray. (Luke 5:12–16)

There are a number of important points to note concerning this episode. First, the leper had an obvious need and He believed emphatically that Jesus could heal him. In other words, he had great faith in Jesus. Second, it simply remained that he convince Jesus to heal him. But Jesus needed no convincing. He immediately reached out and touched him saying, "I will, be clean." And he was. Notice Jesus did not become unclean when He touched the leper, the leper became clean. So, his faith was rewarded.

Third, Jesus kept the healing scriptural by telling the ex-leper to tell no one, but go and show himself to the priest, making a thanksgiving offering for his cleansing (Leviticus 14:1–2). And fourth, Jesus continued His practice of going aside often to pray. This last was perhaps the most descriptive of Jesus. He humbled Himself before His heavenly Father on regular occasions. We

389

sense this practice is what made and kept Jesus empowered to glorify the Father throughout His ministry.

Now we cannot heal the sick or cure leprosy as Jesus did, but we do come often to points in our lives when we need the Lord's help and guidance; points when it is obvious our prayers are in order. In fact, living a praying life is what God would have us do. We are literally to pray without ceasing (1 Thessalonians 5:17). Consistent, sincere prayers followed by our obedience will do the same thing for us they did for Jesus, that is, lead us to live lives that glorify our heavenly Father. **And doing that is why we were born.** Is glorifying God with our lives that simple? It is, and it isn't. We definitely are told to glorify God with our lives. And we are definitely told to pray without ceasing. And generally, one does follow the other. The obedience part is where we fail. Between our sincere prayers and diligent study of God's Word we come to have a feel (via the Holy Spirit's involvement) for how we are to live. And we are truly to comply with the Holy Spirit's direction.

As it happens, we cannot fully obey all we know we are to do and be. We are, though, to keep trying, to keep praying, and to keep studying and obeying God's word. Over time we grow spiritually (this process is our promised glorification) and we grow to be more Christlike. Other people come to see Jesus in us, and by definition we gain ground in our efforts to glorify the Father. That journey is what we are to be about. And Jesus has promised "to be with us till the end of the age" (Matthew 28:20).

PHILIPPIANS 2:9-11

Here, the apostle Paul is writing to the believers in Philippi to encourage them in their faith. Jesus is the ultimate model of faith and serves as the example they and we should imitate. He came to earth as a baby and grew to manhood living out (perfectly) the humble lifestyle of a servant of God and others, this, to the point of a sinner's death on the cross. Notice then in this passage how Paul describes God the Father's response to Jesus' life and death:

> Therefore God has highly exalted him and bestowed on him the name that is above every name, so that at the name of Jesus every knee should bow, in heaven and on earth and under the earth, and every tongue confess that Jesus Christ is Lord, to the glory of God the Father. (Philippians 2:9–11)

Thus, it was Jesus' humble act of submission to the cross (and all that signified) that was the basis for God the Father exalting Him to the position described in these verses. Think about it, what is the significance of having a name above every other name? No one lived like Jesus did. No one loved like Jesus did. No one gave up what Jesus did to bear the burden of death, especially death on a cross. And no one is less worthy than we are to deserve such a sacrifice. Jesus' life and death then literally defines humility, and it was His ultimate act of humility on the cross that led God the Father to exalt Him to the position above all others.

So, Paul's teaching here is that, literally, everyone ever born should acknowledge Jesus' position and bow to Him. Bowing and confessing, taken together, signify complete surrender to Him as Lord. And surrendering to Him as Lord mandates total submission to His will and way of life. **And then Paul goes even further, saying that God the Father intended this, and that**

true belief in Jesus as Savior and Lord on the part of believers culminates in God the Father being glorified. And to glorify God is why we were born.

WOW! Talk about closure! The Holy Spirit, via Paul, put a lot in this verse for us to consume. Jesus is Lord. And He is Lord, whether we know it or not, whether we believe it or not, and He is Lord even whether we like it or not. We are blessed just to hear this truth, blessed to have the opportunity to believe, and blessed eternally if we do believe.

With the knowledge of Jesus' position comes privilege, but responsibility comes as well. Once we've heard the gospel of Jesus, we can no longer plead ignorance of that truth. We can no longer be free of the responsibility to tell others about God's saving grace. We are not told to make disciples simply if we have the opportunity, but to be proactive in that assignment, looking daily for chances to share God's love with someone else, especially with those we love. And why would we be reluctant to do so? It's (very) good news and eternal in scope. No other information we could share carries with it anything close to the same potential benefits. **And we've never been assigned any task from someone with the degree of authority Jesus Christ has.**

1 CORINTHIANS 10:23, 31

Here, the apostle Paul is writing to the church in Corinth, Greece. His purpose in writing is to encourage them as individuals to come together as one membership in reaching out to unbelievers with the gospel of Jesus Christ. They have lost that perspective and are arguing among themselves as to what diets to use, what kind of clothes to wear, the celebration of certain religious holidays, and who is most important among them, instead of focusing on sharing God's love as expressed by the advent of Jesus into the world to save us from our sins. We are to profit from the mistakes they made as we live our own lives within our families, and the world around us. There is no more important message for us to live out than the good news of Jesus' sacrificial death on the cross. He died so we won't have to. As believers we are to imitate Jesus' lifestyle as those who glorify God in all we do. See Paul's advice:

> "All things are lawful," but not all things are helpful. "All things are lawful," but not all things build up. . . . So, whether you eat or drink, or whatever you do, do all to the glory of God. (1 Corinthians 10:23, 31)

Too many believers in that day and ours concentrate on what they can get away with doing and still be considered Christians, rather than how they can glorify God by proactively reaching out to unbelievers around them with the message of God's love. Thus, these verses tell us that simply because something is not necessarily bad, does not mean it's what is best for us, and what we should be focused on in our lives. God would have us develop His positive attitudes in all we do and are.

We can't discuss this subject without considering the influence we have on other people. Our sense of godly priorities in our lives should consistently show in our dealings with other people. And we cannot give too much importance to the word *consistency*. We are all aware how important consistency is; we just don't think about it enough. We've all experienced instances in our own lives or seen them in other people's lives where one thoughtless word or deed has damaged a lifelong reputation and/or relationship. It's that kind of ongoing Christian attitude of love for God and others that Paul is asking the Corinthians (and us) to develop, and it's the same kind of attitude Satan is trying to destroy.

When Paul talks about glorifying God, he is referring to all the things we do and say. This applies to what we might consider major decisions in our lives like who we associate with, and how we think about them and their feelings, and what our plans are for our lives as to school, jobs, marriage, etc., down to smaller daily decisions like what clothes we wear, or making up our beds in the morning, or being a positive influence within our families every day, etc. It's really our whole lives Paul wants us to consider. This, because God wants our total focus on Him, and besides, many times what we consider a small decision, long-term becomes a major decision. And God understands that better than we do.

God has a plan for each of us. And glorifying Him is the most important part of it. What many people don't grasp is that God is love. He loves us with an infinite love, and what He wants for us is best for us, and we benefit hugely when we let God have His way in our lives. Many people feel the Christian lifestyle requires we must give up too much to comply, and that misses the most important part of the Christian lifestyle. **Christians are God's children, part of God's family, adopted into it when they received Christ as their Savior and Lord. And they are permanently a part of it, and as His children our inheritance then is eternal life with Him in heaven. No earthly treasure and goal compares with that.**

REVELATION 21:1–4

This last book of the Bible speaks of eternal things. In this passage it describes the new heaven and the new earth that will come to be when Jesus Christ returns to gather all those who believe in Him. Notice how God keeps His promises and how believers will enjoy an eternity with Him in heaven. John, the author, describes what God's Holy Spirit shows him of the new heaven and the new earth.

> Then I saw a new heaven and a new earth, for the first heaven and the first earth had passed away, and the sea was no more. And I saw the holy city, new Jerusalem, coming down out of heaven from God, prepared as a bride adorned for her husband. And I heard a loud voice from the throne saying, "Behold, the dwelling place of God is with man. He will dwell with them, and they will be his people, and God himself will be with them as their God. He will wipe away every tear from their eyes, and death shall be no more, neither shall there be any mourning, nor crying, nor pain anymore, for the former things have passed away." (Revelation 21:1–4)

This is what heaven is going to be like. The phrase, "and the sea was no more" does not mean there will be no bodies of water in heaven, but is symbolic of sin, chaos, and danger; and these will definitely not exist in heaven. But God will be there, with His presence dominant in every way. His will and nature will control all that is, having taken away those earthly things we dread so much like sadness, worries, sickness, and death.

Time will not be a factor in heaven, nor will things associated with time like decay, aging, and all things temporary. The greatest blessing of heaven will be the presence of God there with us, providing the ultimate in fellowship forever. How that fellowship is defined is unknown, but words like peace, rest, joy, and infinite come to mind as we try to visualize God's presence with us.

The fact that the first heaven and the first earth will have passed away is significant. Thus, the new heaven and the new earth will not be infected with what separates us from God, and that is sin. There will be no sin in heaven, for all residents there will have been glorified, that is, made righteous as Jesus is righteous. His righteousness is imputed to us when we receive His free gift of eternal life, perfecting believers through a gradual sanctification process until we either die and go to be with the Lord, or He returns to gather us for fellowship with Him.

Think about it, there will be no mourning, crying, dread, or pain ever again for those in heaven sealed forever by God's Holy Spirit. God has instructed John to assure his readers (including us) all these former things have passed away. "Passed away" means to go out of existence, never again to be restored. So, to see scripture using that phrase when speaking of conditions on earth that will not be present in heaven we can be assured they will never be felt or heard of again.

This whole passage is an expression of God's love for His children, those who have trusted Jesus Christ's sacrificial death on the cross as payment of their sin debt. Their reward is complete, indescribable, and eternal. As believers we have an eternity to be thankful for, and, hallelujah it begins the very moment we receive God's free gift of eternal life at our conversion.

PHILIPPIANS 4:8–9

Paul is writing to the church at Philippi to encourage them in their faith, and to provide direction for their lives. They, like we, live with their lives broken down into minutes, and hours, and days, etc., and in another way by events, one after the other. So Paul suggests they work to define for themselves what happens in those time segments, and just which events they engage in and why. We can to a large degree direct those different sections. See what Paul tells us about how we can control them:

> Finally, brothers, whatever is true, whatever is honorable, whatever is just, whatever is pure, whatever is lovely, whatever is commendable, if there is any excellence, if there is anything worthy of praise, think about these things. What you have learned and received and heard and seen in me—practice these things, and the God of peace will be with you. (Philippians 4:8–9)

Notice there are two aspects to what we can do to direct our futures: what we let ourselves think about and what we choose to practice or live out of what we think about. Notice, too, it is not so much the subjects we think about that dictate our future, but the type and characteristics of those subjects that have so much to do with how our lives play out in this world.

At this point in his letter, Paul is beginning his closing statements, so what we read here is a summary of what he has already said, a kind of condensed version of the earlier part of the letter. Thus, this is a powerful statement for us to take in, critical even to how we live. **In essence, Paul is telling us to think, not to just react to what life brings us, but to be proactive, to plan (and do) ahead those things and types of things pleasing to God.**

First, in this passage, Paul lists six characteristics of the types of things typical of what God would have us think about, things that are true, honorable, just, pure, lovely, and commendable. Then he lists two conclusions we can draw: (1) These are excellent things to think about. (2) If we do think about them, that is a praiseworthy activity (praiseworthy by God).

If we want to receive praise from almighty God (and don't we all want this?) we now know what to do: think about things that measure up to one of the six characteristics Paul lists for us, and live them out. What Paul is describing then is "thought about" lives, not thought about from our perspective, but from God's perspective. The question for us is, "What does God think about what we plan to do and are already doing?" And then we are to candidly answer our own question.

Paul is disciplined enough as a mature Christian to tell his readers to do as he does, to live as he lives. Have we reached that point? Do other people see Jesus in us? That should be our goal.

Notice the end result of obedience to what Paul is telling us. "The God of peace will be with you." It's not the peace of God we obtain, but the companionship of the God of peace. That's a little hard for us to understand, but picture almighty God Himself in the form of His Holy Spirit **walking alongside us all day, every day**. That is absolutely true of every Christian. As believers we can be confident God knows our every care and need, and loves us enough to provide exactly the help that is best for us.

Our God is a great God, and we can and should take joy in that, and share that fact with others, especially those we love the most. That's why I'm writing you.

PSALM 51:10-12

In Psalm 51 we find a Penitential Psalm by David written after his affair with Bathsheba. It provides us much information concerning what a repentant heart looks like. It is not difficult to understand, full of heartfelt remorse, and loaded with entreaties to God for restoration of his relationship. We do well when we take such wisdom to heart and apply it to our own lives. See this portion from God to us:

> Create in me a clean heart, O God,
>   and renew a right spirit within me.
> Cast me not away from your presence,
>   and take not your Holy Spirit from me.
> Restore to me the joy of your salvation,
>   and uphold me with a willing spirit. (vv. 10–12)

How could we desire more than a clean heart (cleansed by the Holy Spirit) and a right spirit (provided by our heavenly Father)? These are what David is now missing and seeks to restore. And he knows the source of such restoration and goes directly to God with his requests. Notice he wants and needs God's presence as well to be clearly evident in his life. Who better to indwell his heart than the Holy Spirit. And what would surely be the result of God answering this prayer but joy. That joy is not to be short-lived and needs bracing inwardly by a willing spirit for all time. So David is led to pray for that too.

Thus, pending God's favorable response David will be restored from his grievous recent past. Key to his prayer is David's faith, and key to our prayers is our faith. David knew the God he was praying to. Scripture does not describe him as "a man after God's own heart" without cause (Acts 13:22). Nor will we believers be denied forgiveness either if we, too, sincerely repent of our sins, and seek God's mercy. So we can begin to grasp the full scope of this Psalm as applied to our sins of any description. In it we are advised what to pray for: a clean heart, right spirit, God's presence, the Holy Spirit's indwelling, and a willing ongoing spirit. And we are told what to expect as a result: the joy of God's salvation.

God loved David, knew what he needed, led him to pray for it, and provided him the best result possible. As believers we enjoy that same relationship with God. We have prayer access to His throne room and our Lord Jesus to intercede for us just as David did. Hallelujah!!

1 PETER 1:13-17

Every believer is called to be holy. That requires a change from what we think to what God thinks. He is the one who is perfect, with all knowledge and with all power. It's His will, His purpose, and His goals we are to diligently seek to fulfill. He has made us what we are and has a plan for each of us utilizing all the gifts, talents, and opportunities He provides to bring glory and honor to Him. That last thought is the unique goal that only believers have. Believers understand that bringing praise to God is the most fulfilling effort we can make. See these crucial thoughts the Holy Spirit led Peter to write to us:

> Therefore, preparing your minds for action, and being sober-minded, set your hope fully on the grace that will be brought to you at the revelation of Jesus Christ. As obedient children, do not be conformed to the passions of your former ignorance, but as he who called you is holy, you also be holy in all your conduct, since it is written, "You shall be holy, for I am holy." And if you call on him as Father who judges impartially according to each one's deeds, conduct yourselves with fear throughout the time of your exile. (1 Peter 1:13–17)

Notice preparing our minds for action must be something God enables us to do. God would never require something of us that we are unable to do with His help. Thus, because He has made us sober-minded, that is, having serious, temperate personalities, not subject to extreme qualities of emotion or prejudice, we are not to conform to the thoughts we had before we turned ourselves over to the Lord, that is, when we lived according to our former ignorance of God's grace. See Ephesians 2:8–9: "For by grace you have been saved through faith. And this is not your own doing; it is the gift of God, not a result of works, so that no one may boast."

So, as Peter tells us, we are to "set [our] hope fully on the grace that will be brought to [us] at the revelation of Jesus Christ." "Fully" means exactly that. It is only the grace of God (that undeserved love God has for us) that saves us. He loves us in spite of our unworthiness. And as obedient children we are not to be conformed to the lifestyles and principles we had before we made Jesus Christ Lord of our lives. Thus, we are told to be holy as "He who has called you is holy." If we've made Jesus Lord, then it follows we will work toward His likeness in our lives. Therefore, our deeds and conduct will reflect Christ's priorities. And after all, it will be Christ who will one day impartially judge our deeds. Who better could act as our judge than that perfect Son of God who died in our place to pay our sin debt?

Thus, we believers will conduct ourselves with fear throughout the time of our exile. That would be fear as in respect and reverence, not fear as in terror. And this would be our consistent lifestyle while we remain on earth before Christ returns. Surely, that would be the most effective way to glorify our heavenly Father.

Peter saw fit to write of these priorities to believers in Asia Minor, modern-day Turkey. Those believers needed this encouragement, as do we today. And our responsibility to share this truth of God's love is no different than the responsibility Peter had. Such sharing lifestyles honor our heavenly Father and our Lord Jesus. They both are well worthy of our best efforts.

ECCLESIASTES 12:13-14; MATTHEW 22:37-40

The Bible is the Word of God and because of that we should consider every word of it true and relevant. But even with that being true, there are certain verses that seem to stick out and be so vibrant and so strong we cannot help but be struck with the power and wisdom they show us. Such are these two passages. Most scholars attribute authorship of Ecclesiastes to King Solomon. And what we see here certainly fits the image we have of him as being the wisest man to ever live. Matthew the apostle quotes Jesus in those verses shown here. See these verses and how they ring true even now:

> The end of the matter; all has been heard. Fear God and keep his commandments, for this is the whole duty of man. For God will bring every deed into judgment, with every secret thing, whether good or evil. (Ecclesiastes 12:13–14)

For twelve chapters the author of Ecclesiastes has described his life and what he has learned and experienced, and what God has shown him concerning knowledge and wisdom. And here in the last two verses of the book he sums up God's message to mankind. Clearly, we are told the reason for man's existence. And that is to fear God and keep His commandments. "Fear," as used here is not meant to represent being afraid, but fear as in reverence and respect. It is those kinds of feelings we are to have toward God, reverence and respect even to the point of love.

Notice the degree of transparency Solomon tells us will come out during God's end time judgment. Every event and thing ever said or done will apparently be made public, whether good or evil.

Nothing will be kept secret. Everything will be described and explained. And Jesus as judge will make the perfect call as to our eternal destiny.

Matthew 22:37–40 tells us:

> You shall love the Lord your God with all you heart and with all your soul and with all your mind. . . . You shall love your neighbor as yourself. On these two commandments depend all the Law and the Prophets.

Jesus is being challenged by the Pharisees as to which commandment of the law is greatest. Doubtless their intent was to trick Him into naming one which they thought would open a debate whether that were true or not, given the importance of all the commandments. However, Jesus' answer was so all-encompassing, He ended the debate before it began.

But look at what accrues to us here between these two passages: a storehouse of vital information we can apply and share concerning the way to live our lives. At some point we may be so "down," we may claim we don't know our reason for living, but from this time forward that will not be true. Taken together, these two passages literally tell us why we were born. Notice neither passage speaks at all of our personal circumstance during our time on earth. No matter our circumstance we are simply to love the Lord and our neighbors with everything within us, and because of that love, gladly obey His commandments. What a great God we have to simplify things so for us.

JAMES 2:21-24

James is making the point in this passage that we are not justified (that is, found not guilty of our sins) by faith alone, but also by our works, which prove our faith. At the final judgment a person's work gives evidence of true saving faith. And that's only logical; we will live out our faith if it is real. At least that will be our goal. And should we fail in this effort which leads to sin, then we will feel remorse for that sin and immediately repent and seek forgiveness. This was true in the first century and it is true today. Societies change, but human nature does not. See the example of Abraham:

> Was not Abraham our father justified by works when he offered up his son Isaac on the altar? You see that faith was active along with his works, and faith was completed by his works; and the Scripture was fulfilled that says, "Abraham believed God, and it was counted to him as righteousness"—and he was called a friend of God. You see that a person is justified by works and not by faith alone. (James 2:21–24)

So, there is harmony between Paul's declaration that we are saved by grace through faith (Ephesians 2:8–9) and this passage in James. Our works are our lived-out faith, as Abraham illustrated for us. Notice how Abraham's faith earned him the title "a friend of God." Abraham believed God, and that action was credited to his righteousness. He left all that he had and followed God's instructions.

There is a sense though that Abraham's example of obedience to God was done willingly, not reluctantly. He believed God, acted on that belief, and expected to be blessed as God promised (and he was). We can and should follow that same path. Believe in God as expressed in His Word, obey God as commanded in His Word, and expect the blessings outlined in God's Word. Notice how crucial God's Word is to this whole salvation process. Notice, too, God's blessings and promises to Abraham were not completed until long after he died. Thus, so are ours likely to be. Counting on God's faithfulness in the (very) long-term will turn out to be by far the best for us believers.

So, we are not to keep focused on our short-term blessings (i.e., those that come in this lifetime), but our heavenly existence with the Lord forever. Such perspectives will automatically be lived out now by good works, or better worded, obedience to God's laws. And such lives are noteworthy. People will see Jesus in us, God will be glorified, and we will feel led to share the truth of God's love with others, especially those who mean the most to us.

And if so, it can correctly be said we win coming and going, that is, in this life and heaven too. A godly lifestyle adds much to our present existence. Nothing, but nothing, is as fulfilling as leading a lost sinner to the salvation Jesus' atonement bought for them. To know for certain they are heaven-bound and will enjoy an eternity with the Lord is a feeling beyond compare for them and us.

Amazingly, none of this is by accident. God constructed His salvation plan with the best of the best in mind for those who are adopted into His family. And He did it because He loves us. Not a love we've earned, but love coming to us by His grace alone. Faith in the love reflected by Jesus' acts on the cross leads to the free gift of salvation from the Father. Hallelujah! And Amen!

REVELATION 22:20-21

As you can see, I have come to the last words of scripture in my daily Bible reading. And what an awesome passage it is, one of encouragement for us, one of commitment to us, and one with an everlasting promise from our Savior and Lord Jesus Christ. Just look at what we've been told:

> He who testifies to these things says, "Surely, I am coming soon." Amen. Come, Lord Jesus!
> The grace of the Lord Jesus be with all. Amen. (Revelation 22:20–21)

Here is Jesus telling us specifically and emphatically, "Surely, I am coming soon." What a word of good news and encouragement, what a command to us to get ready, and what an implied warning. Notice the response we (that is, believers everywhere) need to (wholeheartedly) provide: "Come, Lord Jesus!" The solutions to all our cares and woes will not ever be provided by worldly wisdom, but only by the coming of our Lord. And so in God's infinitely wise timing Jesus will return one day soon (soon as in quickly, or suddenly, without warning) and we can and should take joy in that fact. And we can and should share that fact with others.

And notice, too, the final blessing we are given: that God's grace (His unmerited favor) be with us all. What better way could the Holy Spirit have John end this letter, and the whole Bible, than to pray God's grace upon us all? God's grace is what we've always needed, and praise the Lord, He has provided it. Look at Charles Spurgeon's take on this last blessing that points up its significance for us: "Whatever you may miss, may the grace of our Lord Jesus Christ be always with you. In whatsoever points you or any of us may fail, may we never come short of the grace of our Lord Jesus Christ" ("Till We Meet Again").

We are to thus never forget, God loved us first, "while we were still sinners, Christ died for us." (Romans 5:8), and through His grace made provision for our eternal life via Jesus' death in our place on the cross. So Ephesians 2:8 really is true: "For by grace you have been saved through faith. And this is not your own doing; it is the gift of God."

2 CORINTHIANS 6:4–10

In this passage Paul commits himself to the ministry of the gospel, describing the many hardships he has experienced and how he has been able to endure those hardships. God allowed those hardships, and at the same time provided Paul the ability to persevere through them. God has and will do the same thing for us. God knows of all we may ever go through, and we can be sure He will not leave us alone in our trials. See Paul's words of encouragement:

> But as servants of God we commend ourselves in every way: by endurance, in afflictions, hardships, calamities, beatings, imprisonments, riots, labors, sleepless nights, hunger; by purity, knowledge, patience, kindness, the Holy Spirit, genuine love; by truthful speech, and the power of God; with the weapons of righteousness for the right hand and for the left; through honor and dishonor, through slander and praise. We are treated as imposters, and yet are true, as unknown, and yet well known, as dying, and behold, we live, as punished, and yet not killed; as sorrowful, yet always rejoicing, as poor, yet making many rich; as having nothing, yet possessing everything. (2 Corinthians 6:4–10)

Over and over Paul speaks of trials, and how God resolved them; pain, and how God eased that pain; oppression, and how God was able to give Paul victory over oppression. How was Paul able to overcome these conditions, the same way we would, via the guidance of the Holy Spirit and the power of God. He was vilified, misunderstood, and wrongly accused. He was physically abused, and challenged spiritually. He was misquoted, lied about, and falsely condemned. Yet though it all, he stayed the course of faith in Christ. And because of that he continued to rejoice in his ministry knowing in Christ he possessed everything worth possessing.

Everyone incurs pain, suffering, and disappointment at some point in their lives. When that happens most of us have trouble not feeling sorrow for ourselves. Many times, when we feel that way, God will bring someone across our path who really does have trials and we come to realize our problems were not as bad as we pictured. Paul's background of suffering was so much worse than what the Corinthians faced they had to feel ashamed.

Paul made many rich, not in material wealth, but with the spiritual values he shared. The eternal life Jesus offered and that Paul preached about is still available today, and it's just as valuable now. And the unique thing about that kind of value is we, too, can hand it out liberally to everyone we meet. We don't have to live perfect lives, or be able to preach like Paul to be a witness for the Lord. It's all a matter of perspective; that is, what we understand as truly real, and valuable and worth both living and dying for. Given the long list of hardships this passage describes we can only conclude nothing we might endure is able to separate us from the love of God. And with that kind of steadfast love, we, like Paul, though poor, have true riches to give away, though having nothing really of earthly value, have everything of heavenly worth.

EPHESIANS 1:15–19

Paul is writing to the believers in Ephesus, complimenting them on their steadfast faith in Jesus and their love toward other believers. And then he goes further, telling them specifically what he is praying for them. He mentions three things. First, that they may know the hope that God has called them to as believers. Second, that they will understand the riches of God's inheritance that will accrue to them one day as saints. And third, the insurmountable power they will have access to as children of God. We, too, can look forward to those same blessings:

> For this reason, because I have heard of your faith in the Lord Jesus and your love toward all the saints, I do not cease to give thanks for you, remembering you in my prayers, that the God of our Lord Jesus Christ, the Father of glory, may give you the Spirit of wisdom and of revelation in the knowledge of him, having the eyes of your hearts enlightened, that you may know what is the hope to which he has called you, what are the riches of his glorious inheritance in the saints, and what is the immeasurable greatness of his power toward us who believe. (Ephesians 1:15–19)

The future hope to which God has called the Ephesians (and all believers) involves an endless and ever-growing relationship with Jesus Christ. That begins the moment of our conversion on earth and continues forever, encompassing time spend on earth and an eternity in heaven. Certainly the length of our hope in Christ is endless, but the quality of that relationship defies description. Notice Paul first prays that a spirit of wisdom and of revelation in the knowledge of Jesus come over the Ephesians to enlighten their eyes such that the significance of their hope in Christ may be made known to them. Without such a spirit of wisdom and of revelation no believer would ever "mine" out the blessings a relationship with Jesus provides. Not only does our heavenly Father love us children so much He provides heaven for us, He adds increased wisdom and revelation to us so we can enjoy and appreciate an eternity in heaven with Him even more.

And how do we grasp the second blessing Paul is praying for, that of the understanding of the riches of God's inheritance? We can be sure our heavenly inheritance will not be measured with units of dollars or by the size of our heavenly home. The sense of Jesus' steadfast love for us, and the security forever that we will feel in His presence will provide joy and peace and harmony and companionship like we have never experienced before. Imagine a new (awesome) revelation every day concerning God's love, power, and majesty that we can share with like-hearted believers who will be just as stunned, surprised, pleased, and satisfied as we are.

And what about God's power, the third point of Paul's prayer for the Ephesians? If we are not overwhelmed by the magnificence of what we experience with Paul's first two prayer requests, the hope we are provided as believers and the understanding of the riches of our inheritance, then the limitless greatness of the power God has and does apply to making our heaven, the heaven it is, will likely be what crowns our overall heavenly experience. It seems inadequate to say we have a great God. It's not enough to just say we love Him. We don't go far enough in our commitments to Him. But we can try.

Let us pray prayers like Paul did, for fellow believers, and for ourselves. Let us live out our faith, and beliefs. And let us continually share what we know of God's love with others.

1 TIMOTHY 4:15–16

This section of 1 Timothy comes under the heading "A Good Servant of Christ Jesus," which is very descriptive. We should all strive to be good servants of Christ Jesus. Up to this point in his letter, Paul has been instructing Timothy in the way of conduct, love, faith, and purity, telling him to devote his time to public reading of scripture, to exhortation, and to teaching. Note how Paul concludes this section, given the importance of these points he has made:

> Practice these things, immerse yourself in them, so that all may see your progress. Keep a close watch on yourself and on the teaching. Persist in this, for by so doing you will save both yourself and your hearers. (1 Timothy 4:15–16)

Paul's word usage here adds an obvious tone of importance, of urgency, of consistency, and of relevance to what he has been saying. Now Paul tells Timothy to "live out" what he has been taught. All these things are applicable to Timothy and to those he will be leading. Timothy is to practice these things, example them, and thus, promote them as God given commands. And, of course, the "things" Paul is referring to are those characteristics he has just mentioned; conduct, love, faith, and purity. Neither Timothy nor we will reflect those effectively unless he immerses himself in them and makes them a part of his spiritual walk. To immerse himself in anything automatically gives credence to that "thing" in his life and makes the fact of that credibility evident to those around him. An example would be Paul's conduct. If it is important to Paul to monitor his own conduct to the point it reflects Christlikeness, then that effort and priority will be obvious to those he influences. **AND GOD GETS GLORIFIED.** So, we easily grasp the significance of such a lifestyle for us. Without question Paul is urging Timothy (and us) to do the same thing with his love, faith, and purity, and for the same reason, that is, so that God is glorified.

The idea is for all those around Timothy to see his progress (and feel led to live a similar life). Paul knows that such a disciplined lifestyle is catching; others will see and be moved and led to also live out their faith. And that's true in our day as well. But it requires a close watch on our lives, a consistent guarding ourselves against the influence of the evil one. No wonder Jesus' "model prayer" includes a phrase petitioning the Lord to "deliver us from the evil one." We must stay alert to his lies.

Notice, too, Paul makes a specific note to have Timothy guard against false teaching. We, too, are to ensure our teaching is always in accord with God's Word. The best and most knowledgeable of teachers can misquote God's Word on occasion.

And as in all aspects of our Christian walk, consistency is critical. Paul tells Timothy to persist (in good times and bad, before the influential and the downtrodden, before crowds or individuals) in glorifying the Father by his unwavering commitment to truth. And notice why this is important: **because by being consistent in all respects (his conduct, love, faith, purity) Timothy will save himself and those he teaches.** And isn't that why Jesus told us to go and make disciples, to lead them to salvation and those they influence.

Isaiah 1:18-20

Isaiah the prophet lived in Judah about 700 BC. God appointed him to go to the people of Israel and warn them of the consequences of their sin. Besieged by surrounding nations, and wracked with sin within, Israel was bound for destruction if they did not change their ways. See below the message God has Isaiah give them. Among all His other wonderful attributes, God is perfectly logical. And it is a most hopeful and logical truth that He has for Israel (and really for us today).

> Come now, let us reason together, says the LORD:
> though your sins are like scarlet,
> > they shall be as white as snow;
> though they are red like crimson,
> > they shall become like wool.
> If you are willing and obedient,
> > you shall eat the good of the land;
> but if you refuse and rebel,
> > you shall be eaten by the sword;
> > for the mouth of the LORD has spoken. (Isaiah 1:18–20)

Notice how gracefully this passage begins. God appeals to their common sense. It is as if He is saying to Israel, "Look, you know you are being disobedient, and that this will lead to no good end. So, why not stop and let us think together about your situation?" God points out how obvious, and how glaring, their sins are. They are evident to Him and evident to the world around them. You cannot hide a scarlet and crimson red appearance, neither can they hide their sins. But there is hope, there is a way for them to go from where they are that will lead to relief from the troubles that now lie ahead. To be as white as snow or wool is symbolic of the purity of a sin-free life that is available to them.

In a very real way this picture also describes our society today. We see a sinful world around us tracking toward destruction that needs to change. But, hallelujah, we have the same hope described in this passage. And fulfillment of that hope requires the same thing from us that Isaiah tells his readers is necessary for Israel; a willingness to change, and appropriate obedient actions. And God is willing to commit to what the results will be of willingness and obedience, "You shall eat of the good of the land." Now those words are not fully specific, but they are specific enough. They have to represent eternal security. They must be talking about the right kind of peace of mind on earth and in heaven to come.

On the other hand, if they (or we) refuse and rebel, they "will be eaten by the sword." We can be sure Isaiah's readers took that to mean a decisive military defeat by their enemies. For us, we can take it to mean whatever is opposite to eternal security and peace of mind, which though not defined exactly, is not good news. How foolish we are to know the truth, to see God speaking to people just like us and to pay no mind to His instructions.

And talk about a final note to this passage that should stick with us, the final verse tells us these words are God's words: "He has spoken." Just think about it, almighty God loves us enough to see fit to speak to us with truth that, if accepted, will make our lives on earth and in heaven more than we can imagine.

So, whether we take the counsel of this passage as sound logic or godly wisdom, it is surely worthy of our consideration and acceptance. And by the way, since God "invented" both sound logic and wisdom, it doesn't matter what we call it. It's His truth.

MATTHEW 5:11-12

Jesus' Sermon on the Mount is perhaps His most well-known sermon. He begins it with a listing of instructions for all believers on how to live their lives. We know that list as The Beatitudes, that is, blessings that come to obedient believers. Though we live in a different society, these thoughts are very appropriate for us too. Jesus does not waste the opportunity to speak truth to the crowds following Him, and no doubt He had us on His mind, too, as He preached then. Notice how relevant this particular passage is to our society:

> Blessed are you when others revile you and persecute you and utter all kinds of evil against you falsely on my account. Rejoice and be glad, for your reward is great in heaven, for so they persecuted the prophets who were before you. (Matthew 5:11–12)

Jesus would have us live lives that honor and glorify Him. Should such a lifestyle upset others, then they have a problem, not us. In Jesus' day and in ours, there are those who find fault with obedient Christians, even to the point sometimes of violent opposition. Jesus warns His listeners of such possibilities and prepares us all for the consequences of serving Him.

Jesus suffered; so as His followers we can expect opposition too. In fact, if we do not experience opposition, it is likely we are not different enough from those around us for them to notice Christ in us. Christ's life was unique, and distinctly different from the unbelievers around Him. So should ours be. Suffering for Jesus' sake leads to rewards, and it is a straight-line function; that is, one follows the other, because Jesus said they would. The timing and type of our rewards is up to the Lord, and might not come to us in this life, but come they will, because Jesus keeps His promises.

Notice we are to "rejoice and be glad" for obedience here leads not just to rewards in heaven, but great rewards. In the first place, heavenly rewards have a connotation all their own. Any reward God provides represents what He knows would please us to the absolute utmost. So if we don't rejoice and be glad not only are we disobeying God, we are missing out on what He maintains will be a great reward in heaven one day.

Though the trials that accrue to us as believers sometimes seem troublesome and impossible for us to deal with, Jesus advises us that we are not the first to be so bothered. When He speaks of the prophets also being persecuted, the thought comes to mind that "better people than we are" have been persecuted before us. It is likely no trial we ever face is unique or has never happened before to anyone else. How many times have you had the thought, "I thought I had problems until I met someone who really had problems." And if Jesus speaks of rewards for us as He has here, we can count on Him both helping us with our trials, but also rewarding us for persevering through our hard times.

So the lesson in this Beatitude is we will face persecution and trials in one form or another. Let us ensure when ours comes to us, they come for Christ's sake, because we have been living in obedience to His will. This world is not our home. The heaven we believers have in store will be infinitely better, and yes, we can and should rejoice and be glad. Who do you know that needs to hear about this Beatitude?

2 TIMOTHY 2:11-13

Paul would have his readers remember Jesus Christ and that includes us. To "remember" Christ entails a deep appreciation of His identity and His earthly ministry, that is, who He is, and all He did and taught for our benefit. Paul's whole life reflected his dedication to Christ, and he keeps on reminding Timothy to keep his focus on Christ. That's an ideal focus for us, too, loving God back for His love for us. See how this passage sums up the results of both consistency and inconsistency in our Christian walk.

> If we have died with him, we will also live with him;
> If we endure, we will also reign with him;
> If we deny him, he will also deny us;
> If we are faithless, he remains faithful—
> for he cannot deny himself. (2 Timothy 2:11–13)

Notice there is no "maybe" or "perhaps" kind of message within Paul's words here. Each of the four statements is an individual "if-then" statement. In each case if the first phrase is true, then the second phrase is emphatically true also. They describe God's nature, and they also describe the way God has constructed His salvation plan for us. Notice, too, how the statements range from comforting and joy-filled principles, to a warning for disbelief, and then back to comfort.

The first statement reminds us there is life even in death for believers who are in Christ. And the implication is that the life we will spend with Christ is eternal. Not only that, the second statement describes our role in heaven with Christ is somehow to be that of a ruler, reigning with Him, again forever. On the other hand, the third statement reflects the result of our denying Christ. He will deny us at the judgment. To deny Him would indicate a permanent attitude of disbelief in Christ's sacrificial death for our atonement. Such a declaration provides evidence for a ruling of "guilty" for our own sins resulting in the separation from God forever for those individuals.

The fourth statement reflects the status of all true believers, believers (in Christ) yes, but weak in our faith, and apt to periodically sin and fall short of God's glory. But praise the Lord, God remains faithful. His love for His children is sure and it is eternal. He is faithful to forgive us of our trespasses as we forgive those who trespass against us. In an earlier letter Paul describes our need to "pray without ceasing" (1 Thessalonians 5:17) for there is always need for our pardon and restoration.

Paul is being realistic in this letter. He knows of his own tendency to sin (even now as a believer), and that Timothy has that failing, too, as do all believers then and now. Thus, we need not fret concerning our failures, not to excuse them, but to recognize God will honor our sincere repentance and request for forgiveness. And in this passage Paul tells us why. God cannot deny Himself. God's nature is one of love. He loves us (His children) with a steadfast love and will never forsake us. Jesus' death on the cross paid all our sin debt forever. This does not present us a pass on sin with freedom from guilt and punishment from judgment via insincere requests for forgiveness, but it does acknowledge Jesus' act on the cross was sufficient to cover all our weaknesses and trespasses. God knows our hearts, and will never deny forgiveness to a sincere believer who is remorseful for their sins. What a great, great God we have.

REVELATION 5:11–14

John the apostle wrote this book from the Isle of Patmos late in the first century. He had been sent there in exile for preaching the gospel of Jesus Christ. There he was shown a vision from God wherein he was taken up to heaven and saw "Him who was seated on the throne" (v. 1) and experienced the praise, honor, and glory that is presented continually to God the Father by the elders, the angels, and other living creatures that reside in heaven. Jesus, the Lamb of God, is there too; He who was slain and by His sacrifice ransomed people from every tribe and nation. The whole experience for John was one of sensing (and describing) the majesty, the splendor, the glory, the honor, and the worship that comes to the Father and the Lamb in heaven forever. Such an awesome experience will be what all believers one day will have forever. See part of what John tells us:

> Then I looked, and I heard around the throne and the living creatures and the elders the voice of many angels, numbering myriads of myriads and thousands of thousands, saying with a loud voice,
>
> "Worthy is the Lamb who was slain,
>> to receive power and wealth and wisdom and might
>> and honor and glory and blessing!"
>
> And I heard every creature in heaven and on earth and under the earth and in the sea, and all that is in them, saying,
>
> "To him who sits on the throne and to the Lamb
>> be blessing and honor and glory and might forever and ever!"

And the four living creatures said, "Amen!" and the elders fell down and worshiped. (Revelation 5:11–14)

We read this and really can't take it in. We don't have a good feel for such a description and how it could possibly exist. But it does exist, it does go on forever, and it is prepared especially for believers by the same God that showed it to John. And what we can look forward to is an understanding of it all. We will be able to participate, to enjoy it ever increasingly, and to share the whole experience with other believers forever.

Notice the focus there in heaven will not be on us. It will be where it should be, on God the Father, and Jesus Christ the Lamb. We will get to enjoy their presence as we praise and worship them. All our singing, all our worship, all our praise, all our honor, all our hope will be in them, but the total experience will be beyond what we can understand now.

Two key points jump out at us in this passage. The first is that both God the Father and Jesus the Son are worthy of all this adulation that is described, and only those two. Their glory and majesty are beyond our comprehension in scope, and endless in duration. And without question or the slightest doubt, we will understand that. So, our participation will be wholehearted, complete, and enthusiastically given. We will enjoy the experience just because it is so correct and appropriate.

Secondly, we will understand only God's grace could be the motive for these provisions, which will make our gratitude all the greater. Only His grace leading to Jesus' sacrifice of Himself on the cross could provide such a destiny for unworthy sinners such as we are.

Something like this is difficult to explain to others. Often the best approach is simply to show unbelievers the scriptures and let them read it for themselves. It is always appropriate though to pray for those occasions; that God's Holy Spirit will enter in and move the reader's heart as only He can do.

MARK 4:35-41

This is a long and familiar passage, and well worth our time to consider. Please look at it again:

> On that day when evening had come, he said to them, "Let us go across to the other side." And leaving the crowd, they took him with them in the boat, just as he was. And other boats were with him. And a great windstorm arose, and the waves were breaking into the boat, so that the boat was already filling. But he was in the stern, asleep on the cushion. And they woke him and said to him, "Teacher, do you not care that we are perishing?" And he awoke and rebuked the wind and said to the sea, "Peace! Be still!" And the wind ceased, and there was a great calm. He said to them, "Why are you so afraid? Have you still no faith?" And they were filled with great fear and said to one another, "Who then is this, that even the wind and sea obey him?" (Mark 4:35–41)

What an amazing story! It's easy to picture, but what does it mean to us in our particular situations? Notice Jesus had given them a goal, to get to the other side of the Sea of Galilee. And they thought they knew how to do that, so they began the trip. But they were beset with storm conditions that soon became more than they could handle. They were fishermen; we can be sure they were doing all the normal things like bailing water and rowing hard, but the weather conditions were seemingly about to overwhelm them. They had not expected such a storm else they likely would have questioned Jesus before they began.

But now they were in the middle of the storm, and Jesus did not seem to know or care about it. That one they would normally have counted on for relief was apparently indifferent to their plight. So they woke Jesus up and protested to Him, thinking they were telling Him something He needed to know about. With three words Jesus solved the problem, and they were amazed. Of course, they were. We would have been amazed too. First, they were confident they could handle the weather, then they realized they were in trouble, and it got worse and worse. Then they called on Jesus and He solved their problem. But they were still in the middle of the sea. They still had to row their way to shore. They still had to finish bailing out the boat. They were still soaking wet. Even after the storm there was work to do to accomplish the task of getting to the other side of the sea.

So it often is with us. We experience trouble and call on Jesus who makes some provisions for us. We had thought we could handle a given situation, but some unexpected things intervened, and we were "swamped." So we call on Jesus and discover He does care and can handle our situations. Yet, most of the time Jesus leaves us with some things to do. And also, most of the time, we live to experience another storm on another day. But if we have learned from the earlier experience those later storms are easier to deal with. Lots of times, too, our storms are of our own making. We go places or do things that are apt to generate storms for us. Jesus is still available, praise the Lord, but He does expect us to learn from our mistakes and we are better off when we do. I have the scars to prove this has been true for me.

PSALM 33:20–22

The author of this Psalm is not listed, but we do have the content to dwell upon, to take note of, and to make a part of our lives. And that is what I ask you to consider, for this word from God, this message, these instructions are precious, meant for our absorption and action. The author obviously has a heart for God and rejoices in God's steadfast love. He wants his readers to benefit from that knowledge too. See these three verses:

> Our soul waits for the LORD;
> he is our help and our shield.
> For our heart is glad in him,
> because we trust in his holy name.
> Let your steadfast love, O LORD, be upon us,
> even as we hope in you. (Psalm 33:20–22)

Note how the first two sentences express confidence in God's love and the third is an earnest prayer for His ongoing involvement in their lives. The psalmist speaks for and prays for others, no doubt especially his immediate family. Notice the three uses of the word *our* in these verses. Such personal possession of God's steadfast love is the essence of comfort and peace and can be yours too.

See God's position in the psalmist's life as his help and shield, and his very soul delights in this fact. When troubles, trials, or temptations come his waiting will stand him in good stead, for God will arrive as the problems arise and provide the support and direction only He can. And God's love is the basis of all the psalmist's faith, confidence, joy, and hope. Nor is there any greater basis for our faith, confidence, joy, and hope either.

So this Psalm is both an example of God working in a believer's life, and an invitation for you to call on Him for help too. Trust in His holy name as the psalmist does, pray for that same glad heart the psalmist has, watching as the psalmist does for God's involvement in your life, expecting God to respond, for He surely will. And when He does respond give Him the thanksgiving He merits, making such prayers a part of your daily life. Over time you will begin to see how God is involved in your life every day, all because He loves you.

HEBREWS 13:15-16

Hebrews presents an effort by an unknown author to encourage Jewish Christians in their faith (and perhaps some Gentile believers too) amid the trials of Roman persecution. While we may not face such defined opposition today, Christians do often face pressures of some sort, complicating their lives and influence. Thus, the same counsel presented here is applicable to us. And certainly, the consistency of our Christian walk is just as important today. Besides there is no appropriate reason for a believer in any era to pull back from establishing their position in Christ in any situation, no matter what society they live in. We have the same God supplying us the same salvation those early Christians had, and He is always worthy of all our praise, honor, and glory. See the counsel we've been shown here:

> Through him then let us continually offer up a sacrifice of praise to God, that is, the fruit of lips that acknowledge his name. Do not neglect to do good and to share what you have, for such sacrifices are pleasing to God. (Hebrews 13:15–16)

Notice the emphasis on praise prayers. We are advised here to consistently lift up sincere praise to God. The physical act of doing such supports the ongoing and increasing spiritual belief we have in God and His presence with us. The author describes these as sacrifices of praise. The time and effort we spend with our hearts focused on God lead to the kind of increasing awareness of God that He wants us to experience. Such spiritual growth equips us to face life's trials and for the opportunities God provides us to be His witness to a lost world.

We may tend to doubt that our prayers provide that sort of ongoing spiritual growth. But Jesus gave us several truths that ensure our prayers are heard and are the means God has provided to grow us spiritually. See Matthew 28:20: "And behold, I am with you always, to the end of the age." If the Son of God has specifically told us He will be with us to the end of time, then we can be sure we are *never* out of His reach, and we can be sure He hears every prayer we ever pray.

Further, those prayers are effective. See 1 John 5:14: "This is the confidence that we have toward him, that if we ask anything according to his will he hears us." So, we can pray with confidence, knowing the all-powerful God who hears us and is with us, also loves us, and has also committed to answering our prayers. The author calls such prayers the "fruit of our lips that acknowledge his name." We get the feeling that's what our lips are for, to yield the fruit of praise to God. What is the purpose of an apple tree but to yield apples? What is our purpose, but to yield praise and honor to God? In fact, we were born to bring glory to God, and if we fulfill that purpose we live the most joy-filled and satisfying life we could possibly live.

And we are not to neglect doing good. If our feelings toward God are such that we continually lift up praise to Him, then surely, we will want to do His will, surely, we will love those people He loves, and surely, we will want those other people to know the same joy in Christ that we know. So, yes, we are to share of our material blessings, and yes, we are to share of our knowledge of God's love, and yes, we are to share the path to eternal life that God's love led Him to provide all those who believe in Jesus Christ. As the Hebrews passage tells us, such sacrifices are pleasing to God. What could be better than that?

1 THESSALONIANS 5:16–18

All believers are to seek God's will in their lives. In this passage the Holy Spirit simplifies that search down to its very essence. As believers we wonder what God wants us to do with our lives, and here we see that spelled out for us. What we see God telling us is to consistently change our attitudes. Notice how "doable" this is. It's up to us then to decide what our attitude is concerning what we face every day. Beware of looking at this passage with an "I already knew that" kind of attitude. You likely did already know about this passage, but do you believe it enough to live it out? Look again at God's instructions.

> Rejoice always, pray without ceasing, give thanks in all circumstances; for this is the will of God in Christ Jesus for you. (1 Thessalonians 5:16–18)

Via Paul the apostle, the Holy Spirit lists just three things for us to do, and He tells us why. First, we are to rejoice always. Even when by earthly standards things are not going well, we are to rejoice. Plainly, we are not to decide whether to rejoice based on worldly standards. Some examples: What "bad" worldly thing could occur that would cause you to lose your salvation, and your eternal future in heaven? Answer: nothing. What circumstance could come upon you that would cause God to stop loving you? Again, the answer is nothing. What sin could you commit that God would not and could not forgive (based on Jesus' sacrificial death on the cross) if you sincerely repent? Once again, the answer is none. The point is, God's love, proven via Jesus' sacrificial death, trumps any and all sin. Thus, we have every reason to rejoice and none to be depressed about. Our mistake is to operate too much of the time with the wrong perspective concerning our relationship with the Lord, and the power of God's grace.

Look at the second instruction in this passage: "Pray without ceasing." Does this mean we are to pray every second of every day? Not necessarily, but it does mean we are to live a praying life all day, every day. For every second of every day, Jesus is Lord of our lives, and all those seconds are to reflect our recognition of His Lordship. Thus, all our thoughts, words, and actions are to be directed toward glorifying our heavenly Father. We are clearly taught in scripture we are to tithe of our income, not most of our income, but all of it. What if we tithed of our time? That would compute to 2.4 hours per day in prayer. Very, very few people would meet that standard. Consider what we do when we pray. We enter God's throne room. Every proper prayer is heard by our heavenly Father. Imagine spending 2.4 hours every day in the presence of almighty God. No wonder we can correctly conclude, prayer is more important than sleep.

And then there is the third instruction in this passage: give thanks in all circumstances. We may not voice our question but we do think, *How could this be?* By definition, we are always in some kind of circumstance, thus, to comply with this command we must stay in "thankful" mode. And many of our circumstances are filled with fear, confusion, doubt, and just plain bad news. Could it be possible that God would and could construct things in our lives that would enable us to comply? Yes, it is absolutely true that almighty God can see to all our circumstances, and give us long-term relief from all our cares and concerns. He loves us and will give us that long-term perspective that leads to our peace.

Notice the bottom line of this passage. It is God's will for us to comply, so He will help us. Therefore, let us give it our best effort.

PHILIPPIANS 2:14-16

Why we do what we do is as important as what we do. God looks on our hearts to determine our motives, and He wants those to be pure and perfect, reflecting true Christlikeness. So, our lives are to be a consistent, ongoing walk with the Lord before the world. That requires we self-monitor our decisions and lay God's will alongside ours daily (before we make decisions). As he wrote this letter to the Philippians, Paul was likely under house arrest in Rome. There he witnessed to everyone he could, from Christian visitors to his Roman guards. So even in such a situation Paul took advantage of the opportunities God provided. See how he worded his recommendations to His fellow believers in Philippi:

> Do all things without grumbling or disputing, that you may be blameless and innocent, children of God without blemish in the midst of a crooked and twisted generation, among whom you shine as lights in the world, holding fast to the word of life. (Philippians 2:14–16)

Notice how Paul starts his instructions. He promotes a clear conscience as to our motives for obedience to the Lord. Implied in this instruction is the thought that we may well be obedient, but sometimes do so reluctantly. Are we ever guilty of such poor attitudes? A classic example of such grumbling and questioning would have to do with tithing. We may give our tithe, but do we do so gladfully and thankfully, and with true gratitude to the Lord for all the blessings He provides us? Do we send along prayers with our tithes that the Lord might be glorified in the use of them in reaching the world with the gospel? Do we include prayers for those lost in sin who have never heard the name of Jesus?

See the results Paul describes if "we do all things without grumbling and questioning." **We become blameless and innocent children of God who are without blemish.** All of us would like to live blameless and innocent lives without any blemishes; and now we know how: stop even thinking about grumbling and questioning.

Our world today is every bit as crooked and twisted as the generation the Philippians lived in. Thus, the opportunities for us to be "lights" is available to us. And Paul tells us how, that is, we are to hold fast to the "word of life." We can generally know how to be such lights without doing it. But if we are going to specifically be the consistent lights God wants us to be, we have to get into the details of that assignment. That will require our shining in every small way, which wind up not being small at all. That's one of the beautiful things about Christianity (or Christlikeness): it involves every area of our lives, and is designed such that every believer no matter their background or location is qualified (with the Holy Spirit's help) to participate. All of us can be obedient within our own circle of influence, and that's exactly what God requires, no more, no less.

If we do that we will shine. We will stick out. We will be different. Other people will see Jesus in us. And that's the way God's goal of taking the gospel to the nations will come about.

That will happen. The point, though, is will each of us do our part? All believers have that privilege and responsibility. So do "hold fast to the word of life." God saw fit to save us believers and to provide us the "word of life." Who are we to keep it to ourselves? There is a whole world out there that needs to know what we know. Let's go and tell them about how much God loves them.

MATTHEW 5:9

In chapter 5 of Matthew, Jesus speaks of the fundamental truths He wants us to live by. As He always does, He speaks directly and specifically so as to be easily understood. This section of scripture has come to be called The Beatitudes, meaning "blessed" or "happy." This, because obedience to these instructions brings godly favor. Jesus spoke about two thousand years ago and yet His words are as applicable today as they were then. The blessed of those hearing Him believed Him and followed His teaching. The blessed of us today believe and obey too. Notice how relevant Jesus' words are:

> Blessed are the peacemakers, for they shall be called sons of God. (Matthew 5:9)

Notice the obvious truths in this verse:

1. We evidently have the potential of making peace or God would not advise we do so.
2. God would have us make peace because He loves us and knows our making peace works to our long-term good.
3. If and when we do become peacemakers, we will be blessed.
4. Thus, we will come to be happy in our role as a peacemaker.
5. What gives us that joy and happiness is that making peace defines us as a son of God.

We might well ask what making peace involves. As used here, a peacemaker is one that works toward promoting harmony among individuals, within the community, and between God and man. That one would naturally not promote disharmony, or be inconsistent in their walk with the Lord. Jesus set the example of being the ultimate peacemaker on the cross as He settled the disharmony we all have with God brought on by our sin. Satisfying the variances among people and countries and between God and man is what peacemakers do. Our role then is simply to imitate Jesus, because we know disunity among individuals is an affront to God, for He loves us all. The obedient disciple of Jesus will be a peacemaker as he lives out his role as a disciple and disciple-maker sharing the gospel of Jesus wherever he goes.

Such obedient believers will be seen as "sons of God," having been adopted into God's family and taking on Jesus' characteristics. True believers will be peacemakers and will be called sons of God. We have that assurance from this verse. And as sons of God, then peacemakers (believers) enjoy all the rights and privileges of being God's children. In our role as peacemakers, we will be unique within our communities, standing out from others who do not know Jesus Christ as Savior and Lord.

Think about the significance of being a son of God. Not only of being a son of God, but also being recognized as such by those around you, believers and unbelievers. Such a status carries with it a great deal of responsibility and privilege. We should not take that position lightly. God does not, nor should we. It cost our heavenly Father His Son Jesus to enable us to gain that position with Him. Men and women alike are given this position as "sons" of God by God's grace through faith, thereby gaining status as a child of God, with all the obligations, privileges, and rights of inheritance that come with sonship. Through the leadership of the Holy Spirit we are empowered with the will and capacity to be peacemakers, lights in the world, and disciples of Jesus Christ making other disciples as we go.

PROVERBS 2:9-10

God loved (and loves) the world with a steadfast love. Because of that love He has made His will for us known in His Word. Thus, we are to give credibility to His Word and make it the road map for our lives. This passage in Proverbs is a classic example of His instructions to us and the result obedience to Him makes in our lives:

> Then you will understand righteousness and justice and equity, every good path; for wisdom will come into your heart, and knowledge will be pleasant to your soul. (Proverbs 2:9–10)

These two verses reflect a result of our heeding God's wisdom; that is, we gain an understanding of His righteousness, justice, and equity. These verses presuppose we desire God's wisdom in the first place (with all our hearts), and make every effort to acquire it. Then God will provide it. Thus, we come to understand these additional three characteristics of God that He makes available for our use. So, in essence, when we seek (and then receive) God's wisdom we become better able to be His disciples and disciple makers in this world. God wants us to be His disciples and disciple makers and makes provision to equip us for this service by teaching us about His righteousness, justice, and equity. Isn't it amazing how God sees to all our needs as we seek to obey Him?

Just imagine what it would be like to know all there is to know about God's righteousness, justice, and equity, plus every good path. Certainly, we would be better disciple makers. "Every good path" must have to do with us knowing exactly how God wants us to make every decision. Notice what part of us God's wisdom occupies, our hearts. And notice, too, how we will feel about knowledge (of God) if God's wisdom occupies our hearts; it will be pleasant to us down to our very souls.

So heeding God's wisdom is obviously the best way for us to live, for His glory, and our sakes too. And it's also best for the world around us. The world gets the benefit of all our Holy Spirit–led decisions and our godly examples.

If heeding God's wisdom is so inherently good for everyone, then it must follow that we should give ourselves over specifically to praying for such wisdom. So, in a way, we have come full circle; we know already we are to pray for God's will in our lives, and we know God's Word is to be the source of our life's direction, so this passage simply serves as a reminder for us to be proactive in such praying and Bible study. We can be sure God will bless such consistent effort.

2 TIMOTHY 4:1–2

God has a message for the whole world. It is contained in His Word, the Bible, and He would have us preach and teach it wherever we go. That word we are to spread involves God loving the world so much that He sent His Son, Jesus Christ, to live on earth and eventually die a sinner's death on the cross to pay our sin debt. That would imply two things: (1) The whole world is made up of sinful people, who all need a Savior. And (2) the only way our sin debt can be atoned for is though Jesus' sacrificial death. Both of these implications are true. So, while Paul waits in prison for his death sentence to be carried out, he writes this encouraging letter to Timothy, and to us, in hopes it will give impetus to all our evangelistic efforts, as we go about obeying God's Word. See what the Holy Spirit leads Paul to write:

> I charge you in the presence of God and Christ Jesus, who is to judge the living and the dead, and by his appearing and his kingdom: preach the word; be ready in season and out of season; reprove, rebuke, and exhort, with complete patience and teaching. (2 Timothy 4:1–2)

Paul charges Timothy; that is, he strongly reminds and commands him to preach the word, the truth of the gospel that describes God's love for the world, reflected in Jesus' sacrificial death on our behalf. Paul is so certain of his assignment by God to share these truths, he tells them God is behind his message, implying its great importance. Jesus Himself will eventually judge the whole world when He returns (appears) and establishes His kingdom. Timothy is to do this "in season, and out of season," that is, when it is convenient, and when it is inconvenient.

The passage tells us that as he preaches, Timothy is to reprove, rebuke, and exhort his listeners. That is, he is to instruct, to correct, and to encourage those who believe. And Paul also tells Timothy he can do this with complete confidence that this is what God would have him do. So can we. Because his message will not always be accepted, Paul urges Timothy to be patient as he teaches to ensure his listeners hear and understand his message.

Ultimately Jesus will return to establish His kingdom, and to judge the living and the dead. In other words, Jesus will overlook no one who has ever lived. All of us will stand before Him to give an account of our lives. That truth should be emphasized in our witness for it is the reality that determines all our eternal destinies.

The message Paul is teaching here is urgent, for the need is great. People die every day without Christ because they have never heard the truth of God's love described in the gospel of Jesus. So Paul urges Timothy to be ready to preach the Word. We, too, need to be alert to every opportunity to share these truths. There is no greater message we can pass on to anyone than the good news of Jesus Christ and His provision for our eternity.

And when we think about it, there is no valid reason for us not to tell others about the love of Jesus. Reality is, He first loved us, and He died on the cross to atone for our sins providing the way to eternal life. If we love those around us, how could we not share this only path to an eternity with almighty God?

Philippians 4:12-13

In the past Paul had been supported in every way by the church at Philippi. And in this passage, he pauses near the end of the letter to thank them. As he traveled around the known world of his day sharing the gospel, he had all the physical and spiritual needs we could logically expect him to have, food, shelter, encouragement, protection, etc. He usually began his visits to a given town by visiting the synagogue there, where he knew he would find godly people, and shared the gospel of Jesus with them. And he went from there, reacting to what happened then. Sometimes he stayed only a few days, and sometimes months or even several years establishing a church. He adapted to the environment he found among godly people, and did whatever was appropriate to spread the gospel. **And so should we**. See this passage where he gives us a hint of the attitude he had:

> I know how to be brought low, and I know how to abound. In any and every circumstance, I have learned the secret of facing plenty and hunger, abundance and need. I can do all things through him who strengthens me. (Philippians 4:12–13)

The secret of his success is one we can use too. He kept his focus on God, and the mission God gave him to share Christ wherever he went. That way he was able to see his circumstances with the right perspective, whether they be good or not so good. He did not waste time, energy, or opportunity. He had learned to face hardships and ill treatment, as well as good times with old friends. He could thus deal with evil men and women and godly folks. He could deal with the rich, the poor, the sick, the healthy, the educated, and the ignorant. Paul saw everyone he met as someone who needed the Lord, and he reacted accordingly.

The last sentence of this passages sums up his position relative to the Lord. "I can do all things through him who strengthens me." This verse applies to us, too, but does not mean God will bless everything we do. Like all scripture we are to read it within the setting in which it was written and in accord with the overall directions God provides us. And that has to do with loving Him with all our hearts, souls, and minds, and our neighbors as we love ourselves. Such a mindset (and heart-set) would lead us to ongoing, consistent service to God and others wherever we are. The word *service* is the operative word Paul lived by. That's what Paul did, he served, that's who he was, a servant. We are to go and do likewise.

God has the ability to see through our make-believe world and still perform miracles. He has the power to change us to His way of thinking, and will, if we open ourselves to that possibility. And most exciting of all He wants to use us for His glory and provides such opportunities (large and small) every day. It has been said many times in different ways but the message is the same, God wants us all to start where we (NOW) are, to use what we already HAVE (in the way of talents and opportunities), and to do what we CAN (for His glory out of a love motive). **Anything less with regard to action or timing is a misinterpretation of God's will for us. And that includes waiting on the Lord which still involves loving Him and our neighbors and living out that kind of heart.**

ROMANS 2:9-11

God will one day judge each one of us according to our works. Paul the apostle is explaining this principle to the Christian church in Rome in this letter. The truth of this passage is very applicable to us in our day also. **Notice this truth applies to everyone, both Jew and Greek** (at that time and now).

> There will be tribulation and distress for every human being who does evil, the Jew first and also the Greek, but glory and honor and peace for everyone who does good, the Jew first and also the Greek. For God shows no partiality. (Romans 2:9–11)

First, consider the idea of works Paul is talking about. He divides "works" into two classes, and calls them evil and good. He is using an analogy here to make a point. He refers to "evil" as works done by unbelievers, people who have denied Christ and His Lordship; those who have not acknowledged Christ's sacrificial death on the cross as payment for their sin debt. Paul is saying everything such unbelievers do is either wrong (thus, evil), or good done for the wrong reason, and therefore useless long-term and evil. So Paul's point is, he calls even the good unbelievers do, evil, because it wasn't done for the glory of God. God's judgment for them will bring pain and suffering, tribulation and distress.

On the other hand, Paul classifies the good works that believers do as good, simply because they did them for the glory of God (not themselves). Such actions for them results in glory, honor, and peace. **So to put Paul's instructions in simple terms, all we have to do is ask ourselves, do we do the things we do to bring glory to God, or for any other reason?** Even if our society would classify what unbelievers do as good, remember that society's thinking is not the best reason for our doing good. To glorify God is the reason we were born. Thus, the principle taught in this Bible passage is, if we are honest with ourselves when we answer that question concerning "why" we do what we do, we will have discovered what the long-term results of our works will be: tribulation and distress, or glory, honor, and peace. So godly lifestyles yield peace for Paul's readers and us, and ungodly lifestyles yield just the opposite.

Remember the criteria mentioned in this passage strongly points up the importance of the relationship believers have with God. When we receive Jesus Christ as Lord, if that relationship is real, then we will "live out" that Lordship, and that relationship will dictate both what we do and the "why" of what we do. So, yes, we will then do good works, but our goal in doing them is to bring praise, honor, and glory to God. That goal will eventually bring glory, honor, and peace to us believers. God is impartial; His salvation plan is for the whole world because He loves us. Find someone to share this with.

1 THESSALONIANS 4:15–18

All believers wonder about the return of Christ. When will it be? What will happen? Will everyone in the world know about it? What will be the result? Paul's letter to the church at Thessalonica addresses typical questions for them and for us. Thus, the general theme of this letter is the return of Christ and its significance. This letter was written from Corinth about AD 50 and thus was almost twenty years after Christ's crucifixion and subsequent ascension back to heaven. In the interim some believers had died, causing concern on the part of other believers as to the eternal destiny of those who die before Jesus returns. The Thessalonian believers needed encouraging on this subject, and so do we. Thus, this passage represents the Holy Spirit's movement in Paul's heart to shed light on this important subject:

> For this we declare to you by a word from the Lord, that we who are alive, who are left until the coming of the Lord, will not precede those who have fallen asleep. For the Lord himself will descend from heaven with a cry of command, with the voice of an archangel, and with the sound of the trumpet of God. And the dead in Christ will rise first. Then we who are alive, who are left, will be caught up together with them in the clouds to meet the Lord in the air, and so we will always be with the Lord. Therefore encourage one another with these words. (1 Thessalonians 4:15–18)

To some degree we can picture this happening, at least for us and those around us. Imagine the scene: clouds, bright light, and loud noises (a cry of command presumably by Jesus, a voice of the archangel, and that of a trumpet blast). And millions of believers perhaps trailing out in the sky behind Jesus looking like angels. How this is displayed before the whole world (at the same time) is not explained. Some people will be awake, some asleep, some at work, some at sea, some doing whatever we all do normally. And not one person will have accurately forecast the date and time. Every single human being will therefore be surprised, caught living out what they are and have been. Paul is not claiming that he will still be alive at the Lord's second coming, but that some believers will be. The point of the passage then is that no believer, (alive or dead when Christ returns), will be left out of the Lord's consideration. The promise of an eternal destiny in heaven with the Lord is, thus, valid for all believers.

Paul declares the authenticity of his teaching by referencing it to a word from the Lord he has received. This is, therefore, not Paul's truth he is relating, but God's, with some direct purposes in mind. First, we note the result of Christ's second coming. Hallelujah! We believers are told we will always be with the Lord. What greater assurance could we have than that we will spend eternity with the Lord? Notice, too, that Paul then tells believers to encourage one another with these words. We are not to become encouraged by these words. That we are encouraged by these words is assumed.

As to the timing of Christ's second coming we are left to do one thing, and one thing only. And that is, to anticipate His imminent return. We are to anticipate and live out the anticipation that Christ will return today; this, as we preach, teach, and example the truth of Jesus' return. Is preaching, teaching, and exampling God's will for us what we normally do? What changes do we need to make in our lives to fit God's will for us as we glorify Him?

LUKE 10:23-24

Jesus' disciples had been with Him for some time at this point in His ministry, and had seen many miracles and heard many of His teaching sessions. This, in preparation for their later roles as disciple makers after Jesus returns to heaven. So we see here then a lesson in perspectives for them; that is, that they recognize the significance of what they had seen and heard and how blessed they had been to do so. With those blessings they had received came the responsibility to go and tell what they now knew to be the good news of Jesus Christ. We have that same responsibility. See Jesus' thoughts:

> Then turning to the disciples he said privately, "Blessed are the eyes that see what you see! For I tell you that many prophets and kings desired to see what you see, and did not see it, and to hear what you hear and did not hear it." (Luke 10:23–24)

If we take these words to mean exactly what they relate, the thought draws our minds to the many prophets and good kings who had come before. They had known of, and sincerely believed Messiah was coming to save Israel, and they naturally would have wanted to see the Messiah and be a witness to His kingdom being established on earth. Yet in His infinite wisdom God delayed the Messiah's coming to that period we read of in the first century. And there were reasons for that. At that time there was only one dominant ruling empire, Rome, and people could thus travel from place to place within the empire with relative freedom. As obstinate and as pagan as the Romans were, they did pretty much allow the Jews and Christians to practice their religions. They had developed a system of roads and shipping, so the ability to travel was much easier than before. The major languages spoken were Latin and Greek, and Paul spoke both, as well as Aramaic and was thus able to communicate well wherever he went within the empire. And probably as much as anything, the gospel spread because the Romans had developed a well-organized tax system (overseen by the Roman army) that brought in regular revenue to support all their endeavors.

After His resurrection Jesus told the disciples: "But you will receive power when the Holy Spirit has come upon you, and you will be my witnesses in Jerusalem and in all Judea and Samaria, and to the end of the earth" (Acts 1:8).

And with God's help the disciples were able to do that; just as we in our time have jet planes, the internet, phones, TV, and email, etc., and thus the capability to communicate the gospel everywhere we want. So inherent in our blessings is the task of sharing God's Word, and with God's help, we have the capacity to do that in mighty ways. Our task is absolutely no different than the one Jesus gave the disciples in Acts 1:8.

Let us not delay for people are dying "lost" every day. Our prayers should be to finish well.

MATTHEW 21:8-11

Jesus knew who He was; the people thought they did. We all have convictions that seem firm to us at some point, but that change over time. This passage describes the people's reaction to Jesus' entrance into Jerusalem for the last time, often called His Triumphal Entry. Within a week Jesus would be crucified. Thus, those people who were singing His praises here, were the same people who shouted, "Crucify Him!" just a few days later. See the Bible's description of Jesus' glorious entrance:

> Most of the crowd spread their cloaks on the road, and others cut branches from the trees and spread them on the road. And the crowds that went before him and that followed him were shouting, "Hosanna to the Son of David! Blessed is he who comes in the name of the Lord! Hosanna in the highest!" And when he entered Jerusalem, the whole city was stirred up, saying, "Who is this?" And the crowds said, "This is the prophet Jesus, from Nazareth of Galilee." (Matthew 21:8–11)

Spreading cloaks on the road symbolized the people's submission to Jesus as king. Spreading branches was representative of the people's sense of nationalism concerning Israel's anticipated military power. So, to say that the crowds accepted Jesus was an understatement. But their perspective was wrong; they had a return of Israel's military power in mind under Jesus' leadership. They saw Him as that one who would lead them to victory over the Romans, and freedom from oppression. "Hosanna" means "O save us," and that's what they thought Jesus was about to do.

Jesus was and is certainly King, the King of Kings, in fact. But His kingdom would not be an earthly one. The people misidentified Jesus. They saw Him as a prophet who had awesome powers, both of which are true, but He is so much more. They saw David as that past leader who led Israel to be the most powerful country in the world at the time. So, it would normally be quite a compliment to be called "Son of David." But the people did not view Jesus as God who had come to earth to save them from their sins. The disciples did acknowledge that, but were still confused about Jesus' complete role in coming to earth, especially after Jesus told them He would soon be crucified. That just did not compute with their logic of Jesus as Lord.

But we know the rest of the story. Jesus is God, and He did come to earth to die in the place of those who believe in Him, paying their sin debt forever. And He did conquer death by rising from the grave, never to die again. So, yes, Jesus was and is worthy of all the praise He received that day and more. We look back now two thousand years and try to picture that event, the people cheering and singing and Jesus calmly riding on a donkey, knowing what lay ahead for Him.

And the reason for it all was God's love for us. God made provision for atoning for our sins by giving His sinless Son to die a sinner's death on the cross in our place. Today, in the press of all our activities, the distractions brought on by the world's problems, and the general ignorance and/or denial of who Jesus really is, we too often find ourselves out of sync with God's will for us. And He would have us love Him with all we are, and other people as well. He would have us keep the same perspective He taught His disciples. That is, "to take up our cross and follow Him." His cross came that day outside Jerusalem, and led to His rising up from the grave on that first Easter Sunday. Our cross involves obeying Him and sharing the truth of the gospel with a lost world. And one day we, too, will rise to be with Him forever.

PROVERBS 28:1

Our relationship with God affects our every attitude with regard to the society around us, and every single interaction we have with others (inside and outside our families). If our relationship with God is one of love and respectful obedience, with His glory being our goal, then that will translate as harmony, concern, and generosity with and for all those we influence. We then are wise when we orient our lives around God's will and His image. See this verse that describes how both the wicked and the righteous are considered:

> The wicked flee when no one pursues,
> but the righteous are bold as a lion. (Proverbs 28:1)

How we view and react to both the good times and the bad times in our lives, that come to us all, will reflect our relationship with God. The wicked (unbelievers) have "shallow" roots. All they have to depend on is their own strength, wisdom, and perceptions of what they face in life. To them that seems to be enough, but long-term it is far from enough. They only see what is in front of them with no proper perspective concerning what is of value long-term. They dodge shadows in life that are not real, but just seem to be real. As the verse says, they run when no one is chasing them. In other words, they are afraid of the wrong things. And they seek help, direction, and comfort in the wrong places, where no lasting power, wisdom, and support exists, not realizing that the lack of love in those places is what makes those sources weak, temporal, and misguided.

On the other hand, an appropriate relationship with God offers eternal security, and (Hallelujah) that same creator God loves us with a steadfast love. Thus, He does have the power, wisdom, and motivation to be the (only) source of direction, comfort, and help we will ever need. Such realizations by the righteous (believers) makes them "bold as a lion," that is, able to deal with the ups and downs of life, keeping the goal to glorify God in mind. That kind of mindset and heart-set on the part of believers sets them apart from society at large.

The key to this difference (and really the eternal destiny) between the wicked and the righteous mentioned in the verse is the involvement of Jesus Christ. John 3:16–17 says it all: "For God so loved the world, that he gave his only Son, that whoever believes in him should not perish but have eternal life. For God did not send his Son into the world to condemn the world, but in order that the world might be save through him."

This truth of Jesus Christ is what the wicked need, and what God wants us to go and tell them.

JOHN 6:66–69

It is a wise person who recognizes words of wisdom when they hear them. But some seem both deaf and blind to Jesus' words of eternal life. It's always been that way. Some people in Jesus' day heard Him speak, saw Him perform miracles, experienced His presence, and still did not believe Him to be the Son of God. We stand amazed at how this could happen, yet in our day don't we do the same thing? And we know the end of the story. We have God's Word to guide us. We have been plainly told of Jesus' true identity, and of the "why" of His coming to earth. Let us be wise in our hearing of God's Word, our understanding of it, and our obedience to it. See this passage where Peter recognizes who Jesus is:

> After this many of his disciples turned back and no longer walked with him. So Jesus said to the twelve, "Do you want to go away as well?" Simon Peter answered him, "Lord, to whom shall we go? You have the words of eternal life, and we have believed, and have come to know, that you are the Holy One of God." (John 6:66–69)

Jesus had been speaking to the people concerning how difficult walking with Him is apt to be. It will involve suffering, rejection, and times of trial. But is well worth the journey. Many of Jesus' early followers were not genuine in their faith. They followed Jesus only to benefit from His healing powers and for His ability to multiply food, that is, they followed for their own selfish benefit.

Notice Peter's answer to Jesus' question. He said, "To whom shall we go?" He implied there is no one else like Jesus, no one else to whom anyone could turn for eternal life. **Peter had distilled the most important question any person could ever ask down to its very essence.** Who or what is the way to eternal life? People are still asking that same question today. There is only one person and only one way. Peter gave us the answer, belief in and fellowship with the Holy One of God, Jesus Christ.

When we sort of step back and consider Jesus, He fulfills all the requirements of a Savior: He had a miraculous birth, led a sinless life, had infinite power to heal and perform signs, He was the wisest of teachers, and has power over death. When we add to this His steadfast love for us that led to His sacrificial death on the cross to pay our sin debt, we can only conclude Peter was right; Jesus is the Holy One of God, sent to earth to save us from our sins. So why so much hesitation, why so much denial of Jesus, why so much unbelief? There are two main reasons. The first reason is ignorance. Many people have never heard about Him and His love for them and what He did because of that love. The second reason is many of those who have heard about Him never quite stop long enough to consider the significance of what He offers. Sadly, they have never seriously addressed the question Jesus asked and Peter answered. Put another way, the question is, "Where will we spend eternity?" Focused on this world, many people miss the message and the life available in Jesus, and the opportunity for an eternity with Him.

Let us be wise enough to recognize the truth when we hear it. Let us be open to that truth, and open to its relevance to us and our situation. Let us not turn away from the only way available to eternal life.

HEBREWS 12:1–2

The author of Hebrews was anxious to draw his reader's attention to the example Jesus set for them while on earth. Those believers then and we now face ongoing trials and threats to our faith. The author would have us change our perspective concerning life from one of frustration and despair to one of peace and joy. And his counsel offers Jesus as the only source of such relief. So, let us take a step back and analyze our condition, where we are, and where we are going. Nothing, and no one else even offers the authentic eternal peace a relationship with the Lord brings. Notice this passage's recommendations:

> Let us run with endurance the race that is set before us, looking to Jesus, the founder and perfecter of our faith, who for the joy that was set before him endured the cross, despising the shame, and is seated at the right hand of the throne of God. (Hebrews 12:1–2)

Notice we are to "run the race of life." That is, go at life vigorously, consistently, and with endurance. We have only one life, the one God provides, the one He gives us and sets before us, filled with various opportunities, choices, and even some obstacles. We are to use it up, not waste it. And we are to do so, looking to Jesus all the while. What could looking to Jesus involve unless it means making Him our standard, our example, our motive, and our Lord? What could be a simpler and straightforward instruction? The author suggests we make Jesus not *a* priority but *the* priority in our lives. We are to make Him the "why" we do (or don't do) anything.

And he even tells us why Jesus should have such a position in our lives. It's because He is the founder and perfecter of our faith. To be the founder of our faith means Jesus created our faith, He thought up the concept of faith. And He put it in place in our hearts. And He made our faith real, a driving force that motivates and encourages us. And He perfects our faith. That is, He grows it, purifies it, and gives us opportunities to live out our faith by applying it in our lives.

And look at what else the passage tells us Jesus did: **He endured the cross. Never, never, belittle Jesus' actions on the cross.** There, He was actually made sin for us; He died that we might believe and live eternally. His death paid our sin debt. And it was for the "joy that was set before Him." Jesus suffered physically, mentally, and spiritually on the cross to an extent beyond our ability to grasp. Yet knowing what His death would facilitate for mankind (salvation for those who believe) gave Him joy, in spite of the pain and shame.

And now, hallelujah! Jesus reigns in heaven. He sits at the right hand of the Father. Surely, such a phrase indicates Jesus has a position of influence, authority, and power. And, praise the Lord, Jesus uses His position to intercede for us with the Father. How could we have a more perfect Redeemer? He died in our place to pay for our sins. He rose from the dead, and because He did, we will too. And one day He is coming back to gather all who by faith believe in Him for an eternity in heaven with Him.

Surely, such a message is worthy of our communicating it to the world. And that's exactly what Jesus told us to do: "Go therefore and make disciples of all nations . . . teaching them . . . all that I have commanded you" (Matthew 28:19–20).

ISAIAH 11:1–3

God uses the Bible in amazing ways to foretell the future and advise believers how to live in the world of their day. It is so universal in application every believer in every era could and can find both hope and direction there. Isaiah lived around 700 BC when the fear of attack of Judah by Assyria was a constant threat to the whole nation, putting pressure on everything they did. So Isaiah's prophecy of a coming Messiah shown in this passage gave hope during a stressful time. God's Word still does the same thing in our day. See Isaiah's words:

> There shall come forth a shoot from the stump of Jesse,
>   and a branch from his roots shall bear fruit.
> And the spirit of the LORD shall rest upon him,
>   the Spirit of wisdom and understanding,
>   the Spirit of counsel and might,
>   the Spirit of knowledge and the fear of the LORD.
> And his delight shall be in the fear of the LORD. (Isaiah 11:1–3)

Jesse was the father of David selected by the prophet Samuel to be king in Judah in 1010 BC. The words *stump*, *shoot*, and *branch* gave indication that Messiah was coming via David's human line. But He would be a greater king than King David. David was also filled with God's spirit, but Isaiah's description here indicates Messiah would have a fuller, richer, threefold indwelling of God's Spirit. It would be of wisdom and understanding, indicating God's sensitivity and leadership, of counsel and might, indicating the capacity to carry out God's plans, and of knowledge and the fear of the Lord, indicating God's perspective, worldview, and holiness. Jesus came and fulfilled all three prophecies as indicated by Matthew 3:16–17, where, as Jesus was being baptized by John the Baptist, a voice from heaven came saying, "This is my beloved Son with whom I am well pleased."

Notice the distinction of Messiah's focus; His delight would be in reverence and obedience to His heavenly Father. We likely don't give enough credence to this last point, focusing on reverence for and obedience to our heavenly Father. **And not just fulfillment of these two roles but delighting in them.** To delight in anything means to gain a high degree of satisfaction, and extreme gratification from it. Do we feel that way about our relationship to the Lord? Are we that "sold out" to His kingdom work and His will for our lives? Do we find pleasure and relief in compliance with His Word? A litmus test of our feeling's concerning our reverence of the Lord is our anticipation of the times we go to Him in prayer. Do we get the peace and direction in prayer that makes them times of joy rather than times of dread or simply when we list all our needs and doubts?

If our prayer times don't lead to rest, hope, and peace, we are missing the greatest joy we could have. That is, fellowship and the sense of God's presence with us. God told us to "pray without ceasing" because He loves us, so there is great benefit available to us when we pray.

1 TIMOTHY 2:5-7

Paul is quite confident of his knowledge of the gospel; that is, the eternal provisions God has made for mankind through His Son Jesus Christ. Paul met Jesus on the road to Damascus years earlier and that meeting will be forever imprinted on his heart. The gospel message is powerful; so powerful, and so all-encompassing, that it is difficult to put it in writing and completely convey the total scope of what God's love has led Him to do. Paul wants to give his readers the same "feel" for the truth that he has. This passage reflects how earnestly Paul is trying to get his point across to Timothy and the others who will read this letter (including us about two thousand years later). So, let us read it as we pray to fully understand it.

> For there is one God, and there is one mediator between God and men, the man Jesus Christ, who gave himself as a ransom for all, which is the testimony given at the proper time. For this I was appointed as a preacher and an apostle (I am telling the truth, I am not lying), a teacher of the Gentiles in faith and truth. (1 Timothy 2:5–7)

Notice Paul's key points: there is only one God, and only one mediator between God and man, and that mediator is the man Jesus Christ. There are no other gods for the various earthly people groups, or separate mediators between God and man for each of the many religions the world claims. It is to be understood that all of mankind needs Jesus, the only mediator, for we are all born in sin, destined to be separated from God forever unless somehow our sin debt is satisfied. He is that one who gave Himself on the cross to pay the sin debt ransom of all who would believe in Him. He, God, came to earth as man to live a perfect life and to die a sinner's death in our place. Further (and hallelujah), He rose from the dead on the third day never again to die. And because He rose from the dead so will we who believe in Him, trusting His death as the full atonement for all our sins.

And Paul maintains he was called and assigned by Jesus on the Damascus road that day to take the gospel message to the Gentiles. So, since then Paul has accepted his mission to preach and teach the gospel of Christ wherever he went. And he urges his readers to believe him. It doesn't seem quite emphatic enough to simply state that fact, so he reinforces his message, claiming he comes in faith and truth, sharing the very message Jesus gave him.

And how could we conclude anything else but that we should do the same thing? Jesus is still Lord, and the need is still there to take the gospel message to the nations. Jesus' command is still just as valid as it was the day He spoke to Paul. We call our marching instructions, "The Great Commission," listed in Matthew 28:19 to "go, and make disciples." It's the same message Jesus gave to Paul.

Paul was not lying when he spoke of his commission to go and tell the world of God's love as reflected in Christ. And we would not be lying either. For God would have us do the same thing. We are blessed to have access to the truth of the gospel, but many people are not so blessed. Imagine living and dying, and never having heard the name of Jesus. That's the fate of many people today. And only we who have heard the truth are qualified to go and tell others. We may not go, but we cannot deny we have been told to go.

JAMES 1:19-21

God's Word, scripture, carries with it the weight and authority of God Himself. This, because His Word reflects Him, His will, His nature, and His purposes. This passage from James is included in a section that speaks of "Hearing and Doing the Word." Hearing God's Word alone falls short of implementing its truth in the world. At the same time, we cannot "do" the Word if we don't know what it is. Thus, the two subjects, hearing and doing, complement each other, as God's Word impacts the world. We are to do both, carrying God's truths with us wherever we go, and influencing all those we meet with godly principles and commands. Naturally then, we also are to beware of words and actions on our parts that conflict with what we know and do of God's Word, for that would surely dilute our witness among those we want to influence. See James' teaching in this area:

> Know this, my beloved brothers: let every person be quick to hear, slow to speak, slow to anger; for the anger of man does not produce the righteousness of God. Therefore put away all filthiness and rampant wickedness and receive with meekness the implanted word, which is able to save your souls. (James 1:19–21)

This passage, therefore, tells us all believers are to be quick to hear God's Word. That is, we are to be anxious to know it and to understand it, and proactive in seeking it with consistent and ongoing effort. The necessary mental and spiritual sweat we put into this activity will stand us in good stead all lifelong. And if ever there were activities that God's Holy Spirit would bless, this kind of effort qualifies, for they define the very purpose God gave us His Word.

And we are to be slow to speak; not reluctant to speak, but careful in our speech least we misspeak, and share a faulty gospel. In fact, the opposite is true, we are to be anxious to share truth with those who have not heard, enlightening them to God's love and His provision in Christ.

And we are to be slow to anger. We might add we are to be patient when we share the truth even when it is opposed, not showing anger or malice toward those who disagree and/or refuse to listen. We will never debate a lost individual into receiving the gospel. It is the Holy Spirit's work to transform the hearts of those we've witnessed to. There is a sense in which we might think of ourselves as being "in advertising, not sales." We are to relate and describe the gospel with love and patience while the Holy Spirit does His transforming work. Any anger, impatience, or violence we might exhibit is not reflective of God's love and righteousness and will not produce those characteristics in unsaved individuals.

Thus, we are to put away any negative or ungodly words, thoughts, or actions, for these will not properly represent our Lord Jesus. Only then can we humbly receive the truth of God's love and provisions for eternal life. Only then will we reflect the love for others Jesus has, and only then will others see Jesus in us.

What is so often overlooked and misunderstood is the significance of the gospel message we share. God's Word is the only route to salvation, and it contains the only truth that saves souls eternally. Thus, the gospel is not just good news, it is the only news that leads to eternal life. For those who believe, they will thus be forever with the Lord. Who are we to keep this news to ourselves?

JOHN 1:32–34

As Jesus began His earthly ministry, He went down to the Jordan river where John the Baptist was preaching and was baptized by him there. This passage describes Jesus being identified as Messiah, Son of God. So now the "news is out," and the world has been made aware of God's appearance with us. Note how this came about:

> And John bore witness. "I saw the Spirit descend from heaven like a dove, and it remained on him. I myself did not know him, but he who sent me to baptize with water said to me, 'He on whom you see the Spirit descend and remain, this is he who baptizes with the Holy Spirit.' And I have seen and have borne witness that this is the Son of God." (John 1:32–34)

See the scene. John has been led to this place to preach and many people came to hear him. So did Jesus, but He was there for something else too. Notice, John tells us that at this time he did not know Jesus was the chosen one, the Messiah, come to earth to save us from our sins. But the Holy Spirit had evidently given John a sign of recognition to look for. See it here in this passage, "He who sent me to baptize with water said to me, 'He on whom you see the Spirit descend and remain, this is he who baptizes with the Holy Spirit.'" Note what John says happened, "I saw the Spirit descend from heaven like a dove, and it remained on him." That's exactly what the Holy Spirit had told John to look for. And a dove was mentioned. This dove coming and landing on Jesus could have been real or simply a metaphor. Notice though, the word *remain* is used twice in the passage describing the Spirit coming and staying on and with Jesus. We can easily picture a dove coming and staying with Jesus as He rose up from out of the water and walked to shore, thus, identifying Him as the Son of God. **One thing is made clear, John was convinced. He had been told to look for a sign, and he saw it exactly.**

So John announces his conclusion, "this is the Son of God." And John the apostle, author of this book, is led by the Holy Spirit to record this conclusion. There are several other points we should be aware of regarding Jesus, His baptism, and John the Baptist's role in it. In the first place, we know John and Jesus were cousins, John being about six months older than Jesus. So they had likely known each other well throughout their "growing up" years. And for those thirty years, we now know John did not know Jesus was the Messiah. Then, too, as Matthew describes this same event of Jesus' baptism, he adds that as the dove rests on Jesus a voice from heaven comes saying, "This is my beloved Son, with whom I am well pleased" (Matthew 3:17). We can't imagine why John did not also record that awesome occurrence, but the Holy Spirit did have both Matthew and Mark (Mark 1:11) do it.

So what is the takeaway from this passage for us? It's that we see here one more bit of evidence that Jesus is God, on a mission to earth to save us from our sins. We now have one more bit of "faith-building" data to absorb, live out, and share. Obviously, God the Father is in all of this, and He has us in mind as He had it play out on earth. What a great God we have!

JOHN 3:17-18

In love and power God sent His Son Jesus Christ into the world to save us from our sins. That event is recorded here by John the apostle under the leadership of God's Holy Spirit. We then are not to see this letter as being from John to us, but from God to us. Given that fact, we see here truth eternal, hope eternal, and life eternal. See how God has John word this vital message to us:

> For God did not send his Son into the world to condemn the world, but in order that the world might be saved through him. Whoever believes in him is not condemned, but whoever does not believe is condemned already, because he has not believed in the name of the only Son of God. (John 3:17–18)

God's purpose is clear, to provide a way for the (whole) world to escape condemnation and be saved. To believe is key, that is, belief in the name of the only Son of God. The concept therefore is belief in the name of Jesus Christ is equivalent to belief in Him. True belief leads to understanding, worship, and obedience. As worded the verse clearly indicates there are only two eternal destinies available; condemnation, and that of being saved; both are eternal in scope. To be condemned is to be eternally consigned to separation from God. To be saved is to be eternally privileged to live with God.

Notice God sent Christ into the world not to condemn the world, but to save the world. People condemn themselves by their refusal to believe in Christ Jesus as Son of God, Savior, and Lord. However, before belief can occur, people have to hear, meaning someone has to "go and tell." Unbelievers in large numbers are not likely to come to us, we must go to them.

God is creator of the universe, so it is His solution to the sin problem (not ours) that must prevail. And His solution involves the cross and Jesus' sacrificial death there. Our solution is apt to be a parade of our good works before God, seeking forgiveness for our sin that way. There is no neutral ground for us to stand on. We are either in Christ or we are not.

This passage also refutes the concept that since there is only one God, as long as a person is sincere in their religious beliefs, any religion leads to an eternity with the Father. There is only one Son of God, only one Messiah, only one Lord who died on a cross to pay our sin debt, and that is Jesus Christ. Thus, we are to promote Christ before the world consistently and without apology. Jesus Himself tells us this in John 14:6. He could not say it more plainly. "I am the way, and the truth, and the life. No one comes to the Father except through me."

ROMANS 10:11-13

This passage is titled "The Message of Salvation to All." It's so interesting that God not only has designed His plan for salvation, but also seen fit to have it recorded in scripture so that it is available to be read, understood, and believed by anyone. Thus, there is no difference in how anyone is saved. See how God's Holy Spirit has Paul word this for us:

> For the Scripture says, "Everyone who believes in him will not be put to shame." For there is no distinction between Jew and Greek; for the same Lord is Lord of all, bestowing his riches on all who call on him. For "everyone who calls on the name of the Lord will be saved." (Romans 10:11–13)

Notice the requirement for salvation: belief in Him. Good works are not mentioned. As much as we might sense that good works lead to salvation, that is not true. Clearly God would have us believe, to have faith in His free gift of His Son in our place on the cross. Nor is there any other way to salvation for anyone. Jesus removes any question concerning that in John 14:6 as He spoke to "doubting" Thomas: "I am the way, and the truth, and the life. No one comes to the Father except through me."

So only Jesus is able to provide eternal life, and He does that only for those who believe in Him. Paul refers to this as "bestowing His riches." What a descriptive way to picture the eternal life Jesus provides. Notice though, the requirement to call on Him. That refers to the acknowledgment by individuals that they are sinners in need of a Savior (and that Jesus is that Savior). But without question those who do call on Him are saved. We get the idea God is always ready to receive us into His kingdom, no matter our location, our circumstance, or our "sin condition." The worst sinner and the least sinner all are to call on His name, and can do so at anytime from anywhere.

Implied in "calling on Him" is the idea of sincerity. And that is as it should be. The relationship (between man and almighty God) such belief leads to merits the most honest of intentions. God is perfect in all respects and our relationship with Him is thus worthy of the purest of motives on our part. Left unsaid in this passage (but covered in many other scriptures) is the motive behind God's provision for eternal life for us believers. **That motive is the most steadfast love we've ever known; love not deserved, but given freely by God.** This last note defines the grace God provides that leads to our heart transformation at conversion.

That fact alone should get our eternal attention. **God loved us first in the midst of our sin-filled existence.** See Romans 5:8: "But God shows his love for us in that while we were still sinners, Christ died for us."

Surely, we all know someone who would appreciate being told of this truth.

MATTHEW 6:11

Jesus knew His disciples (and all of us) would need to be able to communicate with Him. So He instructed His disciples how to pray, and had Matthew record the lesson for our benefit. The result was Jesus' Model Prayer which we call The Lord's Prayer. This subject verse above is part of that scripture passage and concerns "daily bread." The prayer is short:

Give us this day our daily bread. (Matthew 6:11)

Plain and simple, God supplies our daily bread. Thus, we are to pray for our daily bread and continually thank Him for it. He would not have us pray to Him for our daily bread if He were not the source of it. Notice we are to pray only for daily bread, not an infinite supply. We are then to seek God's help every day for our daily bread. The implied lesson here, too, is that by listing bread (a basic need) the verse refers to all our physical needs.

Once we understand that God is the source of our daily needs and that He wants us to acknowledge He is the source and ask Him for them, then our charge is clear. We are to sincerely request all our daily needs and then go about providing them ourselves as best we can. God blesses our request by giving us the wherewithal to accomplish the provision. Thus, most of the time some daily work is required to satisfy our daily needs. We mature spiritually when we see God meeting our needs this way.

When the Israelites were wandering in the desert as they escaped captivity in Egypt, God supplied them manna to eat. It fell from the sky, but they had to collect it each day. They were not allowed to collect more than enough for a given day except the day before the Sabbath. When they tried to, the overage spoiled and was not edible. That manna collected on the day before the

Sabbath did not spoil (Exodus 16:22–26). God obviously wants His children (that's us) to come to Him regularly in prayer for whatever their needs are. Thus, the concept of daily coming into God's presence was born. God knew those Israelites would rather pray and collect manna about once a month, but God knew they, and we, needed to experience His presence more often than that. So, it is out of love for us all that God drives us to Him regularly. We are told the shoes of the Israelites did not wear out during their forty years wandering in the wilderness (Deuteronomy 29:5). So, it is clear God understands all our physical needs, but He also knows we have spiritual needs that require His attention and so He also made appropriate provisions to bring us spiritually before Him.

It's also worth noting God is teaching us to pray for our daily bread, not our daily cake. Those things we need (not just what we want) are the subject of this verse. God is not some sort of heavenly "Santa Claus" that is there simply to provide everything we can think of and want for ourselves.

More importantly, God blesses us spiritually when we come before Him sincerely in obedience to His Word. Thus, we grow spiritually as we regularly come before Him. That kind of spiritual growth in knowing God is really more important than our physical needs. Once again, we understand God's love for us leading Him to provide what He knows we need most.

REVELATION 21:1-4

In this section of scripture we read of John the apostle having been called up to heaven in a vision, and given insight into what heaven will be like, and told to write down what he sees and hears. Thus, we are given information we could have gotten only from God. Much of what John writes is beyond our ability to completely understand. But we clearly see God's majesty and glory on display. In this passage John writes about seeing a new heaven and a new earth coming down from heaven. And God speaks to John promising that He will be with man, and that they will be His people forever. See John's words describing what life will be like then:

> Then I saw a new heaven and a new earth, for the first heaven and the first earth had passed away, and the sea was no more. And I saw the holy city, new Jerusalem, coming down out of heaven from God, prepared as a bride adorned for her husband. And I heard a loud voice from the throne saying, "Behold, the dwelling place of God is with man. He will dwell with them, and they will be his people, and God himself will be with them as their God. He will wipe away every tear from their eyes, and death will be no more, neither shall there be mourning, nor crying, nor pain anymore, for the former things have passed away." (Revelation 21:1–4)

The old heaven and the old earth will pass away, and believers will dwell with God with new conditions and different surroundings, and **God the Father and Jesus, the Son, will be there**. And the beauty of it all will be beyond description. Notice God speaks directly to John (for our benefit), assuring us that He will be with us forever. And notice God spoke with a loud voice, one ringing with authority and clarity. John could not help but understand and record for us to read. These are truths God wants us to learn and remember and take to heart. They are the kind of truths we can learn that will change our perspective about everything we believe and do here on earth. They will reorient our perspectives about every decision we make and give new purpose for our lives. And that new purpose is to glorify God.

Notice, too, what will be absent from our heavenly existence: tears, death, mourning, crying, and pain. And notice what and Who will be present with us. "Behold, the dwelling place of God is with man. He will dwell with them, and they will be his people, And God himself will be with them as their God" (vv. 3–4). What could be more comforting than to be assured almighty God will be with us forever? Two passages in Psalms address this same subject of God's concern and provisions for us with words very poignant:

When I am afraid,
  I put my trust in you. (Psalm 56:3)

You have kept count of my tossings;
  put my tears in your bottle. (Psalm 56:8)

When we are afraid, where better could we go than to the Lord? Is anyone more trustworthy? Who loves us more? Who has more sensitivity, mercy, concern, and power to help us?

Who is more apt to know of every care we have and want to help? We've never shed even one tear God doesn't know about and seen to. Putting our tears in His bottle is a beautiful way to describe this.

God works daily to make every believer's life a heaven here on earth through His love and direction.

MATTHEW 24:1–2

In this passage Jesus foretells the destruction of the temple, that symbol of Israel's God, where they felt God dwelt. We can only imagine what losing such a significant monument would mean to a country and to a people. Because of its religious connotations it would be an even greater loss than if one day we lost our US Capitol Building. Jesus' prophecy happened this way:

> Jesus left the temple and was going away, when his disciples came to point out to him the buildings of the temple. But he answered them, "You see all these, do you not? Truly, I say to you, there will not be left here one stone upon another that will not be thrown down." (Matthew 24:1–2)

This complete destruction happened in AD 70, approximately forty years after Jesus spoke these words, when the Roman army under general Titus (who later became emperor) destroyed all of Jerusalem, including the temple. Israel had threatened Rome with revolution and Titus had been sent to regain control of the land.

This incident points up a number of things. First, Jesus, as God, knew the future. Second, people then, and now, should not think of God as limited in any way. Church buildings are not real churches. We come to a building and worship there, and leave feeling we have met God, but reality is, the people are the church. And we don't need a building to meet God or be a church. Third, we need to remember the first temple (built during King Solomon's reign about 950 BC) had already been destroyed once (in 587 BC) when the Babylonians defeated Israel and took many people into captivity to Babylon. In fact, when Jesus walked through the temple area on that day, the temple (which had been rebuilt by 515 BC) was being expanded to many times the size of the rebuilt temple. That enlarged temple was finished about AD 66 and was only four years old when Rome destroyed it as prophesied by Jesus in this passage.

But fourth and most important, we see God is in control (of everything), not man. He dictates all events, their timing, and the results of everything, down to the smallest details of our lives. Jesus came into the world at exactly the right time to save us from our sins, to live, be crucified, rise again, and ascend back to heaven. And He will come again at exactly the right time to gather those who are destined to live with Him for eternity. Nothing then surprises God, and nothing happens by accident. We believers are blessed to be given a role to play in this whole destiny of man, that is, to go and make disciples among all the nations, sharing the gospel with those who have not heard. God is all-powerful and knows all things, and yet has a specific plan for each of our lives. And while worldly events may seem scary to us, we are told by God to

> fear not, for I am with you;
>   be not dismayed, for I am your God;
> I will strengthen you. I will help you,
>   I will uphold you with my righteous right hand. (Isaiah 41:10)

With that kind of assurance from almighty God, who are we to be afraid of anything? Who do you know that needs to hear this word from heaven? Who can you encourage to receive Christ and gain eternal life?

JAMES 1:2–4

We have here a letter from James, the brother of Jesus and leader of the Jerusalem church, to Jewish Christians. Likely written in the mid-forties AD, to encourage his readers (and us) to be "doers of the word and not hearers only" (James 1:22). Such practical wisdom is timeless in its application and should be lived out by believers in any era. Jesus was tested so it's not surprising that all believers are too.

> Count it all joy, my brothers, when you meet trials of various kinds, for you know that the testing of your faith produces steadfastness. And let steadfastness have its full effect, that you may be perfect and complete, lacking in nothing. (James 1:2–4)

The only way we can "count trials as joy" is if we recognize the meaning and purpose behind them, and still, it is not easy. We can't imagine what it must have been like to be raised in the same household as Jesus. Thus, having watched Jesus' example for about thirty years had to have had an effect on James' perspective on God and family. And then at some point he believed; all he had witnessed over the years must now have made sense. Jesus Christ is Lord, Son of God sent to earth to save us from our sins. So now when such an individual tells us to be joyful during trials, we can be sure that is truly a message from the Lord.

Notice there seems to be no doubt in James' mind that his readers would experience trials. Jesus had been crucified about ten years earlier and by the time of this letter, opposition from the Jewish leadership and the Roman rulers was well established. Thus these tests of their faith James referred to were probably common among believers. So, James' readers could relate to trials, and having to live within a society dominated by unbelievers.

But there was logic behind God's allowing trials to come to these relatively new believers. They needed to grow spiritually, and trials were part of their training process. According to James, trials produced steadfastness. We don't use the word *steadfast* too often, but we generally understand it means fixed in place and not subject to change. So, when used like this we can take steadfastness to be a good thing. Our faith and our commitment to Christ are to be steadfast, not changing in good times or in bad, always steady, even growing over time. So, there is the concept of living this way over the long haul, no matter what happens or where we happen to be.

James, or rather the Holy Spirit speaking through James, maintains that the result of living steadfast in our faith and commitments to Christ leads to our perfection as believers. Like all scripture, it's important that we remember to take it as God's Word, His commands to us. So, when we read that consistency in our faith leads to our lacking nothing, that should make a decided impression on us. What could the concept of our lacking nothing mean? To answer that question, we need only ask ourselves what having faith provides us. We could all make our own list with topics such as eternal life, support in times of trouble, a closer walk with the Lord, kinship with many wonderful people here on earth, and about a million more.

Thus, the next time we are tried we can remember this lesson from James 1, and "count it all joy." Remember this is God speaking to us, and He means what He says. Who do we know that also needs to be reminded of this lesson?

DANIEL 7:13-14

Daniel writes here of a vision he had concerning Jesus and His identity. This passage describes His coming kingdom, His role in the world, and also provides us perspective about who Jesus is relative to us. We believers are to acknowledge that perspective and let it govern our lives. It is so important that we orient our lives around His will and His eternal glory and not ourselves and our short-term views. The position Jesus has as Son of Man indicates both His human and His divine traits. Jesus was fully man and fully God. See Philippians 2:7: "But emptied himself, by taking the form of a servant, being born in the likeness of men."

Here are Daniel's words describing Jesus hundreds of years before He came to earth:

> I saw in the night visions, and behold, with the clouds of heaven there came one like a Son of Man, and he came to the Ancient of Days and was presented before him. And to him was given dominion and glory and a kingdom, that all peoples, nations, and languages should serve him; his dominion is an everlasting dominion, which shall not pass away, and his kingdom one that shall not be destroyed. (Daniel 7:13–14)

"With the clouds of heaven" would indicate Jesus coming with divine authority. His standing before His heavenly Father, the "Ancient of Days," to be presented refers to His relationship to the Father who both acknowledged and introduced Him. Notice He was given glory and ruling authority over all the world's inhabitants. Only His heavenly Father could delegate that to Him. And the relationship that has been in place always between Jesus and His heavenly Father is now indicated to the world as existing. Such authority would not be given to a human. We should remember Daniel is writing about 550 BC so this concept of a heavenly kingdom coming someday is unique.

Everything about this Son of Man Daniel envisions is all-encompassing and everlasting. He will have authority over everyone, and all people will serve Him. His dominion will last forever, and not pass away or be destroyed. Thus, evidently, He has always existed and will live forever, and so He will also reign forever.

So what are to think and conclude? Daniel seems convinced Jesus is (coming as) God, but can we conclude the same thing? We certainly have been advised more than Daniel was concerning Jesus' identity and life while on earth. It's hard to talk about this subject without using the word *faith* somewhere along the line. We were not there when Jesus lived on earth, so if we are going to believe it has to be by faith. And that is exactly what God wants from us. He wants us to step out in faith. So yes, we can, by faith, believe Jesus was and is who He claimed to be. And there is a sense in which it takes more faith on our part to believe because we were not there to see and hear Him personally.

Prayer and Bible study will open your heart to the faith God requires of us. He has "from the beginning" supplied the grace we need for salvation and God plays a role in supplying faith too. It is not a stretch to understand God does it all when it comes to our salvation. See Ephesians 2:8: "For by grace you have been saved through faith. And this is not your own doing; it is the gift of God." It's OK to pray for faith.

LUKE 11:33–36

If we have been blessed enough early in life to hear of Jesus Christ and His love for us, we have an opportunity to both live out a relationship with Him, and to share that knowledge with a needy world. That scenario of both hearing and sharing is God's basic plan of reaching the nations with the gospel of Jesus Christ. As He preached and taught, Jesus continually promoted this concept and would have us do the same thing. Look at this passage of scripture where Jesus uses several metaphors to illustrate this witnessing concept:

> No one after lighting a lamp puts it in a cellar or under a basket, but on a stand, so that those who enter may see the light. Your eye is the lamp of your body. When your eye is healthy, your whole body is full of light, but when it is bad, your body is full of darkness. Therefore be careful lest the light in you be darkness. If then your whole body is full of light, having no part dark, it will be wholly bright, as when a lamp with its rays gives you light. (Luke 11:33–36)

The "lamp" in this passage is representative of Jesus Christ. No one rightly receives the knowledge of Jesus' true identity as Son of God, Messiah, and Redeemer and keeps it to themselves. The light from such a lamp is to be shared with everyone. This knowledge serves to transform our hearts and our perspectives in life. The eye mentioned refers to our spiritual approach to life. If that "eye" is healthy (that is, in sync with Jesus' spiritual approach to life) then our lives are full of godly influence, which is exactly what God wants. That means our lifestyles, our decisions, our words, and our everyday actions are living witnesses of God's love, and thus, other people see Jesus Christ in us.

Therefore, we are to beware of keeping our "lamp" turned off. That is, not living out and sharing the knowledge of Christ that we have been blessed to receive. Having such knowledge is both a blessing and a responsibility. A lamp that is turned off is not serving the function for which it was made. Neither are we serving the function for which we were born if we are not glorifying God with our lives.

On the other hand, turned on lamps bless their surroundings with light. People can see better in the dark when they are in the vicinity of turned on lamps. People around us can see better how to live if our spiritual lights are always on, that is, if our spiritual walk with Christ is consistent through good times and bad. In His infinite wisdom God has seen fit to provide His Holy Spirit to walk with us daily to both remind and guide us of and to His will for our lives. He did this because He loves us with a love so great that He sent His Son to die on the cross for our sins, making a way for us to receive eternal life.

Prayer is the way we access God's love and power. Remember, your prayers are powerful. They are powerful for two reasons: (1) because the God you are praying to is powerful and (2) because of what it cost God to give you the right to pray. It cost Him His Son, Jesus.

2 TIMOTHY 2:1–2

We are especially blessed when we hear the gospel, for many people have not heard this description of God's love. With those blessings come the responsibility to share what we've heard with others. And all believers are to do that daily right where they are, using the gifts God has given them, and the opportunities He supplies. Only in that way will the message of Jesus be spread worldwide. Without dedicated effort we will not accomplish the task. Our busy schedules tend to crowd out time spent in Bible study and witnessing to others, so it is obvious Paul is urging us to prioritize those witnessing efforts. The significance of the gospel should weigh heavily on us. It has eternal worth and is vital to the destiny of everyone. Nothing other than God's salvation plan initiates the path to heaven and an eternity with the Lord. See how logical Paul is in his presentation:

> You then, my child, be strengthened by the grace that is in Christ Jesus, and what you have heard from me in the presence of many witnesses entrust to faithful men, who will be able to teach others also. (2 Timothy 2:1–2)

The grace Paul mentions is a reference to the steadfast love God has for us that we have but don't deserve. Thus, it is this unmerited favor from God that all believers are freely granted by God. And there is strengthening power within that grace that we need to sustain us through the many and varied trials that we face all lifelong. God knows this and makes His grace available consistently for our benefit.

Timothy has been with Paul long enough to have heard him preach and teach the gospel to many different individuals and groups. Again, Paul tells Timothy, and us, to imitate him in doing this. Notice the sequency concept inherent within this practice. Paul teaches Timothy, Timothy entrusts this vital information to faithful men, and those faithful men are to teach others. We see then the connections between the four levels of witness: Paul, Timothy, faithful men, and others. If practiced by all believers, we can easily understand how the gospel would quickly spread. God has given us a wise plan for reaching all nations. Notice the personal responsibility all believers have. And each of us is qualified to participate. We don't have or need particular talents to do this, for as we share the gospel, we are simply relating our own experience of what God has done for us in Jesus. And all of us can do that. And nothing communicates better than true personal experiences.

Paul is writing this letter from prison as he faces death at the hands of the Romans. That surely gives additional credibility to his message. What could be more important than the sharing of God's plan for eternal life? And that's true today too. We have no message more important to share, and no one else does either.

Thus, it is no wonder that Paul encourages all his readers (including us) to share the gospel, especially with the next generation. By definition, we are always only one generation away from ending the spread of the gospel. If the present generation fails in their efforts, no future generation will have access to the truth of God's plan. We can be sure Satan knows this and is making every effort to shut down the spread of the gospel. Notice Paul uses the word *entrust* as he describes the act of passing on the gospel. That word speaks volumes concerning the importance of consistent sharing of the truth by all believers. We believers have been entrusted with this eternal truth. Let us do our part to share it.

JOHN 14:27

If we had to boil down to one word what we want from life, the word *peace* would be the one chosen by many people. Consciously or subconsciously that deep feeling of complete rest and relief is what's on our mind most of the time. And that's been true for centuries with all people in every era and everywhere. And because it's such a bedrock desire of us all, Jesus saw fit to address that mindset and heart-set for us, and to give us counsel on how to achieve it. After all, He does love us, so it follows He wants the best for us, and possessing His peace is a major part of that. See Jesus' words on this vital subject:

> Peace I leave with you; my peace I give to you. Not as the world gives do I give to you. Let not your hearts be troubled, neither let them be afraid. (John 14:27)

Notice in this passage Jesus indicates real peace only comes from Him. There is no mention of our earning Jesus' peace, it comes as a gift. And not only can He provide it, He will provide it. Further, His kind of peace is permanent. Thus, we are wise to realize all this and seek to define and understand this precious gift Jesus is preparing to hand out.

The dictionary definition of peace speaks of tranquility, quiet, and freedom from conflict between people or nations. The Bible definition is much richer. It also includes the condition of our hearts, especially as related to how we stand with the Lord. It has to do with our very lives and how we look at our privileges and responsibilities with regard to glorifying our heavenly Father. Nothing provides more peace than our joy concerning our daily walk with God.

When you think about it, acquiring Jesus' peace is a very exciting concept. He knew that in the rush of our society, from time to time we would be afraid, and that our hearts would often be troubled by worldly circumstances. Therefore, here we have Jesus (ahead of time) advising us of His source of relief for us. So, instead of false, weak, and temporary worldly peace, Jesus advises we take on the peace He offers. And from the wording of this passage, we find we need never suffer from worldly fears or troubles. There is nothing weak, temporary, or limited about Jesus' love, power, wisdom, or strength. It's all available to us as believers.

It's significant that Jesus is speaking here at the Last Supper, only a few hours before His crucifixion. There is a sort of reminder element in all the truths Jesus gave them that evening. For three years Jesus had been teaching His disciples of His identity as Messiah, and proving it with multiple miracles. And now He is about to end the earthly portion of His ministry. And so every word spoken that night is heavy with significance, every truth eternal in scope, and every command ladened with hope.

We see then in this passage a command (flavored with love) to do something that will be good for us. Isn't that just like God? To very gently command us to do something He knows will be beneficial to us personally, and to the world around us if we obey.

So, yes, there is a difference in Jesus' peace and any peace the disciples (or we) can gather from the world. Jesus would soon be leaving the disciples, but He would make provision on the cross for them (and us) to live fearlessly, free of real troubles. Jesus lived that way, and He would have us live that way too. Surely, we all know someone who needs to hear of the peace available in Christ.

REVELATION 14:12-13

John the apostle has been led to write this book of Revelation. Among the things he writes are encouraging words for believers, those who live in this sinful world and suffer for their faith. Thus, they are told not to fear death, but to rejoice in their coming fellowship with their Lord. See these words that are as applicable now as they were when John wrote them:

> Here is a call for endurance of the saints, those who keep the commandments of God and their faith in Jesus.
>
> And I heard a voice from heaven saying, "Write this: Blessed are the dead who die in the Lord from now on." "Blessed indeed," says the Spirit, "that they may rest from their labors, for their deeds follow them!" (Revelation 14:12–13)

Saints, that is, believers, are told to endure, to face bravely and consistently whatever the world brings to them, obeying God's commandments and keeping their faith in Jesus as they do. Such a consistent lifestyle is easier to talk about than to execute. But then Jesus suffered much for our sins, and if He suffered, then it follows that we will, too, as we imitate Him. Thus, believers are not to expect a carefree existence. Keeping our faith in the midst of trials is what God asks of us and expects of us, and what He will help us endure.

Our heavenly Father knows this will be difficult and saw fit to have John specifically address those kinds of fears. He spoke from heaven and told John exactly what to write (for us to read). Those who die in the Lord (from then on) are blessed. To die in the Lord is to die as a believer in Christ. These are the ones who trust Jesus' sacrificial death on the cross as payment for their sin debt, and those who therefore work at obedience to God's commandments.

And the Holy Spirit adds, "Blessed indeed," they will then be able to rest from their labors for all they've done is somehow recorded and will be assessed when their rewards are tallied. Imagine God keeping up with the sincerity of our confession of faith and then with all we then do, and why. Yes indeed, all we do will follow us.

God would not have us be misled. He is very clear in what He requires of us. Just as He very clearly tells us what we will be blessed for. For believers then there are blessings ahead and for eternity. We can only imagine now what rest as defined by God will really mean. We can be sure it will be awesome.

If we need further assurance as to the truth of this passage on endurance see Hebrews 10:35–36: "Therefore do not throw away your confidence, which has a great reward. For you have need of endurance, so that when you have done the will of God you may receive what is promised."

Confidence in God is not misplaced. We can count on God keeping His promises. This is the very kind of confidence we are to live out as we make our daily decisions. And it is the same kind of confidence we are to share with others as they face the same kind of doubts we do.

HEBREWS 12:28-29

Scholars are in disagreement as to who actually wrote the book of Hebrews, but they are not in disagreement as to the depth and power of the truth presented there. In this book we find confirmation that salvation comes through Christ alone, and that His kingdom is eternally unshakeable. Jesus then is the only source of eternal life and we had best establish a relationship with Him. We are saved by God's grace through faith and no other way. There is not more than one way to heaven, and there is not another God who loves us and has made provisions for us to live eternally with Him. See these verses that describe why we should be ever grateful for what God has done for us:

> Therefore let us be grateful for receiving a kingdom that cannot be shaken, and thus let us offer to God acceptable worship, with reverence and awe, for our God is a consuming fire. (Hebrews 12:28–29)

After several chapters describing God's awesome power and majesty, the author draws the obvious conclusion. God is God and we are not. We are to worship Him and Him only. The only proper response to such grace is humble adoration and worship on our part. So, we are to be grateful. We think we know what gratefulness consists of, but do we actually live it out? Gratefulness consists of appreciation for comfort supplied, and for discomfort alleviated.

This passage speaks of our receiving a kingdom. The implication is that kingdom is the kingdom of heaven, that eternal home all believers already have. It's that possession that brings ultimate comfort and peace forever, and per the definition of gratefulness, removes the necessity of our spending eternity separated from God in hell, that destination of ultimate discomfort. So quite simply we are to be grateful on two counts, what we as believers have to look forward to, heaven, and what we have avoided, hell.

Notice believers have received a kingdom (heaven) that "cannot be shaken." Talk about good news. This means several things about heaven. It is for certain and without doubt, God has and is preparing that destiny for all who trust Christ as Savior and Lord, and nothing can stop Him. Secondly, heaven is eternal. Nothing can prevent it from becoming our home, and nothing can ever take it from us once we are there. And third, heaven is that place and condition of infinite, ever increasing, joy. Just (try to) imagine being in the presence of Jesus Christ forever, near enough to hear His voice and feel His love firsthand always.

So, what is to be the reaction of believers to such a promise? It's to be gratefulness lived out as acceptable worship, reverence, and awe just as the passage tells us. And such a lifestyle is not to be a chore or forced condition. As we accept Christ for who He is (almighty God come to earth to save us from our sins), and grow in that knowledge over time, our worship, praise, and honor of Him becomes ever increasingly natural as we become more like Him.

And notice the last point in this passage. Heaven is real; it's especially designed for us believers. And God will be there in the most complete sense, filling our every thought, desire, wish, and anticipation. We can rejoice that our God is a consuming fire for that assures us all our sins are completely forgiven, preparing our natures for all God will have us experience in heaven.

REVELATION 14:12-13

There are seven benedictions listed in Revelation, that is, seven expressions of God's love and good wishes for us to cling to in times of doubt and stress. This passage reflects the second one. It provides short-term and eternal hope for believers (that is, on earth and in heaven beyond). Thus, no matter the temptations and trials we have on earth, we can and should have hope in the future we have with the Lord in heaven. God added such passages to His Word to bring comfort and direction to us in the midst of whatever troubles Satan might bring to us. See this call for endurance:

> Here is a call for the endurance of the saints, those who keep the commandments of God and their faith in Jesus.
> And I heard a voice from heaven saying, "Write this: Blessed are the dead who die in the Lord from now on." "Blessed indeed," says the Spirit, "that they may rest from their labors, for their deeds follow them!" (Revelation 14:12–13)

Plainly John calls us to ongoing obedience to God's will in our lives. He uses the word *endurance* to indicate such obedience might not be easy at times, but to also tell us God loves us, understands what we face, and stands ready to help us. The word *consistent* comes to mind when we consider how we are to react to God's purposes in our lives; consistency in the sense of mindful consideration of God's will when we make decisions and when we seek to live out our faith.

Notice how specific the Holy Spirit was in speaking to John. "Write this," the Spirit told him, and then dictated to John exactly what to say. "Blessed are the dead who die in the Lord, from now on." The Holy Spirit knew what John's readers needed to hear. We are not given a description of those blessings, but we can be sure that when God blesses, all our pain and sorrows are ended. Those who die as believers, therefore, are assured of an eternity with the Lord freed from earth's bonds and trials.

And the Spirit adds the phrase "Blessed indeed," to give further credence and certainty to God's promise. For there is a detail added to the promise tied to the blessing. That detail speaks of the rest from their labors inherent with God's blessing. This, because God knows of their labors and somehow gives those who die in the Lord credit in heaven for those labors. We don't understand all that is involved with this description, but we do know our loving God will provide His children unspeakable joy and rest forever.

One of the things so beautiful and so assuring about all this is that God does not just make all these awesome provisions for believers, **He wants us to know about them ahead of time. He wants us to be thinking, planning, and looking forward to an endless relationship with Him in heaven. Such assurance then provides us the hope and endurance needed to "stay the course" in our Christian walk.**

That's the kind of God we have and the kind of love He has for us.

ROMANS 4:20-21

A man named Abraham lived about 2000 BC in the Middle East. He was a wealthy man and a good man that God chose for a special assignment. God came to Abraham and told him he would become the father of a great nation, a nation especially selected from whom would come blessings for the whole world. At the time Abraham was about seventy-five years old and childless. So you can imagine how surprised and puzzled he was. God simply told him to trust Him and follow His instructions. Look how Abraham responded:

> No unbelief made him waver concerning the promise of God, but he grew strong in his faith as he gave glory to God, fully convinced that God was able to do what he had promised. (Romans 4:20–21)

Abraham exhibited great faith as he and his wife (Sarah) packed their belongings and moved with their many flocks and servants to a land God led him to. He was convinced God was real, that He was powerful, and that He was sovereign. So he gave glory to God, worshipping Him and obeying Him though he did not know how the future would play out. But as the verses says he was convinced God was able to do what He had promised.

That is exactly the same attitude God wants us to have. He wants us to trust Him as Abraham did, even if we don't know the future. God knew that Sarah was beyond childbearing age, and that it would mean Abraham would have to leave his father and his brother and the security they represented. So it would take some miracles for God to accomplish all this in Abraham's life. But God also knew He had a plan for Abraham's life. God also knows our circumstances, where we live, our family situation, and

He knows what the future holds. God fulfilled every promise He made to Abraham. He became the father of the Jewish nation we know today. Within that nation Jesus Christ was born as a man; sent into the world by God to save us from our sins by sacrificing His life on the cross to pay for our sins. That happened in the first century about two thousand years after Abraham lived. So God is sovereign, He controls the future for us all.

God knew that all people are born as sinners and prone to disobey Him. So, because our sins earn us God's wrath, and that such sin on our part is worthy of our deaths, and because God loves us with a steadfast love (though we do disobey Him), He made provision for us to gain eternal life by sending His Son Jesus Christ to die on the cross **in our place.** That's the amazing truth, now we don't have to die as sinners, Jesus took all our sin upon Himself and died for our sins. And we simply have to have faith in God and His truth (just like Abraham did) for God to give us eternal life. And thus, because Jesus rose from the grave (that's what we celebrate at Easter) **so will we. Hallelujah!!**

There is a special verse in scripture that describes this: "For God so loved the world, that he gave his only Son, that whoever believes in him should not perish but have eternal life" (John 3:16).

A simple but profound truth, and very, very true for all who believe. What a great, great God we have!

ISAIAH 40:8

Isaiah was assigned by God to go forth among the people of Israel teaching and preaching obedience to almighty God. At this time, about 700 BC, the Israelites were being threatened by surrounding pagan countries (particularly Assyria) and were searching for help anywhere they could find it. They were leaning toward going to Egypt for help, thinking that Assyria was an enemy common to them both. God had other plans, and this passage very simply describes where the Israelites should have gone for help, and where we should go for help too. See this profound passage:

> The grass withers, the flower fades, but the word of our God will stand forever. (Isaiah 40:8)

One of the amazing things about God's Word is its relevance to all generations in all eras. In both simple and sophisticated societies God's Word finds wide application. This is true because while over time civilizations change and our lifestyles grow more complex, human nature does not change. We are as much afraid of unknowns as those people in Isaiah's day. We love and hate just like they did. And we need God's love and direction every bit as much as they did.

God's Word is powerful because He is powerful. His truths are eternal, and applicable to us all because in His infinite wisdom and power God saw fit to establish the biblical parameters that would govern life generally and specifically for us all. And paramount to everything else, God's love reigns and is the basis for all He has done and will do. His provision for our eternal life expresses the ultimate in mercy, justice, and hope for us, His children.

And God wisely provided His Word to guide us as we make both daily and long-term decisions. Written over fifteen hundred years by more than forty authors, the Bible remains our source of God's direction and His will for our lives. The grass and flowers mentioned in the passage represent the temporary aspects of all life contrasted with the permanence of the truth and relevance of God's Word.

But as important and as worthy as scripture is of our obedience, it won't help anyone if they deny its necessity in their lives, and if they refuse to believe its doctrines. In total it is God's revelation of Himself to mankind. Perhaps not all, but most people will acknowledge they believe in God. That acknowledgment means many different things to many people. The real test of their belief would have to do with whether in addition to believing God exists, they also believe what God says. If His words have no real credibility with an individual, then no matter the depth of their knowledge of scripture, their lives will remain void of any hope of eternal life, and any real awareness of the love of God behind His provision for our eternal life.

So God's Word is "out there," available for us to read and obey, and as true and as applicable as it ever has been. Thus, there is the need for us to translate the truth of God into actions in our lives. There is no more important information we can pass on to our loved ones than God's truth. And there is no more important habit we can cultivate than reading and studying and applying God's Word daily.

EPHESIANS 1:17–19

In the first chapter of his letter to the believers in Ephesus, Paul describes his prayers for them, exactly what he asks of God on their behalf. The very fact that God has seen fit to have Paul record this information for us to read is strong evidence that God would have us pray those same type prayers for ourselves and for other believers in our day. See Paul's heart in this passage:

> That the God of our Lord Jesus Christ, the Father of glory, may give you the spirit of wisdom and of revelation in the knowledge of him, having the eyes of your hearts enlightened, that you may know what is the hope to which he has called you, what are the riches of his glorious inheritance in the saints, and what is the immeasurable greatness of his power toward us who believe. (Ephesians 1:17–19)

Paul writes this letter in approximately AD 62, while he is under house arrest in Rome, about thirty years after his conversion. He had founded the church in Ephesus about ten years earlier. He was writing to encourage them in their faith, reassuring them of Christ's role in reconciling them to God and uniting them with all other believers in His church. So, Paul precedes his instructions with mighty prayers, calling on his heavenly Father to give them (and us) more understanding as to what they have in Christ.

Notice it is the God of our Lord Jesus Christ, the Father of glory, who not only sent His Son to the cross to die to pay the sin debt of all those who believe, but who also provides those same believers with the "spirit of wisdom and revelation" to reveal to them the significance of what He has done. God wants all believers (then and now) to have full knowledge and enlightened hearts concerning the hope to which He has called them. When you think about it, it is only logical that believers in any era have full, and complete awareness of what their salvation is all about. Only then will they be able to live out their lives being proper disciples and disciple makers, looking forward to the rich inheritance God has planned for them, and sharing that same hope with others. And **hallelujah,** every believer has God's immeasurable power working for them as they obey.

Thus, we have been blessed, as were the Ephesians, with (1) the hope of our calling as believers (an eternity in heaven with the Lord), (2) God's power (to guide and protect us), and (3) classification as God's inheritance. This last blessing is most significant. God loves us and looks forward to His glorious inheritance as we eventually will spend an eternity in fellowship with Him. This is how God sees us, His children. What a great, great God we have, who provides for our every need.

We believers today who read this letter are in pretty much the same situation as those Ephesians in the first century. We believe, but our belief is only partial, incomplete, and in "growth mode." At the same time, as it was in the first century, there is a tremendous task ahead of us, for the whole world, near and far, is out there needing to hear the gospel. Thus, Paul's prayer for the Ephesians applies to us too. And it's a prayer we ought to be praying for ourselves and each other. So now we know what we are to do, and how we are to pray.

2 PETER 3:8–9

This passage comes from a section of scripture that discusses the Day of the Lord, that day when Christ returns to gather believers to take them to heaven for an eternity with Him. For centuries believers have questioned the timing of this day and how it will play out. Peter wrote this letter in the late sixties AD from prison only a few decades after Christ ascended back to heaven. So, at this point believers had been waiting for Christ's return only thirty or forty years, and already they were anxious about His delay. We've been waiting two thousand years and still Christ delays His return. Peter's words of encouragement apply even more to us now given the long period we've waited.

> But do not overlook this one fact, beloved, that with the Lord one day is as a thousand years, and a thousand years as one day. The Lord is not slow to fulfill his promise as some count slowness, but is patient toward you, not wishing that any should perish, but that all should reach repentance. (2 Peter 3:8–9)

In the first place, the two thousand years the world has waited for Christ to return is not a long time from God's perspective. It simply indicates the patience God has, and His desire that not any should perish, but all should repent. Look at the facts this passage presents to mankind. God's message in this passage is that Jesus will return at the appropriate time. That fact is not in question. Another key point not in question is, the longer Jesus delays the more people there will be who repent and come to Christ in faith, gaining access to heaven with Him for an eternity.

A third point for us to consider is whether a person lives a long time or a short time on earth, that period is minute compared to eternity. So, our waiting at most is perhaps a hundred years in which we have opportunity to come to Christ in saving faith and in which our eternal destiny is fixed forever, depending on our response to the knowledge God gives us during those hundred years. And lastly the heavenly experience that believers can look forward to (in quality and quantity), is so vastly superior to our earthly existence, that any waiting period would be worth the wait. **We cannot imagine what one moment with Jesus will be like especially when we understand time will be no more; what we call days will no longer be measured.**

God knows what heaven will be like for us. And because He loves us with an infinite love, He longs for an eternity with us as we partake of all that He is preparing knowing what it will mean to us. What this passage gives us is a chance to change our perspective concerning what we think about the Day of the Lord. We no longer need think of it as a far off event that may or may not come about in our lifetime. What the whole concept of that Day provides us (as believers) is a peace concerning our infinite future. It really enriches the witness we can have during our time here on earth. Our message now to those we care about is one of hope beyond imagination, a certainty that will not fail, a future only the God who created us could guarantee.

So, what should be our response to this good news? We are to (1) relax and reorient our perspectives about life here on earth, (2) take advantage of the opportunities that God provides us to share what we know about God and His plans for us with others, and most important, (3) praise and worship the God who loves us so much. To glorify Him with all we have and are is to be our goal here and in heaven.

1 CORINTHIANS 3:13-15

Everyone will one day be judged. Our lives will be evaluated for how we used them for God's glory. Everything we've ever done (and why we did it) will be measured, and (scripture says) tested by fire. We don't know if that means literal fire, or that somehow our lives will be tested symbolically. Either way God will absolutely have us give account for what we've done and judge us accordingly. This concept would naturally follow a completely just God eventually making all things right among all that He has created. Notice how the Holy Spirit has Paul describe this process in this letter to the church in Corinth.

> Each one's work will become manifest, for the Day will disclose it, because it will be revealed by fire, and the fire will test what sort of work each one has done. If the work that anyone has built on the foundation survives, he will receive a reward. If anyone's work is burned up, he will suffer loss, though he himself will be saved, but only as through fire. (1 Corinthians 3:13–15)

The phrase "each one" clearly indicates no one will be exempt from this disclosure process. The word *manifest* would imply all our deeds will be made known to everyone else. Paul makes no attempt to explain how so many deeds, done by all mankind, can be revealed to everyone. He is convinced a God who created everything can also accommodate such a colossal feat. That day refers to what we call "Judgment Day," a day or occasion when all will be revealed, and judgment explained and applied. There apparently will be no time for explanation or discussion by us individually. No opportunity or need for any clarification on our part will be allowed or necessary. We will clearly be identified with our deeds (both good and bad), and we will have no argument as to our guilt or innocence.

Somehow the "fire test" will make our status very clear for all to see, and the sort of work (and motives) we have exhibited will be obvious. Notice some work done will survive, and some burn up. And the criteria for which result prevails seems to be how and whether our work was built on the foundation. The foundation is not defined here, but the previous passage (3:11) precisely identifies that foundation as Jesus Christ. Thus, Jesus Christ, His person, identity, work, words, and authority, will be that basis on which our work will be judged. In fact, He will be our judge.

Thus, those whose work survives will be rewarded, and those whose work does not survive will suffer loss, though that one will himself be saved. We realize Paul is speaking of believers in this passage, and they are by definition saved. Obviously, this passage describes levels of reward in heaven. How that concept will play out is another secret God does not define for us. Again, however, we can be sure in His perfection, our God will do the right thing by everyone.

So, what lessons are here for us? Simply put: (1) All will be judged and rewarded appropriately. (2) Thus, all are responsible for their individual lives and how they glorified God by building on the foundation of Jesus Christ, given their knowledge and opportunities. (3) Our brief lives on earth serve to dictate our eternal destiny. And (4) not mentioned specifically but surely implied, we are to tell the nations about this "judgment policy" God will implement.

EPHESIANS 4:4-6

God sees the church as the body of Christ. This passage addresses that concept and includes details on how we individual believers are to join with one another to accomplish God's will, united through His church. So, it's no wonder we Christians today are urged to actively participate regularly in a local church. We will accomplish more of God's kingdom work together than we will acting separately. We will also grow more Christlike by associating with other believers as we help each other grow spiritually. See how the apostle Paul words this in his letter to the church at Ephesus.

> There is one body and one Spirit—just as you were called to the one hope that belongs to your call—one Lord, one faith, one baptism, one God and Father of all, who is over all and through all and in all. But grace was given to each one of us according to the measure of God's gift. (Ephesians 4:4–6)

Just as each individual has one physical body (made up of many parts) and one spirit that enlivens it, the church also made up of many parts and believers is enlivened by one Holy Spirit. Thus, it is the same Holy Spirit that indwells each and all believers. That one Holy Spirit hears the prayers of all believers, reminds us each of God's truth as appropriate for our many situations, and moves us to respond positively to God's will and for His glory.

Notice the significance of all that's in this passage that is characteristic of every believer. See there the blessings listed that are common to all believers. We all have the same hope and certainty and that's to spend an eternity with our Lord in heaven. We all have the same Lord, Jesus Christ, sent from heaven to earth to do the same thing for all those who believe, that is, save them from their sins. We all have the same faith in Christ, that He is

Son of God, our Lord and Savior, and that His death in our place did, in fact, pay all our sin debt. We all have the same baptism, symbolic of Christ's death as it cleanses us from all our sins through His atoning death on the cross. And we all have the same God and Father, almighty, sovereign, omnipotent, omniscient, and immutable, whose adopted child we are and proudly claim to be.

And last, praise the Lord, we are all saved the same way. Per Ephesians 2:8, that's "by grace you have been saved through faith." And that's according to the measure of God's gift. His gift of grace to each of us is exactly prescribed per our needs and applied perfectly in accord with His measurements, timing, and power.

Thus, believers have much in common and everything in common required for our atonement. God left nothing to chance. We are then commanded to consistently seek the fellowship of other believers, encouraging them in their faith, and being encouraged by them in our faith. In this way we achieve spiritual unity within our church body, solidifying our goals, and thus, making our witness outreach more effective and meaningful in the community.

God foresaw the need for this kind of unity, and via His Holy Spirit provided the necessary heartfelt movements in every believer that facilitated these feeling in us all. What a great God we have.

1 PETER 2:9-10

Peter wrote (probably from Rome) to the churches of Asia Minor (modern-day Turkey) urging them to persevere in their faith in the midst of Roman persecution. In our day, though our persecutions may be of a different nature, we can take comfort that the same God Peter calls on will deliver us. Peter sees the church of his day as a "new Israel," a phrase that could also be applied to the church in our day. Notice how Peter characterizes believers who make up the church, then and now.

> But you are a chosen race, a royal priesthood, a holy nation, a people for his own possession, that you may proclaim the excellencies of him who called you out of darkness into his marvelous light. Once you were not a people, but now you are God's people; once you had not received mercy, but now you have received mercy. (1 Peter 2:9–10)

Most believers today don't think of themselves as "a chosen race," or "a royal priesthood," or "a holy nation," or "a people for his own possession." But what if we did? Seeing ourselves that way speaks of the responsibility God has placed on the church in our day. Too many believers today don't see a real need to actively participate in their local church. They may or may not attend regularly, and hardly contribute to the churches' ministry. But the church was the only institution Jesus saw fit to establish during His earthly ministry. It is God's plan to reach the nations with the gospel through the church, and we as individual believers make up the church. So, Peter's call to us is to live up to the task Christ assigned to His followers when He was on earth.

Notice, too, Peter calls specific attention to what God has done for his readers (and us) already. He sent Christ to earth to call them out of darkness into His marvelous light. What else could that refer to than the gift of eternal life believers are given at the point of their salvation? And they are to proclaim the excellencies of that one, Christ, who called them. Once they were not a people, that is, not part of God's family, but now they are, with all the benefits that accrue to those in God's family. Think about what it means to be a joint heir with Jesus Christ, due the same inheritance in heaven He has. And that's the free gift given believers.

And at one point they had not received mercy, but now they have. Something happened, someone did something significant that made a difference in their lives and in their eternal destiny. That someone was Christ, and what He did was die a sinner's death in our place, to pay our sin debt. And now our destiny is an eternity in heaven with Christ.

The lesson for us here is that we believers have been given so much we should have no hesitation about proclaiming the excellencies of Christ. We have been given a unique responsibility and a unique assignment. We have been clearly directed to go and make disciples (like we are) teaching them all that we've been taught (Matthew 28:18–20). No true believer would deny they owe an ongoing debt to Christ, and that He is worthy of all our allegiance, love, and obedience. Peter's word here is simply another reminder of our call to live out our faith.

ACTS 22:14-16

We likely know the story already of how Saul, the great enemy of God, was converted on the road to Damascus. He met Jesus there and was never the same. God used a man named Ananias to then come to Saul and give him further instructions as to what God wanted him to do. It's not likely we had as dramatic an experience at our conversion as Saul did, but our instructions afterward are exactly the same as his. See how scripture describes the meeting between Ananias and Saul, and what God had Ananias tell Saul:

> And he said, "The God of our Fathers appointed you to know his will, to see the Righteous One and to hear a voice from his mouth; for you will be a witness for him to everyone of what you have seen and heard. And now why do you wait?" (Acts 22:14–16)

At our conversion we probably did not see Jesus, or experience a great light and be "knocked to the ground," or hear a voice from heaven that claimed to be Jesus, like Saul did. But God did in some manner communicate His saving message to our hearts, we did become acutely aware of His saving grace, and we did, like Saul, by faith believe that Jesus died a sacrificial death on the cross to pay our sin debt. We know already, and for sure, Jesus rose from the dead on the third day, and thus we, too, will one day rise from the dead. And there is no doubt in our minds what God commands us to do. That is, to "go and make disciples" (Matthew 28:18). Therefore, in a very real sense we have been advised as directly and as clearly as Saul was about what God wants us to do.

Notice what Ananias said to Saul (from God), "Why do you wait?" The Holy Spirit is asking us the same question, "What are you waiting for?" Are we waiting for God (or someone) to train us? Notice what Saul had already been told to do: "Witness to everyone of what you have seen and heard." We've seen and heard a lot about the gospel, we don't need training to begin to tell people what we've seen and heard concerning Jesus' plan for our salvation. Do we need an opportunity to tell someone about Jesus? We know in our hearts that's not true. We walk by and/or talk to people every day that need to hear the gospel. Do we need more courage? The answer there is probably yes. But God has already told us He will be with us "to the end of the age" (Matthew 28:20) as we go, and we could not have a better helper.

Like Saul, the God of our Fathers saved us, and appointed us in His Great Commission to go and make disciples. Jesus plainly told us in Matthew 22 that the greatest commandment was to love God with all our hearts, and souls, and minds, and that the second most important commandment was to love our neighbors as we love ourselves. So, we know the method we are to use to make disciples; love the Lord enough to follow His instructions, and love others enough to go out of our way to share the truth of the gospel, whether that's next door, or across the ocean.

So, yes, the question is, "What are we waiting for?" We know what God wants us to do, and we know He will go with us.

1 JOHN 5:10-12

This passage discusses the authentication of Jesus Christ as the Son of God. Of course, this truth is the basis of why Jesus' sacrificial death was both necessary and sufficient to pay the sin debt of all who believe in Him. So, it's no wonder John took pains to explain this fundamental truth for His readers (and us). God established this basis for two simple reasons: (1) He loves us, and (2) Jesus' death in our place is the only ransom sufficient to satisfy the debt payment required for the sin of mankind. Thus, from the beginning Jesus' atoning death was planned, and it played out at the appropriate time and place per God's plan. It behooves us then to believe it, take joy in it, to participate in it by faith, and to share this news with the nations, for God would not have anyone miss this opportunity for salvation. We see this in 2 Peter 3:9. We then clearly are assigned the task of sharing the truth of God's testimony concerning Jesus with the world.

> Whoever believes in the Son of God has the testimony in himself. Whoever does not believe God has made him a liar, because he has not believed in the testimony that God has borne concerning his Son. And this is the testimony, that God gave us eternal life, and this life is in his Son. Whoever has the Son has life; whoever does have the Son does not have life. (1 John 5:10–12)

The Holy Spirit could not have been clearer in how He had John describe God's authentication of Jesus' role in His redemption plan. Everyone's salvation turns on their relationship to Jesus Christ; do they, or do they not, believe Jesus is the only Son of God? If they don't, they make God a liar. In Matthew 3:17, the Father spoke from heaven describing Jesus this way: "This is my beloved Son, with whom I am well pleased." But if they do believe, they have life eternal.

Anyone who believes God's testimony concerning Jesus and takes it to heart, living it, sharing it, and taking joy in it, has that testimony within themselves. That is, the significance of it is such that they are bound by it, they cannot keep quiet about it, they must apply it to all their life circumstances, and that lifestyle becomes natural for them. When you think about it, how could we keep the good news of Jesus within ourselves? **And why would we? What possible reason could we use to justify keeping the only way to eternal life a secret? Jesus has told us to "Go, and make disciples." How could that mean anything other than to go and tells His story to an ignorant world and see the Holy Spirit work?**

As believers we have eternal life. But do we really understand how that came about? This passage tells us "God gave us eternal life." If we have it, it's only because God gave it to us forever. And why would God see fit to do that? Are we that worthy? Why us, and not others? Do we really believe John 3:16 about God loving the world so much He gave His only Son to die for our sins? These have been puzzling questions for centuries. Many people have turned away from the gospel simply because it simply did not fit their logic. Who could love that much and that way? God did, and we need to accept that. Faith is the only word we can use to give credibility to the whole act of salvation. It certainly does not fit with man's normal attitude and approach to our relationships and interactions with others. **But if we do believe, if we do have faith, then we are to prove that faith by our lifestyle, by the "why" of what we do, and God's glory will occur to us as we make decisions. And if we give consideration to the blessings we have and where they come from, the fact of God's love will come to us as the only answer that makes sense.**

HEBREWS 9:27-28

Our salvation comes through the blood of Christ. That means it was through His death, and only through His death, that we are redeemed. Redemption then indicates God has made provision for us to live eternally. All people are born sinners, and Jesus came down from heaven to earth to save us from our sins. We die once and after that comes a point of judgment where we each will give an account of our lives to Jesus as the ultimate judge. See this described in scripture:

> And just as it is appointed for man to die once, and after that comes judgment, so Christ, having been offered once to bear the sins of many, will appear a second time, not to deal with sin but to save those who are eagerly waiting for him. (Hebrews 9:27–28)

The first point made here is that man only lives once. There will be no provision for some sort of reincarnation of any individual making it possible for them to have a second chance to believe after death. Thus, we have the opportunity once during this life on earth to believe in Jesus Christ and receive His free gift of eternal life. "And after that comes judgment."

So clearly those who have heard the gospel of Jesus Christ will be accountable for that knowledge. Those who live and die without ever hearing the gospel will be judged based on the knowledge they do have. Romans 2:14–16 speaks to that:

> For when Gentiles, who do not have the law, by nature do what the law requires, they are a law to themselves, even though they do not have the law. They show that the work of the law is written on their hearts, while their conscience also bears witness, and their conflicting thoughts accuse or even excuse

them on that day when according to my gospel God judges the secrets of men by Christ Jesus.

Our perfect God will judge all of us perfectly. It is little wonder then why we who have heard the gospel are commanded to go and make disciples, sharing the truth concerning Jesus Christ with those who have never heard (Matthew 28:18–20).

Jesus came and died once for all, thereby making provision to pay the sin debt of all who believe in Him. Those who recognize their sinful status and repent, trusting Jesus as Lord and Savior of their lives, are given God's gift of eternal life. That eternal life does not begin when we die, but the moment when we are saved, having believed in Jesus Christ, and His sacrificial death as payment for our sins.

We see clear reference in the Hebrew passage that Jesus is coming again. His second coming will be to gather all those (alive and dead) who believe to live forever with Him in heaven. Interestingly, the passage speaks of believers "eagerly waiting for him." And why not, there can be no greater anticipation than the thought of spending eternity with the Lord in heaven. Such a prospect should color every day of our lives and really cause us to live fruit-filled lives with ever increasing joy-filled anticipation of an eternity with the Lord.

2 TIMOTHY 4:17–18

Paul is writing to Timothy describing his close brush with death at the hands of the Romans. He is writing from prison in Rome where he expects to soon be executed. He has had his first trial and evidently was found guilty of some sort of heresy (for not giving the emperor proper allegiance). But for some reason he was not immediately executed, and now writes giving his last instructions to Timothy. Note the confidence Paul has in his faith. Even with the threat of execution hanging over him, Paul remains steadfast in his desire for Timothy to carry on the gospel work, and of his belief in his own eternal destiny with the Lord. See his message to Timothy:

> So I was rescued from the lion's mouth. The Lord will rescue me from every evil deed and bring me safely into his heavenly kingdom. To him be the glory forever and ever. Amen. (2 Timothy 4:17–18)

In a very real way God rescues most of us almost every day. For example, God continually protects us from our own mistakes and the mistakes of others on the road as we drive. And most of us are not subjected to some sort of crippling disease that many others have. Why have we been spared and some others not? What is it that God would have us do with the extra time He has allotted us?

Paul knows he is likely to die soon, yet maintains he will be rescued from every evil deed. The way Paul sees it, the total picture of his life and death also includes what happens to him after his physical death. And he is confident that eternal portion of his life will be spent with the Lord in His heavenly kingdom. So, the Roman authorities were no real threat to him, for his allegiance was of a higher order (as ours should be).

Thus, Paul gladly and with confidence gives praise, honor, and glory to God (from his prison cell). How can we come to that same level of faith? Scripture tells us we can get there the same way Paul did: through living out our faith. From the point of his salvation Paul has continually tested his faith through all kinds of trials and opposition. Before he faced such problems, and as he faced them, Paul did several things. (1) He kept his focus and actions true to God's instructions to him, that is, taking the gospel to the Gentiles. (2) He prepared himself for later trouble by growing spiritually through ongoing prayers, Bible study, and the effort of good deeds as God brought him opportunity. (3) He helped other believers, and he counted on help from other believers. (4) He expected trouble. He knew Jesus suffered, and he knew he would too. (5) His perspective on life included the concept of God always loving him and always being with him. So, during good times and bad, Paul knew he was within God's will and could expect relief even if that came through trials and death.

As believers we have the same heavenly kingdom home Paul has. Thus, we should take the same approach to life and priorities that he did, with the Lord's will and commands making up our agenda. And why not? What on earth compares to the provisions God has laid up for us in heaven? Being realistic, why, here on earth, would a believer even think about a lifestyle focused on self without consideration for God's will for them?

Again, being realistic, how could a believer not love God back for His ongoing display of love for them? A very appropriate prayer request for us all is for a better understanding of the depth of God's love.

1 PETER 1:6–7

Here Peter is writing to the churches in Asia Minor (present-day Turkey), encouraging them to persevere in their faith in the face of Roman oppression. He wrote about AD 62, during the reign of Emperor Nero, some thirty years after Christ's crucifixion. Thus, he is writing to believers who are to demonstrate their faith every day under severe conditions. This passage then should encourage us to keep the faith, too, even though our persecution may take the form of verbal abuse or even indifference to our witness. Notice the subject of this passage is what our witness is to promote, and that is, the praise, and honor, and glory that is due Jesus Christ.

> In this you rejoice, though now for a little while, if necessary, you have been grieved by various trials, so that the tested genuineness of your faith—more precious than gold that perishes though it is tested by fire—may be found to result in praise and glory and honor at the revelation of Jesus Christ. (1 Peter 1:6–7)

Peter acknowledges his readers are believers and knows they rejoice in their faith in Christ's death and resurrection for their sins. Yet still their trials are real and difficult to accept. Peter's counsel to them and to us is to understand that such tests are apt to come during the little while of our lives on earth. Gold withstands tests by fire and is thus purified. Our faith is strengthened, too, by the testing (fire) God provides. See Acts 5:40–42:

> And when they called in the apostles, they beat them and charged them not to speak in the name of Jesus, and let them go. Then they left the presence of the council, rejoicing that they were counted worthy to suffer dishonor for the name. And every day, in the temple and from house to house, they did not cease teaching and preaching that the Christ is Jesus.

Peter's advice to his readers is to live that same way. Our instructions are no different. Promoting God's glory and Jesus' position as Lord are to be our purpose for living. Praising and honoring them should dictate our decisions. After all, what is (even) a lifetime of obedience and suffering to and for them compared to an eternity in heaven with them?

Notice the phrase "if necessary" in the 1 Peter passage. Peter is saying as believers it may well be necessary for us to suffer trials. Why would that be true? What do trials do for us? They give us opportunity to strengthen our faith. Don't athletes push against (lift) heavy weights to strengthen themselves for their upcoming contests? Likewise, God provides us testing times to prepare us for witness time coming later. Then, too, testing provides us opportunities to show the world what our real priorities are. The Christian community in the first century grew rapidly when they saw the disciples living out their faith before them in spite of trials. That is true in our day too. Our examples are more noteworthy than we realize, and every day provides us opportunities to use the influence we have for God's glory.

And that's not an accident. God planned from the beginning to save us individual believers, so that we could grow spiritually (that's called sanctification) as we glorify the Father day by day. Then on that day (the Day of the Lord, when we are glorified and given our heavenly bodies) Christ will return to gather all believers (God's adopted children) to spend an eternity with Him. **WOW! And praise the Lord**.

MATTHEW 16:24–25

If what Jesus said and did during His ministry on earth is worthy of our believing and imitating, then surely, He would make that clear to us, and He did. In this passage Jesus defines what is involved in being a Christ follower, a Christian, and a disciple of Christ:

> Then Jesus told his disciples, "If anyone would come after me, let him deny himself and take up his cross and follow me. For whoever would save his life will lose it, but whoever loses his life for my sake will find it." (Matthew 16:24–25)

To understand this passage, we must have a clear understanding of what "come after me" means. It has to do with following Jesus, that is, of believing Him to be who He claims to be, and doing so to the extent we seek (continually) to be like Him, to obey Him, to trust Him, and to glorify Him before the world. And who He claims to be is Lord, Messiah, creator of the universe, and redeemer of all those who by God's grace and their faith gain His free gift of eternal life.

Such individuals recognize their sinful condition and die to self, that is, they commit to forever put God's will, His glory, and His honor above everything in their lives. It does require us to stop doing some things, and to begin to do some other things, but that is not the point. The point is our establishing a relationship with Christ, making Him Lord of our lives, acknowledging Him as God, as Savior, and as Redeemer. When we do that, our deeds reflect our efforts to obey Him, and become ways we glorify Him, not ourselves.

And we gladly "take up his cross." The cross in Jesus' day meant death, and a cruel one at that. It represented the ultimate in humiliation, suffering, embarrassment, and degradation. And

Jesus expects us to be willing to follow Him to that extent. So we get some feel for the degree to which our perspective concerning "self" is to transform. Thus, we see how the smallest and the largest of our decisions are to all be oriented around God's will and His glory.

Notice though the result of such a "sold out" commitment to Christ (for His sake): we gain (real) life, we save our lives, we don't lose our lives, we actually find our lives. See the summary of our involvement here: (1) We come after Him. (2) We deny self. (3) We take up His cross. And (4) we follow Him. **And praise the Lord, He helps us with all these.** These concepts require facing "everyday" type decisions with Jesus in mind. And by definition, that will involve our sharing this gospel of Christ with others. For surely if God loved us enough to send Jesus to earth to die on the cross to pay our sin debt, that is a message the whole world needs to hear, and we believers have the privilege of sharing it.

TITUS 3:1-2

Paul is writing to Titus whom he left on the island of Crete to continue the work that Paul started there. Interestingly, the instructions Paul gives Titus are appropriate for us in our day. No wonder the Bible remains so popular. Its truth is applicable to everyone in every era. See then what Paul is telling Titus to pass on to the believers on Crete:

> Remind them to be submissive to rulers and authorities, to be obedient, to be ready for every good work, to speak evil of no one, to avoid quarreling, to be gentle, and to show perfect courtesy to all people. (Titus 3:1-2)

We find here seven rules Paul lays down for Christian living. There is no reason for us not to follow these, too, beginning with the command to obey our rulers and authorities. That indicates surely that we know who they are and what they would have us do. And we do. Notice this command says nothing about the competence or the goodness of those rulers and those in authority. We thus are to obey regardless of whether we agree with them or not. Being submissive speaks of our attitudes about how we obey, whether reluctantly or gladly with enthusiasm. Just being obedient does not reflect how we feel on the inside about that obedience. But we are to obey.

What about being ready for every good work? That sounds like we should keep our eyes open for opportunities to do good. And we are to follow through on what we see we could accomplish. We get the idea we are to do one good deed right after another. Once we see a need there is to be no evaluation on our part as to whether we participate or not. Again, our attitude is to be that of

Jesus. He did not judge between helping the poor or the rich, but continually went about doing good to everyone.

Notice Jesus watched his tongue. He did not speak evil without thinking. He did call out the Pharisees when they obviously were wrong and judgmental. But they needed his warnings and would have been better off if they had listened to Him. And Paul tells Titus to avoid quarreling. Most of us are old enough to realize little good is accomplished by quarreling, and good should be our goal, not winning an argument. And then Paul brings up the subject of gentleness. The dictionary defines "gentle" as being free from harshness, sternness, or violence. Doesn't that sound like Jesus? But does it sound like us? And it never will unless we become proactive concerning gentleness.

And what of courtesy, that idea of being marked by respectfulness and having consideration for others? Does that describe us? All of us appreciate being considered worthy of notice, attention, and respect. Courtesy would then be a key part of "loving our neighbors as we love ourselves."

There was a time before conversion, when Titus and all of Paul's readers were guilty of these sins. Now though, as believers, who have they or we to thank but Jesus for our salvation, and holy destiny? Who better than Jesus should we trust and obey with our whole lives? But too often our compromises, our denials, our rejections, and our weak faith are testimonies to our lack of belief. The Holy Spirit, through Paul, told Titus to remind his flock to take on these characteristics. He just as surely is reminding us too.

REVELATION 22:6–7

One of Jesus' disciples, John, is writing here toward the end of the first century AD to some churches in Asia, present-day Turkey. His purpose is to encourage his readers with information about the "end times" when Christ will return. This passage is taken from the last chapter, close to the end of the book. It's some concluding thoughts on the importance of the Bible's message in general, and the book of Revelation in particular. We are blessed when we realize almighty God, who created all that is, loves us and has made provision for our eternal lives. And He saw fit to have the Bible written to ensure we had all the information we need to guide us in our lives. **Notice the emphasis here on the truth of scripture**.

> And he said to me, "These words are trustworthy and true. And the Lord, the God of the spirits of the prophets, has sent his angel to show his servants what must soon take place."
> "And behold, I am coming soon. Blessed is the one who keeps the words of the prophecy of this book." (Revelation 22:6–7)

It is absolutely critical that we believe these words. God went to great lengths to have biblical truths put before us, and He means for us to take them to heart. At this point God has called John up to heaven in a vision to show Him the future. God's angel has been assigned to show John what must soon take place. This angel assures John that what he has seen and heard is true and will take place. We are to believe that too. God does not put random thoughts in His Word for us to discuss. He puts them there for us to believe and obey.

Notice the passage tells us these events must soon take place, and that "I am coming soon." We can take that last sentence as Jesus speaking, assuring us that He knows of our conditions and that He can and will attend to them. As believers this should be very good news for us. Many doubters take issue with scripture here when Jesus says He is coming soon when it has been two thousand years since Jesus spoke those words. In the first place the word for "soon" can also be taken to mean quickly, meaning Jesus will return suddenly when no one expects Him. Secondly, a better analogy of the time of Jesus' return is to picture history as not proceeding directly from beginning to a sudden end, but progressing along a precipice, parallel to the edge and at one point will go over that edge to completion. Christ has good reason to delay His return. See 2 Peter 3:8–9: "But do not overlook this one fact, beloved, that with the Lord one day is as a thousand years, and a thousand years as one day. The Lord is not slow to fulfill his promise as some count slowness, but is patient toward you, not wishing that any should perish, but that all should reach repentance."

Notice, too, the summary of the purpose of obedience to scripture. "Blessed is the one who keeps the words of the prophecy of this book." How one defines "blessed" is a personal choice. But it is truly God's decisions as to how He will define it. And we can be sure God's definition of blessings for the obedient will be far beyond our expectations. We are wise if we seek God's blessings, not ours.

Do we believe these words? Why should we? What are the implications if we do not? God's Word has always emphasized the need for faith on our part. Our exercise of belief by faith is the very essence of our trust that God and Christ are who they claim (in scripture) to be. And it's that kind of trust God wants us to have. **And it's that kind of trust God will give us if we open our hearts to the truth of His Word.**

MATTHEW 11:25-26

The gospel message that Jesus taught and promoted was heard by everyone, the most wise and knowledgeable people of that day, and the most simple and uneducated. Interestingly, the elite of the religious group of that time were the ones who had the most difficulty understanding and believing His message. They were taken up with their own pride and position and were reluctant to give in to His love and mercy teaching. His claim to deity absolutely did not ring true to them. This, in spite of His miracles and His consistent ability to punch holes in their man-made theology. Whereas the poor and less-educated folk believed and followed Jesus, giving Him the praise, honor, and glory He merited. See Jesus' response to this situation:

> At that time Jesus declared, "I thank you, Father, Lord of heaven and earth, that you have hidden these things from the wise and understanding and revealed them to little children; yes, Father, for such was your gracious will." (Matthew 11:25–26)

The tenets and makeup of the kingdom of God require faith and humility. That was true in Jesus' day and is still true now. There is no place for pride and self-aggrandizement in God's kingdom, and yet the scribes and Pharisees of Jesus' day were full of such. Over time they became Jesus' greatest enemies, even to the point of crucifixion. Thus, Jesus prays to His Father, thanking Him for keeping truth from those who would desecrate it, and giving truth to those who believe and act on that same truth. So it was with those "little children," people of little and no influence, who heard and received Jesus' words.

It's still true that two people can see and hear the same message and come away with two entirely different understandings of what they experienced. **A key point in this scenario is that whatever is taken away by anyone from a time of hearing God's truth is given them by God's Holy Spirit.** This speaks volumes concerning the openness with which they heard God's message. God can, of course, do anything, but He generally does not force Himself on anyone. It's no wonder then we are wise to pray ahead of time with the Lord, asking for Him to reveal to us whatever He knows is best for us at that point in our lives.

The gospel is not complicated. God made it so to give people everywhere, in all eras, opportunity to hear, understand, believe, and act on His truth. All of us are born with a sin nature, and the wages of our sin is death. That's because God is a loving God, but also a just God, and cannot abide sin. Instead of having everyone die for their own sin, God loves us so much He sent His only Son Jesus Christ to the cross to die in the place of those who believe in Him, thus paying the sin debt for those believers. Therefore, they come away from the moment of their repentance and belief with all their sins forgiven and possessed of eternal life with the Lord. Such believers are urged to celebrate that experience by water baptism, symbolic of their death to their old life of sin and risen from the baptismal waters to walk with Christ in new life. So, because Jesus conquered death by rising from the dead so will we.

Simple, but profound. Eternal in scope and available to all who believe in Christ. We as believers are assigned the task of sharing this truth with those who don't know of this most significant provision God has made for mankind.

1 CORINTHIANS 2:6–8

Although today we classify Paul a spiritual powerhouse, during his earthly ministry he did not try to impress his listeners with his mental prowess, but kept his messages simple, focusing on Jesus and "Him crucified." Not so, among many other speakers of that day who sought personal recognition and fame. Paul maintained he made no attempt to preach human wisdom but only the word of the Holy Spirit and His power. This, so that those who believed his teaching would have their faith based on God's love and power alone, not on him, or any other human messenger. See more of the "why" of this approach to Paul's preaching in this letter to the Corinth church:

> Yet among the mature we do impart wisdom, although it is not a wisdom of this age or of the rulers of this age, who are doomed to pass away. But we impart a secret and hidden wisdom of God, which God decreed before the ages for our glory. None of the rulers of this age understood this, for if they had, they would not have crucified the Lord of glory. (1 Corinthians 2:6–8)

Paul kept his sermons simple and direct, but for the elect of God (that is, those Paul calls the mature) who do hear and understand Paul's teaching, they received the truth God has for them. The rulers of this age, uninstructed and unbelieving as they are, will find their own messages are temporary and short-lived, passing away over time. Paul's lessons, however, contain that secret and wise message from God which He established before the ages. And God has done so for a reason, and that is, that we who would believe would be glorified in and by doing so. In short, long ago, our loving, heavenly Father not only created all that is in the way of physical things, but established wise and eternal truth as well for our benefit. In His infinite love and wisdom God kept His truth from the rulers of this age, but revealed it to the elect, those chosen ones.

So, as we consider this scripture passage, we sense with awe the love God has for us believers, choosing us before time began to be the beneficiaries of His love and power, and selecting us to receive the truth of His Word. None of the rulers of Paul's day heard what Paul heard from the Holy Spirit concerning Jesus and His true identity as Son of God, come to earth to save us from our sins. For if they had understood as Paul did, they surely would not have crucified Jesus. We know from scripture that Paul was referring to the chief priests of his day, and the Roman leadership like Pilate when he mentioned "rulers of this age." Thus, in Jesus' time on earth there was much in the way of ignorance, even blind, defiant, ignorance, as to who He is. That is true in our day too.

Paul tells us what we know of God's salvation plan through Jesus' sacrificial death on the cross is a secret and hidden wisdom of God, not revealed to everyone. **And it was given to us believers for our glory.** Why us, and not some others? That's a classic question that we cannot answer, but the answer lies somewhere within God's grace, His wisdom, and His infinite power. But we can praise the Lord He did reveal His truth to us. And we can praise the Lord by obeying Jesus' Great Commission to go and make disciples. And so the phrase "for our glory" must have to do with our heart to serve others, our joy, our peace, our salvation, and our "want to" in sharing the gospel of Jesus with the world. When we sense God's pleasure with us as we glory in understanding and obeying His Word, then we have understood the secret and hidden wisdom Jesus wanted us to get from His Word.

PROVERBS 20:18

Almost by definition to live is to desire to plan. We seem to automatically try to foresee the future and make adjustments ahead of time to accommodate our wishes for the outcome of our lives. We are born with the desire to determine our own destiny. Therefore, decision-making is a lifelong requirement. And like everything else in this world some people seem to be better at it than others. Look at this scripture where God provides us some good counsel in the matter of planning.

> Plans are established by counsel;
>> by wise guidance wage war. (Proverbs 20:18)

Implied in this verse is the word *good.* "Good planning is established by counsel." We are wise then to seek counsel when dealing with an area of our lives whereby training, experience, or mental capacity someone else is better equipped than we are to deal with a specific decision in our lives. Such counsel may be expensive, but could be well worth the money, depending on the issue at hand.

Notice the author, likely King Solomon (who by the way was not just the wisest man alive during his reign, but was blessed by God to be the wisest man who would ever live according to 1 Kings 3:12), tells us we can successfully accomplish huge efforts (like war) if we get wise counsel. It's difficult to think of an activity more complicated and more important than going to war. So we are wise to obtain wise counsel. According to Solomon, to acknowledge what you don't know and seek to correct that deficiency before you make decisions is a wise and prudent activity.

Oftentimes acknowledging our ignorance is a humbling exercise. Many a person (even us) has refused to do so to their sorrow. Interestingly, sometimes we don't deliberately act without counsel, it just seems not to occur to us we could be wrong or deficient in knowledge. That can happen in business and in kingdom work too. As we think about this subject, the word *prayer* automatically comes to mind. God has foreseen we believers will (should) always be involved in kingdom work requiring prayerful planning and wise counsel. So yes, per Solomon use wise counsel before you go to war, but use wise counsel before you do kingdom work as well, even, for example a one-on-one witnessing effort.

So the new part of the lesson from this verse is the reemphasis on the importance of being open to counsel in kingdom activity. It's likely even more important than we realize, and that's what God via King Solomon is telling us.

REVELATION 7:9-10

When John the apostle was exiled (for preaching and teaching about Jesus) to the island of Patmos he was given various visions from God. In them he saw something of what heaven would be like. In this passage he describes what he was shown concerning the saved believers in heaven. His descriptions make up what we know as the book of Revelation. Picture this scene as you see it described.

> After this I looked, and behold, a great multitude that no one could number, from every nation, from all tribes and peoples and languages, standing before the throne and before the Lamb, clothed in white robes with palm branches in their hands, and crying out with a loud voice, "Salvation belongs to our God who sits on the throne, and to the Lamb!" (Revelation 7:9–10)

Apparently, there will an endless number of people in heaven, all chosen by God for inclusion, and there glorifying our heavenly Father and the Lamb. The Lamb, of course, is Jesus Christ, given the title Lamb for His role as the sacrifice offered in payment of the sin debt of all believers. Every nation is represented, every group, clan, and tribe, speaking every language, and from every kind of background. Each one special to God and Christ, loved and known by name and life history.

And notice what all these people are doing, standing before God and Christ (we don't sit while we worship our God) in worshipful adoration, singing their praises because that is what we would naturally do when in their presence. It seems fitting that we will be there worshipping clothed in white robes given the perfection Christ's sacrificial death has imparted to us. The palm branches represent the recognition on our parts of the Father and

Christ's positions as Lord and King, worthy of all our praise and adoration.

Notice, too, there is enthusiasm in the worship. Those worshipping are crying out with a loud voice. It is done spontaneously, gladly, and with joy, given our acknowledgment of the love the Father and Jesus have already shown us and the rest and peace we have in heaven with them. We are glad to be there, and assured that we will be there for eternity.

Look at the words we will be lifting up in praise (forever), "Salvation belongs to our God who sits on the throne, and the Lamb." The implication is that salvation belongs *only* to our God and the Lamb. There is no other route to eternal life.

The same author, John, emphasized this principle again in another of his letters, John 14:6, where he is quoting Jesus: "I am the way, and the truth, and the life. No one comes to the Father except through me."

Yes, it is true they have supplied all we have there in heaven, gladly given to us as a reward for our faith in Jesus' sacrifice on our behalf. Jesus, Son of God, Messiah, and King of Kings, saw fit to "leave" heaven and come to die in our place on the cross, atoning for our sins. Our sinless Savior died for our sins so that we would not have to. Hallelujah! What a great, great God we have.

COLOSSIANS 3:15-17

The Holy Spirit has an "every day, all day" kind of intent to be involved with us. Every thought, every word, and every action on our part is to be directed by His influence. Thus, nothing, whether it brings us joy or sadness, is exempt from His attention and concern. And, of course, this works to our benefit, whether we know it or not. God's love is the driving force behind all His involvement and really behind the entire creation process. So, Paul is right on target when he tells the Colossians (and us) to let God rule our hearts; our hearts being the seat of all our actions and motives. See how Paul words this:

> And let the peace of Christ rule in your hearts, to which indeed you were called in one body. And be thankful. Let the word of Christ dwell in you richly, teaching and admonishing one another in all wisdom, singing psalms and hymns and spiritual songs, with thankfulness in your hearts to God. And whatever you do, in word or deed, do everything in the name of the Lord Jesus, giving thanks to God the Father through him. (Colossians 3:15–17)

Notice we get a vote whether to let the peace of God rule in our hearts. We can turn those tendencies God brings to us off, though that would be foolish. Letting God rule in us is an individual thing and a corporate concept for the whole church. God would have us believers involved in both these areas of our lives. And Paul emphasizes this by telling us we should be thankful for this provision God has provided.

Consider that next phrase: we are to "let God's word dwell in us richly." What a concept! Jesus and His life is the Word! So, we are to let Him dwell in us richly. Surely if Jesus dwells in us at all, it will be richly. That has to mean we are to let His full godly nature take control of our nature, thus, providing us the most complete and intimate of blessings and fulfillment. The route then to those blessings and fulfillment is the quality time we spend studying God's Word. **What a gift then the Bible is! And how foolish we are not to take full advantage of our access to it.**

And what does the Bible advise us to do but teach and admonish each other of the wise content there. And part of that involves thankfully singing and worshipping God using the biblical models and examples. How better can we grow spiritually than to spend time in worship alongside other like-hearted believers as we lift up praise, honor, and glory to God in song?

Notice the all-encompassing conclusion Paul provides. "Whatever we do in word or deed, do everything in Jesus' name." There, in one sentence Paul proclaims to believers our privilege and our duty. **Give all glory to God through Jesus. That is to be our life's goal, for nothing and no one is more worthy.**

We cannot overemphasize the role of our thanksgiving in these commands Paul provides. In the first place, this is not just Paul speaking. The Holy Spirit has led him to bring us these requirements to us. Secondly, we are not to be about the business of worshipping God reluctantly. What joy and anticipation are available to believers when they recognize what awaits them in heaven! How could we not be excited about what Jesus is preparing for us? How could we not be thrilled at the prospect of basking in Jesus' glory forever? And how could we not be living now with the great expectation of simply seeing Jesus and Him smiling at us? Oh, what joy lies ahead for us!

1 CORINTHIANS 12:4–7

This section of 1 Corinthians covers the subject of spiritual gifts; those blessings, abilities, and talents believers are given by our triune God to enable them to better carry out Christian ministry within and through the church for the common good. One or more of these blessings are passed on to all believers. Thus, all we believers are challenged via the Holy Spirit to do several things: (1) Determine what our individual gifts are. (2) Cultivate those gifts. And (3) live out those gifts in our community and around the world. This assignment is not to be taken lightly. For only when all believers are carrying out God's mandate to exercise our gifts will His church be the powerful instrument for evangelism and influence in society that God would have it be. Without question God has chosen the route of individual obedience to God's Word for communicating the gospel of Jesus Christ to (all) the nations. See Matthew 24:14 for the culmination of God's plan as described by Jesus Christ Himself: "And this gospel of the kingdom will be proclaimed throughout the whole world as a testimony to all nations, and then the end will come."

And thus, Paul is on solid scriptural ground when he describes how believers can contribute:

> Now there are varieties of gifts, but the same Spirit; and there are varieties of service, but the same Lord; and there are varieties of activities, but it is the same God who empowers them all in everyone. To each is given the manifestation of the Spirit for the common good. (1 Corinthians 12:4–7)

No one has all the spiritual gifts, and not all of us have the same degree of giftedness as everyone else. **But we all do have certain areas or giftedness where we can use what God has given us** to make unique contributions to the spread of His gospel to those around us. And that is what God would have us do. A wise preacher once preached on this subject using a three-point sermon. Those points were start where you are, use what you have, and do what you can. That says it all. Imagine what the results would be if all believers consistently lived by those points. If we could add anything to that sermon it would be to give emphasis to starting now. After all, the problem of worldwide ignorance of the gospel exists now, and people are dying every day without Christ.

Notice how succinctly Paul makes reference to all three persons of the Trinity in this passage. It is the same Holy Spirit instilled in all believers that helps and guides each one to identify, cultivate, and exercise their gifts. It is the same Lord Jesus pointing out the various services that lie in front of all believers daily. And it is the same Father God who empowers every believer's gifts and the results of their using them.

And see how in the passage emphasis is given to the all-inclusive need for the spread of the gospel. It is for the common good of everyone that believers are assigned the task of evangelism. Everyone needs a Savior, and Jesus Christ is that Savior. Many unbelievers don't recognize that need they have, and many unbelievers realize they are missing something in their lives but don't understand what they need or where to find it. Surely it follows that we believers are to use the gifts we have been given to meet the needs of those who have not heard the good news of the gospel.

1 PETER 3:10-12

The presence of God in our lives is directly proportional to the way we live, what our priorities are, and our relationship to God. There are certain beliefs, attitudes, and actions we exhibit that indicate the condition of our hearts, and thus, our eternal destiny. See this passage for God's preference for you:

> For
> "Whoever desires to love life
>   and see good days,
> let him keep his tongue from evil
>   and his lips from speaking deceit;
> let him turn away from evil and do good;
>   let him seek peace and pursue it.
> For the eyes of the Lord are on the righteous,
>   and his ears are open to their prayer." (1 Peter 3:10–12)

Any thinking person from time to time will analyze their lives to determine if the path they are on is leading them to their desired end. Peter writes here of how we can finish well. We all want to love life and experience good days. We all consciously or subconsciously want to enjoy life. The Holy Spirit is leading Peter here to tell us how to find an enjoyable life. Notice our circumstance is not mentioned, thus, Peter's counsel applies to all his readers, in any society, even us now.

According to this passage, apparently, what we say is more influential on how our life plays out than we imagine. When we think about it, that seems logical. Our words in large measure indicate how we view other people, and thus, how they tend to view us and react to us. This applies within our families and outside our families. If we have a loving and understanding nature, that will be reflected in what we say to and about other people, and our relationship with them will tend to be enjoyable. On the other hand, a selfish and critical nature (that is, evil and deceitful) will be easily recognized by what we say, and people are apt to respond to us the same way. This does not lead to good days for anyone.

Notice these verses tell us we get to vote on whether we turn away from an evil lifestyle. It is our choice to do so or not. Doing good leads then to good days. All of us inherently know what good is, and what good is not. We are then to proactively be about doing good. That is, if we want to "love life and see good days."

Peter's counsel does not end there. He tells us to seek peace with others, and not just to seek peace, but to be peaceful in the process. It's probably been a long time since you've looked up peace in the dictionary, but I just did and one of the definitions shown is "harmony in personal relations." I imagine that is the definition Peter wants us to use here. To live in harmony with others will require cooperation between all parties. Cooperation is what harmony is all about. We can't be responsible for the other party, but if we are harmonious, the other party is much more likely to be also.

And then Peter tells us why his counsel always works as we seek to love life and see good days. The reason is the Lord sees everything we do and knows why we do it. And because He loves us, He is open to hearing the prayers of people who consistently do good and pursue peace. He knows we will lead enjoyable lives much more if we are obedient to Him and He has Peter remind us of this.

A very appropriate beatitude is found in Matthew 5:9: "Blessed are the peacemakers, for they shall be called sons of God."

Now that's a title worthy of our striving for.

MATTHEW 16:15-16

At some point in His ministry Jesus saw fit to specifically clarify for the disciples (and us) exactly who He is. All His teachings and all His miracle workings pointed to His identify as God. But to bring closure to that subject Jesus addressed His identity directly. Who better than the disciples who were with Him every day, would know exactly who Jesus is? See Jesus' question to them and Peter's response:

> He said to them, "But who do you say that I am?" Simon Peter replied, "You are the Christ, the Son of the living God." (Matthew 16:15–16)

Think about that scene. Jesus is talking with His disciples, and He asks them, "Who do people say the Son of Man is?" Of course, He was referring to Himself. And the disciples gave Him several answers, naming people like John the Baptist, Elijah, and Jeremiah. But then Jesus sort of stops the clock, asking them who they think He is. **What a personal question! What an eternally important question for every person in every generation to consider and answer.** Most scholars seem to think Peter answered quickly, and that his answer was representative of all the disciples. So without hesitation those who knew Jesus best declared Him to be Messiah, Son of the Living God. Would we need to think a minute about that question? Or are we so convinced of His deity and His relationship with the Father that we would answer as quickly and confidently as Peter did? And if so, does our lifestyle reflect that belief?

And maybe even more telling, would we be embarrassed or offended if asked that question? Should not people who know us well already know our answer to that question? Are we really convinced that this is the most important question we will ever face? Is our relationship to Jesus Christ the ruling measure of our life, on our mind and heart every day, and key to all our decisions and our perspective concerning all we experience?

Jesus goes on to tell His disciples they are blessed (because of their correct understanding of His identify) and that it is His Father in heaven who has revealed it to them. **What an awesome concept! Almighty, eternal God loves us so much He has blessed us with knowledge of the true answer to this most vital question.** When you think about it, that fact carries with it a most significant responsibility, and that is for us to go forward sharing that information concerning Jesus with the world. No wonder at the very end of his letter Matthew is led to describe the Great Commission, God's command for us to go and make disciples of all nations.

REVELATION 1:5-7

Here John is writing to the seven churches in Asia concerning Jesus' second coming. What a glorious day that will be, one that all believers can look forward to. He describes for his readers what Jesus has done for them and some of what our role in heaven will be. We need to remember John's readers were suffering under the oppression of the Romans and needed encouragement. And because we, too, suffer and have trials and temptations, this passage applies to us too. We are wise to take John's message to heart:

> To him who loves us and has freed us from our sins by his blood and made us a kingdom, priests to his God and Father, to him be glory and dominion forever and ever. Amen. Behold, he is coming with the clouds, and every eye will see him, even those who pierced him, and all the tribes of the earth will wail on account of him. Even so. Amen. (Revelation 1:5–7)

From the very beginning of this letter Jesus Christ is central. It is He who we are to focus on and give allegiance to. It is He who died in our place and who is worthy of all glory and dominion forever. **Notice Jesus loves us.** That fact is key to our salvation. God's whole salvation plan is based on His love for us, and it is that love we can count on even in our toughest times. And it is that love we are to share with others by our lifestyles. If others are worthy of God's love, they are worthy of our love. And we are to live out that love.

Notice, too, God has made us a "kingdom," thus, we are royalty, our heavenly position will be that of ruler alongside Jesus. And as believers, we will also be priests, chosen people who now have access to God. As we can now approach God's throne room in prayer, in heaven we will be able to approach the Father directly.

Amazingly, when Jesus returns every eye will see Him. How could that be? No one place on earth is visible by the rest of the world, but we will all see Jesus when He returns, even those responsible for His crucifixion. God who created all that is will take care of the "how" we will all see Him. And as He ascended to heaven in the clouds, so He will return that same way. See Matthew 24:30: "Then will appear in heaven the sign of the Son of Man, and then all the tribes of the earth will mourn, and they will see the Son of Man coming on the clouds of heaven, with power and great glory."

John speaks of people wailing when Jesus returns. Matthew uses the word *mourning* at that same event. Thus, it will not be only the Jews who wail and mourn when Jesus returns. Gentiles, too, from all over the world will recognize they are sinners necessitating Jesus' sacrificial death on the cross to pay their sin debt. Everyone then has cause to wail and mourn, we all sent Jesus to the cross on our behalf. We all will stand before God in judgment for our sins, believers only being justified because of Jesus' atoning sacrifice for them. We believers have a reason to mourn and a reason to celebrate in gratitude for God's gift of His Son, and for Jesus' sacrifice.

Obviously, believers have a story to the tell the nations, and Jesus has given us that assignment.

PROVERBS 4:10-13

Any thinking person wants to be wise, to be able to make right decisions for the right reasons. The book of Proverbs is known as wisdom literature, where God has planted practical words of wisdom for us to use. It remains for us take advantage of what God has prepared for us, for us to put His thoughts in motion in our lives. What a change it will make! People will see the difference; we will feel the difference; and best of all, God will be glorified. See these vital verses; emphasizing for us that knowing is not enough, walking (even running sometimes) God's path is what He would have us do.

> Hear, my son, and accept my words,
>> that the years of your life may be many.
> I have taught you the way of wisdom;
>> I have led you in the paths of uprightness.
> When you walk, your step will not be hampered,
>> and if you run, you will not stumble.
> Keep hold of instruction; do not let go;
>> guard her, for she is your life. (Proverbs 4:10–13)

"Hear and accept" what God has said is the idea, consistently, in depth, and wholeheartedly. The phrase "sold out" comes to mind. And the result, many years of life. This does not mean that anyone who dies young has failed in this regard. It implies God has certain things for us all to accomplish and He will provide ample time and opportunity for us to complete our assignment. And certainly, that means we are to begin now. This, for God has already begun (in every believer) the process of leading, educating, and preparing us for His plan for our lives. There is an old saying that fits the condition of our failing to be involved already in kingdom work.

We are said to be "burning daylight," that is, losing opportunities (never to be recovered) for work that God would have us do.

When we sincerely seek His (specific) will, praying for opportunities, He will provide direction. We already know what His will is for our lives. It's a cop-out to say we don't. Using our present knowledge we could pick up a pen at any time and list a hundred things God would have us do; fundamental things like love the Lord with all your heart, pray without ceasing, make disciples, love your neighbor, stay in God's Word, and worship regularly with like-hearted believers, etc. So let's start with that hundred and begin. God will flesh out His plans for us as we proceed, and we won't burn any daylight.

The passage above does not specifically say it, but it certainly implies God is aware of all we do. He monitors our lives, so we won't be hampered, and not stumble. So "keep hold of instruction." That is, continually seek appropriate application of the truths God has provided. Don't let go (i.e., don't forget and always seek God's perspective relative to what you are doing). Work to think both "short-term" and "long-term," for she (God's instructions) is your life. It's why you were born.

PROVERBS 10:11; 13:14; 14:27

There are certain principles God seems to emphasize in scripture, lessons He wants to be sure we learn. These verses reflect such a principle. We can only conclude God would have us read them, understand them, take them to heart, take joy in them, see the applications to us in them, live them out, and share them with others (who will do the same thing). Let us ensure we note the significance of this truth:

> The mouth of the righteous is a fountain of life. (Proverbs 10:11)

> The teaching of the wise is a fountain of life. (Proverbs 13:14)

> The fear of the LORD is a fountain of life. (Proverbs 14:27)

Given that God loves us with a steadfast love, the "fountain of life" principle is evidently one that would be of great benefit for us to understand and focus on. Why else would He "three-peat" the concept?

So what is this "fountain of life" phrase referring to? It has to do with one's basis for living, our fundamental purpose for being here that God has designed. These verses tell us that those who are righteous and those who are wise have grasped the concept and not only live it out, but speak and teach of it to others. They've made it a practice to model such a lifestyle before the world.

We are told in Proverbs 14:27 the root truth that not only leads to the right path in life, but provides significance and meaning to our lives. That truth focuses on our relationship to the Lord, and it is to be one of fear. Fear as used here refers to the respect, reverence, and perspective we have concerning almighty God. There is a line that speaks of God in the song "Holy, Holy, Holy" that describes this: "For you are perfect in power, perfect in love, and perfect in purity."

If we can develop such an ongoing attitude, every thought we ever think, every word we ever speak, and everything we ever do will bring praise, honor, and glory to God. God showed His perfection in power when He created all that is (and maintains it). He proved His perfect love when He gave His only Son to die in our place on the cross as payment of our sin debt. And He teaches and illustrates His perfect purity in His Word and in Jesus' life.

What is there left for us to do but imitate the righteous and the wise by giving credence to the truth God has provided as the way to eternal life? "By grace are you saved through faith" (Ephesians 2:8). Jesus made it clear: "I am the way, and the truth, and the life. No one comes to the Father except through me" (John 14:6).

ACTS 2:17, 21

During the Last Supper, Jesus announced to His disciples He was returning to the Father. But He promised to send His Holy Spirit to earth to indwell all believers so as to strengthen their faith and continually remind them of all He had said and done during His earthly ministry. This arrival of the Holy Spirit happened on the day of Pentecost, the second of the Jewish harvest festivals, coming approximately fifty days after Passover when Jesus rose from the dead. When it occurred, there were therefore many visitors in Jerusalem for the festival and at this unusual sound they came together out of curiosity to see what had happened. Peter spoke to the crowd, telling them how the prophet Joel had prophesied of the coming of the Holy Spirit, and describing Jesus and His ministry. We are told about three thousand souls were saved that day. We can only imagine what that scene was like. See this passage concerning what Peter said about the coming of God's Holy Spirit:

> "And in the last days it shall be, God declares,
> that I will pour out my Spirit on all flesh,
> and your sons and your daughters shall prophesy,
>   and your young men shall see visions,
>   and your old men shall dream dreams . . .
> And it shall come to pass that everyone who calls on the name
>   of the Lord shall be saved." (Acts 2:17, 21)

The phrase "last days" does not refer to sometime in the distant future, but to that period beginning right then. Jesus started the process coming as the prophesied Messiah providing man's sin atonement through His death, burial, and resurrection. Thus, the Holy Spirit was sent to continue Jesus' work in the building up of the church, as believers spread the gospel to all nations. Therefore, we are in those last days now. Those days have already spanned two thousand years and may seem excessively long to us, but in God's infinitely wise plan for world history, the time for Jesus' return is not yet. There is more to be done, more people God has planned to bring into His kingdom.

The passage talks about prophecy, visions, and dreams which reflect the results of the Holy Spirit indwelling Christians in our time. This is what we are seeing now. Notice how God has aided us in this work with first the printing press, then the airplane, then television, then the internet, etc., all tools we can and should use to take the good news of Jesus to the nations.

And notice particularly verse 2:21. **Everyone who professes Jesus Christ as Lord shall be saved.** That's the concept. We take the gospel to the nations, they hear, they by faith believe, the Holy Spirit does the converting, and they receive God's free gift of eternal life. That conversion then identifies that individual as a child of God indwelt by God's Holy Spirit and **bound for heaven.**

And we are commanded to play a role. No matter our location, or our feelings of inadequacy. God provides all that is necessary if we will but make ourselves available. As an example, all of us can buy and hand out a tract with God's plan of salvation on paper. All of us can unashamedly bow our heads in a prayer of thanksgiving before our meal (in even the busiest restaurant) as witness to our relationship to almighty God. After all what is more important: what the person at the next table thinks, or what our Lord and Savior thinks? So our relationship to God is evidenced in our lifestyle, our priorities, our choices, and our sense of perspective about what is most important in our lives.

1 John 4:10-11

This section of scripture is titled "God is Love." What a title! What a subject for us to dwell on! If we were fully able to grasp this concept, we would be wise indeed. The Holy Spirit obviously wants us to think about this and grow in that knowledge. It's one thing for us to love God. He, of course, is worthy of all our love, devotion, and obedience. But for Him to love us is almost unbelievable. He is worthy, but we are just the opposite, unworthy, born that way, and we live that way. And when we consider the extent to which God loves us it really is unbelievable. So much so that He gave His only Son to die in our place to make eternal life available to all who would believe in Him. See how God has John word this concept:

> In this is love, not that we have loved God, but that he loved us and sent his Son to be the propitiation for our sins. Beloved, if God so loved us, we also ought to love one another. (1 John 4:10–11)

In essence, John is saying it is not surprising that we love God, given his awesome nature, but for Him to love us, unworthy as we are, is the best news we could ever hear. Notice John includes why we ought to love God. It's because He loved us so much, He sent His Son to be the propitiation for our sins. Propitiation means "sacrifice," but with something very significant added. What is added to the definition is "why" Jesus is our sacrifice, and it's for one reason only, to satisfy the wrath of God. When we sin, we incur the wrath of almighty God. So, it is His wrath we must deal with. Since it is against God that we sin, it is His prerogative to choose the payment for that sin. God chose the death of His sinless Son in our place to be the atonement for our sins. And for those who by faith believe in Christ, they are given God's free gift of eternal life.

For the second time in this chapter, John then refers to his readers as "beloved." That speaks volumes as to how he feels for his readers, and for how he would want them to feel about him and each other. The concept then among believers is a complete giving of mutual love, willing to make any and all necessary sacrifices for other believers. So, there is here a "hold nothing back" kind of commitment John is calling for. And he uses God's love for us as an appropriate example. **To put it plainly, if our heavenly Father loves all believers enough to sacrifice His only Son to die for the sins of each of us, then surely we ought to love one another.** Notice, too, that 1 John 4:11 does not give us the option of deciding whether these other believers are lovable or not. We are to be in love mode, not judgment mode.

And that love is to manifest itself every day. How could we claim to love someone and not care enough about their eternal destiny to share God's plan of salvation with them? Jesus Himself tells us to go and make disciples of all nations, "teaching them to observe all that I have commanded you. And behold, I am with you always, to the end of the age" (Matthew 28:18–20). Who better to go with us to "make disciples" than Jesus?

1 THESSALONIANS 5:16–18

From time to time all of us should stop and analyze where we are and where we are going in life. Our lives are not static. Things are moving, situations are changing, and time seems to be flying by. It was like that in the first century, too, and here Paul is writing to the church at Thessalonica with some powerful suggestions as to how to establish priorities. Believers have a head start on unbelievers doing this because they know the Lord and understand more about His love for them which is the basis of our salvation. Everything about the Lord's involvement in our lives has eternal aspects to it. Everything we plan and generate on our own is temporal with only this life and this world situation involved. God loves us as we are (praise the Lord) and we are wise to make God's will our will. When we do, the long-term realities of this life are improved and our eternal destiny is established. Notice Paul's wisdom:

> Rejoice always, pray without ceasing, give thanks in all circumstances; for this is the will of God in Christ Jesus for you. (1 Thessalonians 5:16–18)

If our life perspectives are oriented around the fact of the eternal life we have in Christ, we certainly can rejoice always. That knowledge will be the basis of how we react to all that this life brings to us, whether it be good or bad. Our attitudes, our relationship to others, and our long-term goals will all be established relative to what we know God's will for us to be. We can claim we don't know God's will for our lives but that is a cop-out. We know full well already many things God would have us do, and this passage simply lists three of them. When we get busy doing what we know God would have us do that we might think are minor and unimportant like attending church, treating others the way we want to be treated, being sensitive to the needs of those around us, staying in touch with all our loved ones, etc., then the bigger decisions begin to fall in place. That's the way God has constructed life on this earth.

We are also to pray without ceasing. It's not like we are told to pray twenty-four hours per day, but the passage is telling us to live a praying life, open always to communication with the Lord on behalf of someone else. For example, when a fire truck rushes past you on the road, that is a "live, right now" prayer request happening in front of you. You can be sure at the other end of that trip someone is in trouble and needs your prayers. Who are we that we don't consider praying for them? So, yes, we have many prayer requests personally, and so does everyone else, and we believers have been assigned to pray for them all.

Notice we are also to give thanks in all circumstances. That's a wide-open mandate, twenty-four hours a day. God wrote this through Paul, so it has to be true. Is it possible to give thanks during all the pressures we sometimes feel? Evidently so, for that is exactly what God is telling us to do. Could it be that working at giving thanks to God even in our tough times improves our ability to cope? The more we work at giving prayers of thanksgiving in both good and bad times the more Christlike we become. **God has not stopped loving us during our trials. He will absolutely answer prayers we pray thanking Him for His ongoing love, and for His direction when times are difficult.**

Clearly, Paul has reminded us that it is God's will for us to do these three things. We can obey or not obey, but we cannot claim we don't understand. Obedience on our part is not just wise, it is imperative for a proper relationship with our heavenly Father.

LUKE 13:18-19

God is all-powerful, and capable of mighty acts, and tremendous accomplishments. So sometimes we expect Him to come with enormous effect from the beginning to transform evil to good, and change sadness to joy immediately. And that is not always the case. Often God acts from small beginnings, disguised as minor events or insignificant occurrences. And sometimes He acts slowly, but deliberately. Such was the case within Israel in their thinking concerning Messiah. The people lived under the constant threat of Roman domination and expected that one day Messiah would come with something like a mighty army to defeat Rome quickly in one decisive battle and provide Israel eternal relief. When Messiah did come, as Jesus did, as a baby, they were apt to miss the significance of His arrival. And most people did "miss it." But we don't have to miss it. In these verses Jesus speaks in a parable, illustrating this principle. See how He words this truth for them then, and for us today.

> He said therefore, "What is the kingdom of God like? And to what shall I compare it? It is like a grain of mustard seed that a man took and sowed in his garden, and it grew and became a tree, and the birds of the air made nests in its branches." (Luke 13:18–19)

Now a mustard seed is the smallest of seeds, and a mustard tree or bush grows to twenty or even thirty feet in height, and birds do build nests in mustard trees. Jesus' listeners would all have known this. Such is the analogy Jesus uses as He contrasts His kingdom's modest beginning with its glorious final state that was coming. Jesus' point to His audience then and us now is God often uses our small experiences and our everyday happenings as part of His bigger purposes with huge implications for His glory.

Thus, we are to be ever watchful, and constantly praying and looking for God's appearances in our lives, confident God does love us, He does know of our situations, and He will use us in His kingdom work. Most of us don't occupy important positions, with lots of power, wealth, and influence. But God absolutely has plans for us, things He would have us involve ourselves in, and He supplies opportunities designed especially for us to use the talents and abilities He has given us for His glory. And He couples our obedience with the obedience of others to accomplish His will for the eternal benefit of us all.

Much of the time we don't "see" the bigger picture of what God has eventually in mind for us and our lives and may never realize it all. But that is not the point; we do experience that person in need right in front of us, that circumstance we can help change for the better right now, and that hopelessness we can point toward God's relief and joy, all for His glory (not ours). The "seeds" we consistently plant in the form of good deeds, kind words, and godly wisdom within our own circle of influence, will, with God's help, grow to become a "tree" God uses to establish His kingdom. These verses give us Jesus' thoughts on this concept of small things becoming large for His glory. It is His will and His truth that we are to live out and share with others. It is His sacrifice on the cross that paid our sin debt and made the way possible for our eternal life. God's revelation of Himself in His Word, and the gospel of Jesus Christ described in His scripture clearly outline His (only) way to eternal life. Let us live it and share it.

ISAIAH 6:8–9

In this passage we read of the prophet Isaiah being given a vision from the Lord. We might wonder why the Lord chose Isaiah to speak to this way. Well, we know by his response he is open to seeing and hearing God, and we know by his response he is open to giving of himself in service to God, and we surely know that's the kind of individual God looks for. So, when the Lord asks the question, "Whom shall I send?" it wasn't because He didn't know the answer, but to stir within Isaiah's heart the attitude for obedience that God put there when He created him. Such a scripture passage brings to our mind the thought, "What is my position? How would I respond to God's question of 'Whom shall I send and who will go for us?'" See how this plays out in Isaiah's life:

> And I heard the voice of the Lord saying, "Whom shall I send, and who will go for us?" Then I said, "Here am I! Send me." And he said, "Go, and say to this people:
> "'Keep on hearing, but do not understand; keep on seeing, but do not perceive.'" (Isaiah 6:8–9)

Isaiah knew the people were hard-hearted and unlikely to respond positively to him as he preached the love of God. And sure enough, God tells Isaiah to go, and He tells him the people will not respond, and that they will not receive him well. So, why would God tell him to go? When we go to witness, if we go at all, we tend to want to go where there is at least a chance of a successful witness. And we define success only when someone surrenders to Christ. We are so logical that we look at efforts spent in service for the Lord as an expenditure of our time and we consciously or subconsciously don't want to waste our time. But here we see the Lord telling

Isaiah up front he is not going to be successful in the sense of a positive response to his message. Could it be that this is all part of God's plan? Yes, it very well could.

Notice Isaiah did not say, "I will go" when he heard God ask, "Whom shall I send?" He said, "Send me." The message for us here is that just because a service opportunity seems to be good, we are to wait until God sends us. The very act of our being sent and then going, makes that service successful, and God defines what is successful. In this case God sent Isaiah out to preach to a people who would not respond to ensure their guilt was certain. On judgment day those who heard Isaiah and denied the truth will be standing before the Lord without excuse. They will not be able to say, "I never heard the truth." And God also sent Isaiah out on what seemed to be a fruitless mission to provide the lesson for us in our day that God is Lord. He dictates results in every instance, and it is **His glory that is to be our goal in every type of service act. We are always to be sure our obedience is properly motivated.**

Thus, we are to beware of defining our obedience in human terms. And we are to beware of not considering the "why" of our obedience. Isaiah's response to God's call was not mechanical, it was heartfelt. It would be hard to discuss Isaiah's response without using the word *sacrifice*. And somewhere in our positive response to God's call on us the word *sacrifice* will also appear. Interestingly, however, when we look back on properly executed mission efforts, we redefine what at first seemed to be a sacrifice. Mysteriously, no doubt at God's command, what we thought would be a sacrifice turned into a blessing. With a new perspective, what seemed to be hard at the time, we now look back on and view as well worth the time and effort. **And thus, God is glorified.**

MARK 4:2–9

Jesus had much in the way of truth to teach to those around Him. And He often used parables to do this, a parable being a story with a moral lesson hidden within it. Often Jesus taught mixed crowds, those who believed and were open to His teachings, and others who did not believe and were only looking for ways to discredit Him. This passage is a classic, very familiar to most Bible students, with a message we can take to heart and apply in our day. It has come to be called the parable of the sower.

> And he was teaching them many things in parables, and in his teaching he said to them: "Listen! Behold, a sower went out to sow. And as he sowed, some seed fell along the path, and the birds came and devoured it. Other seed fell on rocky ground, where it did not have much soil, and immediately it sprang up, since it had no depth of soil. And when the sun rose, it was scorched, and since it had no root, it withered away. Other seed fell among thorns, and the thorns grew up and choked it, and it yielded no grain. And other seeds fell into good soil and produced grain, growing up and increasing and yielding thirtyfold and sixtyfold and a hundredfold." And he said, "He who has ears to hear, let him hear." (Mark 4:2–9)

We can liken the seed to God's Word, the truth that Jesus taught. The various types of soil in the parable represent the different responses that came about when the crowds heard Jesus' message. Three of the four soils described produced no fruit. So, we can conclude that many people will hear Jesus' teaching but will not understand the truths He taught, and thus, will have no positive response. Some seeds though fell on good soil and produced abundantly. Notice the degree of success that is potentially available from even one seed: up to one hundredfold of grain.

The parable describes the sowing of seed, but not the plowing of the ground which normally comes later. Plowing the ground would open the soil and expose the seed to the nutrients hidden beneath the surface. Then the seeds would naturally germinate and mature into stalks of grain. God stays with us in this process as He provides the sun and rain necessary for a bumper crop. Thus, in a real and practical way God honors our efforts to sow seed and plow the ground to complement His provision of the natural process of bearing fruit.

So, the analogy is obvious. Our nurturing those with whom we share the gospel will work to provide understanding and belief of God's love leading to their conversion. And God's Holy Spirit works as does the sun and rain to crops, to provide the miracle of belief in the hearts of those who hear and understand God's Word.

And then Jesus provides the punchline, that moment of truth upon which the whole story depends. "He who has ears to hear, let him hear." God provides gospel truth, He provides understanding, and He provides the opportunity to believe. Those who would believe, can believe.

We cannot change a person's unbelieving heart, we cannot cause belief to begin, and we cannot bring about the miracle of conversion. Those are not our roles and God does not hold us responsible for those changes. But we can sow gospel seeds. We can share the truth of God's Word, and we can be involved in the nurture of new believers. Those are our roles and what God has commanded us to do.

LUKE 12:8-9

The word *accountability* often comes to mind when we are discussing God's observations and responses with regard to our actions concerning obedience to His will. It's not difficult for us to grasp the concept that God monitors our every thought, deed, and spoken word. He always knows what we are doing and why. Neither is it difficult to understand that God has established preferred standards for us to meet, and particular things for us to do. In fact, God has gone to great lengths to make such information available to us. The Holy Spirit was sent to lead us to recall all of Jesus' thoughts, and His written word reflects His commands for us. So, for those who are so minded, determining God's will for their lives is easy. Notice Jesus' comments on this issue.

> And I tell you, everyone who acknowledges me before men, the Son of Man also will acknowledge before the angels of God, but the one who denies me before men will be denied before the angels of God. (Luke 12:8–9)

God's monitoring is perfect. Notice the word *everyone* used here. Not one instance in any life escapes His attention, for or against Him. We might ask ourselves why would we acknowledge God before men? In the first place, we would if we were absolutely convinced He is worthy of our acknowledgment. If without question we knew Him to be of such character and nature that we loved and respected His every word and deed, we would certainly obey Him, and "recommend" Him to others. On the other hand, the reverse is true. If we did not consider Him to be noteworthy in any sense, we would not commend Him to others. **If fact, whether we do acknowledge Jesus Christ before men truly proves how we feel about Him.**

And there are positive consequences for our acknowledging Him and negative consequences for denying Him. Notice the different acknowledging audiences, us before men, and Jesus before "the angels of God." We clearly understand acknowledging Jesus before men, but what is significant about a group of angels of God? This passage tells us it is before them that Jesus will declare our allegiance to Him, whether good or bad. We glean something of the significance of that when we consider where angels of God congregate, that is, around the throne of God. Oh WOW! Now we begin to get a clearer picture of what our lives are to be about. The phrase "to glorify God" sums up why we were born and certainly includes "acknowledging Him before men."

So, we have a choice, a choice we must and by definition we do make; to acknowledge Jesus Christ before men or deny Him before that same group. And to not mention Him is to deny Him. Think about that fact, the people we associate with every day either will or they won't see Jesus in us. That's both a tremendous responsibility and an awesome opportunity.

JAMES 4:11–12

Scripture often reminds us not to speak evil of others. Sometimes in unguarded moments such thoughts will spill out of our minds through words of criticism, derision, and even slander. This reflects badly on us and our Lord, for doing so puts us in the position of judging, and that is God's role not ours. See how the Holy Spirit has James word this commandment:

> Do not speak evil against one another, brothers. The one who speaks against a brother or judges his brother, speaks evil against the law and judges the law. But if you judge the law you are not a doer of the law but a judge. There is only one lawgiver and judge, he who is able to save and to destroy. But who are you to judge your neighbor? (James 4:11–12)

First, we are to notice James is referring to how one believer speaks of another Christian brother. We are told in both the Old and New Testaments to love our brothers, not slander them (Psalm 50:19–20; 1 Peter 2:1). Notice these verses do not give us license to "not" love our brothers if they do unlovable things. Our effective witness before an unbelieving world is destroyed if that world sees us slandering a fellow believer. See Jesus' thoughts on this matter: "A new commandment I give to you, that you love one another: just as I have loved you, you also are to love one another. By this all people will know that you are my disciples, if you have love for one another" (John 13:34–36).

If we speak against a brother or judge them, we are also speaking against the law and judging the law. This implies we have considered God's laws but have decided against obeying them. We don't usually deliberately go through those steps, but the results are the same. By judging other believers, we show both believers and unbelievers we think the world should follow our lead not God's. It is as if we are putting ourselves above God and His law. So, by definition, we are not a doer of the law, but a judge. In essence we are writing our own law. This does not glorify the Father and that should be our fundamental priority.

"There is only one lawgiver and judge," and that is Jesus Christ. "He [only] is able to save and to destroy." He came into the world to save us from our sins, and we are to share that truth verbally and as we live out His commandments.

And realistically, how do we answer the last question of the passage? "But who are you to judge your neighbor?" What qualifications do we have and where did we get the idea that we could and should judge our neighbors as described above?

No thinking, true believer wants to put themselves in the position of judge in this manner. Yet sometimes we unthinkingly do that very thing, and we do it before the world. As with any other issue we face, the solution for us is to take this matter of judging to the Lord. Jesus told us, "Behold, I am with you always, to the end of the age" (Matthew 28:20). Why would He tell us that unless it was true? And why would He make that promise unless He loved us? It is true and He does love us. Let us take Him at His Word.

ROMANS 8:28

This passage is in a section of the letter to the Romans titled "Future Glory." It describes a promise and a hope believers have access to concerning their future as disciples of Jesus Christ in this world and in heaven. God is all-powerful, has all knowledge, and loves us with an infinite love. Thus, He certainly has the capacity and the desire to provide for us whatever is best for us, and He does. Notice what this verse tells us God has provided.

> And we know that for those who love God all things work together for good, for those who are called according to his purpose. (Romans 8:28)

We see initially in this verse that God has given certain knowledge to those who love Him. It is one thing for all worldly conditions and circumstances to be put in place by God, but our God has also made clear to us that it is He who has arranged it all. So now we know whom to worship, whom to thank, and whom to praise. And even better, our God has made all these provisions and preparations so that every single one of them interact with each other in ways that work to the good of those who love Him.

Now our "good" is not defined in the verse, but can we doubt that good as determined by our almighty, all-loving God would be anything less than infinite in quality and eternal in scope? We know our God is perfect in power, perfect in love, and perfect in purity, and those perfect qualifications are what He uses to prepare the past, present, and future of those who love Him. **So things do not happen randomly in our lives; our God has a plan for us all, even including the bad things we endure.**

Notice the verse above mentions all things work together for good. So we can conclude there are lessons God would have us learn within even the trials we experience. We wonder why bad things happen to good people (especially us), and that is why. God is always seeing to our long-term good and spiritual maturity is one of the "long-term" good things God knows we need.

The main premise of this passage is that it is based on how God involves Himself with those who love Him. We would translate that condition as those who have been saved, as those who have made Jesus Christ Lord of their lives. It is those individuals who most recognize the significance of what God has done for them via His giving His Son Jesus Christ to die for our sins on the cross. **Thus, it is saved people who are led to really love the Lord for His having first loved them**. Paul has already told his readers in Romans 5:8 that "God shows his love for us in that while we were still sinners Christ died for us." This defines God's grace; His love for us that we did not deserve.

This passage gives us a new perspective about life as a believer. It increases our faith in our Lord Jesus who has promised to be with us "to the end of the age" (Matthew 28:20). **And He will be.**

PSALM 33:11-12

In this Psalm an unknown psalmist, under God's direction, has given us several reasons to praise Jehovah God. In this portion of the Psalm that reason described is that God's will prevails. Whose will would be better to prevail? Who better than the almighty creator of the universe should have their will prevail in all the world in all of time? Look at the encouraging message God has seen fit to provide us, good for anyone in any era to remember, take to heart, and live out in their lives. So let us praise God that He reigns supreme.

> The counsel of the LORD stands forever,
>   the plans of his heart to all generations.
> Blessed is the nation whose God is the LORD,
>   the people whom he has chosen as his heritage. (Psalm 33:11–12)

Notice His wisdom lives forever, relevant in any situation, in any era of time. Notice, too, He has a plan available for all generations; every individual ever conceived can benefit from God's eternal plan of salvation. See John 1:12: "But to all who did receive Him, who believed in His name, He gave the right to become children of God" and 1 Timothy 2:3–4: "This is good, and it is pleasing in the sight of God our Savior, who desires all people to be saved and to come to the knowledge of the truth."

So it would be obvious that any person and any nation whose God is the Lord would be blessed. Who else would bless? Who else loves us to the point of blessing us? And who has the power to bless other than the Lord? So what response on our part is appropriate other than to praise and honor God who loves us so, and has done so much for us? And we who do become His heritage, His gift to future generations as examples of His love and provision.

We believers then are chosen for a specific purpose, to show the world by our lives that we serve a risen Lord, who paid our sin debt on the cross and rose again to live forever. And because He lives, we will, too, with Him in heaven. Hallelujah!!

MATTHEW 20:26–28

There is a natural tendency on our part to want to be well thought of by others, to be considered somehow special, and worthy of respect. Conversely, we don't want to be considered lowly or beneath others in any respect. This was true in Jesus' day too. His disciples were guilty of such feelings and Jesus took pains to clear up this issue using Himself as the proper example. See this passage:

> But whoever would be great among you must be your servant, and whoever would be first among you must be your slave, even as the Son of Man came not to be served but to serve, and to give his life a ransom for many. (Matthew 20:26–28)

Since we all covet good standing, Jesus' words are applicable to us all. In those days, servants were hired, and thus paid (though only a pittance). Slaves were forced into service and therefore not paid. Together, they made up the lowest level of humanity in both the Jewish and Roman society. Thus, anyone who heard what Jesus said would completely understand He was referring to the most reduced status one could imagine, completely subject to the will and whims of others. Thus, this concept from Jesus would be apt to cause much confusion, and even rejection among His listeners. And for Jesus then to point out that was His role in coming to earth, even to the point of giving His life, must have been hard for people (including the disciples) to accept.

So, Jesus is telling those people then and us now to rethink our goals in life, to reevaluate our priorities and motives. That is harder to do than to just think about. The concept of service to others **all day every day,** gets complicated. The idea of "a complete giving up of self" is consciously, or subconsciously, hard to grasp. It's likely something we don't want to think about. We imagine there is too much unknown as to what that kind of lifestyle will lead to. And we picture our being required to give up too much to comply. Jesus is talking about every area of our lives: our time, our finances, our interests, our focus, our motives, our purposes, etc.

And yet we know that is exactly what Jesus did. As to how one does that, it begins with our taking note of our present situation. We are in a certain place, under a given set of conditions, with a given set of talents. At this point we all already have specific responsibilities we need to attend to, and a given set of opportunities potentially available to us. And we need to realize that all of that is by design, God's design. So, no matter our circumstance, **there is a way that God would have us go from here.** This truth applied to the lowest slave in the first century, and the richest, most influential person today.

Thus, we all really have the same assignment: taking what God has provided and using it for His glory. It's a matter of priorities, our deciding to do what Jesus tells us, put the Lord first, others second, and ourselves last. Consistent service brings its own reward. A life well spent this way will glorify our heavenly Father, not us, and it will do so simply because this is the way Jesus has told us to live.

A wise pastor once preached a three-point sermon on this subject. "Start where you are, use what you've got, and do what you can." That works no matter who we are.

ACTS 5:12, 14-16

After Jesus' resurrection and ascension back to heaven, His apostles continued His ministry of teaching and healing among the people. Obviously, God had given them healing powers and they used them for His glory. Such healing did two things: it drew the people to them en masse, and it very much disturbed the Pharisees who feared their influence was being challenged. See these examples of what was happening:

> Now many signs and wonders were regularly done among the people by the hands of the apostles. . . . And more than ever believers were added to the Lord, multitudes of both men and women, so that they even carried out the sick into the streets and laid them on cots and mats, that as Peter came by at least his shadow might fall on some of them. The people also gathered from the towns around Jerusalem, bringing the sick and those afflicted with unclean spirits, and they were all healed. (Acts 5:12, 14–16)

Notice how creative the people were, doing anything they could to bring healing to their loved ones. It was truly an exhibition of faith on their part. No doubt we would have done the same thing. Notice, too, the news was spreading and people from other towns were coming to hear the gospel and to be healed. It sounds ridiculous to us to put people within the shadow of someone and achieve healing, but something very powerful was going on, and the people believed in Jesus as a result.

The disciples had prayed earlier for power and boldness in their preaching, and for God to enable them to perform signs and wonders through the name of Jesus (Acts 4:29–30), and God was answering those prayers. So, for a period of time after Jesus returned to heaven God provided miraculous powers to a select few of His disciples and the number of those believing in Jesus grew rapidly. Evidently, this was God's way of getting the gospel out to the world at large early on. We can be sure of one thing, those people who were healed were no doubt ardent believers for the rest of their lives, spreading the news of what happened to them to everyone who would listen. And so would we be.

But what is the real connection to us now in all this. These things did happen, but it was about two thousand years ago. Is it, and should it be, relevant to us nowadays? When we think about it, it requires as much or more faith on our part to believe these "long ago" events, as it did for those who experienced them. **And that is the point God wants us to understand. He saves us by His grace through faith, and provides us eternal life as a free gift (Ephesians 2:8).** He will keep His promises. The way to eternal life has not changed in those two thousand years. We who come to know the Lord now will spend eternity with those apostles and believers from long ago in heaven together with the Lord, and the two-thousand-year time span will not be important.

So, yes, these scriptural events and those facts are most significant and applicable in our day. We are blessed to have a God who had such events recorded for our edification. And the cross of Jesus is still the most significant event in all of history and always will be.

LUKE 12:4-7

Here is an important scripture passage on fear. Jesus uses the word *fear* five times in just four verses. Jesus knows human personalities very well, and of our tendency to be afraid at the slightest provocation. So He taught on the subject. In the first place, we tend to fear many things, death, the dark, loud noises, people bigger than we are, those in positions of authority over us, and really anything we don't completely understand or can't control. Those people hearing Jesus that day were just like us. See Jesus' lesson on fear for its application in our lives:

> I tell you, my friends, do not fear those who kill the body, and after that have nothing more they can do. But I will warn you whom to fear, fear him who after he has killed has authority to cast into hell. Yes, I tell you fear him! Are not five sparrows sold for two pennies? And not one of them is forgotten before God. Why, even the hairs of your head are numbered. Fear not; you are of more value than many sparrows. (Luke 12:4–7)

The Jews of Jesus' day were accustomed to fear as they lived under Roman authority. And rightly so, for often Roman justice was inconsistent and cruel. Here Jesus quickly gets down to the heart of the matter of fear, telling the crowd to fear only those who have authority to cast (someone) into hell. And the only one who can do that is God. **So fear is a matter of perspective. Jesus' point is we are to give God (and His will for us) priority in our lives, even over staying alive**.

That's a hard lesson to grasp. But it surely plainly pictures how much more God knows about the future than we do, and how much more significant our heavenly existence will be over our lives here on earth. And why not? Jesus will be there in all His glory, more than we can imagine. Further, He and the Father love us and want the best for us. And they, praise the Lord, have the authority, the desire, and the power to create the best for us as believers. I urge you to share that truth with (many) others.

The mention of sparrows gives us important information as to the depth of God's knowledge of world affairs. Even a sparrow dying in the forest somewhere has God's attention. And, if that is so, then how much more attention does He give to our conditions? God knows how many hairs are on our head. We might ask why that degree of detailed knowledge is necessary on His part. It is necessary so that we humans can better understand God's love for us. **This, because our being (completely) convinced of God's love for us is the very basis of His plan of salvation. God's love for us is why Jesus went to the cross to pay our sin debt and the message God had Jesus tell us to share with the world before He returned to heaven.** Having such knowledge and a passion to share it, should be a regular subject of prayer for us.

PROVERBS 1:1–2; 4:1–2

The very first words of the book of Proverbs, when speaking of the purpose of the book, lists knowing and understanding words of wisdom, instruction, and insight.

> The proverbs of Solomon, son of David, king of Israel:
> To know wisdom and instruction,
>   to understand words of insight. (Proverbs 1:1–2)

God puts great store in our learning His way of thinking, understanding His nature, and being aware of His way of expressing His love for us. This, all because He does love us, and He has already made His plans for our lives that are the best we could possibly imagine. See this next passage that is meant to be an encouragement for us to follow through with His plans:

> Hear, O sons, a father's instruction,
>   and be attentive, that you may gain insight,
> for I give good precepts;
>   do not forsake my teaching. (Proverbs 4:1–2)

Now *insight* is a very intuitive word. It is the act or result of apprehending the inner nature of things. So to be insightful helps us see more deeply into God's character and the "why" of His involvement in our lives. Both are very worthy goals for us.

The analogy is that of a father teaching his son and urging that son to "listen up" to his teaching. Thus, as God's children we are to hear God's instructions, and not just hear, but listen attentively. It is as if God knows we humans are prone to "mental laziness" and is telling us to guard against such laziness. Notice, too, that there are no age limits mentioned. Often first-time readers of this proverb are older, experienced, and already set in their ways of thinking. But if they want insight, they must come at it the same way as everyone else. Old ways of thinking and previous beliefs must be transformed into those in sync with God's truths and His will.

Note, too, there is an implied ongoing aspect to these encouragements. They are to be lifelong attitudes. And, of course, that is logical. If godly wisdom, understanding, and insight are truly valuable and fundamental to our living life God's way, then it follows we are to always exercise them. And thus, too, there is an inherent responsibility on all of us to pass along these principles to the next generation. God tells us here His precepts are good and that has to be a "huge" understatement. And if they are good then they are good always, and good everywhere, and thus, should not (ever) be forsaken.

The concepts mentioned in these verses are clear. If we simply read these verses, and give the words their "everyday" meaning, we don't have to be a biblical scholar to see God's (eternal) truth on display. So let us stay in God's Word, study His scripture, commit to memory verses that stand out to us, and live out what we've learned, and we will be well on the way to gaining the insight God prepares for us.

2 Timothy 2:15

My Bible has this verse included under the heading "A Worker Approved by God." From this verse we realize God knows what we are doing and why. And the implication is we will be judged by God as to our lifestyle, that is, whether God approves our words and actions. Paul makes it clear to Timothy that God has a plan for our lives and expects us to live it out. And we can be sure that God's plan for us involves our glorifying Him in all we do and say. And we won't do that unless we make a planned effort to do so. See Paul's encouraging words to Timothy (and us):

> Do your best to present yourself to God as one approved, a worker who has no need to be ashamed, rightly handling the word of truth. (2 Timothy 2:15)

If we are going to give obedience to this verse, it's obvious it has to be on our mind all the time. The verse indicates we will present ourselves to God at some point, and Paul urges all believers to be careful what their record will show. Paul seems to think it goes without saying that we should be kingdom workers, seeking to be about doing good in Jesus' name. We know the truth about what we do, or don't do, and inherently know if it's our best, and if it glorifies the Father. Thus, we will know and feel shame if that's appropriate. We can deceive others, but we cannot deceive ourselves, and we certainly cannot deceive God. He knows our hearts.

Notice, too, it is apparent God expects us to be workers. Thus, if we are not involved in kingdom work, we should be. God made us in His image to glorify Him, and we will not fulfill our potential unless doing so is important to us. We inherently know the difference between kingdom work and earthly work. Thus, we are to work at doing things that benefit others and glorify God. And in our world, there are always many such activities available. They appear before us every day if we just look for them. Choosing such activities should be a subject of prayer.

Notice, too, the key element in being an unashamed worker. It's "rightly handling the word of truth." How do we rightly handle the word of truth? That has to mean: (1) Our spending time in God's Word, seeking to understand it and its relevance to us, and (2) it has to involve our applying it and sharing it. And, of course, "rightly handling" refers to all of God's Word. We dare not disregard any of God's Word. Second Timothy 3:16–17 clears that point up when it starts with the word *all*. "All Scripture is breathed out by God and profitable for teaching, for reproof, for correction, and for training in righteousness, that the man of God may be complete, equipped for every good work."

If we begin our Christian walk with the idea some scripture verses are appropriate for us and other verses are not, we do wrong and severely limit our effectiveness as a witness for the Lord. Being a true believer carries with it the privilege of calling God Father, and the responsibility of glorifying Him with our lives. Part of glorifying Him has to do with the credibility we assign to God's Word. We must remember simply because we don't think certain passages of scripture apply to us, does not mean that's true, and it isn't. God has given us His Word (all of it) to reveal Himself to us, and to assist us in living out our faith. God loves us too much to waste His time or ours, providing us inappropriate truths that would not be of worth to us.

MATTHEW 21:12–13

This passage opens with Jesus in Jerusalem at the beginning of Holy Week. He will finish this week being crucified in our place to pay our sin debt. He finds much activity in the temple, a great deal of which was the sinful exchanges of money to enable visitors to the city to buy animals for sacrifice. See how Jesus responds to what He finds:

> And Jesus entered the temple and drove out all who sold and bought in the temple, and he overturned the tables of the money-changers and the seats of those who sold pigeons. He said to them, "It is written, 'My house shall be called a house of prayer,' but you make it a den of robbers." (Matthew 21:12–13)

Jesus quotes the prophets Isaiah and Jeremiah as He disrupts the activity of the money-changers. His bold actions would have been seen as scandalous by the priests and scribes. But Jesus did this in judgment of the temple leaders. So what is done in the temple has great significance, and is representative of our relationship to God.

It is so in our day as well. Our time in our places of worship is to be special, prayed about ahead of time, and taken seriously while we are there. It is special when like-hearted believers gather to worship the God of our salvation, and God honors such activity. See His Word on this subject:

> And let us consider how to stir up one another to love and good works, not neglecting to meet together, as is the habit of some, but encouraging one another, and all the more as you see the Day drawing near. (Hebrews 10:24–25)

> For where two or three are gathered in my name, there am I among them. (Matthew 18:20)

> Let the word of Christ dwell in you richly, teaching and admonishing one another in all wisdom, singing psalms and hymns and spiritual songs, with thankfulness in your hearts to God. (Colossians 3:16)

Individual private worship by believers is important, but we cannot deny God also calls us to periodically join together in worship. We need the influence of other believers, and they need our influence. Together, we can accomplish more kingdom work than the sum of our individual efforts. The church is the only organization Jesus saw fit to leave behind to function until He returns. And He had a reason for that. His plan was that through the united efforts of His church worldwide the gospel would be taken to the nations. And as a group and as individuals we are given that task.

PHILIPPIANS 4:4–7

Toward the end of this letter to the church at Philippi, the apostle Paul sums up his instructions to the church in an easy-to-understand way, applicable to us today too. We are wise if we take them to heart.

> Rejoice in the Lord always; again I will say, rejoice. Let your reasonableness be known to everyone. The Lord is at hand; do not be anxious about anything, but in everything by prayer and supplication with thanksgiving let your requests be made known to God. And the peace of God, which surpasses all understanding, will guard your hearts and your minds in Christ Jesus. (Philippians 4:4–7)

Notice Paul's mandate to his readers to rejoice. It is as if he knows we are not rejoicing now and should for our own benefit. And if we do not feel like rejoicing, Paul is insisting there are plenty of reasons why we should. And then he goes on to describe some of those reasons.

He begins by telling us to be reasonable. As he would define it, reasonableness has to do with a heart set to consistently seek the best for everyone, and not only us. Thus, over time all those who know us become aware of our tendencies to be gracious, forgiving, and generous with others. Such a lifestyle provides long-term benefits for us and everyone around us.

Key to everything Paul is describing is that the Lord is involved. Paul words that saying, "The Lord is at hand." And He surely is. He is nearby in all our lives every day, for He knows about all we are facing and through His Holy Spirit stands ready to guide us in the way He would have us go. Thus, we can be anxious but we don't have to be, even during our toughest trials. And Paul tells us how to deal with our anxieties, and that is by turning them over to the Lord. So, in everything by prayer and supplication (with thanksgiving) we are to "let our requests be made known to God." That's an interesting concept given that in His infinite wisdom, God already knows what we are going to pray before we pray. So there must be something therapeutic in our sharing our trials with God. And there is, especially if we are thankful for this privilege of prayer. Doing this over time brings us to the condition of seeing our prayers as God sees them, and His perspective is different from ours. His evaluation of our concerns and needs takes into account His will which is to bring us to the point of wanting to glorify Him in all we face, good and bad. And when our life goal is to glorify the Father then we are in sync with His will.

If leading other people to praise and worship God is our goal (for He is worthy of all praise and worship), everything we desire, plan, do, and accomplish (and the "why" of it all) becomes Christlike. This, because Christ set the example. Everything He came to earth to accomplish and did accomplish, including His sacrificial death and resurrection, was to glorify His heavenly Father.

So, Paul is telling all his readers to change their focus to being one of Christlikeness. And when we do, God's peace (not man's) guards our hearts and minds in Christ Jesus. With God's peace guarding our hearts, that certainly implies God's will and way become our criteria for living and that shows up in our relationship with others. Thus, the goals of our lives become love for God first, and our neighbors second, and thus, both God and our neighbors rank ahead of our own focus. That's God's will for us.

ACTS 4:29-31

At this point Jesus had returned to heaven, and the disciples were going about preaching and teaching the gospel. Some people heard and believed, some heard and did not believe. But either way, in spite of commands from the Pharisees to stop, the disciples continued to peach Jesus. It's that kind of spiritual perseverance Jesus' exhibited, and that God would have us imitate today. See how the disciples prayed and what happened:

> "And now, Lord, look upon their threats and grant to your servants to continue to speak your word with all boldness, while you stretch out your hand to heal, and signs and wonders are performed through the name of your holy servant Jesus." And when they had prayed, the place in which they had gathered together was shaken, and they were all filled with the Holy Spirit and continued to speak the word of God with boldness. (Acts 4:29–31)

Notice their faith as they prayed for boldness in their witness, and for God to continue doing healing miracles through the name of Jesus. Those should be our prayers too. Notice, too, they had no intention of stopping their witness and simply prayed for more boldness. They seemed to feel no malice toward those who threatened them nor any fear of what they might do.

. And then they experienced a point where the Holy Spirit came and filled each of them. Since Jesus had returned to heaven, the Holy Spirit filled that void with recall of Jesus' teachings, and direction for their ministries. And there is nothing temporary about the Holy Spirit's indwelling. His is a permanent indwelling for believers. Praise the Lord, the Holy Spirit still does that. And occasionally God will clearly make His presence felt in our lives. Such an experience is one way God strengthens our faith.

A proper, ongoing Christian witness requires our constant attention to the Holy Spirit's leadership. This, because no matter where we are, or what our situation, there is a way we can go from there aligned with God's will. Such consistency in our Christian walk speaks of our whole lifestyle, our very purpose for being born. That's the kind of perspective God would have us develop and adhere to.

The word *boldness* is used twice in this passage. We often pray for spiritual boldness, and it would be well to review the actual definition of the word. It means "a fearlessness when faced with danger or opposition." Thus, we can readily understand how boldness would be needed in our Christian witness, because such a witness is bound almost by definition to bring danger and/or opposition upon us. We see such boldness in Paul and certainly in Jesus. Our being led by the Holy Spirit leads to such boldness in our witness. Obedience to the Holy Spirit's leadership fosters the courage that gives birth to boldness. We may not feel bold about our witness, but we cannot deny (1) it's required of us, (2) we see it exampled in scripture, and (3) it's available through prayer. God never requires anything of us that He does not help us achieve.

John 14:15

We understand by implication that God would have us obey His commandments, not just some of them, or even most of them, but all of them. It would not occur to a thinking person that God would list for us in scripture all He would have us do, and then not hold us accountable for compliance. We inherently know we are to obey God. To tell God, "I know of your commandments, but I don't think they apply to me," would be foolish indeed.

On the night of the Last Supper, Jesus spent time summing up His teachings for the disciples. At one point He specifically clears up the concept of obedience when He says,

If you love me, you will keep my commandments. (John 14:15)

That's a scary thought, for each of us knows how far short of obedience we fall. See Romans 3:23: "For all have sinned and fall short of the glory of God." But it's no consolation for us to realize that everyone else has our same problem.

See more comments from the apostle Paul on this subject:

For I do not do the good I want, but the evil I do not want is what I keep on doing. Now if I do what I do not want, it is no longer I who do it, but sin that dwells within me. (Romans 7:19–20)

Wretched man that I am! Who will deliver me from this body of death? Thanks be to God through Jesus Christ our Lord! So then, I myself serve the law of God with my mind, but with my flesh I serve the law of sin. (Romans 7:24–25)

All of us are born with a sin nature, and we display that nature the same way Paul describes he does. **But praise the Lord! God has made a way out of our dilemma. That way involves Jesus and the cross.** John 3:16 gives us the reason and the way: "For God so loved the world, that he gave his only Son, that whoever believes in him should not perish but have eternal life." The reason for God's provision is His steadfast love. Scripture describes God's love for us as His grace, the love He has for us that we do not deserve. And the way is belief in Jesus. So:

> But God shows his love for us in that while we were still sinners, Christ died for us. (Romans 5:8)

> For by grace you have been saved though faith. And this is not your own doing; it is the gift of God, not a result of works. (Ephesians 2:8)

So yes, absolutely we are to obey God's commandments. How else can and could we show our love for Him and our thankfulness for His free gift of eternal life than to obey His commandments? And when we do fall short of compliance (and we will) we can and should immediately repent and seek forgiveness, even to the point of making whatever restitution to someone else that might be appropriate.

Our great God has made all the necessary provisions for our salvation. He is thus worthy of all our praise, honor, and glory (and obedience). Let us go and share this awesome news.

2 CORINTHIANS 6:16–18

God has already chosen His children, those who will spend eternity with Him. He did that before time began. And yet miraculously we individuals are still free to make our own choices leading to our eternal destiny. This predestination concept seems to conflict with our "freedom of choice" capability, but it does not. Both doctrines are taught in scripture; therefore, both are true. Just because we don't understand them completely does not mean they are not true. Somehow God in His infinite love, wisdom, and power has seen fit to combine them, which allows His grace to have full reign in our lives and at the same time provide us a key role in our salvation. Paul takes these principles and applies them in a lesson for living for the Corinthians and for us.

> For we are the temple of the living God; as God said,
> "I will make my dwelling among them and walk among them,
>   and I will be their God,
>   and they shall be my people.
> Therefore go out from their midst,
>   and be separate from them, says the Lord,
> and touch no unclean thing;
>   then I will welcome you,
> and I will be a father to you,
>   and you shall be sons and daughters to me,
> says the Lord Almighty." (2 Corinthians 6:16–18)

As chosen believers we are heaven-bound (yes, and hallelujah), yet still living with the privilege and responsibility to be the witnesses, the disciples, and the disciple makers God would have us be. Thus, God can and does say He will make His dwelling place among us. And He can and does tell us to be different, to go out from the others, be separate, and touch no unclean thing. And if in doing that we raise questions about our lifestyles, then so be it. That is one of many ways God provides us opportunities to be His witness in this earthly world. Notice what He tells us: He will dwell among us, walk among us, and be our God, and we will be His people. Almighty God is telling us we believers have a unique fellowship position with Him.

Notice, too, what happens if we are obedient: God welcomes us, and He will be a Father to us, and we will be God's children. Whatever else happens to us in this life, it won't ever top those events. So, Paul's lesson for us has to do with us getting and keeping a proper perspective concerning our relationship with the Lord. God saw fit to have Paul begin this passage with the phrase, "For we are the temple of the living God." That has to mean the living God is always with us. It has to mean the living God is always in us. And that has to mean we always represent the living God. And, if we are obedient, it has to mean other people will always see Christ in us.

What is a temple but a holy place where God dwells? So, the title fits us as obedient believers. Most of us don't think of ourselves often enough as the temple of the living God, but He does. He even sees us as His ambassadors (Ephesians 6:20) who represent Him in this fallen world, living out His commands, and promoting the truth of the gospel. Thus, we likely live our Christian lives with more blessings than we realize, and more responsibility. We are wise to pray for more awareness of God's presence in our lives. The more cognizant we are of His presence in our lives the more we come to know of His nature and grace, both subjects we need to know more about.

When we think about it, God wants us to know all there is to know about Him, making it easier for us to live for Him and to share that knowledge with others.

MATTHEW 24:36, 42, 44

We live in a troubling world. There is much we don't understand happening around us and to us every day. There seems to be no end to the heartache we see and feel. But praise the Lord, there is joy available too. God has provided a way to eternal life for those who believe, and the hope of such glory will always be available to believers. So we do have options as to how we respond to worldly circumstances and God's provisions. Thus, the concept of judgment one day is ever present, when God evaluates each individual to determine their eternal destiny. The disciples asked Jesus when this would happen. See His answer:

> But concerning that day and hour no one knows, not even the angels of heaven, nor the Son, but the Father only. . . . Therefore, stay awake, for you do not know on what day your Lord is coming. . . . Therefore you also must be ready, for the Son of Man is coming at an hour you do not expect. (Matthew 24:36, 42, 44)

Clearly Jesus will return in judgment, and just as clearly, the exact timing of His return will not be known. God has apparently made such provisions for His own reasons. But by being secretive about the timing He has created elements of consistency and sincerity in the lives of believers. God tells us in scripture that we are to love Him with all our hearts, souls, and minds, and that we are to love our neighbors as ourselves, and that these two commands are the greatest commandments (Matthew 22:35–40). Thus, our loving God has provided us the key as to how to deal with the "unknowns" involved with Jesus' return. We need only to obey these two most important commandments.

If we live lives given over to loving the Lord and others, that will absolutely color all our relationships and ensure that all our worldly involvements glorify our heavenly Father. **There will then be no concerns as to when Jesus returns in judgment, for whenever He comes, He will find us living in obedience. So consistency and sincerity in our obedience to love will lead to reward. That's always the way God constructs things.**

So when life seems grim, and our options few, let us renew the one option always available, to love the Lord and those around us. Such heartfelt attitudes will always lead to perspectives concerning both the good and bad times we experience that reflect we do realize this world is not our home.

JOHN 3:14-15

Oftentimes in the New Testament the Holy Spirit leads a given author to write making reference to Old Testament events. Thus, that way the Spirit has those New Testament authors tie the New Testament to the Old Testament and bring future prophecy for further proof of God's involvement in the life of Israel. By extension, we, too, can thereby see God's involvement in our lives. At one point during their journey out of Egypt the Israelites became impatient and disobedient and spoke out against God and their leader, Moses. As punishment God sent poisonous serpents among them that bit the Israelites, and many died. When the people of Israel saw this, they repented and cried out to Moses to pray to God to relieve them from the serpents. Moses prayed and in response God had him build a bronze serpent and put it on a pole. Any Israelite who was bitten by a serpent could simply look at the bronze serpent and live. It was simple, but it worked. That's the way God operates.

Here in John 3 the Holy Spirit has John record Jesus' reference to this serpent story as analogous to His dying on the cross to provide atonement for the sin of those who believe in Him. In this way, Jesus emphasizes His future crucifixion as *the* way God provides atonement for their sins. Note this passage in John. Jesus is speaking:

> And as Moses lifted up the serpent in the wilderness, so must the Son of Man be lifted up, that whoever believes in him may have eternal life. (John 3:14-15)

So, in speaking to the Israelites of His day, Jesus reminds them of what happened to their forefathers about fifteen hundred years earlier during the Exodus from Egypt. He likens His being lifted up on the cross to die for the sins of believers, to the bronze serpent being lifted up to bring relief from the serpent bites. Just as all the Israelites had to do was look at the bronze serpent to be cured; to gain eternal life all we have to do is believe in Jesus Christ.

To look at a man-made serpent on a pole was easy to do, so simple probably some of the Israelites did not believe it would help them and they died. Just so, some people today think believing in Jesus is too simple to bring them eternal life, so they reject that approach for salvation, and they die too. Just as looking at the serpent on the pole was effective, thus proving the truth of God's Word to them, believing in Jesus Christ (again believing God's Word) is also effective. **It works, that is the way to eternal life. We cannot earn it in any way.**

Believing in Jesus Christ involves more than just "head knowledge" about Him. It involves head knowledge with faith to the point of living out that head knowledge. Don't you imagine when a given individual in Moses' day who had been bitten by a serpent saw that the nine people in line ahead of them who looked at the serpent were all cured, his faith in his cure would be strong? **Our situation is different. We need more faith than that. We don't have the option of seeing our salvation fulfilled immediately as those Israelites saw their cures enacted immediately. Thus, we are privileged with the opportunity of exhibiting "extra" faith.** Ongoing obedience to God's Word and consistent prayer, and study of God's Word, add to our faith and bring ever-increasing joy in our salvation.

1 JOHN 5:20

God has made complete provisions for the eternal destiny of all those who believe in Jesus Christ. From before time began, He had our destiny laid out, loving us with an infinite love that will never end. Given that all these preparations have been made for us, God saw fit to tell us about it in scripture. Now believers know both about Christ and His coming to earth, and of the results of our trusting His sacrificial death as payment for our sins. This passage from 1 John reflects these truths for our consideration and benefit. Knowledge of these facts carries with it the responsibility to share them with the world. See what John is confirming for us:

> And we know that the Son of God has come and has given us understanding, so that we may know him who is true; and we are in him who is true, in his Son Jesus Christ. He is the true God and eternal life. (1 John 5:20)

As this passage is written, Christ has already come to earth, lived a perfectly sinless life, died a sinner's death on the cross for our sake, rose from the dead on the third day, and later returned to heaven. There He intercedes for us with the Father until that day when He will return to earth to gather the living and dead believers for that final journey to heaven with Him. So, John reassures His readers that Jesus was and is the Christ and gave all believers knowledge of these facts to confirm our faith.

And He did this so that we could and would come to know the Father, that is, "him who is true." What a privilege believers have: they know God. Knowledge of God then is to be our life's goal. So, Jesus came to show us the Father. He told us, "Whoever has seen me has seen the Father" (John 14:9). Jesus is the perfect embodiment of God the Father. So, if we want to know what God is like, look at Jesus.

Notice, too, the next phrase in the passage: "we are in him who is true, in his Son Jesus Christ." Thus, believers are in Christ as He is in the Father. So, there is the potential in all believers then to grow in Christlikeness over time. And that is what God would have us do with the help of the Holy Spirit who God sent to indwell all believers. So, we come to know God through our relationship with the Son Jesus Christ. See John 17:3 for this concept explained: "And this is eternal life, that they know you, the only true God, and Jesus Christ whom you have sent."

The only way then to eternal life is via trust in Jesus' sacrificial death on the cross to pay our sin debt. "He is the true God and eternal life." Christians receive God's grace in order that they might understand biblical concepts and have the desire to live them out. So, God not only loves us enough to send Jesus to die for our sins, He also plants within us the desire and capacity to believe these truths and make them a part of our lifestyle.

All things considered, when God provided the potential for our gaining eternal life, there is nothing more or better that He could do for us. Nothing could be more satisfying, more joy filled, or more complete than an eternity with Jesus Christ. That is the good news that came with Jesus, and that is the good news the world needs to hear and that we are to share.

MARK 15:25, 33–34, 37–39

Jesus came to earth to save us from our sins. The only way to do that was by His death, for we are all sinners and the wages of sin is death (Romans 6:23). So Jesus paid our sin debt on the cross, making salvation available to all those chosen who believe. See some details of the crucifixion:

> And it was the third hour when they crucified him. . . . And when the sixth hour had come, there was darkness over the whole land until the ninth hour. And at the ninth hour Jesus cried with a loud voice, "Eloi, Eloi, lema sabachthani?" which means, "My God, my God, why have you forsaken me?" . . . And Jesus uttered a loud cry and breathed his last. And the curtain in the temple was torn in two, from top to bottom. And when the centurion, who stood facing him, saw that in this way he breathed his last, he said, "Truly, this man was the Son of God!" (Mark 15:25, 33–34, 37–39)

So Jesus was on the cross about nine hours, from 9 a.m. until 6 p.m. when He died. While the Jewish religious leadership did not recognize Jesus' uniqueness, the centurion did. He saw something special in Jesus, and He even correctly assigned deity to Jesus. Thus, Jesus paid our sin debt. And the temple curtain that separated the Holy of Holies from the Holy Place was mysteriously torn in half from top to bottom (opposite to how we would think gravity would do it). Now, figuratively and literally, the common man (even Gentiles) had direct access to God. We praise God for this stark picture of the truth of His love for the world.

We see clearly that Jesus' pain on the cross was primarily mental not physical. He had to be forsaken by God to truly make the sacrifice He did, which was separation from God. He felt the pain of being forsaken more than we ever could.

Without question the most significant part of the whole crucifixion story is that it is the Son of God who made the sacrifice. Thus, God sent His Son to earth as man, who lived a perfect life (fulfilling all Old Testament prophecies), died a sinner's death on the cross, rose from the dead on the third day, and having since ascended back to heaven, now sits at the Father's right hand interceding for us with Him. **And it was and is God's grace that was the driving force behind it all.** Try to imagine if you can God's grand prearranged plan, involving His grace and man's faith, that He put in motion before time began that has played out throughout history, every part of which God monitored seeing to its proper execution. And every single person who has ever lived had a role to play; some played their role, many did not. And for those chosen who responded positively to the Holy Spirit's leadership there is heaven's reward waiting. What a great God we have.

PROVERBS 23:17–18

If we would live well, then we are to bring God into the equation of our lives, seeking His will, and His very heart as we make life's decisions. He is to be our focus and our source of wisdom, and if so, He will be our redeemer and source of direction and protection. See these verses for a proper life perspective:

> Let not your heart envy sinners,
>> but continue in the fear of the LORD all the day.
> Surely there is a future,
>> and your hope will not be cut off. (Proverbs 23:17–18)

The message is clear, we are not to imitate or choose the paths of unbelievers, those whose way leaves no doubt they do not fear the Lord, where "fear" means respect and reverence. There is the sense here that the future holds nothing but judgment and destruction for them. On the other hand, for those who do fear the Lord this way, there is a future. "Future" can be taken to mean a hereafter or heavenly destiny. Those obedient ones then will spend eternity with the Lord they have feared, blessed beyond measure. Their hope is sure, and their destiny eternal. It will not be cut off in any sense, no matter our worldly persecution or trials.

What an absolutely awesome truth! See God leading the author (likely King Solomon) to give encouragement to the coming generations (including us), promising lifelong direction and protection, and an everlasting future with Him. So right now in the midst of what may be (worldly) fears, doubts, or persecution, we see almighty God, who knows what lies ahead for us all, telling us to "keep the faith," persevere, and trust Him with our futures.

When He was here Jesus preached a similar message:

"Blessed are those who are persecuted for righteousness' sake, for theirs is the kingdom of heaven.

"Blessed are you when others revile you and persecute you and utter all kinds of evil against you falsely on my account. Rejoice and be glad, for your reward is great in heaven, for so they persecuted the prophets who were before you." (Matthew 5:10–12)

Notice in the passage in Proverbs our focus is to be on the Lord, and in Matthew, Jesus is speaking and He refers to our suffering "on His account." Clearly, both these passages emphasize Jesus Christ as Lord and that He is to be our life interest and focus. Such obedience provides joy in the midst of sorrow, relief in the midst of pain, and direction in the midst of confusion.

ROMANS 8:1-4

In chapter 7, Paul has been writing about how the Mosaic law binds us. We are unable to comply with it entirely, and Satan uses that sense of failure to depress, deceive, and defeat us. In chapter 8, Paul describes the relief God's Holy Spirit provides and, thus, offers us the only solution: faith in Christ Jesus. See how God has Paul word this way to eternal life for His chosen children.

> There is therefore now no condemnation for those who are in Christ Jesus. For the law of the Spirit of life has set you free in Christ Jesus from the law of sin and death. For God has done what the law, weakened by the flesh, could not do. By sending his own Son in the likeness of sinful flesh and for sin, he condemned sin in the flesh, in order that the righteous requirement of the law might be fulfilled in us, who walk not according to the flesh but according to the Spirit. (Romans 8:1–4)

WOW! What an awesome concept. Herein is described what God actually did for mankind. He provided the only way we could achieve eternal life. Apart from God's provision of Jesus' atoning, sacrificial death in our place, we would still be dead in our sins and destined for an eternity apart from holy God. In the first sentence, Paul gets right to the point of what we now therefore have: "no condemnation" *if* we are "in Christ Jesus."

The phrase "in Christ Jesus" refers to those who have, by God's grace and our faith, trusted in Jesus' sacrificial death as satisfying God's wrath for our sins. God's grace alone has led us to this condition of justified in Christ, that is, acquitted of our sins and perfected for glory. No amount of dedication to compliance with the law on our part could have achieved that status. **At the moment of our conversion our sins are forgiven, and Jesus'**

righteousness is imputed to us, qualifying us for heaven. Our salvation is so secure that, at the same moment here on earth, our eternal life begins. Talk about a hallelujah moment that lasts forever; no wonder we feel such a sense of relief, peace, and joy.

Interestingly, and unfortunately, Satan begins immediately trying to chip away at our faith, but the fact of this passage is STILL IN PLACE. See what the passage says: "For the law of the Spirit of life has set you free in Christ Jesus from the law of sin and death." **We have been "set free" from the very evil influence Satan is promoting.**

We can take joy in that freedom, and in addition to living out that freedom we can share that good news with those around us. There is no one who does not need to hear it.

1 CHRONICLES 29:10-13

Toward the end of his life King David of Israel asked all the people to contribute an offering for the construction of the temple. His son, Solomon, would reign after him and actually see to the construction of the temple. When the people heard his request, they gladly contributed silver, and gold, and precious stones in abundance to pay for the construction; in fact, they gave more than enough. And David and all the people rejoiced at this display of love for God. As a result, we see in this passage part of the prayer of thanksgiving David offers to God on behalf of all Israel. This prayer reflects how we should give, and it reflects how we should respond to God for all the blessings He provides us, for God is the source of all wealth, wisdom, and power. See these four verses:

> Therefore David blessed the LORD in the presence of all the assembly. And David said, "Blessed are you, O LORD, the God of Israel our father, forever and ever. Yours, O LORD, is the greatness and the power and the glory and the victory and the majesty, for all that is in the heavens and in the earth is yours. Yours is the kingdom, O LORD, and you are exalted as head above all. Both riches and honor come from you, and you rule over all. In your hand are power and might, and in your hand it is to make great and to give strength to all. And now we thank you, our God, and praise your glorious name." (1 Chronicles 29:10–13)

In these verses we see a beautiful display of David's love and respect for almighty God. He correctly praises and honors God, giving Him credit for all the blessings he and Israel have received over the years. It is this same kind of praise and honor we, too, are to give God, for He has blessed us as well and He still reigns over all the heavens and the earth. Take time to look at the heavens some starry night and just try to imagine the God who created all that. This same God counts every hair on your head and knows every single thought you've ever had. And best of all, this is the God who created you, and all those you love, and He loves you with an everlasting love. And because He loves you, He has provided a way for you to be with Him eternally through the sacrificial death of His Son in your place. John 3:16 points this out: "For God so loved the world, that he gave his only Son, that whoever believes in him should not perish but have eternal life."

What a great, great God you have. Give Him the thanksgiving He deserves.

1 JOHN 2:15-17

The title of this section of scripture is "Do Not Love the World." We sort of know inherently that it is God's will for us not to "love the world," that is, for us not to give priority to things and pleasures of this world. They are temporary, limited in benefits, and eventually will disappoint us. But knowing God's will in this matter and giving proper priorities consistently to worldly decisions is hard to do. The world seems to want to focus us on short-term results when God would have us focus on eternal things. See how the Holy Spirit has John word his counsel to us:

> Do not love the world or the things in the world. If anyone loves the world, the love of the Father is not in him. For all that is in the world—the desires of the flesh and the desires of the eyes and pride of life—is not from the Father but is from the world. And the world is passing away along with its desires, but whoever does the will of the Father abides forever. (1 John 2:15–17)

Notice the passage talks about "anyone who loves the world." In other words, the priorities promoted in this passage apply to everyone who ever lives. This passage is universal in scope, no matter our age, where we live, or the conditions we experience. The rich and the poor alike are subject to this truth. People in John's day and those of us today are all tempted to disobey these commands. The reason this is true is, as humans we are different in many ways, but our natures are the same. We are all made in the image of God and the sophistication level of our society does not change our natures. So the scripture of John's day is also applicable to our day.

Notice, too, we (that is, no one) can give priority to the world and to the Father at the same time. Obedience to the world and to God do not mix, that is, the love of God is not in those who attempt to be both worldly and godly. We must make a choice, and consciously or subconsciously we do make those choices every day. See how John describes what is in the world: the desires of the flesh, desires of the eyes, and pride in possessions. When we think about it those are the three things we are tempted to put between us and God. Satan is very adept at disguising these temptations as good things that we merit or somehow deserve for all our hard work, and/or good deeds.

Thus, there remains the requirement for us to "train" our consciences to be open to the Holy Spirit's direction. How we do this is very straightforward we fill our minds and hearts with God's truth consistently. Godly people have a "Godward" perspective about life. They spend time in God's Word, and with God's people growing spiritually. They become tuned in to God's will, having made knowing His truths a priority in their lives, putting in the time and "mental sweat" necessary to enable them to properly gauge their various circumstances relative to God's purpose for them.

Note John's comments on the world. It is "passing away." This world's time is thus limited by God. This world as we know it will one day "not be." On the other hand, whoever does the will of the Father abides forever. **Believers (only) then are partakers of eternity.** That's a message we ought to share with a lost world.

1 THESSALONIANS 1:2–5

These entry verses of 1 Thessalonians tell us a lot about Paul's feelings for the Christians in the Thessalonica church. Paul passed through Thessalonica on his second missionary journey and shared the gospel with the people there about AD 50. Now, a year or so later, he is writing this encouraging letter from Corinth. He reminds them of his love for them and his confidence in their salvation. Notice Paul continues to pray for them and their ongoing witness, an example we should imitate. See his words:

> We give thanks to God always for all of you, constantly mentioning you in our prayers, remembering before our God and Father your work of faith and labor of love and steadfastness of hope in our Lord Jesus Christ. For we know, brothers loved by God, that he has chosen you, because our gospel came to you not only in word, but also in power and in the Holy Spirit and with full conviction. (1 Thessalonians 1:2–5)

It's one thing to notice the Christian witness of someone, but even more telling about our own hearts if we can sincerely give thanks to God for those people and their labor in the Lord. So, Paul does not just pray for them but does so constantly. Notice he mentions their works of faith, their labor of love, and the hope in Jesus Christ they exhibit. Those three characteristics reflect a true Christian's lifestyle. Works of faith indicate a proactive witness to all those they influence. Steadfast hope tells us of the end result (salvation for the lost) they look forward to, and the phrase "labor of love" describes their motive in doing all this. And that "love motive" is the greatest characteristic of the three. See 1 Corinthians 13:13: "So now faith, hope, and love abide, these three; but the greatest of these is love."

When you think about it, God already knows of the good work (and the sincere reasons for it) that those Thessalonica Christians are doing. So, what good does it do for Paul to thank God for them? The point is, those thankful prayers Paul prays are indicative of his heart for Christ, and how he grows spiritually when he prays for them. Paul planted the gospel seed in Thessalonica and now he celebrates in prayer what those Christians there are doing as they literally "water" that seed he planted. Surely Paul is encouraging the Thessalonians with this letter, but he is also getting encouraged by them. And he will be a better witness later because of what he sees them doing. That double blessing reflects the beauty of God's love and how it compounds in quantity and quality as all we believers let it play out in our lives.

The enthusiasm of the Thessalonica Christians indicates clearly to Paul the sincerity of their faith, and points up God's election process in choosing them. The Holy Spirit has come upon them in enabling power as they live out their witness. So, when Paul writes to them acknowledging their heartfelt efforts, it will serve to lead them further in their Christian maturity. Their full obedience to the gospel mandates is proof positive of the authenticity of their faith. That holds true among believers in our day too.

So, we see in this passage clearly the value of prayer in general, and specifically for thankful prayers when we plainly see God's presence lived out before us. We believers need to fully grasp the concept that the gospel message we have acquired is priceless in value, needed by the whole world, and is given us with instructions to share it with others, making disciples as we go about our daily lives.

2 TIMOTHY 2:22

Believers who were saved at a young age have an especially good opportunity to live out their faith effectively. They combine their spiritual growth with their physical and mental growth alongside their peers and they all benefit from the process. Timothy is a young man who has been with Paul the apostle for a relatively short time (perhaps just a few years), but has now been given the assignment by Paul to stay in Ephesus and lead the church there. Thus, Paul writes to him with counsel on various issues. The issue in this letter has to do with persevering in the faith during periods of suffering. Living under Roman domination made that a real issue. Notice how personal Paul's letter is to Timothy, and to us. See these instructions:

> So flee youthful passions and pursue righteousness, faith, love, and peace, along with those who call on the name of the Lord from a pure heart. (2 Timothy 2:22)

We all know what "flee" means (to run away from), but when you think about it, it means to depart after having made a conscious evaluation of a given situation concluding (maybe very quickly) that you need to clear the area. We can flee physically, we can flee mentally, and we can flee morally. The youthful passions Paul mentions refer to sinful desires that generally beset us when we are young. So, there is the concept of perfection taught within Paul's letter that we should all be striving for. And such perfection begins with our decision to leave worldliness and pursue godliness.

We are not just to flee from something (youthful passions), but toward something entirely different. And Paul lists four godly goals he recommends as worthy of our efforts: righteousness, faith, love, and peace. We know the definition of those four and would not debate them as being godly. What we seem to doubt though is how worthwhile Paul's pursuit counsel is. After all, how much time do we spend specifically pursuing those four goals. Most of the time we just sort of assume if we do some good deeds and refrain from very many bad deeds, that righteousness, faith, love, and peace will magically come upon us. **If almighty God, through Paul, is telling us here to pursue some specific goals, does it not follow we should pray regularly for those very characteristics, and that we should be about the business of making disciples as we already know Jesus has told us to?**

And notice Paul tells us of a key step we can take in that direction: association with like-hearted believers. That's what those believers who "call on the name of the Lord from a pure heart" do. And it involves active involvement within the only institution Jesus established while on this earth, His church. So, we are not to just attend church, but proactively seek out a role (better, "the" role) God would have us play there.

And as it happens that approach leads to our sanctification and perseverance in the faith that brings on the spiritual maturity and righteousness, faith, love, and peace Paul was talking about. That's how God has constructed the Christian life. So, we are to start our Christian walk as Jesus commanded, with love for Him and our neighbors, encouraging others by word and deed to do likewise.

1 TIMOTHY 2:1–4

Timothy was a young disciple of Paul who traveled with him on several mission trips, and was of great assistance to him. Paul grew to love him and over time gave him increasing responsibility in his ministry. In the second chapter of this letter Paul's emphasis to Timothy was on the importance of prayer. We can understand these instructions as meant for us too.

> First of all, then, I urge that supplications, prayers, intercessions, and thanksgiving be made for all people, for kings and all who are in high positions, that we may lead a peaceful and quiet life, godly and dignified in every way. This is good, and it is pleasing in the sight of God our Savior, who desires all people to be saved and to come to the knowledge of the truth. (1 Timothy 2:1–4)

Clearly, we all are to pray. The four terms listed describing our entreaties to God simply give emphasis to our dependence on God as our only source of salvation. The thought here also has to do with the ongoing aspects of our communications with God. These terms describe a lifestyle and heartfelt attitude, not just periodic prayer sessions when we feel the need for God's help. Notice, too, the emphasis here is our concern for all other people, no matter their worldly status. So, yes, we are to pray for our own needs, but are not to limit our prayers to our personal situations. Jesus meant it when He told us we are to love our neighbors as we love ourselves (see Matthew 22:39).

In the first place the very act of praying is an acknowledgment on our part of God's position relative to us. He is God, and we are not. Praying reflects our faith in Him and our submission to Him for any and all the direction, protection, help, and support we desire for ourselves and others. Paul's counsel to pray for others indicates two things: first, that we know God wants us to feel empathy for others and, second, that we feel bound to obey Him in that effort. Paul confirms our belief that God is pleased with such thoughts and efforts on behalf of others, and that should be of ultimate importance to us.

As always, obedience to God brings desirable results. In this instance, this kind of sincere concern for others leads to peaceful and quiet lives, godly and dignified in every way. Most of us don't think of our lives using those terms, but we have to acknowledge that would be the way God would have us live. Imagine a whole town or city living that way, or even the whole world. There is a heavenly aspect to even trying to imagine such a society.

Paul saves the best for last in this passage. We cannot help but be blessed by the thought that God desires salvation and eternal life for all people. That is not to say all people will be saved, for God has constructed our world such that we humans play a role in those decisions and unfortunately some people will choose to deny Christ. **But we now can be sure that is not God's choice.** Thus, anyone who sincerely repents of their sin and turns to Christ acknowledging Him as Lord, and His sacrificial death on the cross as payment for their sins will be saved. God will not turn any such person away.

Thus, eternal life is there for believers, and those transformed hearts will be concerned for others, and anxious even to please God by our ongoing petitions for them, from kings down to everyone. God has made His instructions clear.

PROVERBS 18:10

God has known from the beginning of time that we will all need His help and protection to live as He would have us live. Thus, He has given us prayer as a means of communicating with Him. It is to be done consistently, and humbly, with a view to our gaining God's wisdom and direction. God provision of prayer is one more instance of His steadfast love in action. See this verse concerning God's relationship to us:

> The name of the LORD is a strong tower;
> the righteous man runs into it and is safe. (Proverbs 18:10)

God's name is representative of Him, and thus, should be kept Holy at all times. To use His name properly or pray in His name is to give Him the honor and glory He merits. Notice the way this verse words that thought. On the other hand, to not reverence God's name is ask for God's wrath. God Himself is a strong tower. That is, He is our source of help, protection, wisdom, and direction. And He has given those who believe in Him and trust Him access to all these at any time. So, by definition, prayer is to be an important part of our lives. We miss out on a lot of God's blessings when we ignore this privilege He has provided.

There is a line that says this well in an old gospel hymn titled "What a Friend We Have in Jesus." The line describes what we lose by not praying:

> O what peace we often forfeit,
> O what needless pain we bear,
> all because we do not carry
> everything to God in prayer.

The righteous and wise person runs into God's tower and is safe. What a neat way to describe the attitude of that righteous person. They gladly and regularly run (that is, they make praying a priority) to God in prayer, sharing what they know He already knows. The idea of telling an all-wise God anything seems to be senseless, but in reality it is a gift of God. When we pray and ask of God what He already knows we need, over time we begin to see our prayers as God sees them, that is, as a means of building an ongoing relationship with Him. And this is exactly what He knows we need.

Notice what we find "in God's tower": safety and security. Consciously or subconsciously safety and security is what we strive for in life. And God has made His security available. Just before He ascended back to heaven after His resurrection from the grave, Jesus gave us an awesome promise. Even though He was going back to heaven for a period of time, He promised us, "Behold, I am with you always, to the end of the age" (Matthew 28:20). He is with us via prayer, for anything, from anywhere, at any time. WOW! What a great God we have.

HEBREWS 3:12-13

The author of Hebrews is unknown, but that he knew Jesus Christ as Savior and Lord is not in doubt. What a powerful letter, without question directed by the Holy Spirit. He seemed to be writing to Jewish believers that he knew and cared about, warning them in love to be consistent in "watching their hearts," lest they not live out the faith they felt. See how the Holy Spirit worded these precautions for the benefit of believers in the first century and us today.

> Take care, brothers, lest there be in any of you an evil, unbelieving heart, leading you to fall away from the living God. But exhort one another every day, as long as it is called "today," that none of you may be hardened by the deceitfulness of sin. (Hebrews 3:12-13)

Notice the first two words, "Take care." It is as if the author is about to warn people of something they already know about, but have taken lightly, not assigning it the level of importance they should. The words *take care* imply it is within the power and capability of the reader to do that caretaking if they just would. He is writing to a group but assigning individual and group responsibility for obedience. Without question the Holy Spirit also has us in mind, including the word *brothers*, meaning believers in any age. So it is Christians who believe, but sometimes doubt their faith, that need such teaching, which includes us all. We get the feeling the author has been there; he knows what it is to doubt.

To doubt often includes evil, unbelieving thinking, that becomes "step one" in a chain leading to disobedience. And the more we disobey, the easier it is to continue to disobey. In a way, we dare not, "not believe." To not believe would mean we have heard truth, and concluded believing it a light and trivial thing that we can turn on and off like a faucet. Thus, we believe when trials come and we seek help, and fall away from the living God in unbelief when things are going well. But belief in Jesus Christ as Son of God, Redeemer, and Lord is far from light and trivial. In fact, it is the (only) way to eternal life, it is the one truth every human needs to hear, believe, and live out (for only living it out reflects true belief). Given that belief in Christ is so vital, then to have that knowledge, to have experienced the gospel truth, and NOT share it, is a grievous sin indeed. No wonder Jesus' command for believers to "go and make disciples" is called the Great Commission.

Thus, we are to exhort one another (other believers) to keep the faith; to stay the course, to continue to believe to the point of obedience and sharing God's truth. Notice the sense of urgency the author adds. We are to exhort one another every day, as long as it called "today." That is, we are to begin now, and continue as long as we have opportunity. Such general exhortation on our part works to build ongoing, strong, and vibrant faith within us.

Jesus' coming to earth begins the "end time," lasting until His second coming. He has come to earth, lived a perfect life, spoken His truth, died to pay the sin debt of believers, rose again, and ascended to heaven. We believers, bonded together in His church, are to be about exhorting each other to believe this truth so as to protect others from hearts hardened by the deceitfulness of sin (which we all need).

MATTHEW 25:31-34, 41

In a general way we all understand that one day Jesus will come in judgment. The whole world, that is, every person who has ever lived anywhere, will stand before Him to give an account of their lives. This passage begins a discussion of that event. It will be a real event. How God will handle the crowd and all the various life stories is not ours to know right now. But we can be sure it will be done with a perfect accounting of even the smallest detail of our lives. So, all we've done, and the "why" of all we've done, will be evaluated by the only one qualified to do so, Jesus Christ. Picture this scene:

> When the Son of Man comes in his glory, and all the angels with him, then he will sit on his glorious throne. Before him will be gathered all the nations, and he will separate people one from another as a shepherd separates the sheep from the goats. And he will place the sheep on his right, but the goats on the left. Then the King will say to those on his right, "Come, you who are blessed by my Father, inherit the kingdom prepared for you from the foundation of the world.". . .
>
> "Then he will say to those on his left, 'Depart from me, you cursed, into the eternal fire prepared for the devil and his angels.'" (Matthew 25:31–34, 41)

Notice there will only be two groups, called sheep and goats. The sheep are analogous to believers who have trusted Christ as Savior and Lord, and the goats, who as unbelievers, have denied Christ's position as Messiah, Son of God, and Lord of Lords. And God's throne will be there, fitting for Jesus to sit on and make His judgments. And the separation of the sheep from the goats will be complete and well defined; no one belongs in both groups. And we see Jesus being referred to as King, as well He should be as King of Kings.

And we hear Jesus speak of the results of judgment; the sheep are called to God's kingdom. Here is a kingdom prepared (by God) specifically for them since the beginning of the world. There, those believers who have been blessed to have been chosen for citizenship will enjoy fellowship with God eternally. Notice, too, this permanent citizenship is their inheritance as children of God.

The goats, however, are told to depart from God's presence. This is an eternal sentence with no hope ever for pardon. They will be subject (forever) to the eternal fire prepared for the devil and his angels. The torment there will be terrible, but just as bad will be the knowledge that it will never end, and that there is no chance ever for release or relief.

So, when will this "judgment day" happen? See Matthew 24:36: "But concerning that day and hour no one knows, not even the angels of heaven, nor the Son, but the Father only."

Our heavenly Father knows, and that's all that's required. But happen it will. Our assignment is not so much to be watching for that day, but to be preparing for it. What more could our loving, heavenly Father do other than to urge us to believe and obey, and to warn of us of the coming judgment for unbelief and disobedience?

ISAIAH 2:11–12

As Isaiah looked around at the world of his day, he must have seen the same type of people we see today; some who know the Lord and give Him honor and glory, but many more who give no thought to God at all, or never seek His will in their lives. Thus, it's easy to see the need for Isaiah to bring the Lord to their attention, to remind people of who He is, and why they owe Him honor, allegiance, and obedience. There is great need in our day, too, for "Isaiah-type" declarations. This section of Isaiah is called the "Day of the Lord." Here Isaiah points out the certainty of judgment and the fact of the dire consequences of sin. See how plainly Isaiah expresses God's coming involvement in our lives.

> The haughty looks of man shall be brought low,
>   and the lofty pride of men shall be humbled,
> and the LORD alone will be exalted in that day.
> For the LORD of hosts has a day
>   against all that is proud and lofty,
>   against all that is lifted up—and it shall be brought low.
>   (Isaiah 2:11–12)

Isaiah sees haughtiness as the main thing wrong with the world. That same pride-filled attitude we see so much of in our day was present in Isaiah's time too. It is as if there is a competition taking place continually in the heart of every human as to who will reign, God or Satan, in that individual. And God always requires first place. And man's "haughty looks" will be brought low. We are not given the definition of "brought low," but it certainly brings to mind our being abruptly put in our rightful place, brought down from the lofty position we think we merit, and having to suffer some painful consequences in the process.

Most of us don't think of ourselves as being very prideful, yet it is pride that sends us into disobedience of every sort against our Lord. At the bottom of every sin is our thought that we have the right to make our own decisions and do anything we wish, all obvious instances of pride having full sway in our lives. The passage above speaks of the Lord having a day, that may or may not be twenty-four hours long. In essence it means God will make the final judgments, He will make the last decisions as to our eternal destiny. No one and nothing but He will be exalted in His day, and that day can be as long as eternity.

Notice, too, that everything is to be evaluated. "All that is lifted up shall be brought low." Not only all people, but every institution, every company, every idea, and every man-originated concept, will be judged, and any that do not honor and glorify God will be brought low. And why not? How and why, can and should, any imperfect thing be left standing after the Lord's Day when He makes all things right?

We have our day as we freely choose to receive or reject our heavenly Father's gift of His only Son. That was the ultimate gift of love God bestowed on mankind. When we pridefully turn that gift down through unbelief, we accrue the consequences of an eternity separated from the Lord.

Conversation about The Lord's Day and our day then are simply phrases that depict the two choices we have presented to us, to fear the Lord, as in reverencing Him, or not. To reverence Him is to both believe in Him (as God come to earth to save us from our sins) and to believe Him as the final Word of God's expression of love for mankind.

So, yes, "For God so loved the world, that he gave his only Son, that whoever believes in him should not perish but have eternal life" (John 3:16) **REALLY IS TRUE.**

1 TIMOTHY 6:17–19

This section of Paul's letter has been titled "Fighting the Good Fight of Faith." And this particular passage addresses the rich within our society, and how they are to fight the good fight of faith. Rich believers are in a unique position, wealthy by human standards, and by God's standards. Inherent in that condition are some responsibilities most individuals don't have. To be rich by human standards is relative. When we think of someone as rich, we have already addressed the question, "Compared to what?" Compared to a billionaire we are not rich; but compared to the vast majority of other people in the world we are rich. No matter the amount of wealth they have, believers are rich, too, compared to unbelievers. Due solely to their relationship with the Lord they have an eternal inheritance of infinite worth. So, this passage by Paul is very relevant to us no matter our definition of rich. See the wisdom God had Paul send us:

> As for the rich in this present age, charge them not to be haughty, nor to set their hopes on the uncertainty of riches, but on God, who richly provides us with everything to enjoy. They are to do good, to be rich in good works, to be generous and ready to share, thus storing up treasure for themselves as a good foundation for the future, so that they may take hold of that which is truly life. (1 Timothy 6:17–19)

Initially, in this passage Paul speaks of riches as defined by material wealth. He promotes the concept of the rich using their wealth for the betterment of society. We picture that in our day as feeding the poor, spending on promotion of the gospel worldwide, and generally sharing with those less blessed materially than we are. Yet Paul warns the rich against depending on their riches for their eternal security. Only a relationship with God will solidify real eternal security. See James 1:17 for the real source of good gifts.

"Every good gift and every perfect gift is from above, coming down from the Father of lights with whom there is no variation or shadow due to change."

Note the idea Paul presents of "being rich in good works" with our earthly wealth stores up treasure for us, and provides a good future foundation. That has to refer to our status in heaven with the Lord who provided our wealth in the first place and knows the "why" of our doing good with it. The right reason for being generous and sharing our wealth enables those believers to "take hold of that which is truly life." WOW! Taking hold of true life is an awesome concept. That could be nothing other than an eternal life with the Lord. Small good things done on this earth merit huge good rewards in heaven *if* done in Jesus' name. Jesus told us why. Remember, Jesus keeps His promises. "And whoever gives one of these little ones even a cup of cold water because he is a disciple, truly, I say to you, he will by no means lose his reward" (Matthew 10:42).

Thus, we are to share our material wealth, and our spiritual wealth. And we are to do both consistently and we are to do both for the right reason, that being to glorify our Lord. And God will take notice. He misses nothing we do, and knows why we do it.

2 CORINTHIANS 9:12-15

Without question God has blessed us. And without question God expects us to share what we've received with others. That sharing brings several results that we might not think about, but are very important. Paul has been traveling throughout Macedonia and Greece. As he visited various churches, he urged them to collect an offering for the poor among the membership of the church at Jerusalem. So, in this letter he is reminding the church at Corinth of their pledge to help in this offering. Such a commitment to help others in need is an important lesson for us. See what Paul advises them and us:

> For the ministry of this service is not only supplying the needs of the saints but is also overflowing in many thanksgivings to God. By their approval of this service, they will glorify God because of your submission that comes from your confession of the gospel of Christ, and the generosity of your contribution for them and for all others, while they long for you and pray for you, because of the surpassing grace of God upon you. Thanks be to God for his inexpressible gift! (2 Corinthians 9:12–15)

Notice the ripple effect coming from the giving of this offering. The offering will not only meet needs in the Jerusalem church, but will be an expression of thanksgiving to God by the various churches for what God has provided them. Thanking God for His blessings is *always* a good thing to do (then and now). And the best way to thank God is to share what He has provided. And surely as they share, those giving churches will also pray for the church in Jerusalem as they collect the offering. And, of course, the Jerusalem church will be very grateful for the gift and will thank both the churches who gave and God for His actions in the hearts of those churches leading them to give. Thus, many prayers will be lifted up by the church in Jerusalem for those other churches who gave. So, praying leads to giving and giving leads to thanksgiving by both the people who give and those who receive the gifts. And everyone becomes more appreciative of God for orchestrating this whole scenario.

What a beautiful scene, believers loving each other enough to support each other, and all those involved giving praise and thanksgiving to God. That's reflective of the wisdom of God putting such generosity in the hearts of believers, leading to a closer relationship among believers and a closer walk with God by everyone. And further, we can be sure that later when the Jerusalem church was more financially stable, they, too, would be collecting offerings for other needy churches as was done for them.

The lesson for us is clear. We are to thank God for what He has provided us by sharing with others. And prayer is the lubricant that smooths the way for this to happen. Prayer will lead us to be sensitive to the needs around us, and to God's direction for us. Prayer will lead us to a right perspective concerning how we feel about sharing. Prayer will lead us to give out of a love motive, not a duty motive. And prayer will bring God's will into the equation, which brings glory to Him for what we do.

Societies change over time, but human nature does not. Most people will be appreciative of being helped in a time of need, especially if the helping individual reflects God's love, not their own generosity. Such giving efforts then provide opportunities to glorify God with a witness for Christ. That's not an accident, it's the way God constructed us humans made in His image.

GALATIANS 3:23–26

People who are not knowledgeable of the gospel of Jesus Christ tend to believe they are saved (that is, given eternal life by God) via living a good life. And their definition of a good life is one in which they judge themselves to be free from very many sins, and wherein they do lots (in their opinion) of good deeds. And that sounds logical to some degree. Good works (and few bad works) should equal salvation, they think. And they live their lives therefore based on their own conscience and will, not God's. So, in a sense then, they believe we can earn our own salvation. But nothing could be further from the truth. In no way does anyone ever earn their salvation. True good works are the result of our salvation and not the reason for it.

God established, and retains, total control of the consequences of sin and of good deeds. We can't because we don't have the power/wisdom to do so, and we have no idea of the significance of sin in God's eyes. He is perfect and would have us be perfect before we qualify for heaven. Since we are born sinners and therefore imperfect from the beginning (and live that way), we can only attain perfection if it is somehow miraculously given to us. And that's what happened when a perfect sacrifice (Jesus Christ) died for us on the cross. See how the Holy Spirit has Paul word this in Galatians:

> Now before faith came, we were held captive under the law, imprisoned until the coming faith would be revealed. So then, the law was our guardian until Christ came, in order that we might be justified by faith. But now that faith has come, we are no longer under a guardian, for in Christ Jesus, you are all sons of God, through faith. (Galatians 3:23–26)

Thus, we might logically ask, "How were people saved before Christ came to earth and died for their sins (and ours)?" Paul addresses that question here and the answer involves consideration of several facts. God created man in the image of God; thus, they inherently knew the difference between right and wrong and could and should make right decisions in those areas. And God's Holy Spirit was also available to guide people who wanted to do the right things to make proper decisions. And as necessary the Holy Spirit was able to provide knowledge to individuals that God would later make appropriate provisions for the sins of those who believed in Him. Which, of course, He did in Christ.

This passage tells us that before the law, that is, the birth of Jesus, people were bound (imprisoned) to keep the law, and were given salvation (or not) based on their heart-based decisions and actions. God, being the just, loving God He is and fully aware of their incomplete knowledge of a coming Savior, could and did make appropriate judgment decisions on behalf of these earliest believers.

So, the passage tells us that initially the law was our guardian until Christ came. Guardian implies the law was our decision-making guide, our source of God's truth, and our "road map" for finding His will for our lives. And the law still defines sin for us, so compliance is always God's will for us.

But now, says Paul, because Christ has come, we are no longer under a guardian. Compliance with the law is no longer the route to eternal life. (We could never do it perfectly anyway). Faith is the route. Christ is the way. His perfect life, coupled with His death in our place (paying our sin debt) was God's plan from the beginning. We are saved by God's grace through faith, that is, belief in Christ. Hallelujah!

1 John 5:13–15

John the apostle is writing to believers, people who have already made a commitment to Jesus Christ. However, just because they have made that commitment does not mean their lives are totally in sync with God's will. Sometimes believers doubt their salvation, sometimes they are not clear on what God's will is for them, and sometimes even believers commit premediated sin. So, there is a need for this reminder from John for believers in that day and our day. Clearly John tells his readers why he is writing. He wants them to be assured of their salvation, and that's good news for us too. We *can* know we are saved and have eternal life. Our heavenly Father has seen fit to provide us this confirmation of our eternal destiny to enable us to better face the various trials and temptations Satan brings us. See John's words on the assurance of salvation:

> I write these things to you who believe in the name of the Son of God that you may know that you have eternal life. And this is the confidence that we have toward him, that if we ask anything according to his will he hears us. And if we know that he hears us in whatever we ask, we know that we have the requests that we have asked of him. (1 John 5:13–15)

In John's day (and ours), it was difficult for believers to be consistent in their Christian walk. This, because Satan is ever alert, continually putting trials and temptations in our paths. So, our faith can be weak at times. But in essence John is telling his readers it is possible for Christians to have assurance of their salvation. Thus, we can know we have eternal life and live out that confidence. What a great gift from God that kind of confidence is. Even in the midst of the toughest of times we can be assured of God's love and provisions for us.

And if that be true, and it is, then our whole prayer life should reflect that assurance. Notice John's words, "if we ask anything according to his will [God] hears us." Some skeptics might claim, they can't pray for what they want and need, but must pray in accord with God's will. If we really consider that complaint, we realize how shortsighted and shallow it is. Imagine praying deliberately for something we know is not the will of almighty God, who, by the way, loves us with an infinite love. Doesn't it follow that a God who loves us enough to send His Son to earth to die a sinner's death on the cross in our place will only have our "short-term" and our "long-term" good in mind. And thus, His will is certainly going to work to our benefit.

The whole purpose of prayer is for us to be able to commune with God. Here, we humans, are allowed to share time with an almighty heavenly Father who loves us and knows everything we will ever pray for, before we pray. God has constructed our universe such that "right" will be the eventual result of every event per God's justice, leading to God's infinite glory.

Thus, our praying in accord with God's will is not only appropriate, but infinitely beneficial to us. God knows (and has always known) what is best for us, and John is being led to simply encourage us to reorient our perspectives around God's wishes rather than ours. We are wise indeed if we let God's will "drive" our prayers.

The first sentence of this passage gives us the key to praying and living per God's will, that is, belief in the name of the Son of God. Belief in Jesus' name is commensurate with belief in Him and leads to the faith necessary for salvation and eternal life.

PSALM 51:17-19

As we read these last three verses of this Psalm, we see how a "blending" of our hearts and our activities is to be accomplished as we engage in sincere ongoing worship of the Lord, and in living out that worship in our lives. This Psalm was written at a serious junction in King David's life just after his affair with Bathsheba, and is thus, especially meaningful. See these verses:

> The sacrifices of God are a broken spirit;
> a broken and contrite heart, O God, you will not despise.
> Do good to Zion in your good pleasure;
> build up the walls of Jerusalem;
> then you will delight in right sacrifices,
> in burnt offerings and whole burnt offerings;
> then bulls will be offered on your altar. (Psalm 51:17-19)

We are to beware of "the routine" of gathering with other believers in regular times of worship when our hearts are not in it. "God looks on our hearts" (1 Samuel 16:7), and knows of the sincerity with which we come before Him. This does not mean we are not to gather with other believers to worship, it means we are to "prepare" our hearts each time we do. Look at the kind of hearts we are to have as we worship: "broken spirits, and a broken and contrite heart . . . He will not despise." This speaks of our recognition of our sinful status (and our remorse over it) and that we come acknowledging God's sovereignty, seeking forgiveness and directions. If God will not despise such sensitive hearts, it means He will embrace and bless such hearts. It means He will hear the prayers emanating from such hearts. And it means He will empower us to hear, understand, and live out the directions He provides.

Thus, David prays that God will "do good" to Zion (God's people, that's us) as He sees fit, and that He will secure their future (symbolized by strong walls around Jerusalem). Therefore, when Israel does come to worship with clean hearts and right spirits, and does perform the sacrificial rites God has commanded, then He can and will "delight" in them and bless their worship. And after such "blessed" worship they will be the witness to the world they should be, and they will bless the world with their outreach of the gospel, and God will be glorified in the process.

And, of course, as we ask ourselves about the application of these truths in our day, we easily see we, too, are to adhere to all God's commands. That is, we are "not to neglect meeting together" in worship (Hebrews 10:25). And we are to come to those meetings with repentant hearts, seeking God's face, open to learning more of His will for our lives.

MATTHEW 12:30–31

To commit to Jesus is to draw a defined line between what we believe and will do, and what we will not. Jesus allows no "middle ground." We are either for Him or against Him. The Pharisees in Jesus' day, and many people today, spend much time and effort trying to live as much as they can according to their own choice of lifestyle without consideration of what God's will is for them. Their first focus is "self" and what "they" want. Their priorities revolve around what they think is best for them. Jesus clearly spoke against such self-bias. See what He taught on this concept of where to place our loyalties:

> Whoever is not with me is against me, and whoever does not gather with me scatters. Therefore I tell you, every sin and blasphemy will be forgiven people, but the blasphemy against the spirit will not be forgiven. (Matthew 12:30–31)

We are not to seek a neutral position with Jesus, to be for Him one day, and against Him the next, to be for Him with one group, and against Him with another group. We can't think about this subject without the word *consistent* coming to mind. We are to be consistent in our walk in and for the Lord. Otherwise, our witness is a "minus." Otherwise, people will not see Jesus in us, for He was the most consistent person who ever lived in His obedience to His Father. Such consistency is easier to talk about than it is to live out. But then Jesus knew that would be the case and made provision for the Holy Spirit to live within believers to guide and remind them of His will.

We often hear of references to the "unpardonable" sin, and that comes from this passage where Jesus defines blasphemy against the spirit as that one sin that will not be forgiven. Simply put, this sin involves the ongoing, persistent, and complete rejection of the Holy Spirit's call to repentance and salvation. Permanent denial then, of the Holy Spirit's message concerning Jesus is grounds for eternal condemnation. Other references to this critical doctrine are found in Luke 12:10 and Mark 3:29. Such denial literally attributes the acts of God's power to Satan.

This sin, by definition, will therefore, only be committed by unbelievers who purposefully and willingly reject the work of the Holy Spirit. Thus, if we worry about committing this sin, that's the Holy Spirit at work within us advising us of the importance of it, and therefore causing our concern; thus, we are likely not guilty of it. Unbelievers would not be concerned, and therefore are condemned.

So, where does this passage leave us? What is the key lesson for us to learn from it? The answers are both simple and critically important. Jesus is Lord, He has always been Lord, and will always be Lord. God loved us so much He sent Jesus to the cross to satisfy the sin debt of every believer. So, when Jesus died there, He atoned for all our sins. And when he arose from the grave, He conquered death forever, for Himself and us. Because He arose, hallelujah! WE WILL TOO. So, no wonder there is nothing "halfway" about our salvation. We are either all in, or not in at all. And that's as it should be. Jesus is worthy of *all* our praise, honor, and glory.

Who do you know that needs to hear this good news?

1 PETER 4:7-8

God's plan of salvation for the world involved a number of important events; Jesus' death, resurrection, and ascension into heaven, plus the outpouring of the Holy Spirit upon believers. When Peter wrote this letter, those events had already happened. And now Jesus reigns at the right hand of the Father, where He remains awaiting the Father's command to return to earth to gather all believers to Himself for an eternity in heaven. See how Peter words this condition:

> The end of all things is at hand; therefore be self-controlled and sober-minded for the sake of your prayers. Above all, keep loving one another earnestly, since love covers a multitude of sins. (1 Peter 4:7–8)

The phrase "the end of all things is at hand" does not mean Jesus' return is certain within the next few days. What it does mean is that all the major events scheduled for Jesus in the Father's overall salvation plan had been accomplished. The only event remaining was Christ's triumphant return to earth. Thus, Peter could correctly say "the end of all things is at hand," and it is still at hand. We can and should expect Jesus at any time and live accordingly.

Therefore, because Jesus could return at any time, there are certain ways God would have us live. This passage mentions three of them. We are to be self-controlled and sober-minded, and we are to love one another earnestly. To be self-controlled is to be focused on Jesus as Lord and Savior and not be influenced by outside sources. Any focus for our lives other than Jesus is a "mis-focus," and results in sin and a negative influence on those around us. When we are saved, we take on Jesus' righteousness, and make His will our will, His words our words, and His thinking our thinking. We not only live Christlike lives but also live such that other people see Jesus in us, and over time they come to think better of God for having known us. Thus, Jesus Christ and the Father are glorified, and that's why we were born.

To be sober-minded is to be consistently thoughtful of others and seriously motivated to be obedient to God. Thus, our perspectives in life have to do with how we can best accomplish God's will, and continually strive to find and execute God's purposes. If we are sober-minded, we will be kind to others, generous, forgiving, and accommodating. For sober-minded people, the well-being of others will come before their own well-being. Such priorities will obviously determine how we pray; calling on God to save, protect, and use all of us for His glory.

But notice how important love is. We are told to above all keep loving one another. Apparently, that means we are to love others whether they are lovable or not. If God loves unlovable people, and He does, then surely, they are worthy of our love. Notice the results of our loving unlovable people: their sins do not dictate whether we are going to love them, and forgiveness thus reigns in society and love dominates the world. Picture that kind of world. John 13:34–35 gives us another result of love reigning described by Jesus: "A new commandment I give to you, that you love one another: just as I have loved you, you also are to love one another. By this all people will know that you are my disciples, if you have love for one another."

MATTHEW 7:23; 12:35–36

Most people seem to think that one day there will be a reckoning where all of us give account for our lives. This, partly because there is certain conscious or subconscious logic to the fact that in the final analysis of everything, "good" should win and "evil" should lose. But that thought has not fully taken root in the average person's life. They are certainly not born with it. And it hasn't taken root because it requires daily consideration, and a daily giving over of self to others. And the carnal person is for the most part self-focused. And that is indicative of our sinful nature showing forth. Jesus spoke of this more than once, and we are well advised to listen:

> And then I will declare to them, "I never knew you, depart from me, you workers of lawlessness." . . . The good person out of his good treasure brings forth good, and the evil person out of his evil treasure brings forth evil. I tell you, on the day of judgment people will give account for every careless word they speak. (Matthew 7:23; 12:35–36)

Notice who will do the judging on "that" day (often called the Day of the Lord in scripture). It will be Jesus Himself. This one who loved the world enough to go to the cross to atone for the sins of those who believe in Him, will on that day turn many away with the words "depart from me, you workers of lawlessness." This will happen when Jesus returns to gather those worthy of spending eternity with Him in heaven. Apparently, the judging will be easy, those who are good will have lived lives reflecting that goodness. And those who are evil will have reflected obvious evil in their words and deeds. We get the idea there will be no options for further evaluation via any sort of appeal process.

Those who are "good" and have done "good" will know it, and those who are "evil" will also finally fully understand they were (and did) "evil." It's not a stretch to define "good" as used here, as those who are believers, who have trusted Jesus Christ as their Savior and Lord. Likewise, those "evil" ones, who must depart from Jesus, can be thought of as "unbelievers," those who have denied Christ's role as redeemer and lived unto themselves.

In his letter to the church in Rome, Paul indicates the importance of our words: "If you confess with your mouth that Jesus is Lord and believe in your heart God raised him from the dead, you will be saved" (Romans 10:9).

People who sincerely do these things have defined themselves as good and identified themselves as disciples of Christ. Followers of Christ will do and be different before the world. When Jesus is Lord of one's life it will show. Our priorities, motives, actions, and words will reflect that Lordship. And that's as it should be. The world should have no trouble identifying a believer as a Christ follower.

It's difficult for us to imagine ourselves standing before Christ and giving the account described in this passage, especially when we know everyone who has ever lived will also be doing the same thing. **But the fact of that occasion is not hard to understand.** Thus, we stand advised of judgment coming. Who do we know that needs to be reminded of this?

James 4:11–12

The Bible is very clear concerning our judging others. We are not to judge others. In the first place, as sinners ourselves, we are not qualified to judge. Those who do judge others are in essence judging God's law. We did not create the law, and our task is to obey it ourselves, not evaluate others as to their obedience. To do so is the height of hypocrisy, for we cannot obey the law and have no right to judge others. See James' counsel:

> Do not speak evil against one another, brothers. The one who speaks against a brother or judges his brother, speaks evil against the law and judges the law. But if you judge the law, you are not a doer of the law, but a judge. There is only one lawgiver and judge, he who is able to save and to destroy. But who are you to judge your neighbor? (James 4:11–12)

We are specifically told not to speak evil against a brother. There is a sense in which we are not even to think evil against a brother. To think indicates we have heard or seen something that triggers our thought processes to judge, evaluate, compare, and eventually speak out against our brother. This whole observing, thinking, evaluating, and speaking sequence is Satan-oriented and inspired. At its base it is the desire on our part to debase someone else and in doing so attempt to elevate ourselves. And thus, it reflects an insecurity on our part concerning our own status.

Our Christian walk is a personal one, and is dictated by our own relationship with the Lord. To cloud it with evil thoughts of others serves only to dilute our commitment to God. Notice the net result of our criticizing others is to lead us to break God's law ourselves. We judge God's law when we do. That is, we make comparisons between what the law says, what we think of someone else's response to God's law, and, by definition, we imply we would not disobey any of God's laws. That whole situation is full of false assumptions on our part.

Notice the result of our judging God's laws: we are not a doer of the law, but a judge. Thus, when we think and speak evil of others we become the very person we are criticizing, guilty of the same sort of trespasses we condemn in others. There is, therefore, an element of thoughtlessness in our speaking evil of others. We have not fully considered our own status as a born sinner also in need of a Savior.

As our almighty creator, God has designed our society with only one lawgiver and judge. He, who saw to our creation, will in the end judge us all. To judge is God's role, not ours. He only is able to save and destroy. He only loved us enough to make provision for the eternal life of all those who believe. So the final question is appropriate for us all. "Who are you to judge your neighbor?" To judge is dangerous ground. We may claim to not be judges, but when we speak evil of others, those thoughts and actions clearly give the lie to those claims.

God is the perfect judge looking at our hearts, not our claims. See 1 Samuel 16:7: "For the LORD sees not as man sees: man looks on the outward appearance, but the LORD looks on the heart."

Those who judge others recklessly break God's law, and in no way honor or glorify the Father.

1 THESSALONIANS 4:14–18

The common thought among many believers in the first century was that Jesus' return to earth was imminent. They believed when He spoke of His return from heaven and looked for Him every day. As time passed and Jesus did not return, Christians began to wonder (worry) about the status of their believing loved ones who died in this interim. Thus, Paul was led here to write about Jesus' return, clearing up the question as to when that would be. It's been two thousand years now and yet we can still look forward expectantly for His return. Paul tells us how that will look:

> For since we believe that Jesus died and rose again, even so, through Jesus, God will bring with him those who have fallen asleep. For this we declare to you by a word from the Lord, that we who are alive, who are left until the coming of the Lord, will not precede those who have fallen asleep. For the Lord himself will descend from heaven with a cry of command, with the voice of an archangel, and with the sound of the trumpet of God. And the dead in Christ will rise first. Then we who are alive, who are left, will be caught up together with them in the clouds to meet the Lord in the air, and so will always be with the Lord. Therefore encourage one another with these words. (1 Thessalonians 4:14–18)

Christ's resurrection is the centerpiece of the gospel; the basis on which we believers place our faith that we, too, will one day rise from the dead. Thus, we can be sure Jesus rose from the dead, and because He did, we will too. Paul reemphasizes that fact and gives us the order of resurrection. Those who have died in Christ will rise first and return with Jesus, and those believers who are still alive at that point will rise to meet that crowd in the air. Notice the sound effects: Jesus comes with a shout of command, and a heavenly trumpet sounds to announce His return. We wonder how everyone in the world will be able to see this great event, for normally no one place on earth provides a view of the whole earth. But then, this is a godly event. He created all that is, and will have no problem somehow showing Jesus' return to everyone.

Don't overlook that phrase "and so will always be with the Lord." That's what salvation is all about, an eternity with the Lord. And here specifically in scripture all believers are promised that reward. Thus, believers know what their eternal destiny is. No problem, disease, individual, or man-made circumstance can prevent that from happening.

Clearly Paul's intent is to comfort his readers with the fact that no believer will be left out. Alive or dead they will either be with Jesus when He comes or rise to meet Him in the air. Paul does not intend to claim he will still be alive when Jesus returns, or that he knows a specific date when Jesus will return. The context is that all believers should live such that they are prepared for Jesus to return during their lifetime. Paul urges us as individual believers to encourage one another with these words. How better to gain a proper perspective concerning the various trials we experience than to recognize this earth is not our home eternally.

Matthew 24:14 adds more information to the timing of Jesus' return. "And this gospel of the kingdom will be proclaimed throughout the whole world as a testimony to all nations, and then the end will come."

We, therefore, have a message we are told to share, a message the whole world needs.

REVELATION 1:3

Here in this last book of the Bible, God has the apostle John summarize His salvation plan through the description of Jesus Christ's purpose in coming to earth, and His resulting death, burial, and resurrection. Through His sacrificial death and resurrection, Jesus conquers Satan and thereby atones for the sins of believers in all history. This book makes clear world history is under Jesus' control and at the end of the age Jesus will return to gather believers to Himself to spend an eternity with Him in heaven. See the promise in this verse of the reward coming to those who rightly receive His message:

> Blessed is the one who reads aloud the words of this prophecy, and blessed are those who hear, and who keep what is written in it, for the time is near. (Revelation 1:3)

Those who know of this prophecy and pass it on to others are blessed. Surely then the message to all believers is that we are to share what we know to be the truth of the gospel, that is, the truth of Jesus' arrival on earth and His life, death, and resurrection. He came to save us from our sins, and we are to "read aloud the words of this prophecy" so that all may hear and obey. It's one thing to know the truth, it's quite another to be so convinced of its validity that we gladly share it with those who have not heard. Given the critical nature of the gospel, we are to make telling others about Jesus the focus of our lives. In this verse then God promises to honor that obedience to His Word by blessing those who proclaim the gospel to those around them.

But it is not enough for anyone to just hear the gospel, we are to "keep" what we hear, that is, be consistently obedient to the gospel's message. Thus when we hear of Jesus' Lordship and sacrificial death in payment of our sin debt, we are to both believe and live out that belief, which includes sharing it. And why not? What more could a holy, loving God do for sinful mankind than to make salvation available through the sacrifice of His only Son, and then make provisions for that truth to be spread worldwide? God did that though provision of His Word, the Bible.

Many people skip the reading of Revelation because they maintain it is difficult to understand, and that is true. Notice, however, this passage tells us we are to read aloud this book. It does not say we are to completely explain every word. Could it be that we can benefit from simply hearing the words of this book? It means exactly that. God in His infinite wisdom constructs His Word such that even as bits and pieces of His words become clear to us we gain insight into His will for us, and direction for our lives. Over time then, we come to understand more and more of God's Word and are blessed because of it. So, with faith-filled obedience we are to study God's Word, with a prayer-filled heart that God's Holy Spirit would bless us with understanding.

And we are to do all this because "the time is near." What could that mean? It has been two thousand years since Jesus came and still He has not returned as He promised. But if we think about it, the time is near for us. We in today's society are two thousand years closer to Christ's return than those in the first century. And think of how many more people have come to believe in Christ (and have thus, been given eternal life) during all those years. That many more people will share eternity with Christ and know eternal joy.

And now we have the opportunity for salvation and eternal life. Hallelujah! Thank you, Lord!

COLOSSIANS 1:21-23

Here, Paul is writing to the church at Colossae, encouraging them to remain firm in their faith. He describes their "pre-" conversion condition and their "post-" conversion condition; the difference being their new hearts. Now, they have made Jesus Christ their Lord and Savior through His grace and their faith. His will, His way, and His motives now dominate their lives. To glorify the Father with their lives has become their life goals. As believers, we, too, are to live similar lifestyles. See the change that has come about in the lives of believers:

> And you, who once were alienated and hostile in mind, doing evil deeds, he has now reconciled in his body of flesh by his death, in order to present you holy and blameless and above reproach before him, if indeed you continue in the faith, stable and steadfast, not shifting from the hope of the gospel that you heard, which has been proclaimed in all creation under heaven, and of which I, Paul, became a minister. (Colossians 1:21–23)

Before conversion, unbelievers live unto themselves, not recognizing or considering the role God and others should play in their lives. The result is an alienated (from God) mind, hostility toward anything spiritual, and thus, evil, Satan-oriented deeds. There are only two approaches to life: Christ-oriented or Satan-oriented. While the vast majority of unbelievers imagine they live good lives, not seeking specifically to please an evil master, their lack of consideration of God's will in their decision making automatically drives their deeds in the direction of self-preservation and benefit. There is no thought of God's glory and majesty in their thinking process.

Notice how Paul speaks about Christ's actions given the self-orientation we are all born with. Christ reconciled in his "own body" (that is, His death on the cross) payment for all our sin debt. The only adequate payment for our sins was Jesus' sacrificial death, for He only lived a sinless life. And He accomplished the death of death through His resurrection. Because He rose from the grave so will we believers.

And thus, we are now alive in Christ, heaven-bound, with all our sins forgiven, making us holy, blameless, and above reproach before Him at the judgment. This, if we continue in the faith, stable and steadfast, not shifting in our beliefs or commitments. This is not to say that after conversion believers live sinless lives. We do not. But we don't live to sin or focus on sin completely as before, and we don't make Satan and his goals our Lord. It can be correctly said believers are not sin free, but they are forgiven, always sincerely repenting of their sins, seeking restoration. Their home already is heaven, and their focus is there. Our knowledge of the certainty of Christ's ongoing forgiveness makes us free indeed of the guilt and the penalty of sin.

Thus, it is the proclamation of this truth of Christ's atonement that we are designated to share with the nations. The good news of the gospel is for all creation in all eras. And why not? It is the greatest news the world will ever hear: eternal life available for all who will believe. We can and should go with joy-filled hearts spreading the word of God's love reflected in Jesus.

LUKE 1:8–9, 11–15

This passage is about a priest of Israel named Zechariah and his wife Elizabeth. They were old in years and childless. Although scripture tells us they were "righteous before God, walking blamelessly in all the commandments and statutes of the Lord" (v. 6) and though they had prayed for a child, they remained childless. Notice how God dealt with them concerning this unanswered prayer:

> Now while he was serving as priest before God when his division was on duty, according to the custom of the priesthood, he was chosen by lot to enter the temple of the Lord and burn incense. . . . And there appeared to him an angel of the Lord standing on the right side of the altar of incense. And Zechariah was troubled when he saw him, and fear fell upon him. But the angel said to him, "Do not be afraid, Zechariah, for your prayers have been heard, and your wife Elizabeth will bear you a son and you shall call his name John. And you will have joy and gladness, and many will rejoice at his birth, for he will be great before the Lord." (Luke 1:8–9, 11–15)

This child came into the world as a herald, John the Baptist, proclaiming the coming of Messiah to Israel. While we can understand such an assignment is of great importance in God's salvation plan for mankind, we might wonder what lesson this passage has for us. And there are several. In the first place this passage illustrates God does (always) hear our prayers. Though God's answer may be long in coming, and not in the format we had prayed about, God does commit to hearing and answering the prayers of His children. So yes, God will answer prayers, but is more likely to answer giving us what is best for us, rather than exactly what we requested. And sometimes that may be a no. Second, sometimes God clearly indicates to us what He intends to do, though likely not by sending an angel into our bedroom. It's more likely He would use some scripture passage of His, or a thought in a sermon you hear, or a word from a Christian friend, etc., to advise you that He has heard your prayer.

Third, many times God answers giving us a much greater blessing than we've requested. After all, the reason He answers at all is that He loves us with an infinite love, and thus, always wants the best for us. So no wonder that son Zechariah had prayed for came, and "was great before the Lord." Fourth, and probably most important, God shows us in this passage when He is answering your prayers, He also keeps the rest of the world in mind and what is best for them too. Only an all-powerful, infinitely loving God could and would see to integrating everyone's individual prayers into His plans for all of us.

God's love for us is overwhelming. His concern for us and our prayers is described beautifully in Psalm 56:8: "You have kept count of all my tossings; put my tears in your bottle." **Just picture that analogy, God collecting every one of our tears and preserving them, thus indicating that if a given issue is important to us it is important to Him. That's the kind of God we have.**

PROVERBS 1:20, 23, 32–33

God has plans for our lives and will not provide such plans without making us aware of every detail, providing everything we need to know that He would have us do. We can be sure He is all-wise, and all-powerful, and loves us with a steadfast love. We can trust that He knows what is best for us and always has our long-term good at heart. See what He says to us in this wisdom proverb:

> Wisdom cries aloud in the streets,
>   in the markets she raises her voice . . .
> "If you turn at my reproof,
> behold, I will pour out my spirit to you;
>   I will make my words known to you . . .
> For the simple are killed by their turning away,
>   and the complacency of fools destroys them;
> but whoever listens to me will dwell secure
>   and will be at ease without dread of disaster." (Proverbs 1:20,
>   23, 32–33)

Wisdom is pictured here as a woman crying out in the "everyday" places we go (streets, and markets), for us to listen and obey her words. Thus, God monitors all our activities and always knows where we are, and provides direction there. And He will certainly make His directions clear so that (if we are willing) we can respond positively to His will. Notice the promises He makes; He will pour out His spirit to us, and make His words known to us. **So God is not going to operate in secret in our lives.** HE WILL MAKE HIS WILL KNOWN. He does this through His Word, our prayers, and other people in our lives.

Notice, too, this passage tells us in a real way that it is dumb (simple-minded) to turn away from God, for it leads to death and destruction. On the other hand, if we "turn at His reproof," that is, turn back from disobedience, God will bless us. Those who are obedient will dwell secure (in this life) and live at ease without fear or dread of bad times. That does not mean that bad times will never come to those who are obedient, but it does mean God will be there when bad times do come to see us through them, and deliver us in ways we cannot envision now. So the idea of us having the faith to persevere in tough situations is inherent in this passage. And it is that kind of faith God wants to see in us, and that He will bless long-term.

So God would have us live out our faith in an ongoing kind of way: daily, faithfully, lovingly, and consistently being His hands and feet in this world. There are many needs among those who live around us, and God loves them too. He has chosen the approach of using His faithful children to minister to those in need, and/or those who are not aware of His love and provisions.

That's our role. And that's not bad news, it's good news; for given the many blessings we have received it is our privilege to be a part of sharing God's love with the world. That's one way we show our gratitude for His love and provisions for us.

LUKE 9:18-20

Perhaps the most important thing we need to know about Jesus Christ is His identity. If we could ever know for sure who He actually is, Son of God, Messiah, King of Kings and Lord of the Universe, then that overwhelming fact alone will draw us to Him in humble adoration, praise, honor, glory, and glad obedience. And if we could possibly add to that knowledge the complete understanding of the significance of His coming to earth as man, and why He came (to save us from our sins) then we could begin to give Him the position in our lives that He deserves. As this passage opens the disciples had been with Jesus several years at this point, and while they were gaining ground on identifying Jesus, they still had a ways to go. See this passage:

> Now it happened that as he was praying alone, the disciples were with him. And he asked them, "Who do the crowds say that I am?" And they answered, "John the Baptist. But others say, Elijah, and others, that one of the prophets of old has risen." Then he said to them, "But who do you say that I am?" And Peter answered, "The Christ of God." (Luke 9:18–20)

The passage indicates Jesus was praying alone, and the disciples came to Him. He had a question for them concerning His identity. It seems likely Jesus was praying for the disciples concerning that same subject, for Jesus was known to pray before significant events, and it is obviously critical that the disciples needed to properly understand His identity. Interestingly, even after His preaching and teaching and miracle working, the crowds still misidentified Him.

Now Peter, speaking for all the disciples, answered the question correctly. But did they really comprehend all that answer implied?

We can probably correctly conclude that at that point the answer is no. A number of later incidents seem to prove this. Shortly after this, Jesus told them for the first time He was going to be killed by the priests and raised on the third day. And somehow that fact did not register clearly the first time they heard it. About a week later three of them experienced the Transfiguration, and they did not respond as if that was as significant as it was. Later some of them failed in their attempt to heal a demon-possessed boy. Jesus identified the cause of that failure as weak faith. And they still argued among themselves as to who was the greatest among them. And there were other examples of Jesus' true identity that still eluded the disciples. **But praise the Lord, when they later saw the risen Lord, they did know who He is. And they lived out that certain knowledge.**

But who do we think Jesus is? And how does our answer correspond to our lifestyles? Does what we claim to believe concerning Jesus affect our burden for a lost world? Is making disciples very high on our to-do list? Our heavenly Father saw fit to include this question-and-answer session in scripture for a reason. The disciples answered Jesus' identity question correctly, but that was not enough to completely motivate them toward total obedience. We could answer that question correctly, too, but we also fall short of total obedience. So what do we do? **We believe, and we pray for greater belief.** See the answer below spoken by a father with a demon-possessed son who wanted Jesus' help: "Jesus said . . . 'All things are possible for one who believes.' Immediately the father of the child cried out and said, 'I believe; help my unbelief!'" (Mark 9:23–24).

That describes us, and our route to glorifying God.

1 JOHN 5:19–21

Clearly this letter is written to believers, those people who are already saved and heaven-bound forever. Yet this letter is full of warnings concerning living for and in Christ, His coming to earth to save us from our sins, and the danger Satan presents to all believers. John's readers in that day are not unlike believers today, saved but needing to be very cautious concerning their lifestyles. His letter is one of encouragement and assurance, full of correct doctrine and appropriate teachings; a letter to be read and reread, and perhaps most importantly, shared with believers everywhere. See John's summary of his message in these last several verses of the letter:

> We know that we are from God, and the whole world lies in the power of the evil one.
> And we know that the Son of God has come and has given us understanding, so that we may know him who is true; and we are in him who is true, in his Son Jesus Christ. He is the true God and eternal life. Little children, keep yourself from idols. (1 John 5:19–21)

John is confident of his salvation and is confident of the salvation of his readers too. And he points that out so as to leave them with that thought, and to give emphasis to what follows: a grave warning for readers in any era, "the whole world lies in the power of the evil one." Every believer needs to be aware of the danger of living in a world ruled by Satan. So, yes, we true believers are eternally saved, but we are still vulnerable to Satan's temptations, and still the target of his daily efforts to distort our principles and lessen our positive influence.

And why not? Who better for Satan to influence than those believers who are known to be such and have a following of people who look to them as examples? The best approach for Satan to bring down God's church would be to try to change the minds and hearts of its members before the world. Diluting the gospel message proclaimed by Christians is Satan's everyday purpose.

But we believers know who Christ is, and that He "has come and given us understanding" of the Fathers' love and provisions for eternal life. Thus, now we can know Him who is true, our heavenly Father. The subject of knowing God is the subject the whole world needs to address in spite of Satan's negative influences.

We believers don't just know God, we've experienced Him, we are in Him and in His Son Jesus Christ. This membership believers have in the family of God is a permanent one, not so much to be proud of, but to be grateful for. We do have access then to the Father, and the eternal life He provided through His Son and the cross.

And then comes the closing sentence of the letter, "Little children, keep yourself from idols." **What a powerful thought.** At first it might seem to be a complete change of subject, but it's not. Idolatry is the threat to belief in Christ. It is the obstacle that will keep us from knowing God. It is the reason lost individuals are lost. Putting anyone or anything between us and Christ and the Father is idolatry of the gravest sort. Idolatry literally defines unbelief in God and will reflect itself in all we do.

Let us take John's instructions to heart and keep ourselves from idols.

2 TIMOTHY 3:16–17

We find Paul here writing about the significance of scripture and how it may be used by believers to prepare them for "good works," and to guide them in their daily walk. It's no accident that God had Paul include these words in his letter to Timothy, for he would need them as well as every other believer. Thus, we can be confident of their appropriateness for us knowing they are God-inspired for our benefit. See how we all are to view scripture:

> All scripture is breathed out by God and profitable for teaching, for reproof, for correction, and for training in righteousness, that the man of God may be complete, equipped for every good work. (2 Timothy 3:16–17)

We notice several points Paul makes. First, he is referring to all scripture, the complete Bible. Second, he assumes Timothy and all believers (including us) will take advantage of their opportunities to study scripture and make that study an ongoing part of their spiritual growth. We can hardly expect to profit from the truths within scripture if we don't read and study it. And third, notice how Paul emphasizes God's role in scripture's origin: He breathed it out. What a vivid description of how deeply God was involved. It gives us the picture of God's truths coming from within Him directly to us.

Scripture is profitable for teaching. What an understatement. God's Word is, of course, the most important book we can ever study, with its revelation of God, and its inclusion of the way to eternal life. All of us are to be forever both students and teachers in God's spiritual school using His textbook. And scripture is also profitable for reproof, that we might use it to analyze our

Christian walk, for it provides the fundamental basis for criticism of our faults.

Scripture is designed to be our guide to correction. It contains the ultimate description of truth and provides the greatest possible example of truth in Jesus' words and life. There is no better standard to lay down beside our lives than Jesus' life, and no better set of values is to be found anywhere than those espoused by Jesus through scripture. Thus, by definition, scripture trains us for righteousness, following scriptural tenants leads us to Christlikeness, and obedience to scripture glorifies the Father. What a book, what a collection of truth, what a standard for us to live by and what an expression of love by our heavenly Father who provided it specifically for us, His children.

And what is the "why" God made His Word available to us? Paul answers that question for us: that we might be real Christians, that we might be competent believers, and that we might be equipped for every good work the Father might assign us.

So, what's our role? Our role first of all, is to begin. No matter where we are along life's path (old or young), what level of spiritual maturity we have reached (high or low), and what our personal environment might be (free or somehow enslaved), we are to begin. And we are to begin now to follow these four purposes Paul has outlined for the use of scripture. We are to apply them faithfully, consistently, and wholeheartedly to the extent we can, to do what scripture offers us, that is, prepare ourselves for good works which is God's will for our lives.

REVELATION 21:10–14

The apostle John wrote Revelation at the direction of the Holy Spirit. This section is titled "The New Jerusalem" and describes what that heavenly city will look like. We would expect God to build a beautiful city, and He surely does, far more elaborate than any man-made city. We cannot be sure if the description given here is literal or symbolic, but if it is symbolic, it is certainly symbolic of something amazing. See what the Holy Spirit has an angel show John:

> And he carried me away in the spirit to a great high mountain, and showed me the holy city Jerusalem coming down out of heaven from God, having the glory of God, its radiance like a most rare jewel, like a jasper, clear as crystal. It had a great high wall, with twelve gates, and at the gates twelve angels, and on the gates the names of the twelve tribes of the sons of Israel were inscribed—on the east three gates, on the north three gates, on the south three gates, and on the west three gates. And the wall of the city had twelve foundations, and on them were the twelve names of the twelve apostles of the Lamb. (Revelation 21:10–14)

And the city was built as a cube: 1,380 miles on each side and 1,380 miles high. And the walls were 96 feet high. See the list below of some of the characteristics of this new Jerusalem:

The wall was built of jasper
The city was pure gold
The foundations of the wall were adorned with every kind of jewel
There was no temple in the city, for its temple is the Lord
The city had no sun or moon to shine on it for the glory of God gives it light

Its lamp is the Lamb

Its gates will never be shut by day, and there will be no night there

Nothing unclean will enter it

The river of the water of life flows through it

The tree of life grows on either side of the river of life

The leaves of the tree of life are for the healing of the nations

The throne of God and of the Lamb will be in the city

They will reign forever and ever

No one will enter it accept those who are written in the Lamb's book of life

And the greatest blessing, we will see His face and His name will be written on our foreheads.

What takeaways can we get from this description? First and foremost is the ultimate glory and majesty of God the Father and Jesus the Lamb depicted. Second would have to be the infinite aspects of their reign—it's forever and ever. And third would be the splendor of the provisions that have been made for those they love, that's us believers, children in the family of God. Every promise ever made to believers is to be fulfilled. **Just imagine the joy, the peace, and the rest of having almighty God and the Lamb look on us with favor forever.**

PSALM 112:1-3

Scripture is full of wisdom literature of all types, so rich and relevant that if we are not careful, we are apt to read it and pass right over truth that we need to apply in our lives. Truth, God has put there seemingly just for us. Such is this passage from Psalm 112. Here the psalmist focuses on the moral character of believers and how such people bring blessings to themselves, their families, and other people in their own generation and generations coming after them. See what is declared for us here:

> Praise the LORD!
> Blessed is the man who fears the LORD,
>   who greatly delights in his commandments!
> His offspring will be mighty in the land;
>   the generation of the upright will be blessed.
> Wealth and riches are in his house,
>   and his righteousness endures forever. (Psalm 112:1–3)

The psalmist has praising God on his heart, and he is about to tell us why. He is excited because the Lord has given him an awesome principle that should be passed on to others. Here he announces that those people who fear the Lord are blessed for they delight in God's commandments. "Fear" as used here means those people respect God, they give Him (and His holiness, power, and sovereignty) reverence, and credibility in their lives. They obviously gladly study and work to obey God's commandments. Therefore, their lives reflect such priorities and it consistently shows in their decisions and influence.

Thus, other people, especially their families, are blessed by their example. The psalmist describes their influence as being mighty (in its good effect), and the lessons they've taught as being worth more than earthly wealth and riches to those who come after them. The psalmist is telling us that the wisdom and diligence God provides for the righteous are how He provides for their material needs and those of their families. And even better the psalmist describes the ripple effect when those same life principles are instilled in those they influence for generations to come. Thus, such a blessed person's righteousness endures forever. Our lives really can have eternal consequences due to God's provisions.

So we see how the world's wealth is not a proper goal, but God's righteousness is. Such a goal has everlasting ramifications in the lives of those around us, and best of all God is glorified in the process.

MATTHEW 21:18–22

At one point in His ministry Jesus saw fit to curse a fig tree because it bore no fruit. It appeared to be a fruit-bearing tree, but upon close inspection by Jesus there was no fruit on it. See this episode as it played out in Jesus' day, and the ramifications of it in our day:

> In the morning, as he was returning to the city, he became hungry. And seeing a fig tree by the wayside, he went to it and found nothing on it but only leaves. And he said to it, "May no fruit ever come from you again!" and the fig tree withered at once.
>
> When the disciples saw it, they marveled, saying, "How did the fig tree wither at once?" And Jesus answered them, "Truly, I say to you, if you have faith and do not doubt, you will not only do what has been done to the fig tree, but even if you say to this mountain, 'Be taken up and thrown into the sea,' it will happen. And whatever you ask in prayer, you will receive, if you have faith." (Matthew 21:18–22)

There are two major lessons we can take from this story. The first has to do with the hypocrisy involved with people who appear to be "fruit-bearing" believers, but they are not. They claim to love the Lord, but their lives do not reflect that fact "lived out." They dress the part, they are often seen at church, and they tithe of their income. When seen only at a distance, like the fig tree, we get a wrong impression. Notice Jesus' reaction to the barren fig tree: He cursed it and it died. The fruit in a believer's life would be disciples. Jesus specifically tells us to go and make disciples. He even commits to always going with us as we go (Matthew 28:18–20). Thus, when we disobey this command, we are without excuse.

The second lesson evident in this story has to do with the importance of faith in our lives. The disciples were surprised at the results of Jesus cursing the fig tree. Such an immediate withering was evidence of two things: the importance Jesus gave to fig trees (and us) producing what they are supposed to produce and the power of faith. There are a lot of things in scripture Jesus commands us to do that are very clear, like love the Lord your God with all your heart, soul, and mind, go and make disciples, love your neighbor as you love yourself, pray without ceasing, and many more. We might think doing these things well is an impossibility given all the distractions and temptations we face. Yet clearly in this passage we see God incarnate telling us they are doable if we have faith and do not doubt; not to mention all the other prayer requests we have such as praying for the sick, the lost, the poor, the hungry, the oppressed, etc. **Jesus Christ, Son of God, creator of the universe, has told us faith is the key to having all those prayers answered. How then could we possibly doubt this fact?**

At the very least then, this passage should encourage us to sincerely pray for increased faith and specific direction in praying proper prayers seeking God's involvement. Without question the almighty God who created us all will surely hear such prayers since He has so clearly indicated how important faith is.

2 TIMOTHY 4:7–8

Paul is writing from a Roman prison to his disciple Timothy. He knows his time is short, and he won't have many more opportunities to communicate. So, he urges him to keep the faith and continue the ministry he has already begun. To make it clear to Timothy, here, near the end of his letter, Paul describes his own situation. We, too, might well take Paul's advice, for the same truths Paul has lived out and is preaching to Timothy apply to us in our day. Notice Paul's confidence in his eternal destiny. As believers we have that same destiny.

> I have fought the good fight, I have finished the race, I have kept the faith. Henceforth there is laid up for me the crown of righteousness, which the Lord, the righteous judge, will award to me on that day, and not only to me but also to all who have loved his appearing. (2 Timothy 4:7–8)

Paul has "fought the good fight," his efforts (against much opposition) to share the truth of God's provision of eternal life to all who believe in Jesus. Paul had traveled the known world sharing the love of God with all he met. He has completed the assignment to take the gospel to the Gentiles Jesus gave him that day on the road to Damascus. And he has not wavered in his faith but consistently suffered hunger, thirst, imprisonment, cold, fatigue, and loneliness, not to mention, storms at sea, beatings, stoning, and one shipwreck.

Thus, he is assured of his final reward. He knows his future contains a "crown of righteousness." That crown is one he merits for his perseverance in the faith, and involves his position with Christ reigning forever in heaven. And Paul knows it will be Christ, the righteous judge, who grants that promised crown.

651

Amazingly, that same God who loves us enough to send His only Son to earth to die a sinner's death in our place, also works in us the will to come to Christ in obedience and love. "For it is God who works in you, both to will and to work for his good pleasure" (Philippians 2:13). The apostle Matthew describes that same destiny for believers in his letter: "Rejoice and be glad, for your reward is great in heaven, for so they persecuted the prophets who were before you" (Matthew 5:12).

And, praise the Lord, Paul assures us that same reward accrues to all believers. How can we deny a God who makes such eternal provisions for us and also draws us to Him in belief?

It's likely Paul had no idea how God would use his letters to spread the good news of the gospel all over the world centuries after his death. If he had known, it would not have surprised him for he knew Jesus as Lord of the universe, he knew the gospel message was eternal in scope, and he knew God's love for mankind was steadfast and never ending. We know those same things, and neither should we be surprised at what our great God can and will do with our meager efforts.

Thus, like Paul we are to fight the good fight. A wise pastor once preached a sermon with three points that describe Paul's ministry. We are to start where we are, use what we've got, and do what we can. That's what God expects of us too. **And He will help us along the way. Pray for that help.**

EPHESIANS 2:8-10

If there is anything we need as lost individuals in this world, it's to learn the way to eternal life. Born as sinners, we are hell-bound if we don't find our way to Christ. God knows this better than we do and has made only one provision for our salvation. That provision involves Him sending His only Son Jesus Christ to earth to save us from our sins. Sinless, Jesus Christ died the death we deserve for our sins, and offered that sacrifice for all who would believe in Him. The church at Ephesus needed to hear this truth no more and no less than we do. So, the Holy Spirit led Paul to outline the way to eternal life for the Ephesians, and preserved that letter in scripture for us. It only takes a few sentences to outline the best news the world has ever heard for all to read and understand.

> For by grace you have been saved through faith. And this is not your own doing; it is the gift of God, not a result of works, so that no one may boast. For we are his workmanship, created in Christ Jesus for good works, which God prepared beforehand, that we should walk in them. (Ephesians 2:8–10)

There you have it, the only way to eternal life. God's grace, that is, the undeserved love we have from Him, prompted Him to send Jesus to die a sinner's death on the cross for all who would believe in Him. Notice this action on God and Jesus' part is a gift, not anything of our own doing. And yet it entails the greatest present mankind could ever receive. And by our God-given faith we can acquire it.

The Holy Spirit has Paul remind his readers in Ephesus they are God's workmanship. He made them and us in His own image. And He had a reason for doing this: to put mankind in place to carry out God's earthly plan for good works, which He has planned ahead of time for us to do. He intends that we should walk in them. What could that mean except that we believers are destined to carry out God's plan on earth? We need to understand clearly that God's plan is the plan for all mankind. There is only one. Everything that has ever happened or will ever happen, has come about because God willed it. Nothing we do surprises God. It will be God's plan that plays out on earth down to the smallest detail.

We have a choice to receive God's free gift of eternal life or not. And we very clearly can say no to the movement of the Holy Spirit in our hearts. At the same time, God knows what choices we will make and has predestined some for eternal life. **So, yes, we get to completely make the call on our relationship with Christ, and He has already made the call on what we will decide.** If that doesn't compute in our worldly way of thinking, that's true. It does not compute using our logic. But God doesn't use our logic. **Both those concepts are taught in scripture and therefore both are true.**

Rather than engage in endless debate of those two principles, we simply by faith need to accept them both as true, and receive God's free gift of eternal life, and be about living out our faith. When we turn our lives over to Christ, He engages the Holy Spirit with our spirit who guides us to live the lives He would have us live. God's overall plan for this world has a special place within it for each believer. God really meant it when He had Paul write that God prepared our good works beforehand for us to live out.

Pray for God to guide you as you travel His life plan for you. He wants you to do that. See Jeremiah 29:11: "For I know the plans I have for you, declares the LORD, plans for welfare and not for evil, to give you a future and a hope."

2 TIMOTHY 2:11–13

To be saved and thus destined to spend an eternity with the Lord in heaven, we simply need to establish a relationship with Christ. This has always been the (only) way to salvation. In this passage, Paul the apostle is writing to Timothy, a young man he had led to the Lord. Paul's goal is to remind Timothy, and have him teach others, about this relationship to Christ that we all need. See how God has Paul word this concept about how we are to relate to Jesus Christ:

> If we have died with him, we will also live with him;
> if we endure, we will also reign with him;
> if we deny him, he also will deny us;
> if we are faithless, he remains faithful—
> for he cannot deny himself. (2 Timothy 2:11–13)

To die with Jesus is to give ourselves over to Him with all we are and all we ever hope to be. If we are saved there has been a moment in time when we chose to follow Jesus. There is a point in our lives when we make a conscious choice to do this. Before that point we lived to "self," and our own goals, wishes, and desires. After that point His will, His way, and His example become our marching orders, and the whole world will see the difference in us. Because of that new relationship we see our past lives laid down alongside Jesus' "perfection" leading to our sincere repentance of our sins. We then receive God's free gift of eternal life and live with Him thereafter in this world and eternally in heaven.

And if we endure throughout the rest of our lives in that relationship, we will not only enjoy heaven with the Lord, we will reign there with Him. We understand the word *reign* in the sense we see it play out in the life of a king or queen in this world. Those people are born into that role, and in the best sense we are born again into that kind of role. We can hardly envision what that will look like in heaven, but we do know that it will be wonderful and eternally joy-filled.

On the other hand, if we deny Christ, He will deny us. To deny Him is to deny Jesus' deity, to deny His love for us, and to deny His journey to earth to live as a man, eventually dying a sinner's death on the cross to pay our sin debt. And it means we do not believe He conquered death by rising from the grave to live forever in heaven. And it means we will stand in judgment one day before Jesus.

And if we are "faithless," Jesus will not be faithless. He will be as faithful and forgiving as His nature allows, never changing in His grace-filled love and mercy for us. So as born-again believers we do continue to sin, but the difference now is we are remorseful about those sins, and we seek God's face in sincere repentance for those sins, asking for His mercy and forgiveness, **which He always provides.** This, because Jesus cannot ever be anything but the perfectly merciful and forgiving Savior that He has always been. Thus, once saved, our salvation is secure and we can rest easy in that security, with ever increasing joy-filled anticipation of an eternity with the Lord. That's the kind of God we have.

2 CORINTHIANS 13:11

In this letter Paul is writing to the church at Corinth in an effort to solidify their faith, and to unify them all in their attitudes toward him as their apostle and founder, and toward each other as brothers and sisters in Christ. He is on the way to see them and is preparing them for his visit so as to minimize any conflicts any of them might have concerning the validity of his ministry and their own relationships with other believers. This verse at the very end of his letter summarizes Paul's prayers for them, and the message of his letter. It also expresses how we in our day should feel and act toward other believers and God's word as our authority.

> Finally, brothers, rejoice. Aim for restoration, comfort one another, agree with one another, live in peace; and the God of love and peace will be with you. (2 Corinthians 13:11)

Bottom line, the Corinthians (and we) can and should rejoice, that is, recognize we are heaven-bound believers, relax, and be confident of what we have in Christ, and let that confidence play out in our decision making and our relationships with other believers and nonbelievers. "Aim for restoration" where it is needed, be open to it, ready to forgive (and forget) slights and trespasses against us. Jesus' model prayer mentions this concept: "forgive us our debts, as we also have forgiven our debtors" (Matthew 6:12). This is an "everyday" requirement for us all.

And "comfort one another." To really comfort one another we need to know about one another, and to have empathy and sympathy for each other. This requires ongoing prayers and interest in what others are experiencing, both good and bad. Notice we are also to "agree with one another." To do so would mean we understand their positions and the "why" of their words and actions, and that we are open to change and edification and not so fixed in our opinions and priorities that we cannot be corrected.

And in summary we are to "live in peace." Living in peace speaks of humility, of willingness to pardon, and having hearts ready to love at every opportunity. There should be a desire for harmony and peace among believers if nowhere else in the world. How else could we best exhibit likeness to Christ? Christ's kind of peace is more than an "absence of conflict," but an ongoing, proactive search for mutual love and respect.

And notice the result of obedience to these five exhortations: "the God of love and peace will be with you." Paul wrote that sentence, but it is truly God speaking through him. **What a wonderful fundamental goal for us all to have, God with us.** That fact gives purpose and meaning to this whole letter. It makes it relevant to every generation of people everywhere. For God to be with us is to know Him, to respect Him, and to love Him, and to have Him on our hearts all the time. And it means we expect Him to be present in our lives, and want Him to be present in our lives. And it means Him being present in our lives will show, other people will see Jesus in us.

MATTHEW 14:25–27

At one point in His ministry Jesus and His disciples were in a desolate place near the Sea of Galilee teaching to a large crowd. In the evening that day, Jesus dismissed the crowd and sent His disciples by boat to the other side of the sea while He went up on the mountain alone to pray. During the night a storm arose while the disciples were far from shore and the wind and waves began to beat upon their boat. See this passage for how Jesus used this opportunity to teach lessons to the disciples and us:

> And in the fourth watch of the night he came to them, walking on the sea. But when the disciples saw him walking on the sea, they were terrified, and said, "It is a ghost!" and they cried out in fear. But immediately Jesus spoke to them, saying, "Take heart, it is I. Do not be afraid." (Matthew 14:25–27)

Now the fourth watch was from 3 a.m. until 6 a.m. so the disciples had been battling the heavy seas (rowing hard and bailing water) for about nine hours. Even though they were good sailors and knew the Sea of Galilee well, they were now obviously soaking wet and very tired. Add to this the fact they were alone. Jesus was not with them. Now picture them seeing someone coming to them, walking on the water. It is easy to imagine them "crying out in fear" thinking it was a ghost.

When someone is terrified to the point of screaming in fear, they have "bottomed out" with regard to their own capabilities to deal with what they are experiencing. We may feel this way sometimes when life seems to come at us with one problem after another, each one of which threatens to overwhelm us. And our solution is the same solution Jesus gives to the disciples in their distress. He tells them He is there, "Take heart, do not be afraid." **And that's what we need to remember too.**

Really these are two points of encouragement and two commands: "Take heart" and "Do not be afraid." First, we are to renew our faith, what we've always believed concerning God loving us and being there for us, is still true, even in our bad times. And we are not to be afraid. To be afraid is to give way to the feeling that God is either not interested in helping us, or is interested, but is unable to help. Of course, we know better, neither of those conditions is true. Yet still, sometimes our physical condition, and the circumstances we find ourselves in, cause us to feel helpless and very much alone (like those disciples felt).

But praise the Lord, as believers we are never alone, and our God is almighty, and best of all, He loves us with a steadfast love. So in the worst of times (and even in the best of times) our God is both available and He is able to deal with our situations. And He wants us to remember that, to take courage in that, and to share that truth with other believers. What a great witness to the world it is when believers "walk" through tough times in faith. So don't waste a trial. Use it to glorify your God who loves you.

2 CORINTHIANS 6:1–2

This passage is part of Paul's discussion of his ministry with the members of the church at Corinth, Greece. He is urging them to make the Lord's work a priority in their lives. He calls himself a "workman with God" for His glory's sake. And it is work, there is an "up early and out late" context to the Christian lifestyle then and now. There is a sense communicated in Paul's letter that believers work with God, not the reverse. The implication then is it's God's agenda that they work on together. It is His glory that is to be uppermost in the minds and hearts of believers. And the task is huge. Everywhere they looked there were needs, people lost without Christ, who needed to hear of His provision for their eternal life. See how the Holy Spirit puts this message in Paul's heart:

> Working together with him, then, we appeal to you not to receive the grace of God in vain. For he says, "In a favorable time I listened to you, and in a day of salvation I helped you." Behold, now is the favorable time; behold, now is the day of salvation. (2 Corinthians 6:1–2)

Paul feels led to disciple the Corinthian Christians. He had planted the church, and is engaged now in discipling them into their kingdom work role. Scholars are not in agreement as to whether this is Paul's second, third, or fourth letter to the Corinthian believers, but it is obvious he cares about them and wants them to grow spiritually. Thus, he appeals to them (this phrase is interpreted "pleads with them" in some translations) to recognize the significance of what God has provided them. The concept of God's grace is huge when believers (then and now) consider their total depravity and unworthiness of God's love. And yet God's love spans the gap sin made between them and Him, defining grace then as God's unmerited favor for lost sinners. Thus, Paul sincerely calls on his believing readers not to receive this gift in vain, that is, with less than an appropriate response to God's love, and Jesus' sacrifice at Calvary.

Then Paul quotes from Isaiah 49:8 tying Isaiah's Old Testament's call to Israel to repent and persevere in their faith to his first-century plea along the same lines to believers in that era. It's easy to relate this message as relevant in our day, too, for believers now who sense the same fears, doubts, and frustrations that the Corinthians did.

See the sequence of God's involvement covered in this passage. Moses, at God's direction, leads the Israelites out of slavery in Egypt in about 1500 BC. Isaiah writes about it in about 700 BC. Paul then references Isaiah's words in the first century AD. And now in the twenty-first century AD we are reminded again of God's work on behalf of His chosen people. So, for about thirty-five hundred years we see God consistently speaking to believers to join Him in His work.

Is there any doubt that God has a plan, and that His grace is still in place? Do we dare to question God's love so evident for all these years? Should we ever even wonder about joining with other believers in God's work? Do we regularly look at our lives and consider what God has done for us already? Obviously, God loves us with an undying love and can and does see to our needs. We've been recipients of God's provisions for our whole lives. Yet many people don't know or seem to care about God's provisions. Surely, God would have us join Him and live out our assigned role.

ROMANS 6:22–23

Sometimes we read the same scripture passage over and over and then when we see and read it again we find there is something there we have not seen before. We don't know how we missed it, but plainly God has opened our hearts in a different way this time and we learn something new, something God has in mind for us at this exact point in our lives. I know you have experienced that, and I cannot help but wonder if this isn't one of those times. I've just been praying the Holy Spirit would show me the passage He wants me to send to you tonight and He definitely showed me this one:

> But now that you have been set free from sin and have become slaves of God, the fruit you get leads to sanctification and its end, eternal life. For the wages of sin is death, but the gift of God is eternal life in Christ Jesus our Lord. (Romans 6:22–23)

The passage begins "But now" something has changed. The reference is that now after their conversion and after they have become slaves not to the world, but to God, they, and we, accrue fruit from their labors. That idea sort of screams at us how important God's will is to us now that we have made Jesus Christ our Lord and Savior. What sort of fruit is Paul talking about? He means that fruit which comes as a result of our transformation. What comes is sanctification, the perfection in Christ the Holy Spirit supplies. It's that process of our becoming ever more Christlike over time. Our perspective on life and the world has changed, our worldview is not the one we used to have, but God's. As believers we now have a new destiny, heaven with the Lord forever.

And there is a reason for this. It's the godly axiom that the "wages of sin is death, but the gift of God is eternal life in Christ

Jesus our Lord." When we sin it's work, and work implies wages for that work. We work to "dream up" sin, and we work to cover it up afterwards. No wonder we wind up tired, depressed, and humiliated. We work at sin, and we are paid what we earn, death. On the other hand, God's gift to believers is eternal life. Not just eternal life, but eternal life in the presence of God our maker, creator, redeemer, Lord, and friend.

Working as a slave of God would be the best way to live even if the gift of eternal life was not the result. But praise the Lord, eternal life is the result due to God's provision of Christ's death in our place to pay our sin debt for us. Surely there is someone in your life who needs to know of God's provision for them.

1 Corinthians 16:22–23

The apostle Paul was a traveling missionary. During the first century AD, he traveled the known world preaching the good news of Jesus Christ, mostly in those countries surrounding the Mediterranean Sea. He planted many churches and usually stayed with them for a while training Christian workers, and helping them get the churches started so they would continue to grow after he left. Often, he would later write them letters answering doctrinal questions they might have and encouraging them to stay strong in their faith. This letter was the first of several letters he wrote to the church he planted in Corinth, Greece. These verses are at the very end of that letter and indicate his love for them:

> If anyone has no love for the Lord, let him be accursed. Our Lord, come! The grace of the Lord Jesus be with you. My love be with you all in Christ Jesus. Amen. (1 Corinthians 16:22–23)

Paul minces no words when he speaks of the importance of love for the Lord. Jesus Christ is Lord, Son of God, who came to earth to save us from our sins. He loves us with an everlasting love and is absolutely worthy of all our love, praise, adoration, and obedience. When mankind ignores or denies the love of Jesus, they are accursed and earn God's wrath and eternal separation from Him. Paul's last words in the letter remind the Corinthians and us of that truth. Christ has returned to heaven after His resurrection and will one day come again to earth to gather those who have believed in Him and take them to heaven to live eternally with Him. So, alive or dead, believers will one day be lifted to new life in Christ. Paul looks forward to that day, and prays for the Lord to return soon.

The grace Paul refers to has to do with the love the Lord has for us that we do not deserve, but that He bestows on us only because of His forgiving love. There is a well-known, Christian song called "Amazing Grace" that beautifully describes the Lord's grace as amazing. So, Paul reminds his readers of the importance of grace and that grace is the source of their eternal security.

A noted Christian pastor and author named Samuel Rutherford puts this whole notion of God's love for us and our love back to him in proper perspective: "My desire is that the Lord will give me broader and deeper thoughts to feed myself with wondering at His love. I wish I could weight it, but I have no balance for it. When I have worn my tongue to the stump, I have done nothing to Him. What remains then but that my debt to the love of Christ lie unpaid for all eternity."

Paul could not wish anything more important on the Corinthians than the grace of the Lord Jesus. That applies to us as well. Paul loved those Corinthian believers and while his letter rebuked them to a great degree, it was out of a loving heart that he wrote.

We, too, need more appreciation for the love of God and Jesus' grace.

1 JOHN 3:16-18

Throughout the whole Bible we find the teaching we are to love one another. We easily understand that's God's will, and the way He would have us live. Yet we see so much of the very opposite in the world around us. Consciously or subconsciously, we know what that "love one another" concept looks like in someone's life. Thus, we are without excuse when it comes to following God's plan ourselves. It's to be worked out day by day in every situation. See how John words this theme:

> By this we know love, that he laid down his life for us, and we ought to lay down our lives for the brothers. But if anyone has the world's goods and sees his brother in need, yet closes his heart against him, how does God's love abide in him? Little children, let us not love in word or talk but in deed and in truth. (1 John 3:16–18)

The "this" in the first verse points us to what follows: "that he laid down his life for us." John is referring to the love Jesus displayed when He laid down His life for us on the cross. And therefore, we can know what love looks like as we clearly see Jesus' example. We can be sure then that God loves us, and we can be confident that His love never fails. And it follows that if Jesus provided such a clear example, we are to live that same way. But we might ask what exactly does John mean when he says we are to "lay down our lives for our brothers"? It has to mean that we are to care to the extent of love, and to the extent of becoming involved physically.

John provides us an example of what that will look like. It has to do with our sharing the world's goods we have with those we see in need. We don't use the phrase "closed heart" very often, but we certainly get the picture here of turning away from those in need and not providing for their needs. John tells us such denial of help is reflective of that individual not abiding in God's love. To abide in God's love means to sense God's love within us, and to do so secure in that love to the point we confidently display it, and share it with others. Thus, to deny a person's needs is to demonstrate we are not living and acting as God does and as He would have us live.

So, John draws the proper conclusion for us. We are to love not in word or talk, but in deed and in truth. Our lives are to reflect the same love for others that God has for us. And that is a consistent love, a love that does not vary with time or situation, and a love that does not choose whom we will or will not love.

James 2:15–16 speaks to this same conclusion: "If a brother or sister is poorly clothed and lacking in daily food, and one of you says to them, 'Go in peace, be warmed and filled,' without giving them the things needed for the body, what good is that?"

Thus, we know what we are to do, and we are told to do so in truth. That is, we are to do these deeds gladly, without reluctance, for God's glory, not ours, being prepared to do so again without being judgmental. Not an easy assignment, but one that reflects godliness in us. Doesn't God do this same thing for us?

REVELATION 1:4-6

John the apostle is writing to the seven churches in Asia, reminding them of the triune God they worship, and of His ongoing love and support for them. This "Revelation" of unseen future events is to encourage his readers (then and now) in their faith and in their commitment to obedience to the commandments reflected in this letter. Thus, there is much for us to learn (and share) from what we will find in Revelation. Notice John begins this passage by describing the source of the grace and peace he wishes upon his readers:

> John to the seven churches that are in Asia: Grace to you and peace from him who is and who was and who is to come, and from the seven spirits who are before his throne, and from Jesus Christ the faithful witness, the firstborn of the dead, and the ruler of kings on earth. To him who loves us and has freed us from our sins by his blood and made us a kingdom, priests to his God and Father, to him be glory and dominion forever and ever. Amen. (Revelation 1:4–6)

Notice at the outset of this letter John claims power to bless his readers by calling into play the Trinity, the three-in-one God they worship: God the Father, the Holy Spirit, and Jesus Christ, the Son. First, it's not enough to speak of God the Father as just the God who is, or just the God who was, or just the God who is to come. We must strive to see Him as John does, as "all of the above," and recognize the "all in all" nature of His love, power, and provision for us.

Secondly, notice John references the Holy Spirt as "the seven spirits that are before his throne." This is taken from where Isaiah speaks of the Holy Spirit indwelling the future King David, and all seven traits characterizing Jesus Christ, Messiah. David is that "shoot" from his father Jesse, and Jesus is that "branch" that comes via David's line that bears the prophesied "fruit" of salvation for all who believe.

> There shall come forth a shoot from the stump of Jesse,
>   and a branch from his roots shall bear fruit.
> And the Spirit of the LORD shall rest upon him,
>   the Spirit of wisdom and understanding,
>   the Spirit of counsel and might,
>   the Spirit of knowledge and the fear of the LORD. (Isaiah 11:1–2)

And third, John describes Jesus and tells his readers and us who Jesus is and what He has done. Jesus is the faithful witness, also the firstborn of the dead, and ruler of (all) kings on earth. Jesus has already loved us, freed us from our sins by His blood (shed on the cross to pay our sin debt) and made us a kingdom, priest to Jesus' God and Father. So, it is to Jesus Christ we owe our salvation, our allegiance, our obedience, and our love. It is His gospel that we are to live out personally and that we are to share with the nations. All this via God's prefect plan of salvation and through the direction on the Holy Spirit who dwells within all believers. And praise the Lord, Jesus is coming back one day to gather believers "to himself" to spend an eternity with Him in heaven.

What better source of grace and peace could John call down on his readers than his triune God? What better source of grace and peace could we call down on ourselves and those we love than that very same triune God?

LUKE 9:26

God would have us establish a lasting relationship with Him; one that is both permanent and apparent in our lives. If it is permanent but doesn't show in our lives, how could it be real? If it is apparent, but temporary, we know God is not in it. So let us "take stock" of the relevance of Jesus Christ in our lives, and be honest with ourselves as we do. For this is serious business for us and those we influence. See this conclusion Jesus provides for us to consider:

> For whoever is ashamed of me and my words, of him will the Son of Man be ashamed when he comes in his glory and the glory of the Father and of the holy angels. (Luke 9:26)

We are well advised to be very clear on what being ashamed of Jesus and His words involves. It surely means first being aware of Him and His message, but not giving any credence to either as we live and make decisions in our lives. Such an attitude would not necessarily mean denying Jesus before the world. It could well simply include having knowledge of Him, and opportunity to give witness to that knowledge in appropriate situations and failing to do so. And the "why" of that failure and missed opportunity is part of this whole process. Why would we ever have knowledge and opportunity to witness and not do so? Are we afraid of something? What could that something be? And how does that "something" compare with almighty God and His will for our lives? And what of the eternal destiny of those we meet who are lost, and leave them still lost? Do we not owe them an opportunity to believe?

And surely being ashamed of Jesus Christ and His words also includes actual denial of Jesus before others. The classic example of this is Peter in the chief priest's house when he denied knowing Jesus at all three different times. This, while Jesus was only a few feet away being "tried" by the Jewish leadership. It's unlikely that we've ever been called on to acknowledge Christ in a pressurized situation as Peter was. But some people have been, and some have died for the stance they took. **So it is appropriate for us to consider the depth of our commitment to Christ.**

Notice the obvious reference in this verse to a day of accounting, a day when Jesus in all His majesty, honor, and glory (and that of the Father) will arrive in splendor to judge the world. For Him to be ashamed of anyone on that day has to involve Him denying them any place in His kingdom, any presence with Him in heaven eternally. And, of course, such a separation would be defined as hell for those individuals.

The very good news, however, is that God forgives such actions on our part. Oh, hallelujah for God's grace, that love He has for us that we don't deserve. Hallelujah for another chance. After His resurrection Jesus asked Peter three times, "Do you love me?" (perhaps once for each denial). Peter assured Jesus that he did. Jesus' words to Peter then were, "Follow me" (John 21:15–19). Those words are key, sinners though we be, at any point we are to repent and start again to FOLLOW JESUS.

ISAIAH 7:9

The timing of this passage is about 740 BC when the Jewish nation was divided into two kingdoms, Israel in the north and Judah in the south. Ahaz was king in Judah and Isaiah was prophesying there. At that time, Israel, under King Pekah, joined forces with King Rezin of Syria to fight against Assyria and together they tried to intimidate King Ahaz to join with them. Isaiah's counsel for Ahaz came from the Lord: Judah should not join that alliance. It was temporary and would not last. At one point in his conversation with King Ahaz, Isaiah urged him to keep the faith, and he worded that truth in a very specific way that rings true in our day too:

> If you are not firm in faith, you will not be firm at all. (Isaiah 7:9)

This verse very clearly advises us of the importance of our relationship with God. It speaks of our faith in God, as being the cornerstone of our position on any issue or circumstance. Believers are to live out their faith. As it turns out Ahaz not only did not join with Israel and Syria against Assyria, but he also sought, and got support from Assyria. Later when Israel and Syria sent their armies against Jerusalem, God protected Judah and they failed to capture Jerusalem. Ahaz therefore might well have assumed his plan worked, but history proved him wrong. Jerusalem was saved, but Ahaz lost potential blessings for dealing intimately with the evil men in Assyria, men who did not believe in the Jehovah God Isaiah worshipped.

We see that same sort of result in our day. We sometimes see what we think are good things happening for the wrong reasons, or accomplished by ungodly methods from ungodly men. Not only is God perfect, His ways are perfect too. Thus, Ahaz believed

Isaiah's counsel, but did not believe in the principles and basic truths behind Isaiah's counsel. **Why and how we do what we do is as important as what we do.** Glorifying God then, in all our ways, is to be our ultimate goal in everything. If Ahaz had understood that, he would never have sought help from Assyria against Israel and Syria. If we understood that truth, we would look deeper into the ramifications of what is apt to result from everything we do and say.

Notice how the verse above gives priority to firm faith. It is as if when we are not firm in faith, nothing we say or do will be faith-oriented at all. Notice the verse above also implies we can have faith and it not be firm. And if weak faith is potentially possible, then we can be sure Satan is supporting it and proposing it for us. And it is only firm faith that stands the tests of temptations and trials. And it is surely firm faith that God wants us to exhibit. And if that's true, **we can be sure God will provide us firm faith if we ask Him.**

And that's what prayer is all about: going to the Lord consistently with requests that are in sync with His will. We certainly get the idea from this passage that if we don't have firm faith in God we won't be stabilized in any worthwhile thing. The concept we need to sincerely grasp is God loves us. And He does so with a love so strong it is capable of completely forgiving our worst trespasses. Isaiah told King Ahaz he need not fear these ungodly neighboring countries and their intentions. And we need not fear such evil influences in our lives either. Firm faith is our answer and God's Holy Spirit is the source of such faith. Thus, if firm faith brings such special benefits to every aspect of our lives, are we not wise to take Isaiah's (and God's) counsel?

MATTHEW 6:13

In Jesus' Model Prayer, we see a petition for God to protect us in our struggle with sin and evil. Jesus knew we would need the Holy Spirit's help in this area, and He wants us to always keep that in mind. We might be tempted not to pray Jesus' Model Prayer because it is so familiar to us that it may not occur to us how very relevant it is. Jesus' actual words as He instructs His disciples (and really us) to pray were, "Pray then like this," and then He recited the prayer He wants us to pray. If Jesus said those words, then He must mean this prayer is always appropriate. See this portion of it concerning our sin.:

> And lead us not into temptation, but deliver us from evil. (Matthew 6:13)

We are then to pray to be spared from difficult situations that would tempt us to sin. God does not tempt us, but He does allow us to experience testing times. We know that all believers do have times of trial and heartache. James tells us how to react to them: "Count it all joy, my brothers, when you meet trials of various kinds, for you know that the testing of your faith produces steadfastness. And let steadfastness have its full effect, that you may be perfect and complete, lacking in nothing" (James 1:2–3).

To be steadfast is to be firm in belief, not subject to change. We can be sure the Lord wants us to be steadfast in our faith. And anything we can do to improve our steadfastness of belief will grow us spiritually. When we do experience trials, we know the Lord has something He wants us to learn. That may be harder to acknowledge than to carry out. But if we can mentally "step away" and look back at our trials sometimes we can get a better overall picture of those trials and how God would have us react to them.

Of course, we are also to pray for wisdom and perspective to "see" what God would have us learn. The point is, be sure we remember God wants us to learn the lessons He presents. He is *not* going to deliberately make His will hard to discern. That goes against God's very nature. He loves us. So when we start praying for God's wisdom, start immediately looking for His wisdom to be revealed and expecting it.

Notice as part of this verse, we are to pray for deliverance from evil, or from the "evil one." That evil one exists; Satan is real, and active in the world. We see his will playing out every day. Jesus knew that would be the case and tells us to pray against his influence. God could have constructed things where we did not need to pray against Satan, but He didn't. He wants us to be involved, and to exhibit the will, discipline, and love for Him that praying to Him against Satan indicates. And that's as it should be.

So, our all-powerful, all-loving, all-wise God has and keeps the "big picture" of our lives in mind. He loves us and has made every provision for our eternal life available. And He has taken the additional step of clearly explaining how we can access those provisions and achieve eternal life right now here on earth. What a great, great God we have.

PSALM 145:1–3

This Psalm is written by King David (led by the Holy Spirit) and reflects praise to God for His goodness and generosity toward all His people, both as a group and as individuals. Notice in these first three verses how the psalmist gets right to the thought of presenting how glad he is and how much he celebrates the idea of praising and worshipping God.

> I will extol you, my God and King,
>   and bless your name forever and ever.
> Every day I will bless you
>   and praise your name forever and ever.
> Great is the LORD, and greatly to be praised,
>   and his greatness is unsearchable. (Psalm 145:1–3)

The key thought here is GOD IS WORTHY of all our praise and adoration, and the psalmist recognizes that, and is thankful for the opportunity to do such. So the Psalm expresses the peace, the rest, and the joy the psalmist gets from such worship. And he commits to do so forever and ever, glad in the knowledge that when we get to heaven all believers will be there doing the same thing.

Notice the first two words, "I will," thus, everyone who sings this Psalm begins by pledging to worship God sincerely, and always. Notice, too, how the psalmist recognizes God's position correctly as his God and as his King. He knows God is great, and he says so; he knows God's greatness really is beyond his ability to comprehend, and he says so. We need to remember God already realizes He is great, and He already knows His greatness is unsearchable for us. But He wants us to realize that too; and He wants us to acknowledge it, and He wants us to do so gladly and with joy.

On earth now some people live like this, and their lives reflect the joy and peace (through good times and bad times) that only such a relationship with the Lord can bring. God would have us all live that way. He loves us all, and He knows a proper relationship with Him defines the best way to live, and He makes such a relationship with Him available to everyone.

John 3:16 is probably the most famous Bible verse of all, as it expresses what God has done for us because He loves us. He has given us the opportunity to live forever, and to spend that "forever" in the best place possible, in heaven with Him: "For God so loved the world, that he gave his only Son, that whoever believes in him shall not perish but have eternal life" (John 3:16).

Having received such a (free) gift, it's no wonder believers can love and worship God like we see the psalmist doing.

MATTHEW 26:30

We don't often think of Jesus singing, but don't doubt He did as
He participated in temple worship throughout His life. This verse
describes Him and His disciples singing a hymn as they ended the
Last Supper. We can't help but wonder what they sang. Tradition
has it that it was customary for the Jews to sing from Psalms 116–
118 as they closed the Passover meal. So picture the scene that
night and see what they likely sang about:

> And when they had sung a hymn, they went out to the Mount
> of Olives. (Matthew 26:30)

> I love the LORD, because he has heard
>   my voice and my pleas for mercy.
> Because he inclined his ear to me,
>   therefore I will call on him as long as I live. (Psalm 116:1–2)

> Praise the LORD, all nations!
>   Extol him all peoples!
> For great is his steadfast love toward us,
>   and the faithfulness of the LORD endures forever.
> Praise the LORD! (Psalm 117:1–2)

> Oh give thanks to the LORD, for he is good;
>   for his steadfast love endures forever! (Psalm 118:1)

What a night! Jesus had taught them concerning His betrayal,
and even pointed out that one who would betray Him. And He
established the tradition of the bread and the cup symbolizing
His body and His blood about to be given in sacrifice for their
sins. Here in Jesus, we have God come to earth in human form,
to save us from our sins. For about three years the disciples had

followed Him around Judea and Galilee hearing Him preach and teach truth concerning God's love for them and urging them to receive Him for who He is, Messiah, Redeemer and Lord. And now it was time for Him to make that greatest sacrifice, His life for our sins.

And notice what they sang about at this crucial time. In Psalm 116 they recognize God has heard their pleas for mercy and they commit their ongoing allegiance and obedience to Him. And they sing of their love for Him, for He obviously loves them.

In Psalm 117 they unashamedly worship Him and praise Him. And they urge all nations to do likewise. For not only does He love them now, He always has, and always will love them. For great is His steadfast love for them all.

In Psalm 118 they give thanks for His ongoing love, and they sing of why He loves them. It's because it is His nature to be good. Thus, His love endures forever. We see them praising God in every hymn. The common threads in each hymn are praise, honor, glory, and thanksgiving to our almighty God.

Today, we wonder how to worship, what to pray, when to praise Him, and who we should tell about Him. And all those concerns are addressed for us in scripture. Every fear, doubt, concern, or anxiety we ever have is covered by His love and exhibited to us on the cross by Jesus' shed blood on our behalf. Every question in our lives that seem so relevant concerning family, work, mission, and use of our time and talents are simplified when we dedicate them all to the Lord.

PSALM 96:7–9

God created and chose Israel, descendants of Abraham, as that nation He would use to bless all mankind forever by bringing them true knowledge of Himself. **It is that truth of God's sovereignty and love all people (Jews and Gentiles) need and basically yearn for.** Here then is a Psalm reminding Jewish readers of the responsibility and privilege they have to share that message, and Gentile readers of that good news God has for them. We, in our day, can and should consider the message of this Psalm both as the source of our faith in almighty God, and as the very information we are to make known throughout the world. See our assignment spelled out:

> Ascribe to the LORD, O families of the peoples,
>   ascribe to the LORD glory and strength!
> Ascribe to the LORD the glory due his name;
>   bring an offering, and come into his courts!
> Worship the LORD in the splendor of holiness;
>   tremble before him, all the earth! (Psalm 96:7–9)

We cannot properly carry out these commands unless we ourselves have already established the Lord as our Lord. Here we see references to all Gentiles ("families of the peoples," and "all the earth") and a call for them to acknowledge God's proper position relative to themselves. Note the word *ascribe* used three times in this passage. It means "to acknowledge," but here it implies more. It adds permanent allegiance, respect, obedience, and ongoing love to our relationship to God.

So we can picture the unknown psalmist, operating under the leadership of God's spirit, crying out to the Gentiles (that's us) to do the right thing, and to do it right now. That is, to establish the Lord as sovereign in their lives, to credit Him with all glory and strength (**which He deserves and which He has**) and to "bring an offering," and in that way live out the love and respect for the Lord they feel. See that last sentence: "Worship the LORD in the splendor of holiness." WOW! What a concept! We are to (attempt) to worship God as He is worthy of being worshipped, that is, with all the (proper) majesty, honor, glory, and splendor He merits, and all the love and humility we (should) feel before Him.

Notice the invitation from the (Jewish) psalmist to the Gentiles (us) to join Jews in "His courts." There is only one sovereign God, and He means for all the earth to join in worshipping Him. Notice, too, we are to tremble before Him. A humble spirit is certainly in order as we come before almighty God.

I urge you to do two opposite things at the same time. Get excited about the God you have who loves you so much, and have peace concerning life here on earth, especially during troubling times. Jesus tells us in Matthew 28:20, "Behold, I am with you always, to the end of the age."

1 CORINTHIANS 10:13

Here is verse that discusses temptations, a common problem among all believers. No one escapes this life without having experienced temptations. You can be sure Satan will see to that. But we can be just as certain that there is a "non-sinful" approach to every temptation we might ever face. Our "escape" may well involve pain, discomfort, expense, embarrassment, etc. but it does not have to involve sin. Most of the time we have generated our own difficulty, by poor planning or misapplied logic. We simply don't think ahead as much as we should, and don't properly evaluate the likely consequences of our actions. God knows that and stands ready to forgive us if we sincerely repent, though He is still likely to allow us to suffer the consequences of our actions. This was surely true in the first century, too, as Paul wrote to the Corinthian church. See the approach to temptation he is teaching us:

> No temptation has overtaken you that is not common to man. God is faithful, and he will not let you be tempted beyond your ability, but with the temptation he will also provide the way of escape, that you may be able to endure it. (1 Corinthians 10:13)

While we might disagree, we are not unique in the likelihood of our facing temptation. We tend to think consciously or subconsciously, that no one has ever faced the array of temptations that we face. Scripture tells us that is not true. In fact, this passage tells us there is not even one temptation that is not common to man. Many people in many eras have already faced what we are facing. And God knows that, and He knows when "our time has come." And, praise the Lord, He is faithful. He consistently makes provision for our escape if we would simply ask Him. The fact of God's faithfulness is both widely known and seldom accessed. We all generally (unthinkingly, having failed to pray) attempt our own solutions to our temptations before prayer even occurs to us. We thereby miss out on God's help and wisdom during our toughest times.

It's interesting that this passage refers to temptation "overtaking" us. It is as if they "sneak up on us from behind." And thus, unexpectedly, all of a sudden, there is temptation upon us, taking over our thoughts and actions before we realize it. Interesting, too, is the fact that God is aware of our ability to resist a given temptation, and so is Satan. Thus, Satan brings to our mind and circumstance our strongest temptation nemesis, that one that is hardest for us to resist. Nevertheless, God enters the picture and constrains Satan's efforts to something less than our ability to resist. And thus, we can escape. Just imagine our God always monitoring our situations to the extent He always knows when we face temptations and which one.

And God will provide a way of escape. That does not mean we will take that opportunity, but as believers that route will always be there for us. Notice Paul refers to our temptation experience as something we "endure." Temptations come, they are very real, they are Satan inspired, but **escape is doable**. We can endure it.

The lesson for us here then is twofold, we need to expect temptations for they will come, and secondly, our God is faithful. He is able to deal with any temptation and will provide a way of escape allowing us to endure. What a great God we have.

MATTHEW 13:31–32

Jesus presented many of His spiritual principles to the disciples in the form of parables, stories of everyday occurrences that had scriptural truth hidden within them. The stories were easy to remember and thus, hopefully the truths Jesus wanted to communicate stuck with the listeners. His parables and their hidden truths find application in our day too. The significant point to remember though is that we are not to just understand Jesus' parables, but to live out the spiritual truths they reflect. See this one concerning small seeds planted that yield a large tree:

> He put another parable before them, saying, "The kingdom of heaven is like a grain of mustard seed that a man took and sowed in his field. It is the smallest of all seeds, but when it is grown it is larger than all the garden plants and becomes a tree, so that the birds of the air come and make nests in its branches." (Matthew 13:31–32)

To understand this parable, we must define the "kingdom of heaven" as used in the passage. It refers to the gospel of Jesus Christ, the truth of God's love as reflected in His sending His Son to earth to save us from our sins. From a small beginning (a child born in a manger) there came a life and a message of eternal significance. Only a few people familiar with God's promise to Eve could imagine such a beginning to the way to eternal life God was providing. And here we see Jesus Himself, who defined that way, telling us of what He is bringing.

It's easy to draw an analogy where the seed is Jesus, the garden is the earth, God is represented by the man who planted the seed, the grown mustard tree is the truth of God's love as demonstrated by Jesus now spread to some degree over most of the world, and the birds and their nests are people, churches, and Christian groups living and sharing the gospel in the world. All this provided and dictated via God's love, wisdom, and power.

Notice where we are in the parable. Jesus has already come. He has lived a perfect life providing the perfect sacrifice for us and our sins on the cross. We believers are in the tree and world having heard and trusted in His Word and life. And we are to "go and tell" the rest of the world of Jesus' identity, and His sacrifice. This, because many have yet to hear, and many have spread false doctrine. So, not all the "nests" are productive. Some "birds" are evil and build destructive "nests." So, the parable also indicates we are to be vigilant, always alert to Satan and his deceit. The kingdom of God is not yet fulfilled; there is more work to do. And we true believers been assigned that task.

Thus, even though at this point we see much in the way of sin in the world, and evil seemingly triumphant sometimes, we are not to be discouraged, the end has not yet come. Our God will be victorious; He will dictate the final outcome in His timing and manner.

ISAIAH 40:15-19

This passage is part of the section in the book of Isaiah that discusses the Greatness of God. Such a subject is one we are apt to skip over, and not take seriously enough. But Isaiah took God's greatness very seriously. He looked around and saw all the things God had created, and marveled at the power and wisdom necessary to create (from nothing) all that he saw. Think about that, knowing Isaiah wrote with no knowledge at all of North or South America, or the two poles covered over with ice and snow, or Africa, or Scandinavia, or Japan, etc. And still he was awestruck by what he saw and did know something about. Notice how Isaiah did describe God's greatness:

> Behold, the nations are like a drop from a bucket,
>   and are accounted as the dust on the scales;
>   behold he takes up the coastlands like fine dust.
> Lebanon would not suffice for fuel,
>   nor are its beasts enough for a burnt offering.
> All the nations are as nothing before him,
>   they are accounted by him as less than nothing and emptiness.
> To whom then will you liken God,
>   or what likeness compare with him?
> An idol! A craftsman casts it,
>   and a goldsmith overlays it with gold
>   and casts for it silver chains. (Isaiah 40:15–19)

You probably have never wondered where the common phrase "a drop in the bucket" comes from, but here is that place. The phrase provides a contrast between God's power and the power of the strongest nation. Isaiah knew that any nation of any size or power was as "nothing" compared to God's wisdom and power. Notice he calls them dust on a measuring scale, that is, they are of no consequence. In those days (not now) the country of Lebanon was known for its dense forests and the abundance of wild game in those forests. Isaiah points out that God is so holy, so majestic, and so full of glory, you could not properly furnish a burnt offering to Him if you used all the wood from those forests, and sacrificed all the game in those forests.

As for idols, Isaiah speaks with sarcasm at the very thought of worshipping something as a God that was made with human hands, no matter their skill or creativity. To Isaiah, such would be the greatest of foolishness, as well as an affront to almighty God.

If no nation can be compared with God, certainly no person could either. Yet in that day (and ours) we tend to give special credibility to some countries and even some individuals due to our impressions of their reputations or history. But we are to beware of making the kind of mistakes Isaiah is referring to. God is God, and we are not. We waste time, energy, and focus when we give more credibility to someone than they merit. Yet we cannot give too much emphasis and attention to God.

God alone merits all our love, obedience, and attention. It is not a stretch to say we are to dedicate our lives to God and His glory. However, the amazing part of His plan is we are not to think of ourselves as giving all of ourselves to God in a conventional sense, where we deny ourselves of worthwhile things and objectives. When we receive Christ as our Lord and Savior, we do dedicate ourselves to Him, but we receive so much more in return, the comparison is overwhelming. God's love and provisions for us during good times and bad, sickness and health, and for eternity with Him, make any sacrifice we contribute seem pitifully small.

PSALM 95:7–9

This Psalm is titled "Let Us Sing Songs of Praise" and there is a reason for that message. It's because God, and He only, is worthy of such songs. And it's because God loves us and wants the best for us, for He knows that when we truly praise Him, we are happiest now, and will know more joy forever. And it has always been that way, God loving His people and always urging them to properly respond to His love and provisions, especially nowadays. A classic example of this is given in this Psalm as it describes the actions of the children of Israel as they traveled though the desert in Sinai after their exodus from Egypt. See this passage, and how relevant it is to us.

> Today, if you hear his voice,
>> do not harden your hearts, as at Meribah,
>> as on the day at Massah in the wilderness,
> when your fathers put me to the test
>> and put me to the proof, though they had seen my work.
>> (Psalm 95:7–9)

Meribah means quarreling and Massah means testing. The Israelites had run out of water and were protesting this condition to Moses, complaining that he had led them out of Egypt simply to die in the desert. That place had been called Meribah, and gained the name Massah, for how the Israelites acted there. And now about five hundred years later God has led some unknown psalmist to write this Psalm reminding his readers, including us, of the sin of doubting God.

These same Israelites had seen powerful evidence of God's power and His provisions for them, evidence such as the ten plagues God rained on Egypt, the crossing of the Red Sea on dry ground and the subsequent drowning of the Egyptian army as they tried to follow the Israelites through the sea. **So the lesson for us is "do not harden your heart" to what you know to be God's will.** Given what the Israelites had already seen, providing them water would be a small thing. And it was. God had Moses strike a rock with his rod and water came forth (enough for two million people).

Beware lest you think God has not made clear to you what His will is; Scripture is full of directions for us. See 1 Thessalonians 5:16–22 for an example: "Rejoice always, pray without ceasing, give thanks in all circumstances; for this is the will of God in Christ Jesus for you. Do not quench the Spirit. Do not despise prophecies, but test everything; hold fast what is good. Abstain from every form of evil."

Doing what we know God would have us do will lead to directions for those many issues that scripture does not specifically address. So TODAY we are to "not harden our hearts," TODAY we are to begin to obey 1 Thessalonians 5:16, so that TODAY we can begin trusting God will give us direction for our lives.

TITUS 2:11–14

In Titus, the Holy Spirit has led Paul to give us a very practical letter, one that is relevant to any society in any era. Here he is writing to Titus, whom he calls "my true child." Paul has recently visited the island of Crete where he planted several churches and has now left Titus there to continue the work of establishing the churches. This letter then is to encourage him in the work and to advise him especially to guard against false teachers. And as Paul does in many of his letters, he emphasizes the connection between salvation and good works. Titus and the believers on Crete (and us) are to live out their faith before the world. See Paul's emphasis:

> For the grace of God has appeared, bringing salvation for all people, training us to renounce ungodliness and worldly passions, and to live self-controlled, upright, and godly lives in the present age, waiting for our blessed hope, the appearing of the glory of our great God and Savior Jesus Christ, who gave himself for us to redeem us from all lawlessness and to purify for himself a people for his own possession who are zealous for good works. (Titus 2:11–14)

Christ has come, and Paul identifies Him as an expression of "the grace of God" bestowed on all who believe in Him. Thus, Paul is not teaching a universal salvation when he says, "bringing salvation for all people." It is for all people, but not all people will avail themselves of God's free gift of eternal life.

Then Paul lists two negative activities they are to renounce, and three positive attributes they are to take on in their lives. They (and we) are to renounce ungodliness and worldly passions, and to live self-controlled, upright, and godly lives. Notice these five activities will obviously be evident to the world around them. Believers then and believers now should (must) ensure what they say they believe is consistent with how they live. Paul could not have been more specific as to the "when" to begin such a witness. He says do so "in this present age," that's right now, right where we are. This as they (and we) wait for the coming of their hoped-for Savior.

That blessed hope is further defined as "the glory of our great God and Savior Jesus Christ" who came and redeemed us from our sin debt. Notice the "why" of Jesus' coming to earth is spelled out for us. It's to purify for Himself a people for his own possession. God chose each individual believer before time began to constitute that group God possesses as His children, adopted into His family, gaining an inheritance like Jesus has. Just imagine it, we believers are joint heirs with Jesus Christ, due the same destiny with Him in heaven forever that He has.

And notice, too, the difference that purified relationship with God makes in our lives. We don't just do good works, we are excited about that prospect, zealous for them, "fired up" even. And we feel that way because done properly, good works glorify our heavenly Father. And as his adopted children we sense that glorifying Him is what we were made for, what we ought to do, and what we gain the most satisfaction from doing. **And all this is because we were made in the image of God, and loving others to the point of doing good in this world is reflective of godliness in us. So now we can see more clearly how the sanctification process (our growing spiritually over time) culminates in our final glorification when Jesus returns, qualifying us for an eternity in heaven with our Lord.**

PHILEMON 4–7

This is a short letter Paul the apostle wrote to a believer named Philemon who lived in Colossae. He is a wealthy slave owner who has done much good for believers there since being led to the Lord by Paul during Paul's ministry in Ephesus. At some point, one of Philemon's slaves named Onesimus fled to Rome where he met Paul and was gloriously saved. He became a vital helper to Paul especially when Paul was imprisoned. The gist of this letter (carried by Onesimus to Philemon) was Paul's attempt to pave the way for reconciliation between Philemon and Onesimus. They are both believers now, and both have been of great service in kingdom work. This passage at the beginning of the letter describes Paul's feelings for Philemon as a fellow believer. See this example of one believer's appreciation of another believer:

> I thank my God always when I remember you in my prayers, because I hear of your love and of the faith that you have toward the Lord Jesus and all the saints, and I pray that the sharing of your faith may become effective for the full knowledge of every good thing that is in us for the sake of Christ. For I have derived much joy and comfort from your love, my brother, because the hearts of the saints have been refreshed though you. (Philemon 4–7)

At the outset of the passage, we read of Paul's prayers for Philemon. The message is clear. We are to pray for other believers. Such prayer support is always of great importance to the one prayed for and the one praying. Paul mentions the spiritual growth that comes to a believer as they share their faith in Christ, and he prays for the continued growth of Philemon's faith. As believers share their faith (then and now), God blesses that effort with increased knowledge of the significance of Christ's atoning sacrifice on the cross. Over time then their witness effectively grows as they confidently and gladly continue to spread the gospel of Christ. That has been Philemon's experience and Paul commends him for it. What could be more satisfying than for us to see someone we led to the Lord out and about doing the same kind of witnessing? That's how Paul feels toward Philemon.

Paul has derived much joy from hearing such good things concerning Philemon's ongoing witness and wants Philemon to know that. We don't have to be the champion for Christ that Paul was to provide this same kind of support for other Christians in our day. We can pray for them, and we can tell them that. And we can follow their example.

Notice the specific compliment Paul provides Philemon. He describes his ministry as "refreshing the hearts of the saints." What a great expression of support. Would that we had that ability to refresh the hearts of other believers too. And we do, because we don't have to do it alone. Sincere prayers for another believer and their lifestyle will surely help, and grow us spiritually. The Holy Spirit caused Philemon's lifestyle to bring much joy and comfort to Paul, and he gave Paul the right words to say to Philemon. If we let Him, the Holy Spirit will do the same for us.

Paul is sincerely appreciative of Philemon's kingdom work, which should be the way all believers feel about the ministry of other believers. Later, Paul asks Philemon to forgive Onesimus and accept him back not as a runaway slave, but as the brother in Christ he now is. That kind of openness and perspective should be part of our witness too. God forgave us, who are we to not forgive others?

MARK 6:53–56

The people of Jesus' day were a lot like us. They hurt when they fell, they ran from things they did not understand, they wanted food when they were hungry, and when they were sick, they looked for ways and places where they could get well. God knew all that and gave Jesus authority to heal and cleanse when He came to earth. So people flocked to Him for help, and brought their loved ones who were sick. And like He does with us, Jesus loved them, and had mercy on them, and healed them. See how this played out back then:

> When they had crossed over, they came to land at Gennesaret and moored to the shore. And when they got out of the boat, the people immediately recognized him, and ran about the whole region and began to bring the sick people on their beds to wherever they heard he was. And wherever he came, in villages, cities, or countryside, they laid the sick in the marketplaces and implored him that they might touch even the fringe of his garment. And as many as touched it were made well. (Mark 6:53–56)

We don't know how many people Jesus healed. What we do know is that He healed any and all who came (or who were brought) to Him and in faith touched the hem of His garment. What we do know is those who knew of His power went about spreading the word of this opportunity for healing, and that when they did that many heard and came and availed themselves of Jesus' power and were healed. And what we should know is that same approach is what Jesus wants us to use today. And what we can be sure of is Jesus still loves those who come to Him, He still has mercy on those who come to Him, and He still heals those who come to Him.

Where we fit in that equation should be obvious. If we need healing (salvation), we should go to Jesus in faith as the people in the passage did. And when we are healed (saved), then we should share that experience with others who need salvation, urging them to do the same thing (as the people in the passage did). The sick people who heard Jesus was available did not have to go to Him. They could have stayed sick, or tried to get healed another way. As it happens, that approach does not apply to salvation. There is only one way to heaven. So we need to make that fact part of our announcement that Jesus is near.

Jesus clearly states, "I am the way, and the truth, and the life. No one comes to the Father except through me" (John 14:6). Jesus could not have made our assignment any more clear. The passage above describes the people "running about" sharing the good news that Jesus has come. Note the sense of urgency implicit in that action. Does it not follow that we, too, should "run about" with our message to those who are without Christ, for their need is urgent too.

GALATIANS 3:19–20

In this passage Paul is discussing the debate concerning how we are saved, by compliance with the law, or by God's grace through faith? He has already stated we are not saved by compliance with the law in Galatians 3:11: "Now it is evident that no one is justified before God by the law, for 'The righteous shall live by faith.'" And he goes on to explain why this is true by examining why the law was given in the first place:

> Why then the law? It was added because of transgressions, until the offspring should come to whom the promise has been made, and it was put in place through angels by an intermediary. Now an intermediary implies more than one, but God is one. (Galatians 3:19–20)

The law was needed, and God provided it because of transgressions, that is, sin. We are all born sinful by nature, and "bound" then from birth to a life of sin, and thus, an eternity separated from God. Therefore, this sin must be clearly defined and specifically dealt with in God's plan of salvation. The Mosaic law was part of a temporary covenant put in place until the "offspring" should come. Along with this temporary covenant came the whole sacrificial system the Jews lived by before Jesus, God's offspring, came. So for centuries sacrificial offerings were made to offset man's sins before God. Specific details were provided in scripture dealing with these offerings, the priests who administered them, and the temple where they were conducted.

But now Messiah had come, "to whom the promise had been made." Jesus Christ, the prophesied Son of God had come, proved Himself by His life and His miracles, suffered through a wrongful death on the cross to pay our sin debt, and rose again on the third day to verify His deity. The old, temporary covenant of law keeping had been replaced with the new covenant of faith in Christ. And that was Christ's sacrificial, one-time death to atone for the sins of all who would believe.

Compliance with the law was still commanded, but not for the purpose of earning salvation and eternal life. The law had never been intended for that, for man could not comply. Those laws had been provided through an intermediary (Moses) who had been advised by angels from a burning bush of his role in God's plan to save His chosen people. Later, that same Moses passed God's Ten Commandments to the children of Israel for their direction and compliance.

But God's second, permanent covenant did not require an intermediary like Moses, for "God is one," totally complete within Himself. We, thus, have direct access to God's salvation plan for our eternal life via His grace and our faith. Eternal life then is not something we have generated, but a free gift from God, not to be earned by anyone.

So what are we to do with this teaching? Do what Paul was doing, share it with others, whenever, and wherever, we have opportunity. That's not just when we accidentally have opportunity, but when with purpose-driven, love-oriented, proactive intent we create opportunities.

JOHN 6:40, 44, 54

Sometimes the Holy Spirit repeats Himself in scripture if He has an especially important point to make. See that illustrated here:

> For this is the will of my Father, that everyone who looks on the Son and believes in him should have eternal life, and I will raise him up on the last day. (John 6:40)

> No one can come to me unless the Father who sent me draws him. And I will raise him up on the last day. (John 6:44)

> Whoever feeds on my flesh and drinks my blood has eternal life, and I will raise him up on the last day. (John 6:54)

Plainly God wants to save us, and if we "look on the Son" and "believe in Him," He will provide eternal life. And He will draw us to Him to accomplish that. The third illustration speaks of "eating" and "drinking" spiritually as we understand the experience of satisfying our physical hunger and thirst respectively. Thus, we satisfy our spiritual needs by coming to Jesus and believing in Him.

And in every case He will raise us up on the last day. We are not sure of all that phrase means, but it certainly sounds like something we want to happen to us. We picture it meaning our being taken to live eternally with Christ. The concept is clear: on the last day, there will be an accounting or judgment process accomplished. As to our lives, all will have been said and done at that point, and we will have clearly indicated our choices by the decisions we have made. The Old Testament speaks to this same event in Ecclesiastes 12:13–14: "The end of the matter; all has been heard. Fear God and keep his commandments, for this is the whole duty of man. For God will bring every deed into judgment, with every secret thing, whether good or evil."

Notice in all three illustrations we see Jesus speaking. It is definitely He who will make the decisions and He who will take believers to be where He is. Being where Jesus is defines heaven. Two of the three illustrations add the concept that this will be an eternal condition. Taken together, which is the way we are to look at all scripture, we see significant promises from God made to each of us as individuals. We don't see the involvement of anyone else in our particular situations other than the Father, the Son, and the implied presence of the Holy Spirit. Thus, the phrase "personal relationship" comes to mind as Jesus evaluates our eternal destiny. **Certainly, nothing is more personal than our relationship with Jesus.**

REVELATION 2:7, 11, 17, 29; 3:6, 13, 22

It's not often you see the same verse repeated exactly in more than one place in scripture. But this is a unique situation. As an old man, John the apostle had been exiled to the Isle of Patmos for preaching the gospel of Jesus Christ, and there was given a vison. God instructed him to write letters to seven churches in what was then called Asia (present-day Turkey). Those churches were in the towns of Ephesus, Smyrna, Pergamum, Thyatira, Sardis, Philadelphia, and Laodicea. Each letter was a different message God had for each church concerning their actions. Several were complimented for being obedient to God's Word, and all were given specific instructions as to how to improve their ministry. But there was one sentence in each letter that was identical for all seven churches. That could only indicate what God wanted all churches in that day (and likely in our day too) to do. Here is that command: "He who has an ear, let him hear what the Spirit says to the churches" (see scripture locations above).

In the first place, obviously, the Spirit is speaking to churches, and we must be willing to listen to what God has to say. That's a big problem for many people. Too many believers and unbelievers never consider God's will for their lives. Thus, they are not open to hearing what the Spirit says. Some are familiar with scripture and know about the gospel of Jesus Christ but haven't made the specific decision concerning their relationship to Him as Savior. There must be a mind and heart set to reorient their lives around the truth of Jesus' sacrifice to pay their sin debt.

The basis of truth in this verse has to do with the fact that God loves the world to the extent He sent His Son Jesus into the world to save us from our sins. We must come to grips with the significance of that truth. Jesus' sacrificial death on the cross was entirely based on God's love for us (His grace), and was the only sacrifice adequate to pay the ransom our sins required. Key to the message of this verse is the fact God's Holy Spirit does speak to individuals, giving them opportunity to believe. In every language and in many different ways, God uses the Holy Spirit to communicate His message of love to us.

Thus, we can be sure the Holy Spirit is at work consistently speaking to churches. Churches are made up of people and it is to these people the Holy Spirit speaks. So, God is not lax in keeping His Word. We might ask what the message of the Holy Spirit is. It is simple but profound. "For God so loved the world, that he gave his only Son, that whoever believes in him should not perish but have eternal life" (John 3:16).

This, and much more, but this succinct verse provides the gist of God's love message, and the way to eternal life for those who do what the seven churches were told to do: hear what they are being told. Thus, the inference is people are to hear, understand, believe, and live out the truth of God's love expressed vividly through Jesus' death, burial, and resurrection.

Those who do truly hear and thus have heard to the point of belief are blessed among all people. They only are destined to spend eternity with the Lord. And we see this expressed seven times. That has to indicate God really means it.

2 TIMOTHY 2:8-10

Jesus Christ came to earth to save us from our sins. So, for all who believe in Him, He provides the free gift of eternal life. Many people don't know that, or have heard about it but don't believe it strongly enough to completely "live it out." They have put someone or something ahead of belief in Jesus for salvation. We can tell they don't believe by their lifestyle. True belief in Jesus will show up in the way we live, what we do and don't do, and what we say or don't say. See this passage Paul the apostle has written to Timothy, a young man Paul led to Jesus:

> Remember Jesus Christ, risen from the dead, the offspring of David, as preached in my gospel, for which I am suffering, bound with chains as a criminal. But the word of God is not bound! Therefore, I endure everything for the sake of the elect, that they also may obtain the salvation that is in Christ Jesus with eternal glory. (2 Timothy 2:8–10)

He reminds Timothy, and us, not to forget Jesus Christ, to keep Him, and His identity as Son of God and prophesied Messiah, on our minds. The concept of Jesus as our risen Savior is to be uppermost in our hearts. Jesus died on the cross for our sins, and defeated death by rising from the dead. Because He rose from the grave so will we as believers. **It's no wonder Paul urges all believers (then and now) to remember they are destined to spend eternity with Jesus in heaven.** It is that victory by faith that assures us of an eternity in heaven with Jesus. Messiah had been prophesied to come as "Son of David," and Jesus was a direct descendant of King David, as Paul had been preaching. Paul had been imprisoned for his preaching and was writing from prison to encourage Timothy in his faith. So Paul could speak from experience that following Christ may lead to suffering. We may or may not face imprisonment for our faith, but following Jesus will certainly not mean our lives will be free of troubles and trials. But it will mean Jesus will be with us as we live every day, guiding us by His Holy Spirit how to respond to our circumstances, both good and bad. See Jesus' own words on this subject of being with us: "And behold, I am with you always, to the end of the age" (Matthew 28:20).

But the word of God is not bound, that is, imprisoned, as Paul is. It applies to all who believe, no matter their background or present status. So Paul is not saddened by his imprisonment. He knows if he does not abandon his faith in prison it will serve to strengthen the faith of his readers, and that is his goal. So Paul feels the salvation of the elect, those destined to be saved, is worth any suffering he might face. Jesus felt that way and it was He Paul was imitating. So should we.

We believers are not likely to forget Jesus. The focus of this passage then is to keep the truth of the gospel in our minds, particularly the centrality of Jesus Christ. Society is apt to come to the conclusion that doing good deeds and not doing bad deeds earns people their way to heaven. NOT SO. We are saved by our relationship with Jesus Christ. Paul puts this plainly in Ephesians 2:8–9: "For by grace you have been saved through faith. And this is not your own doing; it is the gift of God, not a result of works, so that no one may boast."

Isaiah 2:1–3

Isaiah, the prophet, lived around 700 BC in Judah. There he taught and preached the visions God showed him concerning future world events. He prophesied about what he called the "latter days," those times after Jesus' resurrection when the earth comes to be basically given over to sin and unbelief in spite of what Jesus taught and demonstrated by His resurrection. That is, that He is Lord, and King of kings, God, who came to earth to save us from our sins. We are now in those latter days, and thus, ever closer to the time of Christ's expected return as described in this passage. Notice how there will therefore one day be a turning from ignorance to knowledge, from unbelief to belief, and from hopelessness to hope, See how Isaiah words this:

> The word that Isaiah the son of Amoz saw concerning Judah and Jerusalem.
> It shall come to pass in the latter days
>   that the mountain of the house of the Lord
> shall be established as the highest of the mountains,
>   and shall be lifted up above the hills,
> and all the nations shall flow to it,
>   and many people shall come, and say:
> "Come, let us go up to the mountain of the Lord,
>   to the house of the God of Jacob,
> that he may teach us his ways
>   and that we may walk in his paths."
> For out of Zion shall go forth the law,
>   and the word of the Lord from Jerusalem. (Isaiah 2:1–3)

Most scholars interpret Isaiah's words as a description of the time of the millennium, the thousand-year reign of Christ on earth after His return. See how during this time Mt. Zion in Jerusalem will become a focal point of religious worship; Christianity, i.e., worship of Christ as Lord, will become a worldwide belief drawing crowds of people to the holy city. Isaiah refers to Christianity as the "highest of the mountains," that is, Christianity will become the most important religion in the world and will be preached and promoted everywhere. The truth of Christ will flow around the world and there will be widespread evangelism for Christ, people acknowledging Christ's death for our sins and His resurrection proving the "death of death" for believers.

Notice the coming enthusiasm for Christ during this period: people encouraging one another to believe in Christ and to gather in Jerusalem for united worship. Those people described truly want to learn Christ's ways, so they can walk in His paths. So, from Jerusalem will go out God's Word, and out of Zion will go God's laws, all true, all authentic, and all with God's enabling power. So, people will come to Jerusalem in droves where they will receive the encouragement only God's Holy Spirit can provide, and go home "full of the Spirit" to tell others.

There was no doubt in Isaiah's mind that this all will come to pass, and he went about enthusiastically preaching these coming events. His words ring with the certainty of God's power. And we, too, can be confident these times will come. Thus, our assignment is to be an "Isaiah" in our day, to preach, teach, and live out the truth of the gospel of Jesus, proclaiming a coming reign of Christ in the midst of a society that right now for the most part does not believe. The fact of our not knowing when Christ will return should not dilute the enthusiasm we have for the truth of God's Word. Our assignment is to go and make disciples like Jesus did.

MARK 1:32-34

Jesus continued to move around, never staying very long in one community. He had a mission to preach the gospel, not to heal the sick. His healing ministry was an addition to His preaching and teaching ministry so as to validate His identity as the Son of God, thus authenticating His message of the coming kingdom of God. See how Jesus combined both ministries effectively:

> That evening at sundown they brought to him all who were sick or oppressed by demons. And the whole city was gathered together at the door. And he healed many who were sick with various diseases, and cast out many demons. And he would not permit the demons to speak, because they knew him. (Mark 1:32–34)

It was the Sabbath and until sundown the people were limited in how they could move about the community. But when free that evening they quickly brought their sick and afflicted to Jesus for healing. It must have been awesome to see Jesus heal person after person no matter their illness. We have to wonder how those healed people responded later. Did they remember who did this for them? Did they make the connection between His healing power and His divine nature? It's likely the people responded the same way we do when God enters our lives with a revealing action or thought. So, a question for us to address from this passage is how long do we retain that feeling of thanksgiving and Christian optimism after we recognize how God has blessed us in a given situation?

Every obvious instance of God's involvement in our lives should trigger increased spiritual growth and kinship with the Lord. More openness to God's actions in our lives should be the subject of many prayers on our part. We miss much in the way of spiritual blessings when we are dull to God's involvement in our lives. God wants us to know how much He loves us and how much involvement in our daily lives He actually has. So, it simply stands to reason that God will honor such prayers leading to more closeness with Him. And, of course, such increased sensitivity to God's will and actions will change us to the point of other people noticing the difference. And that is exactly what God wants. He wants our worldview to be exactly like His and for others to see Christlikeness in us. That's how our lives come to bring glory to Him.

Notice, too, Jesus healed the sick and cast out demons. That's a little foreign to most of us, but apparently was common in those days. Key to His ability to cast out demons was the obvious power over Satan it reflected. It indicated His kingdom was coming, driving back Satan's earthly kingdom. It provided proof of Jesus' divine nature and His dominion over all of His creation.

Interestingly, Jesus restricted the demons from speaking after He had removed them from someone. They clearly recognized Him as Son of God. But it was not to be their role to announce Jesus' identity to the world. He, by His actions and words, was to announce His true identity. Later, His disciples would declare Him to be God come to earth to save us from our sins. Today, passing along that same message is to be the assignment of every believer.

We can't heal as Jesus did, or remove demons to bring relief to many. But we can love others, serve mankind, share the truth of Jesus' gospel, and support others who do the same. The sick and afflicted came to Jesus. We are to go to them and make disciples. So let's begin.

1 CORINTHIANS 16:13–14

This verse contains some of the closing words of Paul's letter to the church at Corinth, Greece. He has been discussing various aspects of the church's responsibility to take the gospel to the nations, especially making that their focus. He wraps up his message to them with five recommendations. Notice how short and succinct they are. Also notice how applicable they are to us in our day:

> Be watchful, stand firm in the faith, act like men, be strong. Let all you do be done in love. (1 Corinthians 16:13–14)

WOW! Way to go, Paul! If I counted correctly, in twenty words, Paul outlined the job description of what every believer ought to be doing. First, he tells them to be watchful. That covers a lot of ground; watchful in what they say, what they do, what they believe, what they support, etc. and watchful in the "why" of all these. Being that consistently watchful requires a lot of thinking, a lot of decisions, and a lot of work establishing priorities. It goes without saying that for every watchful exercise, there will be decisions to be made that will either glorify God or will not glorify God. That's the whole reason for being watchful.

Paul also recommends they stand firm in their faith. That's a given for us, too, but it never hurts for us to be reminded of that responsibility. And what does standing firm in our faith involve apart from being watchful and thinking about what is going on around us, and responding in ways that glorify God. And what about acting like men? How does that play out for believers? It comes down to what kind of men (and women) are we to be? No doubt Paul was thinking about how Christian people would act. They see situations from God's perspective and respond in kind. And (very important) real believers are consistent in their Christian walk. Consistency is one of the most important characteristics of a believer. It's easy to imagine how poorly a believer reflects Christlikeness when they exhibit "on again, off again" Christianity.

And, of course, we should be strong; strong in the best sense of strength concerning our convictions and our faith. It takes a strong spiritual base for a believer to face all the varieties of temptations and trials that Satan can devise to bring against us. And it takes spiritual strength to continue to get up from spiritual missteps, ask for forgiveness, and begin again to be that disciple God would have us be. And notice the last recommendation involving love that anchors the other four. Earlier in this letter, Paul has already told the Corinthians, "Love bears all things, believes all things, hopes all things, endures all things. Love never ends" (1 Corinthians 13:7–8). Everything those Corinthians were to do should be steeped in love, motivated by love, reflecting love, and encouraging love. And why not? God *is* love. Love is the motive behind why we were created, and why God gave the world His only Son to save us from our sins, and why Jesus came and went to the cross in our place.

Notice that Paul is not charging the church at Corinth (or us) with noncompliance with any of these recommendations. He is simply reminding them these actions and attitudes should be common to all believers in any era. Each of the five recommendations are ongoing, requiring prayer, proactive planning, and consistent effort. Let us then give that kind of focus and obedience to all five.

JAMES 4:6–8

We are to beware of worldliness, that is, giving ourselves over to this world with our time, talents, and purposes. Satan dresses worldly attractions such that we are drawn to them, thinking they will satisfy our need for peace and joy. But such thinking is shortsighted, and we eventually find his influence does not lead to anything worthwhile. Many times, we don't make the effort to really evaluate our activities as to where they are apt to lead long-term. So, we are sort of a "now" society, not considering our tomorrows. People in the first century were like that too. See James' counsel to them and us:

> "God opposes the proud, but gives grace to the humble." Submit yourselves therefore to God. Resist the devil, and he will flee from you. Draw near to God, and he will draw near to you. (James 4:6–8)

If we take the literal definitions of oppose (which is to combat, resist, or withstand) then we get a better understanding of God's response to those who are proud. Thus, to have almighty God against us to that degree is obviously foolish. How could pride then result in anything worth seeking? On the other hand, the humble earn God's grace. Grace is God's love for us that we don't really merit but have because it's God's nature to provide grace to the unlovable. We are born sinners, yet due to His grace, God so loved the world He sent Jesus to save us from our sins.

Therefore, having been given Jesus' sacrifice we are to submit to God. Submit has a "totality" inherent in the meaning. We are to hold nothing back from God. And why should we? He gave us everything we have and are. And it is in that total submission to God that we place ourselves in position to be protected from

Satan. To submit is an act of will. It's the result of our having made a choice, and God honors our sincere choice. Then and only then can we resist Satan to the point of him fleeing from us.

And then and only then will we want to draw near to God. And when you think about it, God loves us and therefore He wants us to draw near to him. **God almighty wants His children near Him in every respect. He will honor such effort on our part by drawing near to us. What better place could there be for God's children than near Him?**

So, some questions obviously come to mind. How can we draw near to God? Is that a good idea? Does being near God bring us more responsibility to Him? What will be the results of our drawing near? In the first place, the passage infers if we make that move toward Him, He more than meets us halfway. This, because He loves us, and He can. We come near to Him in many ways; in our spirits through open sincere prayers, in worship and adoration through recognition of who He is and what He has done, and through our lifestyles given over to obedience to His Word. **God will absolutely bless such ongoing commitment to doing what He has commanded us to do. And clearly, we see what He commands us to do, submit to Him, resist the devil, and draw near to Him. An obedient heart gains God's favor every time.**

This passage in James is a classic example of what we are to share with other people. At some point in life all of us come to recognize our inability to cope. James points us to the solution: dependence on God. So should we point others as James does us.

2 Peter 1:9–11

Second Peter is a letter Peter wrote to churches within Asia Minor (modern-day Turkey) in the mid-sixties AD. He wrote to encourage them in their faith as they dealt with the Roman oppression of their day. Peter began the letter by listing eight qualities for believers to endorse by living them out in their lives: faith, virtue, knowledge, self-control, steadfastness, godliness, brotherly affection, and love. And he even covers the result that will accrue to them by obedience, and that is an effective and fruitful knowledge of our Lord Jesus Christ. On the other hand he also points out what will happen to believers who do not seek to add them to their lives. This passage is literally true for our time too:

> For whoever lacks these qualities is so nearsighted that he is blind, having forgotten that he was cleansed from his former sins. Therefore, brothers, be all the more diligent to confirm your calling and election, for if you practice these qualities you will never fall. For in this way there will be richly provided for you an entrance into the eternal kingdom of our Lord and Savior Jesus Christ. (2 Peter 1:9–11)

Peter calls those who lack these qualities "nearsighted," that is, able to see things close at hand better than those in the distance. Those people see themselves and those right around them clearly, but not God, and not what the eternal consequences of such disobedience will lead to. Peter is writing to believers, many of whom have forgotten how unclean they were before they were saved. They have forgotten the significance of God's salvation and what eternal life with the Lord amounts to. Many believers today live that way too.

So, Peter tells them to "confirm their calling and election" by living per these eight qualities. Notice what Peter advises concerning these qualities. If they and we practice them, we will never fall. What a message! What promise! What better assurance could we have than to be told scripturally very clearly we will never fall if we take on these qualities.

The last verse gives us the eternal hope we need. Compliance (from our hearts) with these qualities provides the rich heritage only believers can look forward to, entrance into the eternal kingdom of our Lord and Savior Jesus Christ. How could the message be more clearly presented? How could we misunderstand this truth? Without question we have presented here a road map to heaven.

Key to following this road map is the diligent effort the passage calls for. Diligence implies consistent, steady, earnest, and energetic effort over time, likely even painful effort at some point. But Peter knows, and we should know, that (1) God keeps His promises, and thus, these are true statements and (2) that the result will be worth the labor.

Sometimes we find scripture that is difficult to understand, and not clear as to how to apply to our lives. But not so in this passage. We don't have to be a biblical scholar to understand Peter's message. And we can be sure we know others who need to hear it. And that's our mandate; we are to go and tell others who might not have heard. That's our assignment and our privilege. What an opportunity we have to play a role (with God's help) in leading someone to knowledge of the gospel. Our effort can and will have eternal consequences.

PROVERBS 23:25

We do not choose the family into which we are born; with great wisdom God does that for us. And He never makes a mistake. It is God's plan that our families are what and who they are. And with great wisdom God's Word gives us much in the way of instruction as to how to live within our families for the long-term good of every member. See this verse for a basic biblical command God has for us:

> Let your father and mother be glad;
>   let her who bore you rejoice. (Proverbs 23:25)

Very clearly God is telling us here to obey our parents. They love us, they provide for us, and their hearts are attuned to our every need whether we realize it or not. Interestingly, the older we get the more important it is for us to obey them. This, because the older we get the more independent we become, the more we make and act out our own decisions, and the more impact those decisions have on the family as a whole and the world around us.

If God blesses us with loving, caring parents and grandparents we are blessed indeed. Lived-out love between parent and child, and child and parent, is key to our building long-term stable relationships within the family, and with people outside our family. Our home-built love capacity will be reflected in the friends we make, the relationships we build up and keep, and eventually the core principles we put into our own families one day. Thus, in a very real way the family is the building block for communities and our country, and we are wise to infuse loving obedience for our parents into our lives.

This is not an accident. God has built such basics into our nature for our benefit. Love is the "glue" that holds families together in bad times, and at the same time gives us more capability to better enjoy the good times. Love is like the steel within a building that provides families the strength and stability to withstand the winds of outside influences long-term. Love then is the key factor in our nature that determines the health of our family relationships. **And we choose whether to nurture that love seed God has planted in us all.** And that is what this verse is urging us to do.

Scripture tells us God is love, and we are made in God's image with that same wonderful capacity to love and feel love. Thus, we are to live out and cultivate family love as we live patiently with our parents, praying they will be patient with us too. One day we are likely to play the parent role, and thus, early on in our lives we need to acquire that knowledge of how important our obedience is to family harmony, and our long-term good. God blesses the family of obedient children and those children are also blessed.

JOHN 1:1–3

Written by the apostle John late in the first century AD, this letter was intended to identify Jesus as the promised Messiah and Son of God. From Ephesus John addressed the believing world of that time to both educate and encourage them in their faith. From the very outset, John speaks of Jesus as always existing with God, and thus, involved with what we call creation. Reference to Him is made calling Him the Word, existing in the beginning with God, and as God. See these important concepts as John begins his letter.

> In the beginning was the Word, and the Word was with God, and the Word was God. He was in the beginning with God. All things were made through him, and without him was not any thing made that was made. (John 1:1–3)

The Old Testament had already described the creation of the world, and man and woman. Their fall and God's punishment comes next. The Law of Moses follows with God's Ten Commandments, outlining the rules God would have man to obey. Since man fails this First Covenant requirement, God proceeds to provide man a New Covenant, the way to eternal life via His grace and man's faith in Jesus' sacrificial death on the cross to pay our sin debt. Four gospel books each provide a picture of Jesus' coming to earth and His life and death here, John's being the fourth.

And so we come to this passage. Quite logically John begins by identifying Jesus as eternal in existence, and all-powerful in His scope. Yet, Jesus had come to earth as man, and thousands saw Him and His miracles, and heard His preaching attesting to His manhood. Referring to Jesus as the "Word" is a beautiful testimony to Jesus' life, for He perfectly lived out God's scripture and is the living essence of God's truth. Only by doing so could and would

Jesus qualify as the perfect sacrifice for us as the atonement for our sin.

Notice the boldness and explicitness of the wording describing Jesus' role in creation. Both positive and negative phrasing spell out Jesus' work. Thus, we see clearly nothing was created apart from Him in heaven or on earth. This, now from the same man who walked the dusty roads of Judea and Galilee, who drank from Jacob's well, and who saw fit to cuddle little children in love. At the same time, He healed the blind, raised the dead, and rose Himself from the grave on the third day, and even now waits in heaven until He comes to judge and take us home to spend eternity with Him.

So, we are impressed. But being impressed is not enough. Satan is impressed with Jesus, but he does not love God nor has he committed to Jesus as Savior and Lord. He has not by faith repented of his sin and trusted Christ's sacrifice as payment for his sin. Believers have done all these things. Thus, we are to take these first verses of John to heart. We are to recognize from them who Jesus really is, Son of God who came to earth to save us from our sins (because He loved us). From this beginning of this book we are to thus be encouraged in our faith. We are to sense an extra burden to share Jesus' gospel with those who don't believe. And we are not to doubt. True believers need not doubt. They have the facts.

COLOSSIANS 4:2

Here, the apostle Paul is writing to the church at Colossae, in present-day Turkey, with instruction on how to live during their turbulent times. They suffered greatly under the Roman domination and needed encouragement in their faith. Paul understood suffering. He wrote this letter from prison, under the threat of death. Perhaps the most important thing they (and we) could do was to pray. Almighty God created us all, is always aware of what we are facing, and what our decisions should be. As we develop our prayer life, we should consider these same instructions.

> Continue steadfastly in prayer, being watchful in it, with thanksgiving. (Colossians 4:2)

We will never pray too much. We always need to consider God's will. He has a plan for our lives, and we should always be seeking to obey Him. As over time we bring our lives into daily compliance with God's will, we will more and more understand His Word and what He has in mind for us. These Colossians were already believers. They knew Christ had come to earth and died a sacrificial death on the cross to pay their (and our) sin debt. So, Paul is encouraging his readers to keep on praying even during the worst of times. That applies to us as well.

Notice Paul tells them to "keep on praying." He is telling us that, too, even though sometimes it seems as if God is slow in answering. In His infinite wisdom He knows what timing is best. And He tells us to be watchful as we pray. The concept of watchfulness has to do with our praying for what we are facing now and what we know lies ahead. So, our prayers are to be timely, and the subject of our prayers are to be the situations and opportunities that lie ahead of us. Interestingly, God knows what we are facing, and what we will pray before we pray. Yet, He wants us to pray. He wants us to put into words the things that mean the most to us. This, so that we will begin to understand our prayers as He understands them. God *always* answers the prayers of believers. But often those answers are not in the format we have requested. This is not unlike how a parent deals with their children. They love them and always consider their requests, but some requests will not work to the good of the child. God always knows what is best for us, whether we do or not, and it's His criteria He uses to answer us.

Notice, too, we are to be thankful as we pray. When you think about it, it cost our heavenly Father the life of His Son Jesus Christ to give us the right to pray. The sacrificial death of sinless Jesus was sufficient to atone for the sins of all mankind. Thus, we are to feel humble gratitude for all God has done for us. In fact, that gratitude for God's love for us that we did not deserve is the very message we are to take to the world. Think of it: there are millions of people in the world who have not yet even heard the name of Jesus. In ignorance they live their whole lives not knowing of the sacrifice He paid. Those of us who do know who Jesus is and what He did on the cross have the huge responsibility of taking His truth to the world. Some people hear and don't believe, some hear and do believe. At some point everyone will give an account of their lives and beliefs to the Lord.

If we are properly thankful for the many blessings God has provided, our prayers will reflect that thankfulness. So, our prayers change from being selfish listings of all our desires, to sincere gratitude for what God in His infinite love has generously provided. What a great God we have!

1 PETER 1:24–25

Written by the apostle Peter in about AD 60, this letter urges
Jewish believers to persevere in their faith, for surely Christians
who suffer will be exalted in the end times. That's just as true today.
Thus, though we are weak, God is not, and His Word consists
of eternal truths applicable in all generations. Within our homes,
families, and society, we are to example the righteousness of Christ
as outlined in scripture. See Peter's summation of these principles:

"All flesh is like grass
  and all its glory like the flowers of grass.
The grass withers,
  and the flower fails,
but the word of the Lord remains forever."
And this word is the good news that was preached to you.
(1 Peter 1:24–25)

This quote from Isaiah 40:6–8 describes the frailty of humanity
contrasted with the permanence of God's Word. The picture is clear
that all flesh (everyone) is "like grass," that is, weak, temporary, and
insignificant. No matter their particular strengths, individuals may
stand out for a while but like flowers they soon fade. But God has
seen fit to provide something we can hang on to, principles that
will always be true, today, tomorrow, and forever, and that is the
Word of God.

We may or may not truly believe God loves us, but that love is
the very reason He has provided us His Word. He knows us better
than we know ourselves, and thus, He is aware how much we need
His guidance. The key question is, do we know how much we need
His guidance? Are we willing to totally yield to His direction in
our lives? And what does that direction entail?

Peter defines God's Word for his readers. It's the good news of Jesus that he has already preached to his readers. And that definition has not changed for two thousand years. It's still the gospel of Jesus. That gospel involves who Jesus is, what He did, and what He will do. Who is Jesus? Son of God, King of Kings, and Lord of Lords. What did He do? He came from heaven to earth as a man, lived a perfect life, and died a sinner's death on the cross to pay the sin debt of all who believe in Him. What is He going to do? He is coming again, returning to earth to judge mankind, and gather those who have received His free gift of eternal life through faith to live eternally with Him in heaven.

So, what is our response to be? It's simple: believe. Believe Jesus is who He says He is, God come to earth as Savior, Redeemer, and Lord. And if we truly believe, we will live out that belief in front of the world. We will love the Lord with all our hearts, souls, and minds, for He alone is worthy. And we will love our neighbors as we love ourselves. And both these love feelings will be reflected in our lives. We will strive for Christlikeness. Other people will see Jesus in us. And, per Jesus' commands, we will make disciples as we go, teaching others to observe all that Jesus has commanded us.

It's significant that Peter describes this message from God as "good news," and we can be sure that phrase came at the direction of God's Holy Spirit. It's not an accident then that what we have been told to live out and to share is good news. Once again, we see evidence of God's love for us. For the truth of Jesus is not just good news. It is far and away the best news mankind has ever received. And when we fully understand that, nothing can stop us from sharing it, especially with those who are closest to us.

EPHESIANS 4:29–32

Paul is writing to the church at Ephesus concerning the "new life" in Christ believers gain when they accept Him as Savior and Lord of their lives. As is true of all scripture these words are as applicable in our day as they were in the first century when Paul wrote. So, it's no accident we see these words as commands, for God knows our character and what we are experiencing at every point in our lives. And just as important, God knows the effects of our actions and words on those within our circle of influence. See these powerful words:

> Let no corrupting talk come out of your mouths, but only such as is good for building up, as fits the occasion, that it may give grace to those who hear. And do not grieve the Holy Spirit of God, by whom you were sealed for the day of redemption. Let all bitterness and wrath and anger and clamor and slander be put away from you, along with all malice. Be kind to one another, tenderhearted forgiving one another, as God in Christ forgave you. (Ephesians 4:29–32)

We see here quite a list of slanderous traits we are to "put away." Notice God would not have commanded this, unless with His help it was doable. Nor would God have added this list to scripture unless we were aware of all of them, and guilty of at least some of them.

So it behooves us to seriously consider this list. What we say and do is powerful and can do both harm and good to others depending on our intent. So Paul refers here to our changed heart intent after we have come to know Jesus Christ as Savior and Lord. Perhaps the most grievous of these sins occurs when we grieve the Holy Spirit. Picture disappointing almighty God to the point He grieves for you and your sin. When we know better but still persist in willful sin, it has to make the very heart of God (who loves us so much) ache with disappointment, especially because He knows (much more than we do) what pain for us such sin will eventually cause.

And notice why God urges us to speak only uplifting words to others, and to refrain from thoughtless comments that corrupt: "that it may give grace to those who hear." There is thus the potential for our being a positive influence on those around us every time we open out mouths. What a huge privilege and responsibility. To thus be able to give grace is to be able to communicate the love of God to those who have not heard, to assure the lost there is a way to be found, and to therefore provide eternal hope that can come only through Jesus Christ.

God has made such eternal life available to those who believe. So in this passage Paul is encouraging those who know the truth to be about the business of sharing it. There is nothing kinder or more generous or more of an expression of love that we could do than for us to share the gospel of Jesus Christ with someone. And surely this fact plays out personally for every believer within their own family. What better message could we communicate than for our loved ones to hear and see Jesus in us.

HEBREWS 2:17-18

In these two verses the author of Hebrews described the High Priest position Jesus assumed when He came to earth as a man, and how in that role He suffered and paid the sin debt of all who believe in Him. Thus, through His sacrificial death on the cross, Jesus paved the way for us sinners to be sanctified (saved and growing in Christlikeness). As a human, Jesus experienced all the temptations we do, without sinning. He understands everything we face and is able to help us through our temptations. We can only cry out, "Hallelujah!" for such love expressed by the Son of God and the Father, and work toward obedience to them with all our hearts. See this important explanation:

> Therefore he had to be made like his brothers in every respect, so that he might become a merciful and faithful high priest in the service of God, to make propitiation for the sins of the people. For because he himself has suffered when tempted, he is able to help those who are being tempted. (Hebrews 2:17–18)

Thus, we see Jesus came to earth as fully man while retaining His godliness. We humans are called His brothers who needed a Holy High Priest to pay our sin debt. And Jesus completely fills that role: merciful enough to go to the cross in our place, and faithful to the point He lived sinlessly throughout His whole earthly life. Anything less and He could not represent humans as their High Priest. Thus, He alone was qualified to be God's sacrifice to atone for the sins of believers. Jesus' sacrificial act on the cross is called the propitiation for our sins. **Propitiation means the sacrifice that satisfied the wrath of God completely, which is exactly the condition we sinners must have to qualify for heaven.**

Now we can understand why Jesus suffered for our sake, and is now able to help those being tempted, which is all of us. His death satisfied our sin debt, and His resurrection proved His deity and everlasting existence as Son of God. Thus, Jesus satisfied His role both as sacrifice and Savior, and He remains Lord always. **What a grand plan God has had from the beginning to provide for those who love Him.**

Jesus' death made eternal life available for all who believe in Him. But some don't, some deny His role, the need for His sacrifice, and His eternal position as King of Kings and Lord of Lords. They may or may not verbalize these beliefs, but their lifestyles reflect them. Thus, not everyone will spend eternity in heaven with the Lord.

Yet there are those who are born, live, and die without ever hearing the name of Jesus. What about them? We can be sure God knows their condition and will deal with them appropriately. God is both loving and just. **We need to be concerned with our condition. We have heard the gospel. And that carries with it the responsibility of obedience to the Lord's teaching and concern for those we can influence. We have some responsibility for those around us who know us and need to hear about God's love for them. So, what are we to do with that information?**

Clearly, Jesus directed us to go and make disciples. Whenever and wherever we go, we are to be Christ's representatives, reflecting Him in our lives. He is committed to helping us do that.

2 CORINTHIANS 5:18–20

In this passage Paul is writing to the church at Corinth concerning his ministry of reconciliation. He reminds his readers of God's provision for their reconciliation through Jesus Christ's sacrificial death on the cross. Thereby, Jesus paid the sin debt of all those who trust Him as Savior and Lord. That provision is what defines God's "new" covenant with Israel. Now, by God's grace through faith, they (and we) can be reconciled to God. Whereas before, no matter their diligence, they could not achieve reconciliation by keeping the Mosaic Law. Nor can we. This concept of "earning" our salvation by our "good deeds" lifestyle is as rampant now as it was in Paul's day. See how God has Paul describe the New Covenant:

> All this is from God, who through Christ reconciled us to himself and gave us the ministry of reconciliation; that is, in Christ God was reconciling the world to himself, not counting their trespasses against them, and entrusting to us the message of reconciliation. Therefore, we are ambassadors for Christ, God making his appeal through us. We implore you on behalf of Christ, be reconciled to God. (2 Corinthians 5:18–20)

To reconcile means to restore to harmony, to determine and settle differences, or to furnish a balancing action or element to a relationship. Born as sinners, we need to be reconciled to God. Knowing this, God initiated the atonement process out of His grace-filled nature. Thus, though unworthy, we can be born again, that is, we can establish a saved relationship with Jesus Christ, and become then a joint heir with Him of His inheritance of an eternal life in heaven.

And with this new "child of God" relationship saved sinners are given, comes the privilege and responsibility to pass on this good news of Christ to a lost world. "Not counting their trespasses against them" is the message God has for the world. That message is called the gospel of Jesus Christ and indicates the only route to eternal life is through faith in Jesus Christ. Clearly Paul identifies the assignment all believers (then and now) are given: go and be ambassadors of Christ everywhere.

Paul can truthfully classify himself and all other believers as ambassadors for Christ. Ambassadors, by definition, stand in the place of their reigning authority. They act and speak on their behalf, seeking to apply their will and rules in local application. So, God makes His appeal through us. In their ruler's absence, ambassadors do not promote their own ideas and opinions, but those of their ruler. It is he they focus on: his purposes, his good reputation, and his plans. And it is his goals they work to achieve.

Paul promotes this teaching on behalf of Christ. It is Christ that Paul would glorify, it is Christ Paul wants to lift up, and it is Christ whom Paul praises; for it is Christ who made all reconciliation possible. Thus, Paul's conclusion has to be "be reconciled to God," not the other way around. We are the guilty ones. We are the ones who need to reconcile, not God the Father, and not Jesus Christ.

Is this command to reconcile a valid command? Do we see ourselves as needing reconciliation every day? Who do we know that needs to hear of God's love, and about His provision for reconciliation through Jesus' sacrificial death?

PSALM 119:149–152

This Psalm celebrates God's Word as the perfect guide for our lives. God saw fit to have it recorded for our benefit. But we must read it, study it, obey it, and make it a part of our lives for its eternal truth to permeate our lives fully. The psalmist lives in this world like we do, and like us he is subject to the same evil forces in his life that we face. So as we should, he prays for God's help, acknowledging evil is present around him, but that God is greater, and His truth is eternal. See how the psalmist words his prayer:

> Hear my voice according to your steadfast love;
>   O LORD, according to your justice give me life.
> They draw near who persecute me with evil purpose;
>   they are far from your law.
> But you are near, O LORD,
>   and all your commandments are true.
> Long have I known from your testimonies
>   that you have founded them forever. (Psalm 119:149–152)

He would have God hear his prayer based on His love, preserving his life and protecting him according to His justice. The psalmist seems to feel surrounded by those who would persecute him for his Christian stance. We, too, see all around us people and societies obviously living outside God's law, whose main purpose is to render God's laws invalid and unknown. But, praise the Lord, the psalmist knows God is near, and that His commandments are true. Best of all, the psalmist advises his readers he has known for a long time that God's commandments are eternal, and that He founded them for all time.

God would have us be assured of those same facts. The Lord is near to us too (always). His Word is still true, permanent, never failing, and always relevant. We need never doubt it. Much less are we to ever challenge God's truth and His purposes in providing His everlasting Word. His purpose is to enrich us with the knowledge of His steadfast love.

The concept of God being near is ripe with meaning. Yes, He is near in every sense of the word. "Near" means He is close enough to hear us, to know our feelings, to fully understand our situations, and to be able to quickly tend to our needs. "Near" certainly implies, too, He has the power to protect, the wisdom to know best, and the love-driven purpose to always help.

Thus, we have every reason to rejoice in God's truth and His provision of it, to obey it, and to share it with those around us. In fact, that's what Jesus means when He tells us to go and make disciples of all nations. And further, He tells us He will be with us always as we do go. What a great God we have!

PROVERBS 2:7–8

These Bible verses describe an example of how God works in our lives. It lists "some" of the things He does for those who study His Word and believe it and see its relevance to them. The purpose of His Word is to teach us concerning His nature and His involvement in the world on our behalf. Getting that knowledge is an exciting prospect; one we should look forward to, for it has ramifications not just to our lives here on earth but for eternity. See this passage:

> He stores up sound wisdom for the upright;
>> he is a shield to those who walk in integrity,
> guarding the paths of justice
>> and watching over the way of his saints. (Proverbs 2:7–8)

We clearly get the idea that God is all powerful, that He knows the future, and that He cares for us long term. Notice how those three characteristics (His power, His knowledge, and His love) fit together, enabling Him to see to every area of our lives. They describe His capacity to guide, guard, and dictate our whole lives so that we accomplish exactly what He would have us do with the talents and opportunities He provides us.

Just look at how the writer (King Solomon) describes God's involvement. He begins by telling us about God's provision for us of "sound" (the best of) wisdom. This, so that we will not only know what to do with our lives but know how, when, where, and why so as to best "glorify" Him. When we speak of glorifying Him, it hints at the idea of God's "way" taking away some of our control of our lives. **And that is exactly right, except He does not take away that control; we give Him control.** The "upright" (believers) will recognize that His will is absolutely best for them, and they gladly turn their lives over to Him.

The Lord then becomes our protector, our shield, and our guard against the actions of Satan, who would deceive us into disobedience if he could. Notice how Solomon describes the life of believers (saints); that is, as those who walk with integrity, along "just" paths, with God watching over our every move. Just the thought of this kind of consistent, heavenly oversight of our lives by almighty God should fill us with confidence, peace, and joy.

In addition to the obvious lessons in this passage there is a powerful implied lesson. That is, **this kind of relationship with God is available to ALL who will trust Him with their lives. So you and I and all who do trust him have access to all He is and all He offers.** These provisions described were amplified when Christ came to earth to save us from our sins. In our own strength no one is able to adhere to all of God's commands, resulting in our "sin condition." Knowing this would be the case, from the beginning God's salvation plan for mankind included Christ's sacrificial death on the cross to pay our sin debt. Trust in that sacrifice has led to the term "believer" for those who do see/believe/trust Christ's death as sufficient to clear our "record" with God of any sin stain. **A very simple, but very profound truth applicable to all mankind.** That kind of loving provision could only have come from God's steadfast love for us.